JoyRiding the Universe
Volume One

JoyRiding
THE UNIVERSE

*Snapshots
of the Journey
Volume One*

Sheradon
Bryce

HomeWords Publishing, Salt Lake City, Utah

JOYRIDING THE UNIVERSE
Snapshots of the Journey, Volume One.

―――――

―――――

Cover art and Calligraphy by Lea Stickles
Book design by Laughing Dog Graphics

―――――

For further information regarding
other materials by Sheradon Bryce,
contact:

HomeWords Publishing
P.O. Box 57396
Salt Lake City, Utah
84157
(801) 265-9272

―――――

LC 93-078950

ISBN 096366360-7

94 95 96 97   10 9 8 7 6 5 4 3 2

PRINTED IN THE UNITED STATES OF AMERICA

To AD
and his band
of joyriders

Introduction

Channeling is a fascinating, although to-date, not a well-understood phenomenon. It has been my good fortune to explore channeling with Sheradon Bryce for the past four years. During that time, I believe we have made an extremely significant contribution to the field of knowledge surrounding channeling.

The topic of channeling often polarizes people into two camps; those who see the channeled presence as an infallible intelligence from another realm—in short, a derivation of our traditional ideas of God; and the second polarity are those individuals who see channeling as a hoax perpetuated and embraced by persons of questionable stability.

Sheradon's channeling belongs to neither of those extremes, so much so, that we have wondered what else to call the phenomenon, since what she does is quite different than much of what is presently called channeling.

Sheradon's channeling state is significantly different than most channeling states. She has no conscious recollection of what has transpired, except for an occasional glimmer. In her full-trance state her personality shifts and she takes on a persona that we call Philip—a kind, unimposing and understated presence. Calling this presence Philip is an over-simplification, since she channels a variety of entities, each having a diversity of expertise and experience. We generally call them all Philip for convenience. We are not sure why she is able to channel like she does, although she does have an enlarged pituitary, which may or may not have something to do with her ability. Sheradon herself has had an exceedingly interesting life, but that will be the material for another book.

The channeling experience can vary widely, from the childlike and innocent profoundness of an entity we call AD to whom this book is dedicated, to entities who present extremely challenging abstract and technical material. There are also entities who are capable of eliciting strong emotional and feeling experiences, like an entity we call Arvana, a feminine entity who has several selections of material featured in this book.

At the very least, channeling is much more than an entity simply occupying and animating the body of the channel. I prefer to think of the channeling experience as a process wherein the mind of the channeler reaches out and touches an extremely abstract world, then acts out and presents that abstraction through the form of channeled personalities.

We know that there are very important factors which dramatically influence the channeling experience. For example, we know that the channeling is colored by not only the beliefs of the channeler, but very directly by the beliefs and expectations of the audience as well. Sheradon's channeling is a process that is in continual refinement, by not only herself, but also by all of us, the people who contribute as an audience.

We are hypnotized in this physical existence to perceive that anything of intelligence must behave, think, and represent itself like we do. To even begin to fathom the abstractions that exist in the universe, our minds must have something they can relate to. The channeled personalities provide the comfort zone necessary to begin to interpret the abstract.

Man has attributed God with man-like characteristics in order to make God more comprehensible. Because of this, the traditional God was made in the image of man—but those ideas of God are a gross over-simplification and distortion about what is really "out there." The channeling explores directly and indirectly what some of the other possibilities may be.

There is a beautiful genius that has shown itself in this channeling that may escape the appreciation of the casual investigator. I encourage patience for those of you to whom this material may seem a little "far out." To many of you, it will be an exhilarating and refreshing breath of fresh air.

This book is a collection of just a few "snapshots" of this material. I only wish this book was ten-thousand pages long instead of some four-hundred. There has been enough material delivered to produce a written work much larger than this. Collectively, the material paints a most fascinating picture of man's journey into physicality. I invite you to go beyond the limitations of the written word to touch the totality of the channeling experience which cannot be adequately captured in this, our first book, *JoyRiding the Universe, Volume One*. It is but a beginning—and the best is yet to come.

Scott Mulvay
July 1993

Snapshots

The Old
Bored Gods

Most of you are actually old bored gods! You have already matured through what you could learn in this existence and much of what you deal with here are recycled issues that you healed eons ago. Let's put it into story form.

There were all these young aspiring gods who were stuck in physicality who came up with a brilliant idea. They said to you, the old bored gods, "A lot of things are being set into motion. Let's help ourselves and the whole universe at the same time. Let's have a birth." That's what you are all doing—you're going to birth a new universe.

So here you were, these old bored gods; you had already gone through your issues, and you did it before physicality was even an idea. You had already graduated from some other school of manifested form. You had a manifested form already—you had gone through the lessons, and you were sitting here half-bored. These apprentice gods came up with a plan that sounded like a good idea because on the other side of it, you'll not be bored anymore!

These young gods knew that they weren't able to pull this off without your help so most of you said, "Oh we can do that—we've already been through all of that." Now the young developing gods thought that if they could get the help they needed, they could get out of physicality and orchestrate a birth of the universe. Additionally, they would be able to merge with twelve levels of creation and wisdom and be able to go back to their origins.

They were really excited. You, the old gods, were tired and bored. You'd made a new planet today, and it didn't look a whole lot different than yesterday's! You had run out of new ideas. So when these young gods approached you and said, "Hey, you're our big brothers and sisters and we have this brilliant idea. You're going to have fun with it," and you, the old

1

gods bought it hook, line, and sinker! "We need some help, and you can do it better than we can." And of course, this was good for your egos, which you, of course, didn't have!

So they told you the plan, and you were smart enough not to get stuck in it. You, the old gods, got guarantees and assurances from some of your friends that you would get out of physicality, if you went into it. Most of you are under contract and you're going home no matter what.

So a lot of you came into physicality because these young gods had asked for your help. And you yourselves went to a higher court to ask for help with it. You asked for a contract so you could go through the terrible dead zone, into the denser portions of physicality, losing your memory and pull off this grand and beautiful scheme. Then you wanted to be pulled back out. You went around and contracted with all your different specialist friends because the young gods wanted your help.

Now the only thing the young developing gods really needed in physicality was life. The only things they really needed in order to pull all this off were an added dose of joy, love, and excitement, and an intensity for life. A lot of you old gods said, "Oh sure, we can do that, no problem." They knew you were bored and they convinced you that you could take a vacation, go through the dead zone, and forget who you were. Then maybe you could get excited again when you got there.

They hired you, the old bored gods, to put a love of life in here. That when this birth would occur—it would be a live birth, it would create a genesis and birth these young gods and yourselves into a new species of entity. Now many of you are going to ride it through in your lifetime. These gods know that if the birth were created out of what is here, its success would be questionable, because hardly anyone on this planet loves life and wants to live. There is no will to live here. Your attitudes have been bored and hopeless. For a live birth, you need a will to live and a strong love of life.

That's why you hired on. Most of you from childhood have sensed a purpose or mission to your life—you knew you were here for a reason. Your reason was to come here and put love and joy into the place. It was to come and have fun, live life, be excited, and you all volunteered because it sounded so good.

So most of you are old gods that can make anything you want—a planet a minute if you like. All of your concerns and issues here are really no big deal, but since you're here, you like to play the games that everyone else is. You like the game of struggle because underneath it all, you are still bored. You still say, "Life isn't that much fun, not that exciting. I'm not having that much joy." But that is what you were hired to do. A lot of you by your natural vibrations are doing it, and other people around you can feel it—but you don't.

You thought that it would be an easy job, but it is a hard one because life and joy aren't here. The people don't want to live. That's why you were asked to come, to instill life in the planet.

You see, your system of reality here is a hodgepodge of everything that has ever existed since the origins, and the origins are further back than you have any idea. If we started with the number thirty-five thousand and put a billion zeros behind it, everything you have become started further back than that. You are a recent addition. You are also a homogenization and a coagulation of everything that has been before you.

They hired you, the old bored gods, to put a love of life in here.

Your bodies contain within them the knowledge of everything that has ever existed anywhere. You are being held in a womb, the mind of a creator/source. You are being held in consciousness. You don't just have one source or "IS," as we will call them. The source has a progenitor who has a progenitor and so forth—just like your pedigrees. In this system of reality, you've never been exposed to the energies and growth potential of more than the three generations of IS's who helped with the creation and support of this universe. At this time you have windows lining up so that the next nine IS's beyond these are going to put their vibrations in here for the very first time. That is going to create a species shift, and your bodies are going to make a biological change.

You see, your planet is the nucleus of it all. It is a *starr*, or a nucleus that clones itself to make a new cell. Your planet is a *starr* maker for a universal birth. It is cloning itself, but you are in the stage where the two cells or planets are still connected.

Now the idea was to build up the intensity and life in this new cell, shove it off from the other and collide and merge with all the wisdom of the incoming IS's. On the other end of this you would become a grander species having the knowledge of everything in manifested existence since the beginning of time, plus the knowledge of the next twelve IS's. You'll do all this in three seconds and it will be the biggest big bang ever!

So this was the brilliant idea these juvenile gods came up with. Of course it was passed on to them from other places. Everyone wants to take credit for it now—then it was a dumb idea!

In all this, the planet has to have enough thrust going out to create a hole in the fabric of the womb of this universe, push through, and birth. But at the same time the mind of your source is going to close down. Everything within this womb, including you and your planet, will be reduced to a single cell and shoved through time and space and genesis into a new universe.

The only problem is that it doesn't want to live. You see, in this single cell you have every possibility, every probable reality, everything you've ever thought but never followed through on—everything that ever existed—and it wants to die. There is no will to live in it. If you punch this out of the womb, it's just going to fizzle—you'll have a still birth.

You have to make it want to live. You were hired on to have fun, good times, to enjoy life, to get excited and find the miracles, to see the marvel and wonder at it. All of that will imprint the inside of this medium so that when it closes down and gets pushed through and touches the medium of genesis, it will say, "I want to live." Then you have a system that is going to grow like crazy. It's going to be totally different than this one, but it will be created by this one. That's what you are all part of.

It's kind of hard to love life and yourself and have lots of fun when you don't have self-worth hormones, and right now your bodies don't have them. You have to want them in order to make them. You see your DNA is a double helix, a twisted ladder of nodules. There are three strands that must be together in order to make you love life, love yourself, and feel good. If these three are in place, you have self-worth, you have love. You also have to put life into this body and it will keep on living even if you leave it and put it in the grave. So these hormones or strands in your DNA were not given to the body, because it would be a cruel thing to do to it until you yourself wanted to live. It was put into motion that when you love yourself enough, you would grow them.

Presently, you are working at growing these rungs. This is going to start putting the life hormone in your body so anything you don't like is going to grow as well as the stuff you do like. Your guilt will be pushed to the max, and all this stuff you don't like can get bigger than life if you let it. But if you are loving yourself, if you like who you are, what you are, that is going to be bigger than life too. Whatever you're focused on is going to be grown.

Once you are beyond your guilt issues, you'll be able to do in a short time what it would take the species a thousand-years to do genetically. If you maintain your guilts, your bodies have ten to twenty-thousand-years of evolution left before they can hold a god in them.

It works the same way with the birth and the planet that has been cloned. You have to choose which one you are going to live in. You see, when your bodies reproduce and clone new cells they are not as healthy as the cells they replace because you don't let enough light in them. But that's not the way the universe works. When a universe clones itself, it dumps off the residue that is too dense and too heavy. In the universal cloning process, the new is always bigger, brighter and more beautiful than the old. That's how the universe works. So in consciousness you're going to have to choose which nucleus you're going to ride on.

It's going to stay stable for a time. The planets are not going to separate yet, and you're going to choose between the two. You're either going to be stuck in your density, stuck in your fear, stuck in all your pain, stuck in struggle and stress on the old side, or you'll be on the new planet and out of those things. You have to have both sides for the birth to occur. The dense part anchors the other and provides a catapult. Everybody is going to go, but you will determine how far you will go according to your attitude.

In the universal cloning process, the new is always bigger, brighter and more beautiful than the old.

To create critical mass for this birth or shift, you need only a slight percentage. But that percentage has to want joy and life; they've got to put in the passion and intensity before it occurs. Otherwise, you'll have to wait for who knows how long for it to set itself up again, and most of you are already too bored to face that again!

The rush of riding this birth through will be the most exciting thing that you have ever experienced. This will be my third birth, and I guarantee it will be the funnest thing you're going to find in the universe, and they don't happen very often. The ride through is worth anything you have to do to get there.

Universally this is a big bang; a universe is going to be born and this comes around in terms of years once every 35 million with another million zeros behind it. And a live birth, occurs only once in every ten of these cycles! That's how long you're going to have to wait if you don't pull this one off. So if you don't learn to have fun and enjoy life now, you have a long time to learn how to do it! I'm teasing, but I'm serious about the time schedule. All you have to do is learn to enjoy life. That's it. You'd think that would be very easy, yet it is the hardest thing to do.

Now, I'm kind of old, but I can claim being young because I was birthed again and again. I've done about everything in the universe you can think of, and nothing compares to the birth process.

In the universe there are different species of entity. You are one species of entity. But there are a lot of species, and I'm not talking about alien brothers. I'm talking about species so abstractly different than you that it's not just the way they look. They have a different function. They run off of different physics principles. I have faces in all of them. I have had a good time. I've had a grand time. In my stories I talk about the young gods, the middle gods, and I talk about the old bored gods. I use the word god because that is what you relate to in your terminology, but they are all quite different species in and of themselves. I've experienced them all.

In the universe, gods merge. I have merged with levels of consciousness, and it is better than anything you have here! I mean, it's real good! I've been just about everything and I still love the thrill of birth. Merging is grand. You are taking you and your entire body of knowledge and you're merging it through another. It is the most fulfilling and complete sharing you can ever have. But in a birth you are doing that with thousands upon millions, amplified by the energies coming in. It is beyond comprehension. It is fantastic!

Most of you have never been through one. Those who have, work at trying to create a new one and to accelerate evolution! I would say that a birth is guaranteed to be the most thrilling thing you've ever gone through. You will never find anything like it.

I would say from the level that I am talking now, I am also where I have even grander parts of me that are yet unable to come in because at the same time where I am and where I come from are outside this womb. So I give you stories and metaphors because that is the easiest way to explain who I am.

Long ago before your universe and what you know as biological life was created, you had a lot of old gods. Now these old gods had young gods going to college and doing projects. There was one young god that was particularly ambitious and by some perspectives a bit of a headache. This young god was an old face of me—how's that for a paradox? This young god decided he wanted to get straight "A's." He was an only child, so to speak, and he didn't think his parents liked him very much because they ignored him all the time—he had all the usual complexes that go with that!

This young god got a brilliant idea in his head one day. He decided for his class project, in order to graduate from god school, he was going to do something so outlandish that he would get some attention. He was kind of insecure, I think!

Now most gods or entities create like you do. One thought leads to another, to another—that's how you create. But there is another species in the universe, and there are only three of them known to exist. I call them space particums because I don't know what else to call them! They are a species independent of everything else. They can go anywhere they want and create totally spontaneous ideas that hinge on no other reality whatsoever. It is the ultimate form of creativity. They are one of the smallest particums you will find, and if one wanted to create right here, it would ignite in a moment, expand out, and create a webbing. As it collapsed back in, it would move to the next place it chose and create again. It just creates webs for life to grow on. From that, sources spring. They are the most spontaneous, independent, originally creative things there are, and I was jealous! Gods can't create that way. Nobody knew where space particums came from, how to make one, or how to catch one, until I caught one—and then I got in really big trouble for it!

Gods, whether old or young, go into sleep cycles. They have to respirate.

So this young god wanted to create something so radical he could get some attention. But as he watched the creations of the old gods, their mistakes, blunders, and successes, to get ideas for his project, he couldn't figure out how what he was learning from the old gods was going to help him learn to create like a space particum. He envied that space particum! If you could create like that you would never be bored, because it was so radical that nothing could interpret it. You would have to try to interpret it from outside the creation and that could take eons of time and that is where the fun came in. He really wanted to be like the space particum, he wanted to be that creative! So he watched all the endeavors of the old gods.

Now gods, whether old or young, go into sleep cycles. They have to respirate. Sources, on the other hand, are a different species and they just source raw material, knowledge-based love stuff, but they cannot think. If a source thought for one second, it would destroy itself and collapse the universe.

Sources and creators are separate. They have always been separate. The source can source the raw material, but if it focuses on itself, it will forget to source the raw material for everything else, and it will fall in on itself. If you encountered one, it would be the most beautiful experience you have ever had.

After the source sources, the creators come along and organize this love stuff and put it on the webs that the space particum left in place. These webs are the same as grid systems and on them, things can grow and coagulate and create life.

So this young god was watching the creators. They looked rather boring because they had always done what they were doing. You don't get new creativity that way. All you do is wait and see what develops from one idea leading to another to another into another. That is why you get bored—you don't have something new to give you *ummph*.

Now gods have to sleep. They respirate. They sleep, go into the source, pull out the raw material, come out, and organize it. That's the way they work. But they can't take their persona into the source. If they did it would destroy the source. So they use a principle called the physics of Self. When they let go and become the whole universe, they retain a single compressed cell of themselves that pulls them back out. They become the universe, they become the source, and this nodule then pulls them back out pulling the raw material out of the source to create from. Self is a physics principle that allows them to go into the source and then be pulled back out without totally obliterating themselves.

These creators do this on a thirty-five-thousand-year cycle. That's as close as I can translate it into your time frame. And this young god watched these cycles and how the gods always improved the new clone of themselves. He was trying to learn from the mistakes of his elders, so he didn't make the same ones. He realized as he watched them that they always sloughed off major pieces of themselves. All the old stuff was thrown away in the respiration. When they were pulled out of the respiration, they had all the new material with which they rebuilt themselves. The old was thrown away.

So this young god realized that if he could pick up all of this residue, the waste material of the gods, maybe he could do something with it. Since it was the garbage or the junk, maybe it held the answers to all the mistakes, and possibly the cure for boredom. So he went around and collected it from all the sleeping gods he could find and started storing it, which got him in trouble! These gods realized that even though they weren't in it or using it, it was still valuable stuff, and besides, they considered it as if it were radioactive waste. If someone was making a radioactive waste dump in your backyard, you'd get a little upset! They were afraid that pulling that much waste into one corner of the universe might destroy the universe.

So a council was convened and the young upstart was denounced as the worst thing that ever happened to the universe! They didn't want anything to do with his hair-brained schemes. They said the time had come to put him out of business. But the elders of the old gods were also at the council and they stood up for the young god. All he wanted was either to learn from the mistakes or to be able to find new possibilities and potentials that the older gods had missed. So the elders prevailed and said that if the young god would protect the universe from his collection, and his experiment from the rest of the universe, they would let him play around with it. But the minute it got out of hand, they were going to pull the plug on it. In truth, the project has not had support from the beginning.

So this young god realized that . . . maybe it held the answers to all the mistakes, and possibly the cure for boredom.

The young god then took the major portion of his own being, making an electromagnetic womb out of his own consciousness, and started holding it. He was not afraid of it, and he told them that he would hold it so that it would destroy him before it could harm them.

Now this young god didn't even know what he was going to do with it. He figured he was going to learn from it and that probably he would get into more trouble for it!

Now if you're a god and you don't want others to know you have a thought, you just kind of blank it off and they never know you have it! It's the same principle you use here. He knew if he could change his focus a little bit, take another part of his consciousness and put it to sleep around what he had picked up, nobody would ever find it, and he would stay out of trouble!

Now the stuff that he was holding was just information, just something to be organized. He was trying to protect it from the gods who wanted him to destroy it, so if he put any thought process in it at all, they'd find it. Since large portions of himself were asleep, not even he would know where it was. He could say it was gone. And so he hid it.

With the remaining portions of his consciousness he started trying to figure out what he could do with what he had. But since he had already closed himself off from what was inside, he had no idea of what was going on. He had found a very small particum in the universe with which he breached this womb ever so slightly. Through the breach from outside the womb, he could peer in to see what was going on, but if he put his thought in there, the other gods would find it.

So he didn't put his thought in there, but separated off more pieces of himself and pushed them through just like amniocentesis (the process of piercing and exploring a mothers womb). He pushed them in with prime objectives to find out what could be done with what was there.

Originally he took five pieces of himself, and this is where my story begins. The first one he pushed in we'll call it P or Philip. It means origins. Its prime directive was to go inside the nodules and find their origins. The second, or A, we call Adraus or Andreau. It was pushed in to search for life, to give life and to create a passion to live. It was to try to see if it could get something to live in here. The third was the D or David. The line of David was the face that was to go in and organize, making the myths, the legends, and the stories that would organize this all into some semblance of reality so that eventually the project could be presented.

Next, since the creation was finding itself to be unbalanced inside, was the L, for Lehma. The L was the piece/peace maker—spelled both ways. It was piece as in chopping up, severing, separating it in order to see what you could get from it and peace as in harmony, balance and flow. He figured that with all these pieces of himself in there, they could work together and figure something out. The last which was also the first was called K. It was the amniocentesis itself—a bridging energy that would allow him to keep track from outside what was going on in the interior.

Once all this was inside, it still had to be closed off again. It is just as with a baby in the womb—you may have an idea but you don't know what it's going to be until it comes out. You can't go in and check on it personally. These pieces themselves were not inside the womb but rather vibratory emanations of them that had been translated through the layers of the womb.

Now this god knew that in its own process of respiration, everything inside would get a ride. So it went to sleep and went into the source or universal heart. Older gods know what sources are and understand their process of respiration, so they organize themselves around sources. Then you have a huge universal heart, the source of all life, because you're going to have lots of large gods sharing one heart. They don't all sleep at one time because they support each other.

This young god was really an old god connected to a shared heart, but he didn't know it. However, the old god was aware of his younger self and infact, it was he that had orchestrated the younger god in his hair-brained schemes.

Now this old god went to sleep in its respiration knowing that his project was safe and that when he woke up, he could figure out what to do with it. In the meantime during the process, as he went into the source, he forgot that he had breached the womb of his consciousness. Now inside, gods were forming and gaining identities out of the refuse. These became most of you, the old bored gods. You were the tired part sloughed off in the respiration.

This is one of the few universes where there are planets. That is how abstract some of these other realities are.

Now these gods that were forming got curious when stuff from this source started leaking through the breach. They loved it; it was a sort of clouded euphoria—it was great! They decided that if they could take this stuff and split it up into a bunch of little pieces, they could shove those pieces into their projects and then see what came out of it. This stuff was wonderful; it made them more alive than anything. It was life to them. This had to be the source of all life—they thought they had found the origins of the universe.

So they took this love stuff and broke it into pieces. They then scattered it to create life for their creations inside. When they did, all these little lifeless junk particles that had been picked up and held, started coming to life. This formed the new young developing gods.

You see, at this point in time, these gods that were forming inside of the womb were oblivious to the fact that they were parts of the source or god that was holding them. They had gone through the big forgetting. So they just played around in here with ideas. They would try them on for size, making and cutting holograms in the space with their different ideas. Then when they weren't looking, this life stuff and the space junk started coagulating onto the holograms, and a form of life started happening within the womb. Inside the womb layers started forming, each trying to gain closer access to the love stuff. This created rapid organization of the layers inside the womb. The old bored gods were created.

The true source of this creation's origins was asleep and holding it. And that source came out of its sleep not too long ago in your present time. In all that process it was never able to see what was going on, and it couldn't put its head inside to look without destroying it because if you take a personality into a source you will distort it and destroy what it is holding.

This god realized that what he had created was a sterile medium, because his project had no thought processes from him. This meant that he, for a god, had gotten as close to creating like a space particum as anybody ever had because there was no way of knowing what the creation was going to be. In the process of this god's sleep, all sorts of things occurred inside—hierarchies, systems, realities, planets. This is one of the few universes where there are planets. That is how abstract some of these other realities are.

This god was outside feeling the pushing on the edge of the consciousness from inside the womb which began to wake up. It knew that what was developing and incubating inside was grand because it was getting some messages through the breach. But it had no idea what it was. So it put another layer of itself to sleep to hold that layer, and another layer, and another layer just to protect itself from waking prematurely. This created the generations of IS's and faces holding this reality from outside the womb. It knew the moment it awakes completely it would close down to a single cell and create birth. Anything that is not it, is going to get shoved out, and that is when you have birth. But it's not quite ready for that yet. The stuff inside has to want to live.

You could say that this god is all these layers that create and makeup the outside of this womb. These layers are his faces, and this is where I come from—I am the faces as well as the owner of the consciousness that makes up this womb that is holding this reality as it plays. The faces that were originally projected into the womb have split and incarnated. The original ones were very strong entities because they were core gods, but they split and split and split far enough to get subatomic structure, mass, and matter.

The A strain is dead except inside the womb, and most of what is here has been corrupted and closed off. That is the passion for life. The L strain also exists no where else but inside the womb and it too, is rare. So, if this birth is pulled off, these gods will be resurrected, so to speak. If not, they cease to exist for all eternity.

The P was the first one in and it went scouting for origins to see what needed to be created. Then it called for the A, the D, the L, and the K. They stayed together for a while after which they fractured into large pieces and then separated and homogenized into the waste nodules. You are the experiences out of all these gods.

Now with all these extra layers that have been created to hold this universe while you play and as you gain a desire to exist as individuals, along with your steady growth and expansion inside of it, you were taking up too much space. So this god was told that he had to go on a diet or wake up and close down because others wanted some of the space. Space is limited because you can't create space without a space particum, and you can never tell where they are or when they are going to do their thing—push the fabric and create. So the council told the god to go on a diet, but they didn't know what he had been growing for eons. So he fessed up and they said that since it was junk anyway, "Dump it." But he protested that there was something growing inside, alive and viable, and he said he wouldn't dump it. They put a bunch of stipulations on him, but he said, "I can't do that because I gave it free will. I wanted creativity out of it."

Free will is what this sterile medium was all about. You can do anything you want and be protected and have the universe protected from you at the same time. All this has been going on inside here—and outside, and now when you are very close to being able to pull this off, they want to pull the plug on the experiment!

The word went out that a project was growing, and some of these other bored gods wanted to come in and figure out what was going on.

And so at that point in time, there were arguments and arrangements and different things happening. A council was called and some of the members had actually participated in the experiment. The council was going to determine whether the experiment was going to continue. It's not that they are going to pull the plug, so it's nothing that you have to fear—remember this is a story to approximate something that is quite abstract.

At the same time these young gods inside saw some windows lining up. They realized that if they could line them up and stir up a fuss, they could pull the entire council in, smack them with their life force and creativity, and prove their value and validity from within. Then they could gain at the same time the force and movement they needed to pull off the birth.

This is a mass event. This is where your images and pictures and stories about mass ascensions, people just popping off the planet, come from. The word went out that a project was growing, and some of these other bored gods wanted to come in and figure out what was going on. So it's inspection time! That's why you have entities on the inside telling you you'd better get your act in order. But there is nothing to worry about! You're such a novelty that even if your act wasn't in order, they'd still leave you alone—you are a creative endeavor.

When this started moving—when enough of you started screaming to get out—you set up a resonance that finally started waking up these layers.

My job from the outside is to make good the contract some of you hold that assures your ride home when the time is right. This contract assures that no matter what, you will go home. Many of you have had a know-ingness about that since you were very young—you've always known you were going home this time. You came here to have joy and *live life*. This will give the new universe the life it needs to create a most beautiful birth.

My portion of it all is timing and orchestration. I keep track of what is going on outside the womb and inside the womb from this layer. I have many faces inside and have incarnated 85,000 times and loved it. I have ascended 960 embodiments. Some of my faces, just like some of yours, have gone haywire. I still love them. Others of those faces are very beautiful, very intricate, very important parts, because this is a project that everybody is involved in—not just one or two here and there.

You've had teachers through the eons and their main job has been to teach you to love yourself and to know you exist. Most of you don't understand free will. While you are held in the womb, you couldn't die if you wanted to—not permanently. The greatest free will you are going to be given ever is the free will to exist or not—granted for the first time. This is the ultimate act of free will and unconditional love. It will be self selected and chosen. So through the ages there have been many teachers with one message, "Love who you are. I am. I exist."

Now you could look at yourselves as being made up of a lot of waste products and that might help you understand why you don't like yourselves because you were all originally rejected. But if you do like yourself then that's great, because you are getting the refuse to like itself! That's a pretty fair accomplishment by any standards. But a lot of you don't realize that you are a whole lot more creative than a lot of gods that have come along for a long time. It is because you were left to run free and wild inside here. Everything you ever thought, any possibility you ever came up with can be a reality in the new universe. You know how your hawks and eagles soar? How many of you have ever tried to become one? In the new universe you're going to have flowers that can feel, trees that can think, and birds with your intelligence, because it was a possibility that you gave them here. The rose that smells and feels so wonderful when you touch its petals—you're going to have roses that can feel *you* back. You are a lot more creative through your ignorance than you would have been with someone telling you what to do.

You are very literally the creators of the new universe because no one else has participated in it. You know how you feel when you are trying to create something and you have a million thoughts running through your head—so many that you end up not doing anything? The new you, in the new universe will be able to do everyone of those thoughts with ease. Here you have a dead zone and a separation. You use your dead zone for your atmosphere and gravity. That is what gives you the friction to stay in orbit. But you never knew you had a dead zone, so your next universe won't have one. Your desire to live forever? Those in the next one will be able to do so with ease. All of your dreams will be birthed there as potential. Here the best you can do is to make a hologram and hope you fall into it. There, the inhabitants will be the gods that you dream of being. ▲

The Grand Gift and Treasure of the Body

These bodies are one of the grandest gifts and the grandest opportunities any of you will ever have. Originally, when you created this whole system of reality that you call the planet, you as the apprenticing gods that you were helped to design and create it. But you couldn't walk with your creation. You couldn't touch it. So in your own ideal you wished to have an embodiment that you could actually walk, talk, and be part of the planet with.

This initial embodiment was actually created before your present embodiments were. Anything that comes upon your plane or that comes into manifested physical reality of any form is always created in thought first. Back to your perpetual question of the chicken and the egg, which came first? In creation, it is always the finished product which comes first and then you figure out how to make it.

For example, with the rose you didn't just put a bunch of cells together and a bunch of organic matter together and hope it came out to look like a rose. That is not what you did. The whole vision of a rose was there first. In other words, you or the creator felt a creation or an ideal, but didn't know what to call it and didn't know what it was. The source formulated it, and in thought it became a rose, and in thought it became the finished product. Now that it was a finished product, it had to be created in cellular matter so that it could be physically manifested. This is how all things are created, whether it is your bodies, your planet, or anything upon it. If it is manifested physically, it is created from the same principle. You take the end ideal and then you fill in the pieces, and that is what all of you are doing with your lives.

The rose was embraced. When it was embraced, you gave it fragrance, you gave it touch, you gave it velvety petals, and you gave it thorns to protect itself. But, these were all the ideals. Then to move it from that, you had to take it into the light, to be held into the light so that it could then be put into a holographic imprint. The ideal was in the thought. From there it goes into the light to be put into a holographic imprint and from there the holographic imprint will begin to magnetize to it cellular and molecular structure to fill in the pieces of the hologram that was created from the light.

At this point in time you take the finished ideal into the light. Now you have a holographic imprint from it that cellular structure and molecular structure begins to fill in upon and pushes all the way down to the single cell. This is how all things are created. You have a single cell that is put into a medium to grow, and become the rose, but it will also evolve. In other words, everything that the rose was as a finished product is now in the single cell. This single cell is so single in its consciousness and so single in its oneness that it doesn't even know what it will be yet. That is part of its mystery. It is part of its love for life. That is part of its growth—the ability to go from that single cell to see what it will become. Your bodies were the same way.

You only see yourselves as being limited by these bodies because you don't understand the precious cargo that they are.

When this planet and this whole system of reality was created, you wanted to be in vehicles that were capable of holding the full-fledged god that you were. You were totally unlimited outside of this reality, and you still are. You only see yourselves as being limited by these bodies because you don't understand the precious cargo that they are.

Your ideal was a physically manifested body that could actually hold a living god, and do anything that the living god would want to do. One that would give you sensory perceptions. Outside of a physical embodiment, you have no sensory perceptions. You have a form of sight, but you do not have touch, you do not have smell, you do not have taste and many of your other sensory perceptions without a manifested vehicle—a body.

The ideal was now to give the god an embodiment that could touch the rose that it had created into existence. You took the body into the light to build a holographic imprint. The molecular structure started forming and you took it down to the single cell. The single cell was then implanted into a system of reality that would allow it to grow and to evolve into a physical vehicle that would hold a full-fledged, one-hundred percent, functioning god within it. As it did this, your embodiment started into an evolutionary process.

The gods that you were and the sparks that you were, were already birthed and loved into existence previous to this. Now the single cell was put into a medium called an evolutionary cycle. From there it began to grow and evolve into a physical embodiment that could hold a living god.

You are all at the interim stage of that. In other words, these embodiments are at a point where they are just now beginning to make an evolutionary cycle in their brain capacities and in the body capacity to be able to hold a living god, totally and completely in them. But they are young. Look at these embodiments as young children. You don't punish a young child because it can't do what the adult does, yet most of you do that with your bodies! These bodies are in an evolutionary cycle that is very, very beauteous and very loving.

This experience with these bodies is the grandest experience any of you will have, but the bodies of the humanoid species are evolving. The light that you are is already mature. It knows all things. It is complete, but the two are trying to come together. In other words, the light that you are can see it as the end product, and so it gets very anxious. It wants these young bodies to hurry up and grow up and be able to hold it because it is excited for that! And so you are at a juncture. For quite a few thousand years on your planet now, the light that you are has been trying to inhabit these bodies and coax them to hurry up their evolutionary process.

But all of your bodies upon this planet could be considered a child's body. It is like the five-year-old child and your light is a graduate student, and it wants to know this body and play with everything it can. These evolving bodies cannot do it yet. You are at a stage where you can change them and you can start altering them so that they can, but they are not complete in their own growth yet. Right now they are at a point where the more of your own light that you bring into them and that you expand and grow into them, the more you are facilitating the transition. Your evolutionary and biological bodies that you have all been dealing with are in puberty. They are in the place where they are beginning to make the transition to where the entity that you are and the light that you are can fully begin to start living in them. Some days it works better than others, so to speak. You have some days where you can live closer to them, and you have more joy. There is an excitement because you brought that excitement for life with you.

The light entity that you are is excited for this embodiment because it is going to be its own when it is done. It is going to be its vehicle for touching and for embracing. It is its grandest gift and it is excited. So whenever the light that you are comes close to these bodies, it brings grand joy because of the excitement for it.

But you get disconnected and stuck into your biological personalities. As you get stuck, you often forget the light that you are, and this is where you see the limitation. Then you see the body as a limitation. You see it as being in your way. You see it as slowing you down from everything you want to do. None of you were forced to take a body. You asked for them, and you didn't ask for them in order to be punished. You asked for them because they were a grand gift and a treasure.

The cells in your bodies know how to build another universe just like this one.

Within these bodies lie the mysteries of eons. Look within these bodies. The bodies have evolved from a singular cell. Since they have evolved from a singular cell, your cells within your bodies know everything your progenitors have ever thought. Your cells in your bodies have the knowledge of this whole universe. The cells in your bodies know how to build another universe just like this one. They know its secrets. One cell in your body holds the mysteries of the universe, its creation, and how to do it. One cell in your body holds that much information.

If the entity light that you are can actually come together totally, one-hundred percent with this biological embodiment and the biological personality that you are having to deal with, you will bring the two worlds together totally and completely and end separation forever.

But in the meantime these biological bodies can't always hold the whole light that you are, because they are still evolving. Your brain system is still a little primitive for it. It is evolving and it is growing. It is a beautiful creation just the way it is right now and that is why you wanted them, but it is evolving. You wanted to be so intricately part of them that each of you were willing to go into them before they were finished. You were willing to go into these bodies long before they were ever at the state of holding a full god just because you wanted to get that close and to have that opportunity earlier on in the game.

You are playing around in these biological embodiments, living in them, expressing in them, but you are also cursing them a lot. You are also very harsh and very hard on them. Most of you don't get after a baby or a child that can't do adult things. You realize that the child is growing, is evolving, and one day it will be able to do adult things. Your biological bodies are the same way. They are beautiful creations just the way they are.

You came here because of the knowledge contained in them. The body that each of you is living in remembers the entire emotions of this whole planet. It has the feeling tone of the entire planet. Your bodies are a living testimony and a living history to this whole planet and it is a treasure beyond your measurement, and that is why you came here. That is why eventually all of you will take one with you when you choose to leave this plane, but it is a matter of learning how to manipulate it here and learning how to live in it, with it, and love it while you are here.

You are not totally limited. You are only limited because of your perception and because you believe yourselves to be limited. When you can move past that, these bodies will grow at light speed. You are on an evolutionary hill. It is like you are on the last leg of the uphill journey and then once you get to the peak, it will all be downhill or smooth sailing after that. These bodies are totally changing. They are getting ready to make a species change. They are getting ready to make a break or shift in the entire genetic structure of the humanoid species. This is a very precious and beautiful time for these embodiments.

Since this is where you are, it is also a trying time for many of you because the bodies are going through emotions. They are going through feeling tones they've never felt. They are experiencing their power. They are experiencing their limitations. They are experiencing all things at once. That is because they are learning to be all that is. When they are all that is, which means to be the source of the universe, which is what each of these bodies have the ability to be, you are going to experience everything. You are going to experience the ups and the downs. You are going to experience everything that has ever been created. You will personally experience all this, and it will be beauteous. If your personalities see everything as a struggle, then it is going to be a harsh time. It is one of the most beautiful times upon your planet, and it should be seen as such. ▲

The Consciousness of the Body

Originally each of you were light entities and light beings, and you wished to go into physicality and live in this expression here. You wished to live among the things that you had been creating, visiting and seeing. You began designing and creating embodiments that would allow you to live here biologically as one of the creations on the planet. During the primitive state of the planet, you began to develop your future embodiment. In the same way as a child's body matures into an adult embodiment, so too, the species had to develop from a primitive instinctual state into one that could hold the totality of your consciousness as light entities within them.

Biologically you began to create embodiments that would literally hold you in physicality, allow you to experience here, to share the sensory perceptions that this planet offers, and to enjoy life in this expression. Ever since, the body has been going through its own development to evolve it into a species that would be able to hold a full-fledged god within it.

Originally, the body was just a mass of elements from your planet in different combinations. To begin with the body didn't have any more consciousness than a plant or anything else. Each species began to grow its own consciousness, and in that primal stage it was just cellular division. Dividing the cellular structure was the limit of the consciousness. Originally the body or cellular mass could do no more than re-create itself. From that point it evolved the survival instincts of animal behavior so that it knew how to preserve itself. Eventually, as it began to evolve and grow, it was stimulated through emotions and through feelings that were added down the line when the light beings you are began inhabiting them.

Outside of the embodiment, you are each beauteous and have the ability to breathe life into anything you do. When you began to merge into

21

the biology of the physical beings, you were creating and began sharing in this experience. It created a synergy that began to put life into portions of the embodiment. You put feeling tone in it. This created an emotional body out of it, but it also allowed the body to feel that it was somewhat alive. The body began to become much more animated. It had much greater freedom of movement, and it could now function in a whole different perspective.

The light consciousness that you were wanted to be able to express in physicality and be conscious of that state, but the biological embodiment at that time was not able to allow you a full conscious connection with it. So as you were re-creating the brain system to hold you, you also began to re-structure the solar-plexus and the entire feeling and emotional centers in order to handle biologically what you were as light beings. You did this because you wanted to be able to embrace the totality of this planet. This re-creation of your brain and feeling centers began to evolve the species much faster. As it evolved, the biological embodiment began to think itself to be conscious and alive. The consciousness really belonged to the light entity that was sharing its perceptions, but now the body thought it was conscious.

When the light entity was put together with the body, the entity be-came the consciousness and the body became the vehicle. In their synergy the body moved into its own particular movement and reactions to life. The body didn't know that it was sharing and thought that the consciousness was its own. It began to think it was alive. It started to see itself as that consciousness, because it didn't realize that there was anything outside of itself. This is when the body actually began to develop its own conscious-ness from the consciousness of the light entity.

Because it thought it was all the same package, it began to create the images for the light embodiment to manifest into. The light entities that you were had become so entwined through the entire body-mind system that you resonated with that body. You were such a part of the body that as soon as your light was gone, the body thought itself to be dead and would create physical death for itself. It perceived that its consciousness was gone and it no longer felt alive. The body had become so dependent upon your own light that in its absence it would revert to its own lifeless, unanimated form that it was before the light entity was inhabiting it.

The body began to be aware of what was going on because you the light entity was beginning to understand it yourself. Anything that the light entity understands through the body, the physical embodiment assumes is a portion of its own consciousness and can use it as its own.

The body is still biologically evolving, and when you love it into existence, it will live forever. There will be no death process, and the body will be a living entity. Now it is a cellular mass, a biological species, that is run by the light that you are. You give it life, but as soon as you allow the body to move into its own consciousness and evolve its connection with yours, the body will move into full animation and will be a fully alive species.

The body in the process of all this began to understand emotions a little. It began to understand some of the various charges it was getting from the different things that were happening to it. It didn't understand where it was all coming from. It didn't know where the consciousness was. It didn't know that it was both a physical and a spiritual being. All it knew was that it was beginning to feel some form of consciousness. It realized that it was thinking. As it started to think and feel, it also wanted to know who and what it was. To answer these questions, the body started creating its own images. This is where your original images that all of you deal with came from.

The body is still biologically evolving, and when you love it into existence, it will live forever.

You see the light entities that you are, are so fleeting in your thought that you could move a mile a minute. The body was too slow and cumbersome for you. Since you were sharing with the biological being, every thought that you had was telling the body it had to shift or change in order to match it. As light entities in these bodies, every time you change your thought about what you are or what you are not, you actually change the direction for the whole body.

A light entity thinks, and whatever they think is created. Whatever they project in thought will be created and manifested for them, but the physical embodiment cannot work the same way. After the light being and the embodiment came together and the body started to think it was conscious, the light entities would think different things about themselves in consciousness. It was like playing games with yourselves in consciousness, imagining yourselves in different roles and using different faces. Each time you would do this, the body would shift in order to create the image you were holding.

You would look at the different bodies and think, "Well, if I had a different model, I could do it a different way. If I had different legs, I could run faster. If I had a different face, I could look different. If I had a different coloration, or different color eyes, I might like it better." As light entities you were very creative, and at that time you were not as tied into these bodies as you are now, and you allowed your minds to explore these different possibilities at a mile a minute. The whole time the body was trying to keep up with you and to evolve into what you were envisioning. The body was not capable of the quantum changes that you, the entity, was. It was an evolving biological entity, evolving within a time-space medium, and it took time to change.

The biological species was so slow in its evolution that the light entity had to find something to entertain itself with. So it merely enjoyed seeing itself in all these different embodiments, lives, and experiences it could create. But since the body and the entity were now somewhat connected, the body thought that all these perceptions were its own. The body began to feel that these were all the things that it was supposed to be.

Originally when you first began your connection with these embodiments you put in an evolutionary path for them so that they would evolve at a more rapid rate. Your children, for example, grow into adults because they were given an imprint within their cellular structure to become adults. So too, you gave a life path to these embodiments that you were playing with. You would merge with it, and give it a direction to grow in order to hold the totality of you and be one entity. If it was given the path and allowed to follow that path, it accelerated the evolution of the body and its consciousness.

But because the embodiments and brains were so unbearably slow to the entities, they never completely merged. In the meantime the entities' minds were running off a hundred different perspectives of directions. So instead of getting a biological embodiment that would normally just evolve according to one plan, you have all these embodiments trying to create the thoughts of the entities in all these different images in which they saw themselves.

Let's say the light entity is only feeding the biological embodiment a dozen different visions of itself, and many of these entities were feeding a whole lot more than twelve images of themselves. Now you have a biological embodiment picking up on that and trying to create every one of them. But it doesn't know how to do it because it must work through time. This creates a grand conflict within the embodiment. So it pulls in one thought of the entity and tries to create that, then the next thought comes in and it tries to create that. It keeps changing, and this is how disease was built in these embodiments. As the biological embodiment would try to change to match the thought of the light entity, it would set a whole cellular response in motion in order to grow according to the thought that it perceived to be its journey—the direction that it was supposed to go. But it had so many signals and directions, that it genetically started setting itself on many courses that were not compatible.

The light entity did not realize the embodiment was putting life into all of its thoughts, but it is the nature of the light entity's thought process to put life into all of its thoughts. The biological being has now been set on multiple courses. The life of each idea tries to create the embodiment in a different direction. Molecularly and cellularly each of those is already started into movement and become part of the evolutionary process. It is a disharmony in the organism, and you have diseasement for the first time in the body. This happened because the light entities couldn't focus on what direction they truly wanted to go.

Because the embodiments and brains were so unbearably slow to the entities, they never completely merged.

Prior to this the biological being was evolving extremely rapidly by any standard. Now it was beginning to slow down because it was diseasing and conflicting within itself. Since at this time it was still a primitive vehicle, anything that would cause an overload would shut it down. The conflicting signals and directions had confused it. It didn't know what to do, so it shut down and would not evolve.

The body had tasted the love and joy of the light entity, and it craved that life force. It had to have that but it didn't know how to get it. It went within its own being and used its own primitive consciousness to try to form an image of what it was supposed to become. It would feel the consciousness of the light entity and try to create a composite picture of the light entity and what the light entity wanted. The biological embodiment would then take this picture and say, "This is what I am; this is what I am supposed to be." It used that composite for its image to grow into. It would say, "This is how my biological being is supposed to be, because this is what consciousness says I am."

Some of you today on this planet are still living out evolutionary processes that were put in motion eons ago by your progenitors. Whatever image was settled on was a statement to the biological being to create the physical genetics to match that image. Many individuals are still living out of their genetic structure. The biology continues to try to fulfill that whole image it embraced ages ago. This is when the original image began.

When the biology settled at last on an image, it gained an increased sense of identity and consciousness which accelerated its evolution once more. Again the light entity and the biology were able to come closer together. The closer the entity can come to the biology the more life it gives to the embodiment. The light entity puts life into anything it touches and it will live in a whole animated form.

At this point in time, the light entity was merging more fully with the biological being, but it was also being trapped by the images in the genetic structure. The light entity hadn't understood what had happened. It didn't realize the grand respect, almost worship that the body had for it. The consciousness that was forming in the body tried to create everything that the entity thought. It didn't see the entity as separate from it at this time. It assumed that it was its own consciousness, and out of its great love and respect for it, it determined to create and be everything that had ever been thought through that consciousness.

These embodiments are working from survival behavior. That means that whatever they need to create or re-create will be genetically encoded as part of the evolution of the species. If the entity is off playing in other realms and experiencing the non-physical, the biology can't understand all that. Whatever the entity thinks of biologically or physically, it will create. Its intent is to maintain and become all that, for that is what it considers to be its direction. Whatever you the entity living in these bodies feel about them or think about them, back as far as your generations go, actually goes into your cellular genetics to alter and change this body to match the thought of the entity. This is basic survival behavior. It is what your bodies were designed to do. The light entities became a little impatient waiting for them to evolve and catch up with them. They didn't realize what they were doing to the whole species. And now you light entities come into them, get stuck, and sit and curse them because they are not living up to your image or expectations of them.

The body is now trying to move into a new perspective of evolution; it's beginning to understand consciousness. The entity is now a cross between a light entity and the biological being, and most of the thought processes that go through your heads are associated with the biology or physical existence. So you have a biological body trying to live up to the physical expectations of the hybrid entity that now inhabits it. Those expectations are what it sees as necessary for it to evolve to.

Understand that the entity you are is not totally within the embodiment but surrounds it at all times. This means that the image that you hold for your embodiment is also contained out in your field, the area surrounding your body. This field we call your mind. It is your non-physical mind. This is what holds the image for the evolution of the body.

Most of you upon your plane spend most of your time worrying about physical existence, and this is what keeps you dense. You spend most of your time dealing with the day-to-day physical life, and this is what you are feeding these bodies to have them evolve to. The more you allow the body to evolve into light or into a grander expanse of what it can be, the more you accelerate its evolutionary process—but this hasn't happened for some time. It is starting to shift now, but for the longest period your planet has been rutting in the focus of physical existence. Non-physical reality was unheard of.

Now you have physical embodiments that you are trying to evolve into light. These embodiments are fearful of that because they haven't known what light is, and you haven't been telling them. They didn't realize that the light entity is what has been evolving them all this time, what has been living with them, and what gave them a consciousness to begin with. They are beginning to realize that you are intending to evolve them into a much more expanded form to be able to live with them in both the physical and non-physical worlds.

Most of you upon your plane spend most of your time worrying about physical existence, and this is what keeps you dense.

A lot of you on this plane now, in your various paths and disciplines, are trying to promote your physical embodiments into expanded and spiritual perspectives. This will take a little time, because you are showing them something that is so nebulous that the body isn't able to hold an image of it in order to grow into it. The biological body must hold an image of something, if it is to grow into it.

All of you are trying to grow into the non-physical, even if you are not in conscious pursuit of it, because all of you on this plane are always seeking death. Even when you are trying to enjoy life, you are usually planning for death or for the world hereafter. But your ideas are nebulous about it. The only real spiritual image you've been holding for your body to grow into is that it must die. So your whole life you prepare to lay it down. When you are in this perspective, it's not going to evolve very rapidly.

As you begin to understand that perhaps you don't have to lay the body down, you start trying to move the embodiment into spirit and expanded perspectives. Most of you don't know what that means or what is out there waiting for you. You still cannot hold an image or ideal for the body to grow into. That is why if you can really understand a concept like ascension, that understanding actually holds an ideal that the body can grow to match. Your understandings so far have been very limited. What you hold are pseudo-images or ideals. The body for quite a few generations now has been balking at the unclear directions of its entity. It sits in the same old ruts, because it doesn't know where to go. It has virtually lived out every image that the original light entity put in it. It is at an evolutionary crossroads. It is capable of evolving into a whole different perspective, but it needs input. Anything you embrace about you as an image it will create for you, but you entities living in these bodies are not embracing your own physical and non-physical nature, and you're not giving the embodiments their new direction.

Without that direction these bodies are just going to pass around the same old images. Your bodies have to have a blueprint to grow into or to live up to, but you as light entities don't even hold a vision of life for these bodies. You wish you could get out of them or wish you had a different one. So the body is going to find its own images, and it will get them out of social consciousness because it knows it's okay there—it knows how to function in society. If you as the entity will not give it an ideal to evolve into, it will find its own, because it needs one for its own survival.

Because you have not consciously been trying to direct the development of the body, the embodiment had to provide itself with its own survival consciousness. The bodies have been developing their own consciousness because the light entities weren't paying enough attention to them. Your social images in this plane have become your prime survival instinct for these bodies. You have to match the image, you have to have something to live up to, and whatever you are is never good enough, because the moment you do get good enough, the body ceases to evolve. But long ago you built into these bodies that they must evolve, so the body will find an image one place or another. Because you're not telling them what to be, they will try to live up to everybody else's expectations.

In the consciousness that these embodiments are developing, they have learned how to access your field or non-physical mind in order to feed themselves the images they need. When you are around other people, it will access their images and start living them, because you the entity are not giving them a picture of their own perfection.

Your fields are quite flexible and a lot bigger than most of you think. These bodies have learned how to use your field to create and access gestalts. All the body wants is for this light entity it adores to give it some direction, but for the longest time it has been ignored. So it creates these gestalts or coagulations of images to substitute for the direction that the light entity is not giving it. The body has to have an image to live up to, and your social gestalts are always willing to provide one. Unless you give your body an image to live up to, it will always try to match someone else's expectation.

All the time you are all telling yourselves that your images aren't good enough. Nothing's ever good enough about most of you on this planet. You are always running yourselves down. You never look right, you never feel right, you never act right. You are always looking and striving for something different. That tells your embodiment, "Do not accept anything I send you. Go seek for something else." So it does, and it goes out through your field and pulls in other people's images and tries to live up to them.

Your atmosphere and your gravity is created out of the prevailing attitude of consciousness on the planet.

In the earlier days of this planet when you as light entities were just beginning to overlay these embodiments, your planet had a fairly pure atmosphere and gravitation. What you term your atmosphere and your gravity is created out of the prevailing attitude of consciousness on the planet. When you created this planet you gave it a very beauteous atmosphere. Your whole attitude was very synergistic with life. The attitude of every species on the planet was one of harmony and one that perpetuated life. The whole planet was one consciousness, what we will call a pure or unaltered consciousness. The consciousness of any species living on the planet then was one of life and joy. Everything, including the primal human species, lived with this atmosphere around them. The entire planet lived in joy, life, and harmony. There was no diseasement and there was no death.

When the biological embodiments learned to access your mind, that also gave them access to the entire mass consciousness of the planet. Up to that time each species just had its portion of mass consciousness. When these embodiments accessed through your minds into mass consciousness in their efforts to find images, it changed the entire consciousness constructs for the planet. You had these light entities running around in biological embodiments. Anything that any one of them was doing in a physical body affected the entire consciousness. Because they were in a physical body, they were out of harmony with their natural state, but they were still light entities that gave life to everything they thought or touched. This is when your diseases in these embodiments, began. It is also when the embodiment started seeking other images, and in doing that it actually attached itself to the atmosphere of this planet which is what began to create the gestalts here.

At this time the individual biological entities started putting out gestalts or images around themselves in order for them to have a story to evolve to. The embodiments had to have a story to grow into so they created one. The original gestalt was just a story the biological being was creating for itself to evolve to. When it did this, however, it also imprinted that image into the atmosphere, and therefore, into every other species on the planet. That is when everything, including your plant and animal kingdoms began creating death. Prior to that time nothing died—your trees, your plants, and your animals didn't even know disease. This is where some of your stories about this planet being a grand paradise in its early days came from. It was a paradise for a long time. It lasted until your embodiments began creating their own images and gestalts.

Now these gestalts were just strong coagulations of similar images in this pure atmosphere. They attached to it so that it was no longer pure joy and pure life. Prior to this all of your life forms had the ability to access this pure, free-flowing consciousness to have the connection they needed for life. When they sought that connection, all your plants and animals started running into these gestalts that the biological human species had been creating for its story. These images and pseudo-life forms taught your animals to behave almost like the human species. They taught them to evolve differently, how to create disease, and how to create death.

About this time the light entities started realizing what was going on. They had shifted their focus for a while and had been off in all these other realms playing. So, they brought their attention back and focused more intently on the embodiments, to evolve them more rapidly for themselves. All of you now are still experiencing the direction and intensity of this focus to evolve.

It was going to be a little harder than the light entities had thought. Some of these images that the body had picked up by this time were so strong and so burdensome that the light entity felt that the only way to get rid of the image was to lay the body down and pick up a new one. Hopefully the new embodiment would have different images that it could evolve it through. They still didn't realize that the embodiments held in their genetic structure everything that the light entities had ever thought, and that it was the body's intent to create it all.

For a period of time there was a grand decline in the consciousness levels and evolution of the embodiment. You became intensely focused in the embodiment and gave life to everything that the body had perceived to be the direction it was supposed to go. As you actually lived in all these different directions and images, it became too burdensome, and you created the death process so that you could pick up another body. You hoped that succeeding generations each would have fewer images as the images were lived out and the bodies laid down.

In the beginning the death process took thousands of years, but you rapidly moved it into occurring every few years to speed the evolution. The life expectancy, at one point, was under twenty-years, because you wanted to lay them down as fast as possible and hope that you laid the images down with them.

Since that time you have lengthened the life span again in order to give you each, if you used it, more time to evolve these embodiments. The embodiment is finally ready to hold a whole entity. The entire brain system, and several other features that are needed to hold that entity that you are, are finally grown within these embodiments. Biologically, these bodies could hold you now, but they have to be activated. There are portions of the brain that you have been using elsewhere that need to start coming on line here. You are actually going to move more fully into these bodies and give them full life.

Right now the body still thinks it has its own consciousness, and there is a kind of tug of war going on between you. But these bodies are becoming conscious enough that they can function somewhat even when you are not in them. Also now the biological image of the embodiment survives the death process to some extent even though the light entity goes on to a different perspective.

At this present point in time you are learning to live fully in these bodies. You are creating them to be a whole living entity.

At this present point in time you are learning to live fully in these bodies. You are creating them to be a whole living entity. As the light entities that you are, you are in a position now, as you yourselves become more fully awake and aware, to take this body and add a few finishing touches and transform it into a vehicle to hold the totality of you. Originally that was the dream of this universe. That was one of your primary reasons for coming here—you each wanted to have a vehicle or embodiment that would fully house a complete, whole god. You wanted to be able to live in it, to express, to feel, to enjoy, and to have all of the sensory perceptions. You wanted to be able to use these things to interpret everything else you experienced anywhere.

In an expanded consciousness, and in other states of reality outside this one, each individual has a core, a central area within which they can create, experience, and interpret everything through. Being the young gods that you were did not mean that you did not have such a core, but you each wanted an individualized one. These embodiments will allow you to have your own medium to interpret every experience you ever have. That is why the body is so important and so valuable. You came here to this universe to pick one up and call it your own.

In your older generations of consciousness,—and not from a principle of hierarchy—but in the realms that existed before this one, each of them have their own embracement vehicle through which they can experience and interpret everything they ever experience. Now, each of you have an embracement vehicle as well. Physical existence was your way of getting one. As the gods you are, you designed these bodies to be that for you, and you will keep coming back to them until you have evolved one that you can take with you.

When these bodies are fully functioning, they are capable of interpreting any experience you will ever have in any reality, literally and in every aspect of the experience. There is more in that statement than you are able to appreciate at this time. These bodies will be a treasure beyond your comprehension.

In the mean time you are putting consciousness in the embodiments so that eventually these bodies will be a living consciousnesses in and of themselves, working fully and compatibly with yours. This body is at a point of evolution where all this can be realized, but you have to be able to move into your feeling tones to teach and evolve it. It is the last leg of the journey, and the most challenging.

The more you move into your feelings, and that is what you are all doing, you are literally giving consciousness to the biological being, but until you get this embodiment to a point of being a living consciousness of its own, you are going to run into a transitional pattern in your evolution. That portion of you that perceives pain, rejection, loneliness—the portion that deals with these types of attitudes in this plane is going to be very sensitive as you move into your feelings. This is coming out of the portion of the consciousness of the body whose function it is to monitor how it thinks about itself. And now this portion is becoming alive. The whole body is becoming a living consciousness, so it is going to react to its genetic patterning and to any physical stimulus at all, and it is scared half to death. You're putting consciousness in something that previously wasn't conscious. The body is becoming more aware because the light entity is. The body is becoming more sensitive and vulnerable. All of the attitudes that you don't like to deal with are coming out of the consciousness of the body and are going to start surfacing.

A long time ago this embodiment learned how to deal with minds. It learned how to use your mind to connect with images; it knows how to play the gestalt game. And now, as it becomes more aware of itself, it will perceive the slightest influence from any of these gestalts. Some of your first awarenesses on this planet are going to come through the consciousness of the body, and they may be a little painful.

You are allowing the whole body to become a living mind . . .

The body learned to access the mind on its own, before you as the light entities could evolve it to that point. It knows how to perceive energies, it understands levels of consciousness, and it knows when and what to accept and what not to. It had to learn to because it wanted to live, and it had to have an image to grow into, and you, the light entities, were not giving it one. Now, as it is becoming more aware because you are, it moves into a greater sensitivity to the influence from these realms. That portion of you that can feel rejected or hurt. That portion that is open to all these types of feelings is going to become more and more sensitive as the body becomes more conscious.

The biology evolves in stages so it is not going to be a constant thing. You may think that you've gone through it, but it is likely to resurface each time the body becomes awake for a time, and you're going to go through a period of sensitivity.

Understand that in consciousness, the light entity has every gift that any of you ever seek. You already know how to use them, but you are trying to teach the biological embodiment these things. All of your gifts, your psychic abilities and non-physical sight, must all come through the consciousness of the body as it evolves along its path toward holding a full-fledged god within it.

Left to their own devices, these biological embodiments evolve at such a slow rate that it would be eons down the road before they would be at the place you wish them to be. This is reflected in your children. The human species is one of the slowest to mature on the planet, and for a long time they are unable to fend for themselves. This is because your embodiments are one of the latest species added to the planet. The species that were here before you, living in the uncorrupted atmosphere, evolved at a much faster rate. The rate at which their offspring mature, reflects that rate of evolution. Your embodiments are of recent advent to planet earth, and they have been evolving very slowly. That is why your children grow so slowly in their early years. It is what keeps them dependent for so long. This entire lengthy process of the evolution of the consciousness of the body is what is behind every dependency issue that you or this planet ever had.

On one level you realize this. Your entire medical profession is actually trying to accelerate the evolution of these embodiments. When the embodiment becomes diseased, it means that it is trying to go too many directions at one time. So in many instances the medical profession literally cuts out unwanted directions or images through surgery. A lot of the prescriptions, drugs, and techniques that your doctors are using work on the body in an entirely different perspective than what you understand. In most cases these things allow the light entity that you are to come into a more singular focus with the body. You see, every time the body goes into disease or disharmony, you have to focus upon it because you care about it—you give it self-attention. When you do that, what you are really doing is focusing back into the embodiment and how you want it to be. If you are sick at the time, your focus holds a vision of it not having the illness, getting rid of it. Your medical profession is a system created to help you focus back into your embodiment. You need to focus back on your body more, but you don't know exactly how, so your body helps you out through illness. When you have a cold, for example, you wish you didn't, and so you hold an image of yourself being free of the cold. That actually holds you in a different image to allow the body to evolve into. In many cases the medical profession helps to eliminate certain images or structures that are hindering the evolution of the body so that a more singular focus can be created.

Each of you need to realize that while these embodiments may seem like a limitation to you, they are not necessarily a limitation in the way you perceive them to be. See them rather as your own children, your own child. You love your children. They slow you down, they holler at you when you are in the supermarket, they want a lot of attention, but you still love them. If you could give the same kind of consideration to these embodiments, you'd get along a lot better, a lot easier, and you'd evolve them at a much faster rate.

By the consciousness perspective of the light entity that you are, these embodiments are juvenile. Your consciousness is so expanded that the embodiment is a real limitation to you, but they don't have to be. Just realize that you came into them for a reason. You are loving them into existence;

you are allowing the whole body to become a living mind, entirely awake and alert, so evolved in its own right that it is sensitive to everything in existence.

You start loving these bodies into existence when you come to peace with them, loving you just the way you are, loving you completely, relaxing and allowing your images to drop—is a whole lot easier than surgery. Besides if you are the god living in this body and you keep adding new images, that's what you are telling the body to be. You won't be teaching it to live forever. You won't be teaching it to evolve in consciousness. All you'll be doing is seeing the body as a prison, and you'll use your fantasies and your images to entertain you until you decide to get out.

Be friends with your body, respect it. Genetically speaking its roots go back eons farther than yours. Remember that all on its own while you were off playing your games in other realms, it chose to live. It loves you as the god of its being. You are literally creating it now into your ultimate expression, your grandest creation. When you are done with them, these biological embodiments are going to be the synergy of your living mind and living consciousness. They will be the entire interpretive mechanism that you will use in every consciousness experience that you will ever have anywhere. These embodiments are more valuable to you spiritually than these brains are to you physically—they are really much more valuable.

You came here in order to get an embracement vehicle, an embodiment—no one forced you to come. So come to peace with your bodies, no longer pushing new images upon them. Just allow them to be, loving them into existence. That loving into existence is going to come through a relaxed state as you put joy in them and in every facet of your life. The body responds to joy; it is the ultimate body response that can be created. In spirit there are other concepts and constructs that are grand and wonderful, but in the body, joy is the ultimate expression now. After joy it can begin to understand the lessons of passion, and other vibrations of life. But right now joy is the grandest thing you can teach these bodies. Joy is the ultimate expression it can know here. Love your bodies, put that joy in them, and allow them to be your most joyous expression. ▲

You start loving these bodies into existence when you come to peace with them, loving you just the way you are . . .

A New
Breed of God

Would you describe for us what we have to look forward to when we make the jump to the other side?

You know all the wildest ideas and fantasies and what the good stuff is? Amplify that about a thousand times and then you're close!

The one thing that all of you want here actually boils down to a feeling of freedom. That freedom is a freedom to be you. It is a freedom to manifest and to be the god that you are. When you hit the edge of that, you move with a velocity that you have never experienced. It is the biggest rush you will ever have in existence, until something better comes along. There are some better ones—I've tried those too!

When you hit the edge of that, everyone of your barriers and everyone of your inhibitors are released. When I talk about inhibitors, I don't mean the moral ones. I'm talking about the ones that repress you and keep you from doing things. I'm talking about the ones that keep you as the rigid adult, the one that tells you, you can't do anything. When you hit the edge of that, you are so free that you will dance and laugh and sing like you have never done in your soul before. Amplify your wildest expectations by at least a thousand times, and that is what is there. It is the biggest rush, the biggest thrill, the biggest exhilaration you will yet find in your existence. When you've done it, you will wonder why you didn't do it ten-million-years ago. Then you'll realize that you had to go through all this so that it would be even more impressive. It is a thrill.

Moving to that side is the birth into being your own god. Inside the womb of this physical existence, you are still at the mercy of everybody around you. You are gaining your own strength so that you don't have to be, but it is a fact of the schematics here. You're going to be affected by what you are around. Inside the womb you are in a subjective reality. You are subjective gods. You can do some things, but that process of getting outside of this womb objectifies you into full-fledged godness.

I guarantee you, your ideas of what a god is and what a god really is, are two different things. A lot of you have a very solemn idea of what a god is—that would be rather boring! Your god has arms, legs, a head—and he's very solemn and very punishing. When you understand what a god is, it is so different than all the ideas and the myths ever were, you will wonder where they came from. When you make that last journey through the womb, you go back into the wholeness of the universe. It is the biggest thrill you will ever find—I guarantee it.

A lot of you have a very solemn idea of what a god is—that would be rather boring!

From that point you are unlimited. Right now even your ideas of unlimitedness are a limitation! You can take what you would consider to be your most unlimited thought and it is limited by the very fact that you thought of it! When you get to that point, it is a space of intensity of love. That love is different than what you are expecting too. It is an intensity. Right now you are all being held in it. It's an unconditional love. It is so unconditional you can't even feel it.

You came into these bodies to gain sensory perception so that when you break the edge of that womb, you can *feel* it. Up to that point in time, no god that ever journeyed in it could ever feel the love. You just are it, and it is so unconditional that to you right now, it would feel like this air sitting on your hand—it is that unconditional. When you get clear in your vibrations to such a point where you can breach and break the womb of your own consciousness and go out and into that objectification, you'll take your sensory perceptions. Then you'll be a god that can feel the raw stuff, and you'll be a god that knows how to use it.

You here are a new breed of god. I'm not saying that to flatter you. It is a truth. Originally there were sources that could do nothing but source. Creators organized it, but they didn't ever know how to make the stuff. This experience here is to teach you to do both. You will be a new breed of god that can source your own material and create with it at the same time. There has never been a god like that before. You are a new breed of god and I would be very proud of it. That's what is waiting for you on the other side. You will be able to play in the universal raw material and you will learn how to make your own, and you're going to start by loving yourself into existence. Then you can create because that's what you are all doing here. You are organizing your lives minute by minute. Then there are a few other bonuses waiting too. You'll be a new breed of god and some of the first ones to be born. That is grand.

Our time is up. I love you. I have had a grand time with you. I appreciate you for allowing me to come visit you. Be at peace, not in pieces! Be in love and joy. You are gods and I love you as the gods you are. Have a good time. Good night. ▲

Ascension

Your Planet is preparing for a mass ascension. It is a scenario that has been planned for a very long time. A lot of your stories through history and your prophecies have led up to and are explaining the mass ascension from this planet. It is occurring because a lot of you, for generations, have been crying for an end to separation. There is a burning inside to be complete, to be whole, to go home. When enough of you shared these same feelings, you created what we term critical mass within your beings. You were making a statement that you now wanted out of the game you've been playing for eons of time.

When you created critical mass, there was an opening made, and now the creator is coming in to facilitate and to help with what you are asking for; not to interfere with it, but to open a space for the creation of a window and a way out. If you are truly wanting out of the separation and back into you, there is a window to do it through. A portion of what we are here to do is to facilitate this windowing.

Your critical mass has also created a domino effect within the universe. It has awakened several generations of IS's, and as they awaken, they are removing their separations too. They also want to know you, their children, so to speak, so they are making the motion, the movement, to come here for the very first time ever. They are finally realizing the desire you hold to rid yourselves of separation and they are answering your call. You have created a window in time and space where all of these sources can align and come into this plane. They are moving in and you are moving out in consciousness to meet them. This mass ascension is really only a by-product of this coming together to rid the universe of all the separations that have been known for as long as you, any of you, have ever been in existence.

From a physical perspective, how is all of this going to take place?

Understand that anything that is not formed into a gestalt or a conscious ideal, you can't do here. There are those of you that are consciously carrying the intent to ascend. Until there are enough of you to believe in it and embrace it as fact, it will not be easy for any of you to do. A lot of you will do it one at a time, here and there, and as you do this, it begins to build a gestalt or a framework for others to follow and do it also.

Basically, the mass ascension is going to be a "birth process". When enough of you upon this planet reach critical mass, you will shift vibrations, and as that vibration shifts, many of you will ascend. As you ascend and move off the planet, you will pull the planet behind you. We use these terminologies to help design a picture for your minds. You are not going to sit down with each other and say, "Well, we're going to do this next Tuesday at twelve o-clock." What will happen is your vibrations are just going to, all of a sudden, hit a peak. In other words, you're not going to be forewarned about it. It's just going to happen.

Many of you will be the forefront of that, but everything will ascend. In other words, those of you with the strongest vibrations are going to be at the head of it; not out of hierarchy, as we will talk about later, but there will be enough of you to create the velocity needed to pull the planet behind you.

There will be many who will be upon the planet who will be doing whatever function they are doing at the time, and there will be those who just pop off all around them. Many upon the planet won't understand what happened, but at the moment of that mass ascension those who pop off will pull everything else, which means everything will be changed in a twinkling of an eye. As it begins to move, the other IS's that you have coming in are going to meet off your horizon. As they meet and collide off your horizon, you will be pushed back into your own point of joy. You will have ended the separation within you. You will move into a place of being objectified—being your own god, your own creator—whatever term you wish to use.

These events occur only every so often, and this is just what your planet is getting ready to do and many of you upon it, in physical life now, are going to experience it.

I understand from your perspective how ascension could occur, but the word ascension holds such an emotional load for most of us on the

planet—all the beliefs we have about it—like lifting off and going into the clouds, etc.

We prefer to use the phrase, "Taking the body with you." We choose to call it that because we have issue with the word ascension too. It has a lot of connotations and people use those connotations to tap into the very gestalt that will prevent them from creating it for themselves.

Understand that ascending simply means to climb or to move as you would on a ladder, from one point to another. You will ascend as far as the vibration you carry allows. Ascension is a vibration, and you've all been ascending since you stepped into physical reality. You are ascending in that you are moving from one evolutionary step to the next, to the next, to the next. As you move, you shift the vibration of your body.

It is a very natural process, but the people on your planet see ascension as something beyond their capability. In truth, a lot of your ascended masters are not as far removed from you as you believe them to be. Yes, they ascended because they created a vibration that resulted in a distance or gap between you. This is why many of you see them as superior to you or far removed from you, or a grand source of light and information to you. It is because their vibration is a distance from your own. Since it is, it appears that they are superior to you. That is not the case. All that has occurred is that they have vibrated at such a rate that there is a larger distance between you.

Many of you feel that being an ascended master is as far as you can go and it is not.

Many of you feel that being an ascended master is as far as you can go and it is not. A lot of your ascended masters are still in the process of ascending and will continue their ascension process as long as they are open to it. Some are ascending beyond where they originally ascended, but there are also those who remained right where they originally ascended to. That means that some haven't evolved. That means that some are not able to see the expanse of the universe, and they are therefore, as limited as you feel here. Others do have a stronger vibration that allows them to see a broader spectrum, but that's all. It does not mean that they are necessarily superior. It means that they knew how to raise their vibration. This came from knowledge, this came from light, this came from loving their own beings. All they did when they left this planet was raise their vibration to such a degree as to create a vibrational difference between their embodiment and the physical plane.

There are a lot of you upon the planet that have made a conscious decision to go through the ascension process when it occurs. Understand that there will be those that will ascend right along side of you and they're not doing anything about it. In other words, from your perspective, they're not on the path, they are not trying to ascend. They don't even know what it means but they're still going to go because they are open and that openness is shifting their vibration.

Because of the beliefs you have about ascension a lot of you are looking for the dramatic ascension that will feed your egos. Others seek ascension out of fear and out of many attitudes that actually create an inability to ascend the body. There are still others who think it's a good idea but it's not something they embrace within their being as part of their knowledge base. A lot of you want to ascend to have proof or validation that you've made it, are worth it, or have done the whole process right. A lot of individuals in your time and space are looking to ascension as a way to prove they are on the right path.

From a scientific standpoint, what is happening within the physical body to set this ascension process into motion?

In order to ascend you have to change your molecular structure to a different vibration than the earth and everything else is vibrating at. To do this you have to completely restructure the whole physical genetic structure of these bodies including your DNA to teach it to move at light speed. Realize that what you're trying to do is build a totally new cellular structure for these physical embodiments. You're trying to take them out of the dense molecular structure and build a new holographic light principle for them.

Because you are focused in this reality, you are not always aware of the non-physical part of you. That non-physical part of you we refer to as the light of your being. It is the intelligence that keeps your heart beating, your lungs functioning and your other organs working without your conscious thought. The light of your being sits behind your heart where your new embodiments are always being created at every moment. It is the holographic light imprint that your cells use to build and grow upon. As your light embodiment changes with your evolution, it will also change the holographic patterning for the new cells that are being built to restructure the molecular pattern of these bodies.

A lot of you are now holding love in your beings, and you allow yourself to be in a place of bringing in grand amounts of light. As you are doing this, it moves to a place wherein you are beginning to create new holographic imprints for yourselves to build upon. As you do that, the imprint goes out, and the cells begin to build upon that. You have some now that have been built upon a new light principle and they are bringing in a grand amount of spirit. These future bodies will be created to hold greater amounts of spirit because they are being built from the light principle which is fed by love and the joy of living.

The frequency called joy is where thought breaks into light. That is your goal and that is the reason why most of you want to ascend. The ascension process is equal to grand amounts of joy on a non-stop basis. You can measure your success by seeing how well equipped your body is to hold those intensities of joy.

The ascension process is equal to grand amounts of joy on a non-stop basis.

You make changing the body's molecular structure sound relatively easy in some regards, but it would seem that there are some big changes in store. Can you give us some insights into what our bodies will experience?

The body will go through a lot of change and some of these bodies are more upset about the changes than others. You actually have a body consciousness and the body consciousness with some of you is very high strung and very uptight. Some body consciousnesses are just laid back and they say, "Okay, I've heard this story a hundred times. I don't believe you anyway." It depends on what mode the body consciousness is in and how uptight it is. So first of all, realize that when your vibration begins to change and most of you are going through different phases of this, the body will become more paranoid than at other times.

There are also different things that happen in the connection between you and your body. Some of the experiences you have will depend on the way your entity and the body work or don't work together. If you start feeling fear or if the body begins to feel fear, go into the body. Become more connected with it. It will start creating more trust and if there is fear or anxiety, go into the fear and anxiety and say, "Okay, I'm listening to you. Tell me the story and tell me what is really in here." Then take it down into the feelings and the fear, and the body might start talking to you and telling you what's really bugging it. Also, every time you get into a new energy that your body's not used to, these bodies immediately go into anxiety and say it is bad. Whenever you're bringing in new energy, a new vibration into your body, it will have a tendency to put the body and you into anxiety. You all do this. Every time you get into anxiety if you could look at it and say, "Okay, "I'm in anxiety. That means a new vibration is coming in. Let me see what is going on and why my body isn't liking this or handling it." Then you can start short circuiting the actual fear. Develop a rapport with your body. The body will learn trust and you will learn trust with it.

Understand, these bodies were built in density. They have not been understood. They have not been programmed. They have not ever been taught to ascend. You've been, for the last eons of time, teaching them how to die, not how to live forever. This physical embodiment was created to live forever, so ascension is going to be one of the most natural things for it to do. But you have eons and eons of physical genetic programming that says they cannot do this. The truth is that a lot of you are already going through an ascension process right now. You have been for years, but you're not aware of it and don't realize that's what you're doing. What you have is a body that is becoming more non-physical and because of your belief system, you're expecting it to work in the same old physical way. It won't work that way any more and it will never go back to where it was. It is changing and altering. You are changing its molecular structure and you'll learn a different way of functioning it. You're actually teaching these bodies to be more light. They are becoming non-physical while you're quite in them. It is not a matter that you will work to a certain point and then suddenly shift or change and become non-physical. You're doing it while you're trying to live in these bodies. As you do that, each step of the way creates a place where this body simply does not work the way it used to. That is not necessarily bad, but it can be frustrating unless you understand it and just allow yourself to work with it.

Also, when you are evolving in consciousness, these bodies begin to feel less and less supported unless you work with them. The reason behind that is you, the entity, are refining your vibration and you are becoming more non-physical, so this body starts feeling like nobody is home. When you're dense, it says, "Oh good, the owner is home. We're happy, we're healthy, we're having fun." The more refined you get in that body, the more frightened it can become and with some of you, the body will even some-times set up rigormortis because it doesn't think you're in it even though you are. This is not common, but it does happen. It is because the body is predisposed to the feelings of death and it just starts shutting down and quitting. So mentally and with feeling, keep a very good close connection with your body and mind at all times. Go into the feelings. Feel it. See what the fear and the anxiety are about. See if there is something you can do about it.

These bodies know how to handle everything that is ahead of them, but they've been taught for so many eons to die that they're afraid that if you start changing your consciousness and going in new directions, you're going to create death for them. They are afraid that evolution is going to create death for them at a faster rate than if you just left them alone and let them do it by themselves. Look at the body as having its own consciousness, then allow yourself to connect in your inner being with the body's consciousness and communicate with it. For a lot of people this might sound funny, but when you find it, it will act sometimes like a bratty, snotty, little child. It will act like one that does not trust you, doesn't believe a word you say. You'll wish to talk to it and work with it and it will kind of thumb its nose at you in the beginning and say, "I've heard this story from you so many times and you never followed through. Why should I listen to you now?" That is where the trust has to begin.

You're actually teaching these bodies to be more light. They are becoming non-physical while you're quite in them.

The thing that none of you trust is physical existence. You designed these bodies, you created them, you came into them. You know there is support, but the body says, "Where is it? Where are these invisible life lines that are holding me out here in this medium called time and space . . . and I don't like this feeling." It would be the same as if someone were to take you out to the edge of a cliff and hang you out over the edge. That is how the body often feels. It takes the brunt of all your feelings so it feels like it is being held out over the cliff with no support so it responds with fear. I would say, always, if you have fear that there is something wrong with the body, that it is not functioning the way it should, that you might have a problem with it, get it checked. At that point, there will either be something manifest that you can externalize and work on, or you will get a clean bill of health and then you'll realize that other things are going on.

How can one develop the "being" to perceive the love one needs to have for these bodies and to assist them in this process of evolution?

The individual who begins to realize that the journey is what it is all about and begins to love where they are and comes to peace with physicality and comes to peace within themselves, are aligning themselves to ascend at a much faster rate than other individuals might do. If you have fear of death, if you have ego wanting the drama or the validation that you have done it, if you have any of these forms of images or wanting to change the body, it is not going to cooperate with you to do it. In order for you to ascend these physical embodiments back into the spirit from which they came, you have to become so totally attuned with them that they will function and do everything that you ask them to do.

One of the first steps in truly ascending the totality of your physical embodiment is going to be loving yourself completely, exactly the way you are. That is where you will begin to find the joy. It also requires that you move into a place of stepping outside your images and stepping back into the joyful moment—loving life just as it is. We don't mean to settle, we mean to accept and love life the way it is as you evolve your consciousness into greater joy. When you can move into the joy for life itself, when you can move into the wonderment in everything there is, you are moving into the ascension process and you are on your way back home. ▲

The Side Effects of the Genetic Shift

Your body is going through a genetic reconstruction. In the process of doing it, many things are going to happen and change in it.

The heart center in your being is an electromagnetic sac. In the heart center you have two pacemakers. You have a natural pacemaker which is on the front, and you have a second one that is being created on the back. The second one on the back is going to be for the newly evolved species and body. Some of your hearts are fluttering, palpitating, flip-flopping in your chest, and when you go to the doctor he says there is nothing wrong with you—but here, have some pills!

What is happening is the bodies are biologically reconstructing this new pacemaker on the back of the heart. The back one is beating at a higher vibration. Your heart gets two signals and the chest is kind of trying to figure out where the arrhythmia is. It kind of flutters, palpitates and can't figure out what is wrong with itself. Because the number one killer is heart disease on this planet, you tend to go into fear if this is happening to you. I would say, if you have problems, go to the doctor anyway because it will alleviate your fears, and fear is your worst enemy.

Most of you think that since you're trying to evolve, that if there is something physically wrong with you, you've failed. Always, if you have physical difficulties going through your process, it is not a failure. If you're upset and mad at the body, you're going to aggravate your problems with it.

Since it is going through a genetic reconstruction during this time period, your body is not always going to be one-hundred percent up to par to your ideal of how it is supposed to be. Be gentle with it. The heart is one area of change. Livers have a tendency to act up during these time periods also. Be gentle with them too. You might have a tendency to go through fatigue, and your mind will go through this real spacey time period where it won't focus on anything. It is just like you're out in space, going crazy, or senile because the thought was there and you lost it. You'll go through it and it doesn't matter what your age is. It has nothing to do with senility!

Most of you consider that all your memory is held in your head. If all the memory that you're using is held in the head or brain, you are stuck in the rut of primitive or first brain. Your mind is your electromagnetic field, your auric bands, or whatever you wish to call them. Your field is your mind. The thing in your head is your brain. The brain only holds temporary memory called behavior, instinct and survival—that is all it holds. The mind is where your thoughts and your concepts come from and it is surrounding your embodiment. You are learning to access more parts of your mind, your fields, but since you've been in a rut, you're used to your brain picking up things easily. You're expanding your mind now so instead of the data you want being here in the head, it's further out in your field. The brain goes out to pick up a thought in the field, tries to bring it back, but it doesn't remember the path, so it drops it. In mid-sentence the thought disappears when it was right there. It got glitched, it disappeared.

You will all go through it and it doesn't matter what your age is. If you're older then you say, "Well, I'm going senile." But people will go through it even in their twenties. It has nothing to do with senility, but the brain is learning how to access further and further reaches of your own mind. Sometimes it just doesn't do it perfectly yet, that is all.

In order to go through a genetic shift you have to dump the old memories out of the body and out of the DNA structure. That old memory is emotion. Anything that was ever emotionally embraced by any of your predecessors, you're dealing with right now in your body, unless you've cleared it.

If you look back on your lives, most of your experiences which were real powerful and intense experiences in which you had an emotional embracement, were traumatic. Most of them were painful, real miserable, and very emotional. There is some love coming in there now though. Look at your pattern and realize that your ancestors were probably into more drama and trauma than you are. When you're going through your genetic reconstruction, you're going to have to dump that cellular memory and put in what you want, so that this body you're living in matches your mind the way you want it to.

Right now, your bodies are being run by everybody else. They are being run by your ancestors, your neighbors, the dog on the street, and the checker in the grocery store. You have circuitry connected and set up in all these places, and your bodies are used to being run off everything and everybody else. Part of your process is to dump that. A lot of you are doing that by dumping your images. Some of you are doing it by other methods and means. Whatever works for you, do it. You have to get to a place of being so at peace with you that you run your own mind, you run your own consciousness, and you tell the body what to do, not the other way around.

In the meantime, the skin and the nervous systems take an enormous brunt from the evolutionary changes. The light of your being goes through the nervous system. All these little nerves, clear up to the spinal column, is where the light entity that you are lives. The light that you are can refract, be diffused, or directed, but it doesn't bend. Have you ever questioned, "How do I take light and make it be a body?" You designed almost a fiber-optic system called nerves and nervous system to get the light of your being to take shape, to make arms, legs, and etcetera. Therefore, when you're raising your light, your vibration, the whole entire nervous system is going to take the brunt of it. If you have some blockages in it, a lot of you will end up with lower back pain. You can get pain shooting into your legs, arms, and also, numbness sometimes. Everybody can be different with it. If you have a predisposition genetically to back problems or if you've had an injury in the lower back, your solar-plex or sacral area, they may start acting up. You're going to run more light through there than you're used to, and you're going to have some pain.

You have to dump the old memories out of the body and out of the DNA structure. That old memory is emotion.

Also with this, sometimes the body will go into involuntary shudders, shakes, and convulsions. As the light of your being moves through the body, it electrically triggers the nerves and so they will seem involuntary. Not all of you will have all these symptoms, I'm just telling you some of the different symptoms. Again, if you ever have any problems, do go to a doctor because then the doctor will tell if there is anything wrong or not and then you can release some of your fears.

As the nervous system and the spinal column start taking more of a brunt, if you have scar tissue, if you have any kind of blockage in there, it is going to be more aggravated, more painful, and you're going to have a few little difficulties. Your skin is a receptor for the light. When the light comes in and out, it has a tendency to burn it. Sometimes, when you're dumping genetic information, you can dump so many toxins that your skin can rash. With some people it will go to a point of almost lesions from the dumping. Not all of you have to worry about getting lesions, but that is something that can occur. You can have all kinds of skin difficulties, problems and ailments with the evolutionary process.

If you could look at it, the genetic shift and change that you're going through is almost like trying to take a cat and turn it into a rhinoceros. If you were a scientist and doing this in a lab, you'd be very gentle about it because you'd know it would take quite a bit of doing to get that cat genetically, skeletal-wise and everything else to end up being the rhinoceros. When it is happening to your own bodies, you're not very gentle with yourselves, and you all get very critical with it.

The bodies will also go through fatigue. The fatigue comes from several things. It comes partly from the evolution that is going on with these bodies, but it also comes from jumping dimensional realities. The body can go through periods of fatigue unlike anything it has had. It doesn't have to have them and it can have them for periods here and there where any physical activity is an effort. Talking is almost an effort. To do anything is almost an effort. The body fatigue level is such that it just can't function, and some of you will get to a point where it just says, "I can't and I won't." If you're down on yourselves and critical, you're going to have more difficulty with it.

Would you talk a little bit about the immune system and what happens to it during this evolutionary process?

During the evolutionary process the immune system will go through a period of shut down, but it does not have to be long-term. Most of you will go through periods with it. You're trying to re-program it and restructure it to the new body, the new you. You're generating all this love, all these intensities, all this beauty of who and what you are, even down to the point of, "I'm god and I want to live as a god in this body." You're putting all these intensities in and trying to force it into the DNA.

If you're putting foreign things in your DNA, the body is going to attack it. The DNA is so protected that the body immediately sends out antibodies to kill anything foreign. You're putting all your beautiful, loving, new positive attitudes right next to your DNA to go into your DNA. Because the body sees those attitudes as something foreign to it, it tries to kill them.

You're not getting anywhere with that. So instead, what you're doing is taking all these attitudes, all the new you, and you're kind of putting it in repositories. Rather than completely trying to insert it into your DNA or into your neural memory, you are storing it. You're storing it in these repositories to go on line when you're ready for it. Otherwise, when you start the creation of the life hormone through all your new attitudes, the body's natural resistance comes up and kills it, because it is foreign to it.

So you're learning how to hold them in little repositories. This is why a lot of you have said, "I've changed my attitude and I feel really good," and then you have a bad day and you say, "Why doesn't anything work?" It is because it has not gone on line yet, it is not part of your physical structure yet, so therefore, it is going to have to be a conscious effort to make it work.

Your DNA strand looks like a twisted ladder with little nodules on it. In order to get out of the physical attitude, you have to grow three new rungs on your ladder. These are the self-worth rungs.

The genetic shift and change that you're going through is almost like trying to take a cat and turn it into a rhinoceros.

You were not given them in the body at birth or ever. The reason is that if you have those and you're not clear, you could destroy yourself, the planet or anything else. This is your power. The god-in-a-body is the last three rungs and some of you will go onto grow a fourth and fifth. But you have to have these last three rungs to gain your entire god power in this body. You can't do it until you're worth something, which means you have to love yourself in order to grow them.

These last three rungs are made up of these little nodules. You are setting these little nodules of thought there in the pocket around your DNA. "I love myself." "I'm all right." "I'm okay." "Here is some joy." But you're not using the hydrogen bonding to hook them into your DNA to imprint your cellular structure. If you did, the body's natural resistances would say, "Here is an alien, kill it." So you hold them until you get enough to pretty much build a new rung on your ladder. Then the whole entire immune system of the body has to shut down to rescript the DNA.

That is the only way the DNA can be rescripted. It will have to stay shut down a minimum of twenty-eight days to imprint this new material. Your immune system will try to get you to a point where it knows that you're not going to get any contagions, where you know that you can have some help and you're going to be all right for a period of time. The simple cells in your body, the ones that have to be able to carry this DNA, take twenty-eight days to reproduce. The immune system shuts down so it won't kill the new material. When it has shut down, your body runs off the adrenal system and your adrenal system kicks in harder than it ever did before.

Some of you have had almost this real stressed edge, and you don't know where it is coming from, but it almost feels on one side just a total fatigue of the body, almost where it wants to die. This process creates an edge, a very sharp edge and most of you will recognize it. The immune system will try to stay down for six weeks if it can, because that insures more of the DNA will be rescripted into the genetic memory.

When it shuts down you need to be gentle with your bodies. Love them. Do not get ornery with them. Just know that they are going through something right now, and they're going to come back out of it. A lot of you don't let them stay down long enough to let the whole DNA rescript, and so, you'll go through a series of these. Some of you will usually go through a major process or major illness at some point when it is rescripting. Most of you won't do it on an ongoing basis. Most of you have already done it at least once in your life. You'll do it once and it might be a period of months or years before you'll do it again.

Something similar happens in your brain with your neurons. Most of you are evolving masters, but you are still going to get into some anger. Many of you have already gotten past that point. Anger is the most misunderstood thing you have. Anger is the emotional story you put on something that isn't anger at all. It is creation.

The neurons in your brain look much like a tree with branches. That is the easiest way for your mind to look at them. In order for your brain to continually and habitually maintain your new progress and your new evolution and growth, it has to go on line. Whenever the neuron fires, it fires from the core and goes out through the branches. This connects thoughts—one thought to another—and this determines your behavior. Whatever is closest to the core or the center of the tree is going to have the biggest brunt of everything pushed through it.

Your brain is trying to learn new thinking processes. You can't attach them to the center of the tree or the middle of the neuron, because the brain and thought process already run through the core. You're going to have to put the new attitudes and thinking in as a very fine sliver of neuron just like a tiny, fine branch on the outside edges of the tree. All of your new thoughts go out on the edges just like new growth on trees do.

All of you are going to require some event in your life to put those on line so that they are permanently yours. Most of you will use intensities through the brain called rage to do so. There are other ways of doing it, so if you don't get into rage, it doesn't mean that your brain isn't going on line.

You can be a very gentle, loving, beauteous person, and free of all the angers and rages. But when you have enough of these tiny fibers to go on line, the vibration or the intensity which you call anger or rage runs up the spine, through the nervous system, shoves into the brain through the hypothalamus, and turns all these neurons on.

Anger is when you repress it, shove it down, and don't allow it have its course. Then it sits like a pressure cooker. What you call rage is a negative in your minds. If you called it Kundalini you would believe it to be a beautiful experience, but it is the same energy, it is the exact same life force. It flows up the spine, hits the hypothalamus and reprograms it. As it does that, if you have an issue with your own creative life forces, you repress it. In that repression, it boils up again, and you call that anger and label it rage.

Anger is the emotional story you put on something that isn't anger at all. It is creation.

When this first starts coming up and rising very fast, it will scare your body. You might still call it rage and anger, because when it rises that fast, your body says, "Oh, this is scary. Since this is scary, it must be anger." The body puts all these emotional stories called anger around it instead of calling it love.

The body will spontaneously start shoving that up the spinal cord. When it does, it takes all the life that it built at the base of your spine and with a velocity force it up through the brain, to the hypothalamus to reprogram the pituitary, into the neurons, and puts all your new thought processes on line. Without that, all they are are good ideas and they never become part of your reality.

Many of you need to be gentle with your system because it might be one that was programmed by your ancestors and your predecessors for rage rather than for the love or what one would call the Kundalini. You have to be in a place of being willing to let go of your judgments about what is happening. As soon as you can quit labeling it and calling it bad, you'll change it and quit repressing it. Then you'll start feeling it for the love that it is as it starts rising. But for a lot of you, your systems are so afraid of expression that it holds it down. When it finally comes out, all of a sudden you went weeks, months, and years, without lifting your voice, and now you're screaming at the top of your lungs at somebody! It is your own system opening up to let this go on line. You have to learn to be gentle with yourselves. If you can be gentle, then you can patch up and repair the damage after you scream!

What about the flip side of anger?

Laughter is the best thing you can do. It is the prescription for anything. Laughter in your being actually activates your diaphragms, messes with your solar-plex, pulls the energy up, and it is the absolute best thing any of you can do. I would say, laugh as much as you can!

Just as many of you repress your anger, you repress your laughter also. If you notice, when you're laughing, you hold your chest very tight. If you can let it open, and let that laughter out, it will move the diaphragm, and the rib cage, which moves the back, stimulates your spinal column, and lets the light move up into your brain faster. So I would say laugh—laugh your heads off! Laugh your way back home. Laugh your way into health. It is the best thing any of you can do in these bodies. These bodies were created for fun, joy, and to live life to its fullest. Anything that enhances that, do it!

There are two things that you will all learn about gods. One, they all know how to have fun and two, they are lazy. They don't expend any energy when they don't need to! ▲

From the Mush Into the Butterfly

Can you give me some insight? I'm feeling discouraged, depressed, and very detached from everything. Why?

Most of you are feeling new things you've never felt before, so you're having to find an old label for a new thing that your brain is getting tired of trying to figure out. The brain says, "I can't compartmentalize this. I don't know where it goes. I don't know what it is; where can I shove it?" So it will take it and shove it into the old emotions.

Feel what you're calling your discontent. Go into it, don't be afraid of it. Amplify it. What is there? What are its components?

I don't know how to define physicality any more.

You can't define physicality any more, but do you know what that means? Isn't that what all of you have been trying to do, or at least say you're trying to do? You're all trying to move past the physical attitude while you're in the flesh. This is the insanity that ensues with it. Go into it some more.

It feels like there is no anchor in physicality and yet there is no way out and that I'm stuck, with no movement in a place that I don't like.

Okay, keep going into it. Take any one facet of those. Are you stuck? Or have you finally touched your freedom and you're scared to walk in your freedom? Follow the part that is scared. The one that says, "I'm stuck right here." Find it.

I don't know where to go. Everything I see in physicality is not interesting, there is no focus for me here . . .

Um hum. Okay. What else?

I have no idea where my passion is.

Most on this plane don't ever have the faintest idea what passion is. Most of you, what you call passion is repressed anger that you've repressed so far that you can't let it out and say (angrily) "This is my passion!"

Your passion probably doesn't lie in the earth plane. Go in there and find out where your passion lies. Take the part that feels stuck. The part that says, "I'm stuck in this god forsaken place that I hate". . . say that real loud inside and feel what comes up with it.

You're smiling!

I know!

That is not good for discontent!

Part of me wants to laugh!

That's what I want you to follow. Go into the part that wants to laugh—this will get you out of your game. Follow the laughter. Your entities aren't stuck any place. They are too unlimited. Go into the part that wants to laugh about it. Ask it if *it* is stuck.

It's telling me I'm free and I don't know it!

So your discontent is that you finally achieved the freedom you said you wanted your whole entire life, but now that you have it, you don't know what to do with it. So now what *are* you going to do with it? Ask the part that was laughing—that seems to be the part that knows what is going on. Find the part that is laughing. Whine at it and I want you to be melodramatic! Whine and cry your poor woes to the side of you that is laughing! Get into the "Woe is me. I'm so stuck. I'm so stuck. I don't know where I'm going to go."

Try each of these on the part of you that is laughing. See the response. See if it laughs harder! Now take the, "I don't know where I'm going to go," and see what its emotional reaction is. Now take, "I'm bored half to death." What is its reaction?

Ask it to give you a feeling about your life. Let it just feel because it is not going to give you the direction in verbiage. Ask it to feel if it knows where it is going to take you. Ask it if it can let you feel the passion that it has for your life—which you think you don't like. What is it giving you?

The message is I have a grand life, but then there is another part of it that's just total confusion.

You're going to have confusion at first, if other people aren't running your lives! This is contradictory to what everybody thinks it's going to be. The stability for most of you comes when other people tell you how to be, what to do and how to act—that's what you call stability! The minute you break the circuitry and you have nobody sitting and telling you how to be, what to do, how to act—you feel chaotic. All of a sudden those ends of your circuitry that were attached to other people are frayed wires which don't know where to connect and stabilize.

You have always said you want peace—but you'll hate it because it's boring!

I've always told you these two things. First, none of you like peace—and yet you have always said you want peace—but you'll hate it because it's boring. Second, you're going to hate your freedom. You could have freedom any minute you're willing to have it, but the psyche has to shift in order for you to have freedom. If it maintains a rigid definition of "Here is who I am, and here is what I do," you'll never have freedom. As soon as it loosens its bounds on that, you feel chaotic and psychotic. The only thing that is wrong with you at that point is that you're in your freedom.

But is there a part of me that is ahead of my psyche?

Yes, otherwise you wouldn't find the part laughing at you! The part of you that is laughing is the part of you that already went ahead of you, made the road map and it sees the road clear and exactly where you're going to go, and so you are *its* hindsight. You know how you all laugh at hindsight? That is your future self—you're *its* hindsight and it is laughing at it!

There will be a day in another reality, after you leave this place, when all of you will sit around some big huge table, drinking your coffee or whatever you do and you'll sit and laugh about these adventures that you were so uptight about!

Will I still be here! . . . there's a part of me that wants to walk away from all of this.

From the planet, from everything?

From everything.

I know, but why? Many of you say, "I can push myself, I want to take advantage of all the energies coming in, I'll take it as far as I can go," Then you end up where you are. That is your psyche cracking. You all have been through it before. You touched home. You finally touched you. You're so close that you touched it, but you can't find the doorknob because your nose is stuck on the door!

When it comes right down to it, a lot of you say, "Why in the hell am I here? Who put me here? I feel like I'm in a prison camp." But there is another part of you that also knows you are intelligent. You wouldn't have done this journey if there wasn't a reason—or least you hope you're intelligent!

You are touching your freedom. Freedom is the most frightening of all things. The only fear you will ever legitimately find is the fear of your own freedom because you're on an edge that asks, "Where are you going to go?" It says, "The whole universe is yours. Make a direction." Then you sit here and say, "Okay, but these forty, fifty people that are telling me what to do. They're not telling me what to do right now so I don't know where to go!"

Take the void that you are feeling, the complacency or whatever you want to call it. Jump into it. Just take it right now and jump. Say, okay, *I'm leaving*. Do it right now. You're a god—you can do it. Build your intensities. I want you to get to the serious part—this will be fun for you. Get to the part of you that is so sick and tired of being on this stupid planet, with these stupid limitations. Take all of that frustration and say to yourself, "Okay, I'm a god. Right now where I sit, I'm going to end it."

Do it with seriousness, and you'll have an experience with this, I promise. In this moment right now, call every force in your being. Say to yourself, "Right now where I sit, I don't have to go through a death process, I don't have to go through an ascension process, I can end it right now." Pull all of your forces up, your frustration, your irritation at not liking where you are. Build them up and command your universe, right now, to get you *the hell out of this place* and do it with determination like you mean what you say. Don't question it. If you don't feel right about doing it, then don't do it—but don't question it. Don't go in there and say, "Well, am I doing this strong enough or not?" Go in there and use every ounce and every force of *ummph* you can come up with. Command you to get out of this place— *now!* Take it and explode your energy into it. The energy in your being, in your heart, explode it into that. Use your whole entire force. Use every energy you can get up right now to get you out of this. *End it.*

Now let your energy flow to your base seal and float up to the crown of your head and go with it. Drop the body. Let the next wave of energy come in behind it. Now command your psyche to be able to interpret the next wave of energy. Balance down.

Now feel where you're. Now feel you. What's going on inside there? Where is your vibration now? Let yourself see if you're through with your temper-tantrum and if a gentleness hasn't come over you.

See, whenever you're wanting to end something and get out of it, that tells you that there is something in your psyche that needs to be thrown out. That's the easiest way to look at. Your psyche is not going to sit there and scream and cry and nag and create discontent unless it is trying to motivate you into doing something.

Freedom is the most frightening of all things.

When you get into that state, you wouldn't necessarily say you were suicidal, but you could be because you want out bad enough—but you're not going to really do it. So if you want, use the metaphor that, "Hey, I'm sitting here right now and I'm killing this, I'm causing death, I'm severing it," and see if you're really that determined or not. Pull up every ounce and every bit of energy you have to end it. Feel yourself going into your brain and breaking the cord. Go back into it right now for a moment. Pull up your power, if you really want out. You have to go with a determination that you're going to actually sever your existence with physicality. On the other side, that's not really what is going to happen. You can rest easy with that, but you have to have the determination. Go into your brain. Your brain will show you where it is. There is a place in there. Just go in and break the cord. Go in. Find the cord. Break it, knowing that when you break it, death occurs. Break it. Break it. Did you break it?

I chopped the hell out of it!

Okay, now feel where you are. On one side you're going to be emotionally fatigued from what you just went through so that is not the feeling I'm looking for. Go beyond the emotional fatigue from what you just went through and feel where you and your body are now. What you effectively did is you told your brain to isolate the area of your brain that was your irritation. You told it to go into the part in your neuron system that was causing the problem and cut it off. You went in and chopped off your confusion. You actually severed the neuron that was causing it to fire. Now how is your body feeling—except for the emotional fatigue?

More of a gentle peacefulness there. But there is still an intensity in my solar-plexus to get out.

Then go in and use every ounce of that frustration. It wouldn't be there if you weren't going to use it. So rather than letting it keep nagging and irritating you for days, use it. Build it up and amplify it, exaggerate it as much as you can. If you can take it and pull the power in there, you can actually blow a hole right through your brain and into another reality. When I say blow a hole in your brain you'll think, "Whoa, that sounds dangerous!" These are just microscopic holes, but it actually will break through the membrane in such a way that you'll touch what you're crying to reach. So use it. Use it and bring it up in a force so powerful that you bring it up and you can explode it. Your determination is that you want out so bad that you're going to sit there and you're going to mediate death to your life.

You have to be passionately intent with it if you have that much frustration. You're going to go in there, you're going to cut it, and you're going to have to take about two days off work when you do it because you will not be in a state fit to do much of anything. From that, your psyche will begin to repair and heal. After about a forty-eight to fifty-six hour period you're going to start coming up with a whole new look on life. If you go into those feelings as I have described, on the other side you'll find out that you're not really wanting out of here.

All of you here are strangers in a strange land, and that is the bottom line. This is not home to you. You weren't created for this reality. You weren't meant for this reality and these bodies are about as foreign as you can get to you. That is also part of the joy why you came into them because it was a novelty. This is probably one of the most limiting forms any of you have ever been in. You could say that most of you eons ago evolved past this limitation and now this is almost like creating paralysis to you. It would be as if you've used your body your whole life and all of sudden something happens and you're paralyzed from the neck down. That is how you all feel in these bodies. There is a part of you that knows your power and your ability and it creates a frustration to be limited in this form.

So you're going to pull that energy and that power up and everyone of you will have to use it at least once in your life. Some of you have already used it. Some of you will use it multiple times. To some people this is when they get into their big intensity, they hate god, they're going to kill god—you've heard them all. Everybody is different with it.

Your identities are made up of a whole lot of layers, just for simplicity sake. Those make a cocoon over the Self that you're creating. You're the butterfly trying to come out of your own chrysalis. Most of you can see the beautiful butterfly floating. You can see the chick that has become the chicken, but you never think about what it took them to get out of the cramped space of the shell or the cocoon.

You know how tender the wings are on the butterfly, but do you know what a butterfly goes through in the process of changing from a caterpillar to a butterfly? Most of you say, well it makes a cocoon and comes out a butterfly. If you want to break it down, the caterpillar makes a cocoon and turns to mush. It doesn't just change from being a caterpillar. It actually creates an acid that totally destroys it, and if you were to break it open at that point, it is not a caterpillar. It's a green mush. There is no resemblance

You're the butterfly trying to come out of your own chrysalis.

of any life form at all. It actually totally dissolves itself so that it can reconstruct itself.

Most of you have seen the size of a cocoon that your butterfly emerges from. You have a butterfly that emerges from a cocoon a third its size. That is cramped—totally cramped. What do you think the butterfly is going to go through in a feeling sense to break through that cocoon? Cocoons are not indestructible, but they are hard enough. If you put a fair amount of force on it and can't break it, what is the butterfly inside of it going through to get out of it, with its tender wings and legs?

Right now you're in a mush stage and the chrysalis stage. You are in the process of the mush and you want to break out of the cocoon at the same time. Technically you can because time is simultaneous. So you're sensing a part of you, right now in the body, is in the mush stage of the caterpillar, but there is a part of you that is in the chrysalis stage with the wings that are trying to beat against and make a hole in the cocoon to get out. You're also sensing the butterfly knows how to fly, because you've breached your second brain. And so, you're seeing you to be all these at once.

So which stage is going to be preferable to you? If you were living these all at once and you are in the physical body going through the mush, you're obviously going to prefer . . .

The advanced stage.

Yes, and that is where the temper-tantrum is coming from. So instead of just staying in the mush, if you can use your determination whenever you get frustrated. It can be one of the most powerful tools you can use. Just don't be afraid of it and use it. Pull it up, use it and let that begin to crack the edge of your cocoon so you can emerge, so that you can do it quickly and simultaneously. You're actually going to take your intensities, get as mad as you can, as frustrated as you can, and punch a hole so that you can at least view the finished product. If you are here in the mush and you can view the finished product, it gives you stability. It gives you a sense of, "Okay, its worth going through this, if that is how I'm going to look."

How many of you think a caterpillar knows what is happening to it? It's a molecular thing that happens. How do you think the caterpillar feels when its body secretes an acid that turns it to mush, and it is conscious through the whole process? How does the caterpillar feel? Emotionally, psychologically, what is that caterpillar going through as it sits and is consciously aware of its body going into mush for the transformation, and it doesn't know what transformation is? This is the only time it has been through it so it has no idea what is going on. It is molecular. It doesn't know what it is going to be. It doesn't recognize that its even going to become a butterfly. What would it be going through?

Confusion, frustration, fear . . .

Everything you said you are going through. When it is in the process of doing that, what do you think the caterpillar wants to do?

It wants out of there!

It is in the cocoon of its own making. That cocoon of its own making is for protection to hold it together during its transformation. ▲

Creating the Beautiful Space[*]

The best gift you can give anyone—yourselves, your loved ones, the planet as a whole—is the gift of the walk of a master or to be able to see the god in all things. You don't take time to do it. None of you do. When was the last time you just sat down and felt the appreciation of you? When was the last time you sat down and appreciated all the little quaint things you do? When was the last time you sat down and appreciated your own uniqueness. When was the last time you took time to appreciate all of these little insignificant differences about you?

Do you know all those little things that you consider so insignificant are what makes you, you. It is what makes you beautiful to everyone, including yourself. But you as a people, on the whole, are not taught to appreciate yourselves. You are taught exactly the opposite. You are taught to find out what is wrong and what is bad. You don't take time to praise your own beauty, and when you do, you take it and try to create a puffed up intellectual beauty. "Yes, I'm beautiful, I know that, I am beautiful, yes," and you try to convince yourself. When was the last time you took time to realize how beautiful you really are? Have any of you even done it, ever? No. You do it from some parts and you do it a little bit and you do it here and there but you don't have an ongoing appreciation for you. You don't allow yourself to stay in that beauty.

Take yourself for the moment now and feel your own beauty. Let yourself feel beautiful right now. Feel what a beautiful individual you are and feel all of your walls against it. You've never taught yourselves or allowed yourselves to find beauty in you. Do it. Generate how beautiful. Create a feeling of beauty. Let your whole entire body, your whole entire being feel beautiful.

*This piece was originally delivered as a meditation.

63

We're not talking sexy. We're not talking an image. We're not talking a picture. Let yourself take the moment and simply just feel beautiful. You don't have to create a picture. It is a feeling. Let your body inside realize its beauty. Put yourself into a space where you just feel beautiful, very beautiful inside. But notice your resistance at doing this if you have it. If not, feel how wonderful you feel. Feel the gentleness that is there. Feel the lack of fear that is there. Feel the intensity of love that you are. This is what you are wanting everyone else to instill in you. This is what you're asking the whole world to show you—how beautiful you are. But nobody has the time to do it. They are all taking time to prove how ugly they can be, because that is how they feel about themselves.

If somebody could instill in you and help you create that sense of just feeling beautiful about yourself and being in that beautiful space, that would be a gift. That would be the grandest gift you could have in physicality. That sense of beautifulness is where you are going to learn about love. That sense of feeling beautiful is where you are going to learn about joy. That state of beautifulness is where you're going to learn about intimacy and sharing. It is all right there. The world is too busy. It is not going to do it for you. Whenever you can hold an image of beauty for another individual, this is the gift you are giving them and they don't even know it.

Do not fear things. Don't fear loss as permanent. Yes, if it appears, acknowledge it and let yourself go into it; feel it, wallow in it and then put the beauty back in it. That beauty is god. That beauty is the essence of you, and if you take an individual and hold them in that image of beauty, you will help them walk in their own power and become that. That is the best gift you will ever give anyone.

So in these times when you fear and there are many of you that are fearing for your children and loved ones, send them beauty. Send them a sense of their own beauty. Not the fear of losing them, not a fear of loss, but instill in them a sense of beauty.

If you could maintain that sense of beauty all the time, you wouldn't be seeking to leave here. You wouldn't be seeking to try to get out of physical existence all of the time. You'd be in a place of gentleness, where anything you had to deal with, you would have the strength to do it. That gentleness, that beauty, is a state of god. So when you can see anything in a state of beauty and a state of god, no matter how ugly it wants you to believe it to be, you have given it a gift and you have lifted it.

This world is going to need this and so does this planet, but if you can't see beauty in you, you're going to have an awful hard time helping it out. If you can take all of these atrocities, all of this ugliness it wants to show you and hold it in beauty and touch the beauty and feel the beauty in it, you are lifting it. You are lifting you, because you cannot feel beauty directed at someone else unless that beauty is you and going through you.

If you take these words and feel them, you will know that it is truth. The only thing any of you have ever sought in existence is to know that place of beauty. That is all you have ever wanted. That place of beauty is what you are seeking when you ask for wholeness and to get beyond your limitations—to truly feel beautiful. It is why you want relationships. It is why you want everything you want. Whatever it is, you are wanting it to instill in you this sense of beauty.

That sense of beauty is god, and it was always there. It never went anywhere.

That sense of beauty is god, and it was always there. It never went anywhere. You are just trying to convince the world that you're not beautiful. You don't want to believe how truly beautiful you are, so you are trying to put out this picture to the world, "I'll prove to you how ugly I can be. I will prove it to you." As a planet you've been going out of your way to try to prove to everyone how unbeautiful you really can be because that is how you feel about yourselves. You say, "I'm this unbeautiful in here, and I'll make you know so. I'll prove to you how unbeautiful I am."

It is not a truth. This is the largest untruth there is. That beauty is there because it is god. It is part of all of you, but that is what you are running away from. Anytime you are running away, you are running away from that state of beauty. Anytime you hide, that is what you are hiding from. Anytime you are scared of love, what you are scared of really is knowing your own beauty and feeling beautiful. When you feel beautiful, all of your images feel vulnerable, but you have a strength with that beauty because you are not looking for anyone else to instill it in you.

Let yourselves go into your own beautiful space. You need it. With the planet going through its changes and its metamorphosis, you're going to have to stay in your state of beauty to keep from being pulled into its proof of how ugly it can be. That beautiful space, if you will let yourself feel it, right now, is the deepest state of you that you have ever felt. Let yourself feel that beautiful, that approachable in spirit and you will feel that connected at all times. That is your shortest course to feeling connected, to feeling loved, to being with god, whatever your term for it, it doesn't matter.

Just let yourself feel beautiful. When you feel beautiful you are in a state of intimacy which means a state of intimacy is a state of sharing love.

If you want to love anyone else, to help them in their life, you have to be able to touch that state of intimacy in your own being in order to send it to them. You have to be able to see yourself in beauty. When you can feel that beautiful space, when you can just get to a point where you just feel so beautiful, and I mean every cell of your being can feel beautiful, then you will begin to understand what love is. When you feel that, you can then instill that in others and that is the best gift you will give anyone, including yourself.

If you can let yourself move into that state of beauty and feeling beautiful, you can send your feeling of beautifulness to another individual and embrace them in beauty. Connect with them and feel them. Feel them in that same state of beauty that you are feeling in yourself.

You will end their war because when you feel beautiful, there is no war left in you. If you can do that there will be no war in them either because that is all any of you want is to be able to be beautiful and to feel it. When you've held them in an image of god, you've removed all of their ugliness. They have no excuse for saying they are ugly inside any more, because that is the time they were truly loved. In doing that, when they go in there to try to dredge up all of these terrible things inside, when they get through with all the intellectual mind play, all they are going to find is a sense of beauty and love. Nobody could ask for a grander gift than that. When you touch that beauty and love, all you have is the desire to live, the desire for existence. Their decision will be made and you will have had a hand in making that decision.

The same goes for the planet. That is why when one focuses upon all of the atrocities—your pollution, your pain, everything—you are just reinforcing it. While by some perspectives it would be considered irresponsible just to focus on the beauty, you are giving it the best gift you can give it because when you can focus on the beauty of everything, including this planet, you have given it the gift of life. You have given it the gift to know that it is god, and it will make its own decision having considered two sides of the story.

If you don't have that beauty in there and you've never found that beauty in there, you have only one side of your story. That is a story of ugliness because that is what everybody has told you for eons of time. They haven't taken the time to let you feel your beauty. They have not taken the time to help you learn beauty. All man has ever done on this planet is to teach each other how ugly everything is.

The gift of beauty is the best gift you are going to ever find or give. All of you have been indoctrinated into your ugliness long enough. Most of it was self-done. You bought other people's truths about ugliness, but you did most of it yourself. All of these judgments you've made on yourself are trying to prove to the world, "See I'm as ugly as I want to be." That is your way of trying to hide that beauty in there. Your whole population spends more time teaching and reinforcing ugly.

Ugly is judgment, that is all. There is no such thing. You can take your most ugly thing and in it there is something of worth and something of beauty that occurs from it. Within your beings there is nothing ugly about any of you, either. But you enjoy feeling that way. You enjoy feeling not loved, because you've been taught that. Let yourselves feel beauty and you'll do more for you, more for mankind, more for the planet. More important, it will do more for any of those that you are trying to send love to. Feel beautiful, because when you are feeling beautiful, there is no judgment.

When one focuses upon all of the atrocities—your pollution, your pain, everything—you are just reinforcing it.

Judgment is polarity. Judgment means that you are away from being god. In that state of beauty, when you let yourself feel beautiful, there is no judgment unless you were using it as a resistance to feeling beautiful.

When you feel beautiful, the next magical thing happens. It is called the magic of wanting to be you, and wishing to share and express. Feel how beautiful and loved you are. Notice that when you get into that state, all you want to do is share. This is called a state of abundance. Whenever you are in a state where you want to share, you are in a state of abundance. Feeling beautiful is a state of abundance. This means that you are willing to touch the universe and let the universe touch you and to share with it. It means that you are willing to quit trying to do it all by yourself. All you had to do is let yourself feel beautiful and it was always there. That state of beautifulness in there is abundance, and it will lead you into more abundance than most of you know. Anything outside this state of beautifulness is lack and the only thing that you are lacking is the eyes to see how beautiful you are.

If you haven't the eyes, or the embracement of how beautiful you are, that is the only thing you can lack. However, it is enough to put you into your whole mode of lack, loss, and perpetual motion. Then you start trying to create lives to prove it—to prove how ugly you are, how unloved you are, how unbeautiful. You set up all these things in your life to reinforce your feelings of a lack of beauty. The grandest gift a master can ever give is to instill beauty in another, and they can't do that unless they are abundant with beauty themselves.

The only key you need to unlock the whole universe and put it at your fingertips is to allow yourself to feel beautiful because that means you are equal to the universe. It means you are in flow. It means you are allowing the universe to touch you and when you feel beautiful, do you feel defensive? You don't have to. When you feel beautiful, all of these things that you want out of just disappear. When you feel beautiful, do you feel vulnerable? No. There is a sense of anticipation. There is a sense of expression. There is a sense of deep sharing and a curiosity for life. That is real beauty. If you learn nothing in life except this lesson, you've learned life because life was created to show you, to allow you, to comprehend your beauty, but you got mad at it. You've been trying to throw a temper-tantrum to prove how it didn't work. You've been trying to prove how you're not beautiful because everyone knows that beauty is appreciated and things of beauty are loved by all.

When you go truly into that beautiful space, there is no longer the fear of being loved. There is the actual desire and motivation to go out into the world and be you and be loved. It actually generates the desires and passion. That state of beautifulness will instill more passion than you will ever find any where else, but it will also attract beautifulness back to it.

Just let yourselves feel beautiful. You don't spend enough time doing it. I love you very, very much, and I do find beauty in all of you. I see it and feel it and I know it. It is time for you to know it and to allow yourselves to feel it. ▲

The Evolution of Man's Brain

When each of you as gods decided you wanted to live in physicality, the biological brain had to be adapted so that you could use it differently. Otherwise these brain systems would have been just the same as any of your animal's upon the planet and would serve basically one function.

This biological brain is simply your primitive brain or your primate brain. The biology of your physical embodiments and the biology of the planet are a little bit different. If these embodiments were at the stage that the planet itself is, through its own biological evolution, your brain would be much different than the ones you're using now. You would have one basic brain and this brain would be for instinctual behavior and animal behavior. Each of you already have this within your brain systems. This portion of your brain is dealing strictly with the primitive or the survival instinct, the animal behavior.

Your brain today has basically three functions. You have primarily your biological brain from the planetary system. But you also have portions of your brain that were developed later to help you evolve these biological embodiments.

Each of you are a biological entity, but you are also a light being. When your light hit the edge of time-space medium, you refracted into multiple pieces. When you refracted into multiple pieces, each of those portions sought out an embodiment in physicality. When it did this, some portions of you went into your past, some portions went into your future, and some right now into your present time. If you could see it as a nucleus of light hitting the edge of the time-space medium and at the edge of the time-space medium it refracts. When it refracted, portions of you went into all different time periods—forwards and backwards, historically speaking.

The body has a biological time clock, and so, only bodies have history in that perspective. The light you are went into all the bodies at the same time. This is why it is considered simultaneous time by our perspective. The body does not understand simultaneous time in the same manner as the light that you are does. Since you are a light being living simultaneous lives, any embodiment that you were in needed to be aware of all the rest of the light that you were. This was necessary in order to allow you to have a continuity, to understand everything that you were learning and to embrace everything that you were.

The core of light that you were hit time-space. When it refracted, let's say it refracted into ten particums. (Most of them refracted into more pieces than that.) Let's say each of those ten particums went into a different time in history. Each of those went into a different perspective of history by the reckoning of the biological time clock of bodies.

Each body knows its own biological time clock, so therefore, it has a beginning and an end. However, light doesn't. Light cannot comprehend linear time. Since light cannot comprehend linear time, because it is in all places at once, you have the ten particums of you that came out of the same core, and from what they understand, they're living all ten of these lives at the same time. The bodies aren't necessarily living them all simultaneously, but the light is. Since the light that each of you are is living each of these lives at the same time, you have simultaneous time.

Biologically, you do not have simultaneous time. Biologically, you have linear time. Light and spirit have simultaneous time and do not comprehend or know linear time. So the light particums that you are now, the core having split into ten light particums, for example, each went into a different biological functioning. This allowed them to have the perspective of linear time. However, since it was a light particum, it cannot be separated into linear time and must be doing all things at once.

When you put yourselves into these embodiments, a portion of you had to be able to keep track of where the other parts of you were at any one given time. At that point in time when you chose the embodiment to move into, the brain structure was not equipped to handle simultaneous time or to even understand it. What you had to do is actually grow a new apparatus of your brain.

At this point in time, the second piece of your brain was grown. This second piece of your brain is totally equipped to keep track of every piece of you no matter where you are, past, present or future. It keeps track of and actually holds all of the experiences that the core of light is having in all ten of its expressions. So this portion of your brain literally keeps track of you so that you are focused here. Then you as that light particum can focus into this body in this time and this space but still keep track of all of the other experiences you're having. This allows you to gain wisdom at a much faster rate, since you're sharing the experiences of and learning from all the other particums.

This second portion of your brain has two functions. One, it keeps track of all of your lifetimes. It keeps track of what you term past, present, and future lives. This portion of your brain has two sets of chemical membranes in it and works from a much more chemical principle and light principle than the rest of it.

One set of membranes keeps track of your light from a linear perspective. It says, "This is this linear lifetime. I was birthed here, I will die here, and this is where I'm in the progression." It keeps you, the light that you are, focused in linear space. If the chemical membrane for your linear set of membranes in that portion of your brain becomes weak, damaged, or is penetrated, this creates symptoms like those of Alzheimer's Disease. An individual has learned either how to break the membrane, how to transcend the chemical membrane or how to change it. And so they get out of it, and when they come back in, they're not sure which portion of the linear space to come back into! They might get out of it and jump around. They might jump from being a sixty-seven-year-old to a twelve-year-old. They might then go to twenties, to forties, to thirties, to teens.

When you go into a past life regression, you're actually going into your . . . own brain and understanding it through this second brain structure.

The second portion of this brain function runs the whole totality of all your other experiences, simultaneously. This is what individuals do when they go into a past life regression. All they are doing is penetrating the chemical membrane of that portion of their brain and going into that experience of light in another existence at that same time.

The particums refracted from the core are all living at the same time and don't know that they're each in a linear perspective. This portion of your brain literally keeps track of all of them, so that you can interchange experience, interchange information, attitudes and perspectives.

Some of you are so tied into the linear perspective that the chemical membrane is very hard for you to penetrate in order to go into another experience. Therefore, a lot of individuals might never be able to penetrate it to find a past life or other experience. When you go into a past life regression, you're actually going into your own mind, into your own brain and understanding it through this second brain structure. That is why, since you're understanding it through this brain structure for this current time, it has to be interpreted here through whatever your belief system, your attitude, and what your language is now.

You penetrate your own chemical membranes within that portion of your brain very easily by altering your own brain waves. In a regressed state, a relaxed state of mind or hypnosis, an individual is actually penetrating their own chemical membrane within their brain. As they are doing this, they will actually pinpoint into one of these other perspectives of light, their own light, living in another embodiment in another historical time or linear space. They will perceive all of the perceptions of that portion of their light, but they will have to perceive it through the embodiment they're in now and the way this brain structure is functioning.

That light particum could be in another embodiment some place else having an experience. Its experience is going to be a little bit different than your interpretation of the experience here because it has to filter through your brain system in this present time. That is why when you go into regressed states, you often have difficulty with names, dates, and places. Those are things understood by that light particum in that linear space. It doesn't interpret well into this one. Through its chemical membrane, the brain structure will actually distort or change it to perceive it here and now.

The brain functions by triggering electrical charges across these chemical membranes. Let's say a certain chemical charge is needed in order to interpret an experience, and this brain system that the light is in now isn't picking it up. You're going to have a glitch or a piece of memory out of that one that can't come through to this one because the brain structure won't interpret it. This is why often when you try to understand past experiences or regressions, you're going to miss pieces of it. This is also what happens in many channeling experiences.

In many channeling experiences, this membrane portion of your brain is the one that is primarily used. It allows the actual light particum to travel through simultaneous time rather than being in linear space. The membrane allows it the freedom to go into simultaneous time, in all its perspectives, wherever they are and translate them back through this brain system. When most individuals have guidance or when they are channeling, they are simply penetrating their own chemical membrane in their brain. They are actually stepping into one of their own experiences in another time and space and are literally learning how to interpret it into this one.

Let's say the core split into ten different light pieces and is living in ten different historical linear spaces biologically. That means each of those lights has a different embodiment. Everyone of your embodiments carry a different chemical structuring in their brains.

Let's say you have a portion of you that lived a thousand-years ago in your terminology. The chemical structuring and the electronic firing of that brain is different than yours today. That means that when that information is trying to be translated and understood by this brain system, there are going to be pieces and glitches and things missing from it because your brain system runs on a different chemical and electrical basis than that brain system did. It would be like trying to send Morse Coding and one person sends it very rapidly and the other can't interpret it that fast. Since they don't, they catch pieces of it and these pieces seem to form words, images or pictures.

Your brain systems are working on a different firing pattern than they were even a hundred-years ago.

That is what is happening now. Your brain systems are working on a different firing pattern than they were even a hundred-years ago. They technically are working at a different rate of speed, so therefore, anything out of your past that is trying to come through is going to come through at a different rate of electrical and chemical firing than your brain system uses today. Your brain says, "Well here is the first couple letters of the word. I'll fill in the word."

You often do that when people start talking. They start to say a word and you fill in the word for them in your own mind before it is even spoken. Your minds do this with the past. When your past is trying to be translated into these brain structures, the past is firing at a different rate of patterning, and therefore, it looks like it is going to have a certain image or certain picture.

This changing of your chemical and electrical firing is what allows you to grow into your brain systems so that you know that you're not five-years-old any more. There is a minute portion of this brain system that is almost like a clock that doesn't let you back up. It continually fires at a much—I'll use the term rapid, it is a little bit different concept—but it would be much as if it changes its speed. Let's say that if you were one-year-old, it would be at a slow pace. If you're two, a little bit faster so that you can no longer interpret the one-year-old. By the time you're five in a linear space, it is firing at such a rate that you can no longer relate to the younger age. This is actually what allows the light that you are to keep track of linear time and space in these bodies, because the light does not understand or comprehend linear time.

This portion of the brain is literally designed with a mechanism of its own to keep you up-to-date with where you're supposed to be. That means that this portion of your brain is actually firing differently than it was a year ago or even a month ago. It allows it to pick up speed so that you can't back track and lose your focus in linear time.

So now you're trying to connect with something that you term your past or past experience. It is going to be firing chemically and electrically in a different pattern than where your brain is now. Since it does, you don't have the same interpretation. This brain will try to interpret it according to where your brain is firing now. Since it is slow in comparison, your brain will try to fill in the pieces. Your past life or regression is coming so slowly that your mind just wants to fill in the pieces and get it done with. That is why sometimes it doesn't match what you find historically. Your mind will fill it in with what it understands now, rather than the true picture or the true understanding.

There are also portions of your light that went into what you would call your future. Since they are your future, the chemical firing and reaction of that portion of your brain that is dealing with them is working at an even different rate. So if you try to connect with these future lives, it would be similar to connecting with a past life. If you tried to connect with it and bring up the information or translate it from there, you're still going to have the same difficulty translating it across the chemical membrane and the firing sequences.

We've been discussing the second brain. The brain of simultaneous time or the brain that deals with linear time and space, we will refer to as the time-space portion of the brain or the light brain.

In the beginning, the second portion of your brain or your time-space brain was very open. Since it was very open, you knew every portion of that light particum at the same time. That portion of your brain was simultaneously aware of every one of those ten pieces that had fractured from the core light.

But problems began happening. Let's say that you were in a situation and you were grandly at peace—no problem. But one of the other ten light particums from your same core light was under predatory attack. That entity portion of you that was under predatory attack would make the brain structure react in fear to preserve it. You, sitting in your historical time-space, would do the same thing, and you didn't need to. Because you were so open to understand and be aware of all of your perspectives at the same time, it began to give you problems. It actually moved it to a place where you would be triggered by one of your other light particums in another experience that had nothing to do with you! All of a sudden, you could feel that you had to flee, because something predatory was coming upon you. It had nothing to do with you in that time and space, but you felt it. This began to create confusion for all of you. If one of the light particums, wherever they were in linear space and time, began reacting to all the others, it was very chaotic for the individual.

At [one] point in time all of you upon the planet could read each others thoughts. You didn't have language.

At this point in time all of you upon the planet could read each others thoughts. You didn't have language. This portion of your brain is also the portion that interprets thought waves. It is what interprets everything else from the planet and actually allows you to communicate. So this portion of your brain does not only work with linear time and space, but it also deals with what you call your telepathy. Since you could read each other's minds and brains, you would begin reacting to what everybody else was thinking. This was the beginning of social consciousness on this planet. This was the beginning of your very first gestalt here.

The lights that you were came into these bodies, built the second brain, and adapted them for your own use. Not only was the core light that you were in ten different linear perspectives making you react, but so was everybody else on the planet. Anybody else who came into contact with you in your state of telepathy, whatever their mind was doing and whatever they were perceiving, was also triggering this portion of your brain and creating the same behavioral instincts for your body. It began to become very chaotic! You got to a point of not wanting to read everybody else's thoughts and not wanting them to read yours because everything you thought, so did they. Everything you felt, so did they. Everything that you were reacting to, so did they.

You began altering your chemical firing and your electric charges in the second portion of the brain so they couldn't be interpreted any more. You literally shut this portion of your brain off so that all it did was focus you here and now. You didn't want any other focus or anybody else's input in it whatsoever—including your own. Each of you individually began to alter your whole chemical responses in this portion of your brain so that it would actually filter out anybody else's thoughts. Each of you began to develop your own individual Morse Coding, chemically speaking, that no one else could penetrate.

Since each of you altered these portions of your brain and changed them to fit your own purposes, it is very difficult for anybody else to get into them or to understand them. It is even difficult for each of you to get through this portion of your brain. Your whole chemical membrane and the firing system for this portion of your brain became just like your own fingerprint for this existence. In other words, nobody can penetrate that unless they know your exact access code, so to speak, or your exact way of chemically firing in this portion. This portion of your brain is so intricately yours, that nobody else can get through it unless they are a portion of you. It is so intricately yours, that even your own guidance has difficulty getting through it! That is why it is very difficult to have clarity in this portion of your brains. This is why it is very difficult to use it or to heal it. But, it can be used, it can be dealt with.

This is the portion of your brain where most of your own guidance is going to come through when it comes through the brain system. This is the portion of your brain that was actually created for the light, so therefore, it is the light brain and deals with the time-space medium. It interprets and is intertwined with your primitive brain in order to create a synergy for the body and the light that you are to live together.

The next or third portion of your brain, we're going to call the interpretive portion of your brain. In your light brain and the interpretive brain there are major portions that seem to be dead or totally unused and your medical profession does not understand them or what they do.

When your light became so entrapped in these brain systems that they no longer could get out of them, and they could no longer get out of the biological species or linear time-space, you actually had to find a whole new interpretive way of getting into it. This led to the development of the third portion of the brain. Many of you have not yet accessed this portion of your brain. It is usable, totally functionable, and is there. This is the portion that you will use for your higher expansions of consciousness and evolution. It was created for interpreting higher consciousness into the light brain and then into the primitive brain. Your second brain or your light brain became so enclosed and encased that you could no longer interpret your own guidance, so you began to create this interpretive brain.

This interpretive brain can interpret from the feeling center into an intellectual understanding or comprehension. In its pure state it can take you into evolution and expansion of consciousness. When you began to use this third portion of your brain your intellects were born.

Originally, your first brain only gave you the animal behavioral instincts. The function of the second brain, or the light brain, was to keep track of the light, access the guidance of the light, to keep the light in the body and functioning. The third brain had to be developed to get you out of the density that you created by putting the light so deep into biological structuring. The third brain was added to interpret it so it could understand your own light and be able to get out. It was created to understand the animal behavior and actually evolve yourself out of the biological animal behavioral instinct.

In your solar-plex region you have other gray matter and we'll call that the solar-plex mind or the heart mind. This was designed to create and receive feelings—it was your feeling center. The gray matter in the solar-plex mind and the gray matter in the third brain were added at the same time. They work together in order to get you out of the density you created by entrapping your light in your second brain or the light brain.

The solar-plex mind or the heart mind was created to receive all feelings or abstract thought. Since the light was shut off in the light brain, you weren't interpreting it because you didn't really have a package to do that. When that second portion of your brain was added, it was to hold the light in these bodies. You hadn't comprehended that by holding the light in these bodies that it would become as any other animal upon the planet. You didn't quite realize that; and therefore, you sought a way of gaining once again, your higher guidance and to have a connection with the universal principle. The solar-plex mind was added and created for that purpose. It was created to feel, so it and the interpretive portion of your brain were created to feel and work together in order to help the light brain get out of the animal instinctual behavior.

The solar-plex mind was created to bring in the abstract thought or lesson, feel it, and send it up to the interpretive brain. The interpretive brain would then interpret it into a language, a sequence of Morse Coding if you will, or chemical and electrical firings to help these instinctual humanoid species to get out of the density they were in and evolve this biological vehicle into a vehicle that the gods could use for their own purposes.

The solar-plex mind was created to bring in the abstract thought or lesson, feel it, and send it up to the interpretive brain.

At this point in time, this interpretive portion of your brain was created to work in harmony with the solar-plex mind. If the two worked in harmony, the abstract thought or feeling would come into the solar-plex mind, go up and be interpreted by the interpretive brain, push from there through the light brain and light centers into the primitive brain to mature and evolve the biological species. If it needed to, it could actually change biologically anything that needed to be changed in the bodies.

A ll of the altering of your genetic structure comes from this portion of your brain where it actually connects the interpretive mind to the light and primitive brains. Where these three come together is the portion of your brain that deals with your genetics and the physical imprinting. When you began to use that imprinting the species grew. At that point in time, the species changed and altered dramatically very, very quickly. The fastest biological evolution these vehicles have ever had is when these three came together and worked.

But at that point in time the light brain moved into a place of still wanting to have a different thought process and firing sequence than everybody and everything else. So once again, it began to create another chemical membrane around it and actually altered the new genetic packaging it was creating. Because the individual's light wanted to still be isolated from everything else, it started setting up chemical and electrical firing as a barrier around the interpretive brain, and now you're entrapped in the genetics. Now you've literally cut yourselves off from even using the interpretive brain portion of your package. That portion of your brain package is dormant.

It was fully functioning for a period of time. During that period of time you used it enough to change the genetic structuring and that genetic structuring is being passed down. But you genetically predisposed these embodiments not to use that portion of the brain, because you set up a chemical electrical firing around it that enabled you to no longer get into the interpretive portion of your gray matter. When this interpretive portion of your brain begins to be fully functioning, it will step you outside of this physical expression. It is what is going to evolve you and expand you. Most of your journey is to release a lot of this limiting chemical structure in your brain. Much of that comes from releasing the old attitudes that created it, in order to create a synergy where you can use the whole totality of your brain system.

The interpretive brain is not going to be functioning and fully opened again until the solar-plex mind and the heart mind are opened up, functioning, and sending its messages into the interpretive brain to be interpreted. Right now the solar-plex mind has either shriveled on a lot of you and so is not working the way it could or it is working very little. What it brings in it shoves in the genetic memory portion of your brain to be interpreted in genetic memory, then shoves it into the light brain, which shoves it into the animal or primitive brain. Since it does this, anything that comes in that could be able to evolve you into the higher level of consciousness is actually being shoved into your animal behavior and instinct. The portion of the brain called the intellect is what creates your genetic structuring. It is where the three tried to come together, and at that point in time, the interpretive mind tried to move into a place of overcoming the other two and their limitations. But, since it did not fully overcome them, you ended up with a portion of your brain that establishes your genetics, passes them down, but also has established an intellectual mind.

Your brain systems translate. They do not think. They do not create thought.

That portion of gray matter in your solar-plex region, we label the fourth mind or fourth brain. Actually, your brain is simply for receiving thought. I would prefer to call this fourth mind the solar-plex mind, because it actually deals more with non-physical input or thought feelings than it does with the interpretation of it. Although mind and brain are terms that are commonly used interchangeably, we generally refer to the brain as the physical portion of the thought process and the mind as the non-physical portion of your thought process. The mind is actually the auric field, electromagnetic field, or what we like to call the biofield that surrounds your embodiment.

Your brain systems translate. They do not think. They do not create thought. All they're doing right now is actually taking everything that comes into the mind or biofield, interpreting it and using it. They are actually just receiving thought and interpreting it according to your attitudes, your belief systems, your perspectives, and creating your realities out of it.

The solar-plex mind or the heart mind is actually your feeling center which allows you to go into your interpretive portion of the brain. A lot of you are not using it to the depth that you need to in order to create the electrical charge to re-awaken that portion of your brain.

Your brain systems work from an electrical and chemical charge. If you're going to get into this interpretive brain portion, you're going to have to create the electrical and chemical charges to wake it up and use it. Until it is awakened and is being used, it is just going to appear to be dormant.

This interpretive portion of your brain is still connected where you want it to be and is functioning there. That is why it feels as if somebody is controlling your life. That is why it feels as if your guidance can't be heard or can't be seen. That is why it may feel as if your life is going on without you. It is either running off the animal instinctual behavior or that portion of the interpretive mind in the non-physical region and you're just not aware of it because it is not interpreting through.

The solar-plex mind has the ability—when you use a feeling tone and you take it deep into your feelings and understand your feelings—to actually recreate the chemicals that are needed for that interpretive brain. The more you feel, the more you're creating the electrical and chemical charges that you need to link your entire brain system together so that it functions as a whole.

This is what awareness is. Self-awareness comes when you're fully aware and the consciousness of your whole brain system is working together. Right now you have your primate brain working on physicality trying to keep you alive, you have your light brain working and playing in other realities and other realms, you have your interpretive brain working in a non-physical region, and you have your solar-plex brain, closed down or off in most cases. You have this other portion where the three had come together and facilitated genetic evolvement, and that's the only one that is working. Since that is working, it is tying all of the brain portions together through your genetics right now. What this means is that your genetic structuring is the point that is tying the primitive brain, the light brain, the interpretive brain and the solar-plex brain all together as your genetic packaging. That is why most of you are running off your physical genetics rather than off of your mind.

How does the pituitary contribute to the functioning of all these portions of the brain?

The pituitary system and the pineal system are light sensitive, which means that they were originally designed as an appendage of the second or light brain. The pituitary and the pineal system were created to help direct the light that you are into the totality of the rest of your embodiment.

In all animals on your planet, the pituitary system is what orchestrates or controls the light that flows within the animal. When you moved into these biological embodiments they already had a pituitary system. It was much different than the pituitary system you've evolved into now. The pituitary system actually responds to light. Whenever you move into grander spaces of light within the embodiment, the pituitary system opens. As it opens, it begins to create the synergy for the brain systems within your head. Whenever there is more light in your embodiment, it is going to come through feeling yourself into love, into life. As you feel yourself into that joy and bring those levels of joy back up into your embodiment, that begins to trigger the pituitary system. When it triggers the pituitary system, the pituitary system being at the center of your brain structure begins to open.

Bringing those feelings of joy very deeply into the totality of your life is what is going to trigger that brain back into complete openness.

As it begins to open, it begins to chemically change the hormones and the electrical firing of your whole brain system. When the pituitary system is open and functioning, it actually can work to tie all of the other brain structures into one synergy so that they work in harmony. If the brain structure is not working in harmony, then you're going to have diseasement in the body, you're going to have aging in the body, and you're going to have disconnection between the various portions of the brain. This is why there is so much emphasis put upon the pituitary system in the brain. It is not necessarily what you term a third eye. The reason that working with the pituitary can give an individual more expanse of knowledge and more expanse of understanding is because when it opens, it actually interprets. It actually ties into the interpretive brain as well as the primate brain, and the solar-plex mind and the light brain. It ties all of them together into that synergy so that you're actually interpreting the feeling in the whole brain system.

The pituitary system controls everything in your whole body, including the flow of your fluids in your body, and the control of whether you sleep or are awake. All of these things are orchestrated by the pituitary system in accordance to the needs of the light in the body. So whenever the body biologically gets too void of light, the pituitary system goes to work and actually begins to try to create a new balance. Your blood pressure is run through the pituitary system. A lot of other things are run through the pituitary system in its effort to try to create grander light or grander amounts of energy or electrical charge for the entire embodiment.

To open the pituitary system so that it opens the brain requires grand amounts of love and grand amounts of joy. Realize that the only time the joy is going to reach the levels needed in order to open that pituitary system is when the solar-plex mind is opened by bringing in the feeling.

There are many ways to facilitate this. You can meditate upon it. You can try to open it, you can do any of these things you wish to do. The fastest and easiest way to do it is just by feeling joy. When you bring the vibration of joy into your embodiment, it has to come through the heart. Whenever you're feeling joy, it is felt in the heart center or solar-plex mind and flows into the entire embodiment from there. Joy is one of the few vibrations upon this planet that is isolated and concentrated into that heart-mind center. Since joy does that, it activates it. When it is activated, that immediately sends a signal to your pituitary system, allowing the pituitary system to relax open. As it relaxes open, it moves into a place of triggering the entire brain so it works as the interpretive package it was intended to. When it does this, you move into states of awareness, you move into states of psychic abilities, and you begin to view different perspectives.

It is within all of you to be able to have a fully functioning brain. Even if genetically, you have been predisposed or passed down into generations where the brain is partially closed, where the brain does not fully work because of the chemical membranes that have been designed in it, everyone of you, simply by feeling those levels of joy, bringing that into your being and allowing yourself to vibrate at it, have the ability to change your brain system very fast and very easily.

Most of you do not allow yourself to stay in those levels of joy long enough to recreate the chemical membranes that your brain needs in order to create the harmony in it. The joy and bringing those feelings of joy very deeply into the totality of your life is what is going to trigger that brain back into complete openness. Even in an individual whose brain is partially damaged, partially closed, is not functioning properly, the easiest way to heal them is to put them back into a state of joy. Bring the joy back up into their life again, and this will actually teach their entire brain system how to work around those damaged portions and either heal them or to actually move into that interpretive brain and begin to function out of it and use it. Joy is the grand healer of the brain and the grand healer of the totality of each of you. ▲

Core Lifetimes and the Time-Space Medium

A core lifetime is when the light from the universal principle penetrates the time-space membrane. If you could see it, from your perspective this membrane looks like a mirage of jello. That is the easiest way to explain it. From outside of it, it looks as if you were looking in your beautiful night sky, but you know how your mirages wobble. It wobbles like that, and its substance is like looking through clear gelatin.

The core light, core lifetime, is the entity, you. When you are at that speed, you travel so fast that you cannot be held. In order to see itself, the light penetrates this membrane, this jello, this gelatin of time-space. It penetrates so fast, just like a laser beam, that it cannot stop to check out the experience. In its traveling through that membrane, it leaves a holographic imprint of its journey. It would be like burning a laser beam through a steel door. The metal is all warped, and you can't see the laser beam any more. All you can see is the path of where it went.

The core life is the exact same thing. The core life or the core light traveled through the gelatin membrane called time-space at such a rapid rate you couldn't see it, and it left a hole or an imprint from its journey, just like the laser beam on the steel door. Now you come along and examine the door to try to figure out what made the hole, and that is what you call your lifetimes. This would be much like taking a big, thick steel door, burning a hole through it, and then sitting around analyzing every inch and every speck of the entire metal to see what made the hole.

Because of the way time-space is made, this planet, your lives, are all a hologram—everything you see. In the membrane of time-space, in the gelatin, if you used a laser beam in jello, it would melt it, but it would fill back in. With light in the time-space medium, it is the same way. The core light, penetrates through it at such a rapid rate that it melts it almost behind it, pulling the gelatin back in, creating a hologram of its journey, and giving life to everything it passes through.

The time-space medium was a membrane created out of possibilities. So whatever portion of the membrane the light penetrates will determine which portion of the membrane it gives life. The core light went through, penetrated, created a hologram, a very straight hologram. It couldn't see itself, but as it did that, it was so high powered with love and life, that it gave life to the jello around it. Each of you are taking a piece of that, calling it yourself and dissecting where the light went through. Your lives, as it were, are the study of the paths of the light through this medium.

From one perspective, it was only one light that traveled through and it imprinted the whole thing. This is why you live all of your lifetimes in one lifetime, or you can spend as long as you want and thousands and thousands of them playing around trying to dissect what you are. When the light made a hole through the gelatin, the hologram, the portions of the gelatin that it gave life are like little worms trying to inspect where the light went through. It would look much like your brain systems. If you could actually watch your neurons firing in your brain system, it looks the same way. They get out and jump back in, because they are not perceiving themselves to be mini-lights. They jump back in to try to see the rest of the story. You are all trying to see the rest of the story. You want to see how it ends. So from one perspective that is why we say also, you are living what has already been lived. The core light, having gone through the gelatin, lived it all because it gave life to it all.

L et's look at it another way and we'll put a different persona on time-space. Let's say that time-space is a physically manifested entity with a genetic structure. Let's say that it has a body, but it doesn't look like yours. Let's say that its body looks like a piece of gelatin, just like what we've already described, but it is a fat, rich, genetic, story. That is its body. Let's say in the abstract that this entity is an entity that is a manifested entity, just like you are, that has a different body. This entity, when its body is manifested, looks like a membrane of gelatin. But it is vast and rich in genetic heritage and memory, because it went through all these experiences just like you do, but they weren't in bodies quite like these.

So this entity, the gelatin entity, which is what you call the time-space medium, has a body; a total genetic body. The light penetrates, like we said.

As it penetrates through, it leaves a hologram of all these little life essences. Each one of these little life essences picks a different genetic memory out of the body and gives itself a face. So now, where the light penetrated the body of the gelatin entity, it ran into the vast genetics, all of these stories, all of these faces, everything it had gone through on its journey.

When the light went through it, it left the hologram or it left the path of its journey. The light and the love was so intense that it created life; it gave life to every one of the genetic structures. This is like its DNA structure around the wound where the light went through. Each of these little particums starts trying to heal the wound in the gelatin. This is its way of healing itself. If you cut yourself, your body goes to work in the same way the gelatin body starts working to heal itself. As it does this, each of these little light worms, all of a sudden, start seeing that they are alive just as how most of you take your skin for granted unless you hurt it. Then you start to notice it. Each of these little particums in your strip where the core light went through is starting to play with one of the genetic memories. Since that genetic memory gives it a whole story of who it is, it now thinks it exists and is a person.

Because of the way time-space is made, this planet, your lives, are all a hologram— everything you see.

In one sense each of you are like antigens or antibodies trying to heal a larger body. Each of you think you are a person, but you are just one of these antibodies in the gelatin body. The light went through it and gave life all around it. It created a wound so it had to start healing itself, but the wound was life giving, so it created everything to be alive.

Because you are all out of the same gelatin body and the same light that penetrated it, you could say everyone of you is the same person on this planet. Everyone of you in a very legitimate way is a face of each other. So which one of you is the real you depends on which day of the week it is and whether you like you or you like somebody else better.

Now light, in the larger perspective, spirals. You're just on a piece of it so it looks like it only goes straight. You assume that light does not bend, and therefore, does not create a spiral because you are only playing with a part of it. Light always spirals. The light went through the gelatin in a spiral motion, and it is going to return. The speed, the velocity, and the intensity of the light penetrating the gelatin membrane will determine how close of a circular motion it makes. Here you believe light is one speed, but that's because you are just playing with one piece of light, the straight part. Light has different speeds. You can see that in your different frequencies, they are also light.

Light travels at different speeds, different velocities, it has different cycles. You could visualize this light like a loose spring. You could take this spring that normally would be a foot long and stretch it out ten feet. Your mind knows what that would look like—the coils are farther apart. If they are, then each loop is going to be separated from the last one. If it isn't stretched then each spiral of the spring is next to each other. So also, if the coils of light are tight, each time that the light comes back around, it is going to be very closely connected to the last loop. Your universe was created out of a spiral that was very tightly wrapped. One way of looking at it is that each loop became a dimensional reality.

See it all as being a tight spring with each revolution touching the next so there are no gaps. That is how your universe here was created in a virtual no-time and no-space. Each loop is a dimensional reality. You stretch them apart, and you assume that you are separate. If you left the spring as it was, it would be tight. If you stretch it, it would assume that each revolution of the wire is separate. Since it sees itself as separate, that's also what you do.

When the time-space was created for this system that you're living in, it was created by a light-thought principle that was very tightly wrapped and then stretched. Each time the light penetrated the gelatin membrane, it made the next revolution and penetrated it again and again until it went through the whole membrane. That is how come you have linear time to begin with. Because the coils on the light spring are so close together, you can take this time space gelatin after the light has gone through it and expand it, just like a regular spring. When you do, there is a gap between all of the loops, and these gaps and loops are what you are calling you, your time, and your objective space. You are merely seeing the little straight portions of the same large spiral of light separated from itself. It is like looking end to end down the top of a stretched spring.

The light was trying to see itself each time it burned a hole through the gelatin. It made a very fast revolution, so it would have a chance of glimpsing the effect of the last revolution. Each of you, are this light glimpsing itself down the small portion of the light that intersects the jello; glimpsing yourselves through the separation of seconds, hours, days, and geographical space. It allows you to watch your idea of yourself evolve to the finished ideal. It is called evolution, and its called manifesting, and the process is the same at whatever level of creation. All of this is a little difficult to talk about because we are talking about something that is non-linear from a linear perspective.

Let's say that the core lifetime had an ideal. That ideal is the basic thought. The thought will go first and then the light is the following spiral. So let's say that this core entity, you, is at one end of the spiral you're about to create. First you put out the thought or ideal. In this case it was a finished body that you could live in on this planet, a body that could hold a full-fledged god. Immediately, the thought runs ahead of you in the time-space medium or whatever you are going to use.

Light is trailing thought, so the light fills in the thought through the medium. This gelatin, you see, is an entity. It just looks different than you do. It is an entity that is so vast, so rich, that from it you can get any material, any information, anything you need. So here you are, the entity, and what you want to create is a body that will hold a full-fledged god. The thought will go first through the medium to begin to collect upon the thought what it needs to build this. It is much like going into the universal genetic pool and pulling out what you need.

So the thought will go first through the universal genetic pool to collect what you are going to build this on. The light will also go at the same time the thought does, but the thought travels so fast that the thought has already arrived at the finished idea at the same time the light is starting to spiral to create it.

When the time-space was created for this system that you're living in, it was created by a light-thought principle

So if the light travels in a very tight spiral, it will be able to keep brushing against where it just last created and see on each revolution what its last step was. Then when it reaches the thought, it has the knowledge of every step and every increment of organization it took to get the end result.

Let's say that you're the entity. You've already gone through this process. You've put the thought out; the light is creating the spiral. The thought that went out first, already has every piece of data you need. But it's in a pool and it hasn't been organized. The light is organizing it. You've put out the thought for the possibility you want. As you put the thought out for the possibility, it is already created. It is already done. Since it is already done, the light now will start your own spiral to create it into a manifested form. ▲

The Creative
Possibilities
of Limitation

Y ou all create your reality whether you want to admit it, whether you realize it or are consciously doing it. Everything in your life you have created. Actually, if you were willing to sit down and take the time, you could see where you have created everything that you have.

Within your beings, the portion of you that sets out to create your reality will usually do it by default, because you don't consciously put in the intent in everything that you wish to have. Realize that you are such intricate beings that you can't just sit down and say, "Okay, I want a new car in my driveway right now," and it will happen. You are so multidimensional and you already have so many belief systems, so many different characteristics within your own being and your own personality that every time you try to manifest anything consciously, it takes all these into consideration. All of your hidden agendas, all of your attitudes, and all of your belief systems come up and make a composite picture. When you try to manifest anything consciously, it just puts that as data into the large computer bank to see what you are going to get.

Let's say that you moved to a place of trying to manifest a car in your driveway, a brand new one. First of all, none of you really know what you want! You start out with an idea and you change it and change it and change it. So several days later you are still trying to manifest the car from a conscious perspective, but you have already changed the model, make, color, and everything else on it several times. The thought has never been released so that it can be manifested back to you. This is the first issue.

Next, all of you have hidden agendas. You can try to talk yourselves intellectually into believing you can manifest, but a part of you says, "Well, this won't work. This can't work," so when you finally try it, you only intellectually talk yourselves into it. As you do this, you can generate enough feeling tone to put a good impact in, but underneath it all you know that you've never done it before. Since you know you've never done it before, it puts it in a place where you are actually nullifying what you are trying to create.

Your realities are created minutely and intricately down to your very last detail. Look at it as a giant computer having to take every little piece of data and create your reality out of it, and that's what you get. Everything you think about yourselves, everything you think about reality, everything you think about any aspect of your life whatsoever, are little pieces of data being fed into a large computer. The large computer puts them all together, makes a synergy out of it, and says, "Well, this is what the reality will be."

The lives that you are living . . . are usually about ten years behind the thought process that created them.

Let's say we've put in ten or fifteen parts of, "Yes, I can get this new car in my driveway." That goes into it. But we've also put in five parts of "I can't do anything." That goes into it. Let's say that we've put in fifteen or twenty parts of hopelessness, that goes in. The "I believe in struggle," attitude goes in there. "I really don't deserve it," that attitude goes in. "I can't do it," that attitude goes in. "I couldn't afford the insurance payments on it, and what about the taxes on it?" That goes in. And this example is just one little area of your life.

Let's take the larger perspective of the rest of your life. You are constantly feeding in all these thoughts about your reality. The only reason you would be sitting down trying to manifest the new car that way is because you know you couldn't do it any other way. In other words, if you know that you can have anything you want, you will not sit down and have the desire to have to try to manifest it in your hand. The individual who wants to try to manifest it in their hand is the individual who doesn't know they can create it.

You actually came here to create through a creative principle. When you are outside a physical embodiment, your thought is reality and whatever you think, automatically manifests. This is possible in the body also, but you have a time-lapse here. You are actually using time as a buffer to protect yourselves from manifesting everything too fast. The amount of thoughts you have about yourself and about your life in one day is approximately ten to fifty-thousand thoughts. If you were to manifest every single one of those thousands of thoughts you have per day, look at what your life would do on an hourly basis! You actually use time as a medium to buffer yourselves. This is what makes it a very creative endeavor here. It allows you the opportunity to make a synergy of your entire thought process, not just one little intricate item that you want to manifest. Everything you feel, everything you think, everything you desire out of life, is like data being put into the large computer. The large computer puts it all together and says, "Yes, this is what we will create."

Your physical embodiments are the densest portion of your reality. Dense does not necessarily mean there is anything wrong with it. You came into them because you wanted to be in them. It is a matter of learning to deal with them, learning to understand what you came for, and why you are in them. Your body is totally, one-hundred percent your past. It is your past physically, because it was created out of your progenitors.

Also, your physical embodiments right now are emotionally a product of your past. What you are going through in these bodies right now is actually where you were in thought months or years ago—most of you, years ago. Your body is just representative of the time-space medium that you are living in. The lives that you are living in these physical embodiments are usually about ten years behind the thought process that created them.

Your present moment was created ten years ago. This means that you are going to get the new car in your driveway, but it will probably be ten years down the road, and it will be a ten-year-old car at that point in time! So then, it won't be the new car any more, it is going to be the old one.

To create and to manifest in your current now you have to let go of your past. You have to let go of where you were. This is one of the hardest things to do, because the physical body is actually created out of the past, lives in the past, and manifests from the past. Your bodies are a composite out of everything that has been in your physical ancestry as long as your bodies have been on the planet. Therefore, your body does not know how to be the future. It knows how to be the present, and it knows how to be the past. That is all it knows how to do.

In order to manifest something immediate and spontaneous, you have to teach the body how to be the future as well as the present, so that you can go into the future in thought and bring it back to the present. But most of you are taking it into the past. You have to cut your past. You have to sever that and release the images that hold you in the past in order to bring yourselves into a current, present, now. As you do that your manifesting comes much faster.

The other factor you have to realize is that you didn't come here to manifest spontaneously. You came here to live spontaneously, yes, but outside of an embodiment you can create anything you want in thought. You come here and expect to still be able to do that. You can, but because the body is a primitive vehicle, is evolving, and is a young child, it cannot keep up with where your light and your thought processes are. The body lives in the past and you knew this when you came into them. In other words, you didn't come into them so that you could sit and manifest the gold in your hand. Yes, you can all do this, and yes, eventually you all will, but it is a matter that you came into the body for the limitations it gives you among other many beautiful things. The physical body is the most creative endeavor any of you will have, and you came to be able to manifest creatively through the embodiment.

Every last little detail in your lives, you have all manifested, everyone of them.

Outside of the body you can manifest anything you want, at will. That became little boring, so a lot of you said, "Well, what if we go into a medium, or a vehicle where we can't manifest at will, then we are going to have to be creative about how we manifest what we want."

So you came into the bodies to learn how to manifest creatively. It was not necessarily the top choice to be able to manifest it in your driveway immediately nor to be able to manifest it in your hand immediately. You could already do that. You came to learn the limitations of time and space. Through learning the limitations of time and space, you could learn how to creatively manifest a car. You could creatively learn how to go through the lessons of what it takes to get a new vehicle in your driveway, whether through working, through paper work with the bank, or through whatever method you take.

Most of you don't take credit for everything that you manifest in your lives. Every last little detail in your lives, you have all manifested, everyone of them. But you don't take credit for them. What you want are the big dramatic things that are just going to pop up for you. Yes, eventually they will be there, but the individual that knows that everything they need is always cared for, that everything that they always want is there, is the individual that will be able to manifest through this earth-plane existence, because they allow a relaxed place where everything can come in and be manifested when they need it and as they desire it.

However, most of you don't allow yourselves to know that you can manifest this way and want the big things now. If you knew that your bank account was always all right and there was always enough for everything you needed, you really wouldn't worry so much about trying to manifest a large lump sum, right now. Yes, it might be fun. It might be a good parlor trick to do so, but it wouldn't be something that would be of necessity.

When you move into the earth plane, many of you don't realize that you can still create and have everything you want. Most individuals who want to manifest the gold in the hand right now, are individuals that do not know that their needs are cared for and that they can have everything and anything they want. So they want to do it in the big dramatic of the moment. They want to be able to take the big dramatic experience and say, "Here is the gold in my hand, I proved I can do it."

This is not to put down anyone wanting to do this, because manifesting from that perspective is very grand and you will all do it. But as long as you are cursing and warring against these physical embodiments and your physical limitations, you will never learn how to manifest that way.

First of all, you came here to learn the limitations of creation. You came here to learn the limitations of manifesting. Once that lesson is learned and has been understood, you will learn how to create everything you want with flow. Then you automatically move back into the place you were in, in a non-physical reality. However, an individual that seeks for the big drama or the golden bar in the hand, so to speak, is an individual that doesn't know they will be cared for. If you don't know that you are already cared for, you will never create that with consistency.

If you are wanting to move into a place of learning how to manifest and manifest with regularity, look at it to come from natural events. Your lives are created with flow. They are created from natural events and natural experiences that are in your control.

Yes, you can facilitate them, but most of you wait until you get into a crisis. You say, "My bank account is too low, I'm in a crisis and I want the gold here and now." If you are into flow all the time, you would understand that if the bank account is in crisis, that you're just at a low. There is a reason for it, and you're going to be out of it in a few days or few weeks. You wouldn't worry about it, and it would just take care of itself. However, most of you, because you manifest sporadically, so to speak, and don't keep it up on a constant basis, you hit and miss. You get a large manifestation here and one there, because your ego is looking for the drama. If the ego is looking for the drama, it will make crisis in order to have the dramatic episode to pull you out.

If you had what money you needed in your bank account and somebody gave you a thousand dollars, you wouldn't think a whole lot of it. However, if you are an individual that is continually looking for the golden bar in the hand, so to speak, then you're going to be the same individual that will use crisis in order to create stimulation. If you put yourself into crisis where the bank account is gone, then if somebody gave you a thousand dollars in the hand, it would be the biggest drama you've had in a long time, and it is a prize. You are very grateful for it, it also feeds the ego.

Your lives are created . . . from natural events and natural experiences that are in your control.

If you want to learn to manifest and manifest all of the time, see it in your life. You do manifest your lives moment by moment. If you can manifest your lives moment by moment, you can create anything you want, but let it come in its natural space. If it comes in its natural space, then you are just going to evolve into a place that you will think, "Well I'd like an extra thousand dollars," and it will pop in there, but it won't come out of crisis.

Right now you've all taught yourselves how to design, manipulate and manifest out of crisis. When you get into major crisis and have major need, then you will do it, and when you do it, it is dramatic because you just saved your own life so to speak. You just pulled yourself out and so you use this to prove yourself to be the gods that you already are.

Know that you are already god and you came into a medium to understand the limitation, to work with it, to heal it and to heal yourself. If you just knew that your whole entire life was cared for, that it was always exactly as you needed, and you always received everything you wanted and desired—not just needed, but desired—then it would just always be there. But when you don't live that way and you don't know that you are taken care of, then you are always going to look for the drama. If you are always going to look for the drama, then your psyches will create the crisis to actually mirror the drama and make it look bigger to you when you get the dramatic effect. This is the way a lot of you manifest. It is just a matter of changing your perceptions on it. ▲

Myth as
Personal Truth

Myth is a way of taking an abstract thought and unifying it into a common language. In a larger perspective each of you are light that came from an abstract thought. To put that into an understanding is going to require a myth to explain it. Since you came from an abstract thought, you've had to have a way of explaining yourselves and realizing what you were. This is where a portion of myth comes from. In the larger scheme of things your universe was created out of a principle you don't understand. Since you don't understand it, you have to make stories about its explanation. These stories are what you call myth.

In your common language, most of you consider myth to be totally fictitious or to be an untruth. Myth is not necessarily fiction or untruth, it is a modeling or a metaphor to explain reality. The only thing that all of you have in common are your experiences. If you do not have common experiences, you cannot talk to one another in common language. Your myths are a way of taking universal or common experiences and putting them into a unified language so that you can all share.

Everything that you live in this reality is a myth simply because what you are living, experiencing, or believing is actually a representation of something else. All of your religious structures are a myth. They are a myth trying to explain creation, reality, a way of life. Your science is a myth because it is taking the components that it understands and tries to create a story out of them. It does not understand the entirety of any given situation. None of you here do as of yet. You take bits and pieces, and as you take a piece you try to make a story about where it came from.

Let's take a story about one of your natural elements. Your rain comes from the sky, so to speak. Eons ago individuals saw the rain coming from the heavens and thought god was crying. All they knew is they had a tangible thing they could touch which was the rain and which was abstract to them. They didn't know what caused it. They didn't know where it came from, so that kept it in the abstract. For their own minds they created their myths or stories of the creation of rain—that it came from a crying god.

You do likewise to everything in your reality. Your psyches cannot handle not understanding what is going on. One of your main priorities in coming here was to write, so to speak, an explanation of how you work, why you work and how you do it. Your psyche was created to write this explanation. When you start doing anything in your life, your psyche automatically has to have a reason for it because that is part of its programming. It begins to make myths or stories about your life to tell you what your reality is.

Myth is not necessarily fiction or untruth, it is a modeling or a metaphor to explain reality.

All of you are in the process of living different realities and experiences. This makes it quite difficult to talk common language. People throughout time and history have come onto your planet to try to create unified myth or a unified reality. They have tried to make a common language with which everyone could communicate. Most of these are what you now call religions.

In any given organization or in any given situation, the participants have a unified theory of how they agree to view reality. For example, your creationists believe that the earth and this whole reality was created by a god and that it just happened. Scientists see that as quite ludicrous and so they try to find an explanation down to the minute detail of how it was created. You have your creationists and your evolutionists. Each one of them weave and create their myth or their own story about reality. All along the way they find new pieces of it.

Your psyches were created to deal with new input, but they really don't like to. They are much like individuals who go to work, but don't really like what they're doing. Your psyche is the same way. Your psyches always seek to find a unified ideal or idea so that it can cease its expansion. It always likes to take the path of least resistance, which will often be to go into an organized philosophy, system of dogma, or religion.

The traditional organized religious thought creation, for example, was done one way and there aren't any ifs, ands or buts about it—this is how it was created and don't ask questions. The psyche feels quite secure and safe with this. It knows that it isn't as simple as it sounds and it knows that there is much more detail to it, but it is willing to just take that and use it. Your psyches like to have something that does not clutter them. They like being told, "Here is what it is. Take it, use it and don't ask questions."

From a larger perspective, your science is actually what is evolving because it is willing to ask more questions. When you are willing to ask questions, you open up your self and your psyche to a greater understanding, and you expand your myth. Your science was just not satisfied with the mainstream religions, so it created its own religion of trying to find the answers within the cellular structure and within matter.

Both science and religion are creating a myth. They are creating a story, a philosophy, a belief about reality, how life was created, how it exists, what it came from, and where it is going. The myths they create are ultimately a simplification or an incomplete story of how things actually are.

Many individuals can stay in one philosophy and one system of belief and never be bored with it their whole life. Their psyche is so rigid, compressed and so tight in that belief system that unless it is fractured, split, or altered it is not going to find boredom with it. It will find that it has a sense of security, a sense of peace that is there, and it will not give that up. It becomes stronger and stronger with time.

When the psyche begins to be pushed, then it begins to look for a new myth to create stability. Your journeys in life actually lend to a movement or fracturing or expanding of the psyche. Whenever the psyche becomes disturbed, the psyche will then begin to seek out an explanation for its disturbance. It will seek out a new myth. The way the psyche becomes disturbed and seeks to create a new myth is when your reality presses against the belief you've bought into.

Let's say that you are in an organized system of belief or religious structure which does not allow you to act in certain mannerisms or behaviors. Since that is its belief system, you've spent a lot of your life not acting in those mannerisms. You've built an immediate guilt response around it, or you've built up a belief system that says, "This is taboo and we do not do this." Then one day you find yourself in a forbidden situation and the psyche does not understand it. The psyche thought it knew the myth. The psyche thought it knew the totality of your reality and understood it. Now you bring in a new experience which actually goes against it or challenges the psyche's positioning. When it challenges its positioning the psyche begins to seek out an excuse or reason for your new behavior and feelings. It will try to either put you back in the old myth through guilt, or it will try to take the old myth and expand it into a new philosophy. The psyche says, "Well, we have to make an exception here," and it begins to find some loopholes in the existing myth or the existing belief system in order to allow you to expand in the way you really wish to be.

The myth is the creative portion of reality. An abstract idea comes in as a feeling tone, and from that feeling tone, you actually use your mind to be creative with it in order to explain a whole story. Your myth or the way you live life is actually a very creative principle. This is where your creative potential comes from at this point in your journey.

Whatever your perspective is at any given moment is your current truth. What your truth is today will be expanded tomorrow, the next day, and the next. What your truth is ten years from now will be different than your truth today. It might have some of the same components or it might have deleted some of them. It might have completely altered and changed, but your myth is your constant ongoing story. It is what you take with you out of this reality. It is your way of explaining something that you have no other way of explaining.

What your truth is ten years from now will be different than your truth today.

Let's say that you took a religious organization that had ten-thousand members in it. Everyone of those ten-thousand people would have a different view of god. Their views might be similar in a generic way because of the premise or the belief system that is holding the organization together. But each of them will view god and all of the components in the religion slightly different. Each of their individual truths about god would be different.

You cannot say that your truth is the only truth. Your truth is your truth, but each individual's truth is their truth too. Truth is basically your view of reality at any given moment. In other words, when you were five-years-old, your truth might have been mud pies and toys, and you might not have ever comprehended driving a car. You might not have ever comprehended going to the moon. You might not have ever comprehended the career that you have now chosen for yourselves. At five-years-old these things were not a portion of your view of reality. So as you evolve and expand in your consciousness the horizon widens. As the horizon widens, you begin to see new truth, you begin to see new ways of looking at things, you begin to see things that you never saw before.

Your planet is going to move to a place of unified myth. This has happened in smaller perspectives. Religions have tried to unify the myth. Your ancient Greeks, Romans, and even your ancient Egyptians, each in their own way had their own myths or unified way of looking at life. Science today is creating a unified myth by trying to create a perspective of how to look at life. Each of these are very legitimate in their own way, but what you actually need on this planet is one unified myth that pulls them all together and allows everyone to live their own creative truth at any given time.

If you could move into a unified myth or unified view of reality, all of you would see your own intricate place in it. It would not move it into a place of one unified religion—that is not what it would do. Each individual with a scientific bent would be able to have that reconciled with every other aspect of reality. An individual with a religious bent would understand why they are in a religious bent and the purpose it is serving. You as a people would understand your angers. You would understand your frustrations, and it would lead to a place where you would not have the warrings you have with each other.

Now when I suggest a unified myth or unified system of reality upon this planet, you may think, "Well, good, that will be my truth and everybody will live life the way I see it!" That is not what this means. It means that each individual will have an intricate place, and that place will be very well respected. It will be understood what archetypical forms they are dealing with, what myths they are dealing with and the biology of the body they are dealing with at any given time. There would be allowances made for each individual, and it would not create the states of disturbance that you now have upon this planet.

Once again, myth does not mean it is fictitious. It does not mean that it is an untruth. It is just a way of explaining what you are going through, what your life is, and what it is all about when it is so abstract that you don't understand it to begin with. To be able to live here and even begin to fathom any of these experiences, you have to have some form of story to put it all into. It is much like playing a game where somebody gives you a couple of letters of a word and you fill the rest in. You all enjoy this type of game. In the abstract it is the same way. You fill in your understanding of life with myth. The myth is creation. It is creativity. It is your life. It is the fun thing that you came here to learn how to do. Taking the components of it and weaving your own story is called life, and it makes each of you individual and unique. ▲

The Development
of Consciousness

Y ou were all thoughts within the mind of your creator as the creator saw itself in different directions, different ways, different actions, and different movement. If it needed something solved, it
created something to solve it with. It was a grand game of psychological constructs for it.

At this point the creator that was thinking this all into existence became aware within its own being of what it was doing. It found that it had
great love for what it had imaged into existence in its own mind and in its
own thought. It moved into a place of wanting to give it life. Therefore, it
endowed each particum which was originally its own thought, so that the
creator or the source would see itself in a particular role. While it was in a
particular role, it would embrace that, give it a package that we'll term your
"intent package," for it to exist and to become alive because the creator
found that it lacked all of these different faces.

It loved the way that it did different things. It loved all of its own
creations and its own thought. So it moved into a place of giving a portion
of itself to all of its own thought, and it loved itself into existence. When it
did this it took all of these individual thoughts that had originally been
within its own mind or within its own consciousness, and individuated
them out, giving each of them an intent package.

The intent package was their programming for existence; it was what
they had done in the mind of the creator, the faith of the creator itself. The
intent package contained all the input necessary for each of these individual
particums to actually go into existence, experience existence, live through it,
and live up to the total intent of the creator.

In the ultimate whole the creator loved all of its creations; so therefore,
it loved them clear into existence. In this intent package each of you were

given, the creator saw its own self living a certain particular role or certain particular way within its own consciousness, and gave a package of life to each particum. This intent package was then birthed with the particum into physicality, into a physically manifested reality—this one or another. It would then take these individual particums, isolate them so that the creator could experience itself through them, and hopefully move them into a place of individuating and becoming its equals.

A portion of this intent package all of you received was the original intent of your creation within the consciousness of your creator. In whatever way, the creator saw itself playing out the role was a portion of your original intent package.

Another portion of your original intent package was a desire to maintain and remember everything you had experienced so that the creator of your being could have a more full experience of manifested reality. You were created and given a module to maintain and remember that, and we will label that a "soul". It was created to take every experience it had ever had, imprint it, hold it, maintain it for record so that the source or your creator would be able to fully embrace that experience.

The creator loved everything within its own consciousness so grandly that it wanted it to exist. A portion of your intent package was to exist and to come alive because the creator was trying to make all these faces of itself, its own consciousness, come alive. It wanted to actually embrace them each individually rather than just being a mass within its own consciousness. Your intent package contained your original intent or your original face of your creator. It contained within it a memory chip, if you wish to term it, called the "soul" to record the experiences of this individual particum. It also contained within the package the desire to want to live and to exist. It also created time and space, a medium for holding each separate from the other so that they could live out their intent package. The whole intent package was to become a different face of the creator in consciousness.

This was how you were originally created into existence. At this point you are just consciousness particums out of your creator—you are not a full consciousness. You have the ability to be the total consciousness, but you presently are just particums out of it because your source and your creator saw itself in all of these different faces, and it loved them into existence.

Each of you are one of those different faces. As it loved each of you into existence, it wanted you to become equals to it—because you already were. You were portions of its consciousness, so you already were it. But you were in a place that you were minute portions of its consciousness. So now, instead of being one consciousness, you are particums of consciousness. Each of these particums of consciousness, because of their intent package, could not interconnect fully with each other. The creator kept them separate in consciousness so that they each had a package that would allow them to develop their own consciousness as they would develop back into the full awareness of the creator. This was one way of birthing what you term *creation of spirit*. This is how one form of it is done.

Each of these particums were held in an intent package and loved into existence by the creator. They were faces of the creator. Everyone of you are a face. So as you were loved into existence, you began to feel some separation from the creator. You had originally been one full complete total consciousness and now you are a part of consciousness, not a whole consciousness. This put you in a place where you felt oblivious of knowing who and what you were. This created your original separation.

Your creator saw itself in all of these different faces, and it loved them into existence.

You could not function as the whole consciousness or the whole creator or source any longer. You had the full ability because you were *intended* to be and already were one of its faces. As you took that and moved into your medium called time and space with your intent package, you felt separated. Since you felt separated from your wholeness, you felt rejected by it. You felt as if you had no way of knowing. This is where your lack of ability to know the larger picture began to come from. This is why all of you within your being knew there was something much more conscious, more knowing, grander, and larger than your own beings, because you came from it. Now you were a particum of it.

The soul portion of you was like a chip in a computer and was created to hold data. It was created to take the individual particum or individual face of the creator, hold it in the time-space medium, and record everything that the creator experienced as that face. The soul was originally just designed to hold data. It was designed to retain anything that this face, this module or particum did on its journey so that the creator could embrace itself physically manifested through these particums.

These particums all of a sudden started knowing that they were separate. They were originally one consciousness. Now they're particums of consciousness which meant there's some little bit of recognition of consciousness within them, and so they began to see themselves as separate from the whole. As they began to see themselves separate from the whole, it created within their being an overloading of this soul memory. They saw themselves separate from the whole and therefore were no longer connecting with the larger consciousness to maintain the total knowingness. Since they no longer maintained the total knowingness, they felt separate from it and were more isolated into their individual packages.

At this point in time that little spark of consciousness that came as a particum of the larger consciousness of the creator started hurting because it was separate. It wasn't the same form of pain as what you term pain now, but you translate your pain from that.

The creator was one whole consciousness and was still trying to connect, communicate and view all of these particums within its own consciousness. Each of these little particums are one of you. You are each a face of the creator. Now that the larger source of the consciousness cannot connect with them—you have separation, which is much like having glitches in your consciousness. Whenever any of you are trying to think something and it is just not there, you have a glitch and it creates a frustration. All of a sudden these individual particums within the consciousness of the creator started having glitches.

The consciousness is trying to maintain its continuity and its flow. It is trying to move it into the whole entire knowingness of what it originally was, but each of these particums, because of their intent package, is now a glitch. Every time you in your own minds get a glitch or when you're trying to think of something and you have it right there and it is gone, it frustrates you. These little particums with their intent packages were glitches. Since they were each a glitch, all of a sudden that glitch would trigger something within the consciousness. When it did that, it created frustration for them.

This is the beginning foundation of what you term struggle upon your plane now. One of the most frustrating things for most of you is when you're in a thought, the thought seems to flee from you when you just had it. It is very frustrating to you. Those particums that each of you became and these intent packages, are the same. They were glitches within the larger consciousness of the creator. Since they were glitches, they were now conscious that didn't have the whole picture and it created frustration. The soul wasn't created to record frustration because the creator was love, joy, and totalness. It didn't know or have the experience of frustration.

So here you have an intent package, one of you with a soul. The soul was not designed to understand or process any form of struggle. You now have frustration because it perceives itself to be a glitch in the consciousness of the whole. As it does that, the glitch will actually create frustration within you. That frustration manifests itself as struggle in physical existence.

Now the soul which could not understand or interpret frustration begins to develop a little bit of independent consciousness based on struggle. The glitch creates an electrical charge. As it does this it starts triggering your consciousness. As it begins triggering this consciousness, it starts to remind you of your whole intent package—the intent to become a creator or the same essence—and that you were a face of the creator.

But the soul doesn't have that awareness of that intent in the same way, because it was created to record the data of the creator. It wasn't created to necessarily make new creators but just to record data. So you're giving it all this information that it doesn't know what to do with. Now it has to begin to process it. As it begins to process what is coming in, it is becoming overloaded. In this overload it is much like any electrical circuit that becomes overloaded: it starts sparking and creating a form of pain.

Now you have a consciousness and a soul. But it was a portion of a consciousness, not the whole consciousness of the creator. This particum out of the mind of the creator is now seeing itself separate. That means it is beginning to wake up, or it is beginning to have some form of an intelligence. We will label this artificial intelligence, because if it was in the larger intelligence it would be the whole creator. But these are faces of the creator trying to be grown and inspired into being a whole creator on their own. Therefore, that is why we will label it artificial—not that there is anything wrong with them. The reason it is artificial intelligence is because it isn't a full consciousness yet. It is not consciously aware and awake. These little particums because of the sparking and because they are a glitch within the larger consciousness are waking up a little bit and are beginning to try to create artificial intelligence. It is trying to draw from that conscious particum to tell it what it is and to try to explain to it artificially what the wholeness of the consciousness is.

The artificial intelligence perceives all the incoming consciousness as struggle. You have incoming consciousness, but it doesn't know what it is or what to do with it. So, as it comes in, it is trying to understand it. Since it does not understand it, it will create struggle for it. If you overload anything with data it cannot understand, it will go into a form of frustration. This frustration creates greater separation

That little spark of consciousness that came as a particum of the larger consciousness of the creator started hurting because it was separate.

103

You have all of this consciousness within the intent package, and remember each of these intent packages is one of you. You have all of this consciousness within you that is struggling to tell it what it is. It is trying to tell the intent package and trying to grow it into a full consciousness equal to its creator, but you don't have a mechanism within there yet to form that.

If the creator had wanted you all to be clones, you would have been. The creator or the source you came from wanted each of you to be individual, which meant that each of you needed to develop your own consciousness package—the totality of your own consciousness. This was the form designed to create a place wherein you would first develop out of that consciousness particum. That is part of your intent package, a form of artificial intelligence leading you to intelligence, leading you into your own consciousness.

So, now these particums are in frustration because the consciousness particum within them is trying to tell them what they are. It is trying to say, "We are a creator, we are a god." The growing consciousness can't interpret it, and doesn't know what to do with it. As the larger consciousness comes in, it is creating struggle. All the struggle that comes into your life is trying to understand consciousness. Anything that you understand is not struggle. The spark is waking up and trying to create its own consciousness. As it does, it finds this form of struggle.

Struggle is termed pain of the soul. The soul hurts because it is awakening. It is beginning to create an artificial intelligence within it. As the soul is awakening and trying to become conscious. It is aware that it is separate from the whole consciousness. Since it is aware that it is separate from the whole consciousness, it begins to trigger a short circuit which it interprets as pain. What it will do now is begin to find a way to heal the pain. As it develops a way to heal the pain, that is how it is going to create intelligence and individual consciousness.

The internal portion of you hurts. The hurt is because there is incoming data that cannot be interpreted. Since the incoming data cannot be interpreted, it is creating a frustration for it which is struggle and pain. That pain can become very deep as that consciousness is starting to awaken. As it is awakening, that artificial intelligence is also waking up and trying to become fully aware, awake, and conscious. As it is doing that, it will come up with pain, and most of this pain is a separation from the larger consciousness. It is because, "Here is something, and I should know this. I already know this somewhere." It is because that conscious particum within your intent package was part of a whole consciousness that knew it all. It was fully conscious. That consciousness package says: "Here's something coming in and I should know this. I do know what this is but I can't find it." It is because it is separated from the whole rest of the consciousness of the creator.

Since it is separated from the whole rest of the consciousness of the creator, it feels that it must have done something that was wrong and was kicked out. It feels like it has been rejected. It feels like there must be something wrong with it because it can't process properly. So it hurts. This is one of the forms of the original separation. It hurts, in consciousness. Since it hurts in consciousness, it will develop or design a way to heal. It will design a way to quit hurting.

The pain from the soul as you deposit it in your being, lasts for eons. It is because it has never been dealt with.

One way of stopping the hurt is to develop image and ego so you don't have to feel it. But the fastest way to heal it and the surest way to heal it is to develop the consciousness. Pain in the soul is the consciousness that was the larger you trying to tell you something. It is trying to tell you something and the artificial intelligence within you that is trying to wake up can't relate—it knows it, but it doesn't know what it is. Healing comes for the soul when you become conscious. Each time you hurt within your being, take that hurt and find out what it is telling you. That puts you into consciousness and eases the pain.

When most of you feel pain you cover it up. You add another layer to your image. You build stronger walls. You build stronger barriers, blockages, so you don't feel the pain. It doesn't heal it, and it does not make you aware or conscious. That covers it up. That is why the pain from the soul as you deposit it in your being, lasts for eons. It is because it has never been dealt with. It is because you are covering it up. You're putting one Band-Aid on top of the other, and you've built a beautiful image of whom and what you think you are, but you don't know anything in consciousness. You haven't embraced anything in consciousness.

To truly heal it, and to truly heal you deep within your being, you need to go into a space of understanding, and you're only going to do that through feeling what is there.

The consciousness comes in. If you allow it to be felt, it may hurt, yes, but the understanding will come with it. When you have done that, it gives you an emotional embracement which is consciousness and intelligence, and then the little artificial intelligence particum that is waking up heals because it *knows*.

Knowingness is the healing principle. As it comes in, it heals, you gain the knowingness, you gain the wisdom, and you grow in consciousness. Consciousness in its true understanding is what is alive. Everything else is variations or distortions of it, but consciousness is truly alive, and it is joy. ▲

Archetypical Gestalts, Metaphors, and Channeling

A psychological gestalt explains patterns and behaviors about the entirety of any given subject. You could say from a larger expanse, or from our perspective, physical reality is just a psychological gestalt. It is just one course of experience among a myriad of experiences or psychological gestalts available throughout the universes. A psychological gestalt is a non-physical, universal perspective and understanding of a particular reality, whereas a consciousness gestalt is man-made, collective consciousness defined by a particular set of beliefs. Religions, cultural beliefs or political ideologies are examples of consciousness gestalts. A consciousness gestalt is a much more limited understanding of a reality than a psychological gestalt. However, these consciousness gestalts can be very powerful, and have a life of their own fueled by the collective beliefs of all those who participate in them. Consciousness gestalts are the formation that eventually will evolve into psychological gestalts, or a more universal understanding.

Each of you within physical reality are actually trying to build your personal consciousness into your own psychological gestalt. You are evolving your consciousness into a framework to explain everything you do by a given perspective. These frameworks or understandings are unique to your experience here in physical reality. If you took these same beliefs and ideas and put them into another psychological gestalt other than physical reality, they would mean something totally different, or even perhaps appear absurd.

The consciousness gestalts you have created in this reality dictate how you function and what you do in any given situation. Most people on your planet are stuck in consciousness gestalts or in their cultural and religious beliefs, and have forgotten to continue to expand their consciousness into an understanding of the whole psychological gestalt of physical reality.

The larger consciousness gestalts tell you how you live and die, and what to do. They explain physical reality for your consciousness so you have a framework from which to understand it. But if you're evolving your own consciousness into your own psychological gestalt, you will eventually let go of the need for other individuals or gestalts to explain to you how your consciousness should be developing. As you are in the process of developing your consciousness, you go through many experiences. However, most of you now take those experiences and filter them through the light of the consciousness gestalt that you are currently in, to explain what you're doing and why you are doing it.

When you originally began to become stuck in your minor consciousness gestalts, you needed ways of getting yourself out of them. You needed ways of seeing physical reality and other realities in a different light. So at that point in time, some of your neighboring realities—which are psychological gestalts in and of themselves—began to filter through to you, a few minor psychological gestalts from their realities in order to infiltrate them here to allow you to expand into them. A psychological gestalt will have all the behavioral patterns for a given reality, and this can be represented as an archetypical stereotype or referred to as an archetypical gestalt.

Your neighboring realities had different forms of gestalts than you do here. They began to let you borrow some so that you could learn from a different perspective. So let's say they have a Christ consciousness, as it were. Your Christ consciousness is different than Christ the man—they are two different things. Many of these archetypical energies, and a lot of what individuals are channeling, are the Christ consciousness gestalt—it's belief systems and metaphors. They are archetypical energies, that is all they are. This archetypical gestalt—the Christ consciousness gestalt—explains to the individual a whole way of philosophy and a whole way of psychologically viewing reality.

The basic metaphor of the Christ consciousness, as it were, is an individual that comes innocent into the world. As they come innocent into the world they are raised into greatness. As they are raised into greatness, they then try to elevate the consciousness or help the world. From there, they are crucified or killed for their journey and for what they have done.

If you look at your lives, this is the actual stereotype almost all of you are living. It is called a savior-martyr syndrome. Maybe you don't compare yourselves to Christ, but you technically come into the world as children, innocent. You move from there into understanding, elevating your consciousness, and from there you move into a place of trying to do your best for the world—doing what is right, doing what is proper and elevating consciousness. From there you feel that you are just stoned or crucified for what you are doing.

These stereotypes or archetypical forms have actually existed in your reality for eons of time. They are not new. In other words, Christ wasn't the first Christ or the first individual to portray the same set of psychological thinking, functioning, and reasoning. The only difference is that the one you call Jesus became noted after death, simply because of the mechanics around it.

For eons of time upon your plane, there have been many who have birthed into any one of several of these psychological gestalts or archetypical stereotypes. It is a way of growing and enlightening oneself upon this plane. Prior to coming here, the individual might go through and pick out a psychological stereotype for physical reality much as you would clothes.

What you're experiencing as behavior here and what you experienced as behavior in another reality, are going to have two different results in both realities. In physical reality, it would be one reaction. In another reality, another reaction. If you dropped a ball on the planet here, you know what would happen. It would drop in a certain way and at a certain speed. If you dropped it on the moon, it is going to have a different reaction. Your psychological gestalts are the same way. You can take the very same action, put it into two different mediums of psychological functioning and end up with two totally different results.

The Christ metaphor existed a very long time before what you term Christ the man came into existence.

The Christ metaphor existed a very long time before what you term Christ the man came into existence. It is a stereotype which is a functioning of brain schematics, emotional attitudes, and a functioning of a philosophy of life, all put together. You take this as a package, much as you would putting on clothes, and put it into a new medium called physical reality and see what happens.

A Christ metaphor or Christ archetype is one of these packages that a lot of you on this planet are living right now. It is trying to move you from the state of just being mere man into a state of being god. In the metaphor that most of you are using now, Christ the man became Christ the god, and that is what all of you are trying to do. You are trying to elevate your own consciousness out of just mere man as the primate animal into a place of man as god.

Let's say you took the same archetypical energy or stereotype and put it into two different cultures on this planet. If you were in the Orient living through the belief system there, you might term it Buddha. In another culture it might be Mohammed. In yet another culture it is going to be Christ. It is the same energy, the same stereotype, but because of the belief systems and attitudes of the people in any given area, it changes and alters to fit their belief system.

Christ the man is not what people are accessing or channeling when they are channeling the Christ consciousness or Christ, as it were. Each of you within your beings have a portion of you that is your own Christ consciousness. This is a stereotype out of an archetypical psychological gestalt. A portion of the basic metaphor is to elevate or evolve out of primitive man, out of the innocence of man, into god or to elevate man to god status.

When you worship god, when you worship a Christ, you are worshiping the metaphor. You are actually paying homage to a metaphor that you are trying to become part of rather than actually worshiping Christ the man. The two stories are different. The actual life of Christ the man, is different than what your metaphor and belief system is around the life and death of the man. This is also very indicative of how individuals will take anything— and it doesn't matter what it is—and filter it to fit their belief system. Rather than finding out about Christ the man, they will accept what the gestalt explains Christ the man to be. Therefore, if they are going to channel Christ or Christ consciousness, they will channel it according to the metaphor of the gestalt and the belief system around it rather than actually channeling Christ the man.

Nobody upon your plane is channeling Christ the man. Christ the man, is not accessible upon this plane, but the metaphor and archetypical energies are. Christ the man is going on with his own journey. This doesn't mean that he doesn't love you. It simply means that in his own evolution, Christ the man, is now, even in your own terminologies, Christ the god. It means that he is evolving and growing in his own perspective and his own light. Those who channel the Christ consciousness, are channeling their own consciousness. The reason is, most of you selectively chose what you term the Christ consciousness, as a metaphor to psychologically live your life by. Whether you term it Christ consciousness, Buddha consciousness or whatever, it is all basically the same type of a stereotype. The role is basically the same, it is an elevation of man to the recognition of god.

Most of you because of this time period upon your planet, chose to be birthed under this understanding to help elevate the consciousness of primitive man into a consciousness of a god and to actually elevate the whole consciousness and the physical embodiment to be able to hold a god in it. That is what you came here to do. Most of you that are birthed here in this physical incarnation, brought that as your stereotype to evolve into a psychological understanding. Each of you will do it in a different way. In other words, each of you brought your own Christ consciousness. This is a portion of your intent for the life package here. A portion of it was to elevate the consciousness you're evolving in from mere man into an understanding of god-man. That is what Christ is, god-man. So each of you brought this as a stereotype or a condition for this life to be in. Since you brought it, most individuals that are channeling Christ consciousness are channeling their own beauteous consciousness and their way of filtering and seeing that metaphor in life.

When you worship god, when you worship a Christ, you are worshiping the metaphor.

Since you are individually dealing with a Christ consciousness and filtering this physical reality through that, you will literally view that according to how you see your journey upon life. Since you use the metaphor of a Christ consciousness as a underlying psychological gestalt for your reality here, how you view your life here will tell you how you view Christ. That is why most individuals see more grandness after death than they do in life. It is simply because they do not see life as being much more than a lot of trauma and drama and they want out of it. Since they are wanting out of it, they will worship the death of a Christ, which means that they are actually worshiping their own death in order to relieve themselves from physical reality and then step into something they consider grander. The worship of the death of Christ is worshiping the death of god-man, which means that you are seeking and looking for the solace and the beauty that comes with death. This is an individual who does not see much beauty in life, but sees beauty in death.

Quite truthfully, most of you on the planet fall into this category. Most of you enjoy life somewhat, or on some days, but you would prefer to be out of here. So you spend your whole entire lifetime actually preparing for death! You don't prepare to spend your lifetime learning how to live and enjoy life. Since that is what you do en masse, then anything that you would see as an archetypical energy or form is going to take on the same coloration. That is what you have done with the Christ consciousness. You have quite literally given it different form than just elevating it to god-man. You've now given it form to be a symbol for you to worship life after death, rather than learning how to live in the current moment. If you don't learn how to live and enjoy life here, you're not going to like it when you leave here either!

A Christ consciousness is just a stereotype. There are other forms that each of you take. For example, anybody that comes to a place of being famous by your terminology, is an individual who is working through a psychological gestalt that they have borrowed to learn with. In your physical reality here, you deal more with consciousness gestalts than you actually do with psychological ones. Even those of you that are using a psychological gestalt such as physical reality or a Christ consciousness, filter it through your consciousness gestalts and lose a whole lot of the impact in translation. Other realities use these archetypical forms and by your terminology, they're simply gestalts of psychological reasoning. An individual can pick up one of these archetypical forms and actually go into it, express through it, and realize all of the different avenues of learning. In other words, each one of these archetypical forms in another reality is a metaphor for life. The individual goes into them and very quickly learns all of the behavioral patterns such as, "If I act a certain way, this is the reaction, if I psychologically work in this direction, this will be my reaction." And so they will take it, move into it, and live it very rapidly. So in other forms of reality, what you term a Christ consciousness here, is like a degree of learning or schooling. Here, you have your grade schools, one through twelve, and then you have graduate courses. In other realities, various psychological gestalts would just be different schooling experiences. Each one is a different stereotype, a different metaphor for reality, in a different psychological gestalt. So what you would do is take psychological gestalt A and live it. Then you would take B, live it, C, live them, until you had gone through the whole schooling.

A Christ consciousness in another reality is just one of these psychological gestalts. It is a schooling. In the reality where it was formed, which is a reality parallel to this one, everyone takes that as a psychological gestalt. It is just a learning experience. They might have multiple Christs all at one time, just as you have a lot of first graders here, a lot of second graders, and a lot of third graders. You wouldn't necessarily say any of them are higher or lower than any others, but they are just where they need to be for the learning experience.

These gestalts or archetypical metaphors, came from a parallel reality next to yours. That is how they mature and grow and learn. Therefore, everybody that filters through those realities, goes through the same metaphors or the same classes.

When you started filtering and bringing these metaphors here to live through, you started making hierarchy out of them. In other words the Christ consciousness in that reality would technically be about a fifth or sixth grade education in that perspective or the reality it came from. When you put it here, all of a sudden you made it a metaphor for your entire life, and so you start putting a hierarchy on it. The metaphor is one that is elevating man into god-man. For primitive man, which is what you've been on this planet for a long time—it is very beautiful, but it is still seeing yourself as primitive man. You're still seeing yourselves as connected totally to physical reality. You're not allowing yourselves to see other possibilities anywhere else.

In other forms of reality, what you term a Christ consciousness here, is like a degree of learning or schooling.

Because you are so isolated into this reality believing yourself to be physical and nothing more, you will filter everything through that belief. So therefore, when you bring a metaphor that says here is a way of elevating you from primitive man into being god-man, you all jumped at it. That is why this metaphor is extremely prevalent upon your planet. A lot of you are dealing with it and working on it, whether you call it a Christ consciousness or not. As I said, each culture will put a different name on it, but it is still what you are endeavoring to do.

Since that metaphor has been upon your plane for quite a period of time, you've had different generations and different people working through it. You will see that a lot of the people in your history that you term spiritually famous, have all had the same type of a mechanism or stereotype. The role and their life might be different, but you could quite literally put it in the same perspective. Some of them had hard, harsh childhoods or innocent ones. They grew, they put their word out into the world, and then they were crucified, killed, or persecuted for it.

You can put most of the grand people on your plane into the same category. You can put your Ghandi in here. You could put many other beautiful people in there. They have all lived a life, and as they lived this life, they were also killed for it in many cases. Sometimes literally and sometimes not so literally. In other words, sometimes they were just stoned, so to speak, with words and verbiage because of what they were doing and speaking about.

You've had eons of time where men upon this plane have been using this stereotype without an understanding. It is just a borrowed psychological format—that is all it is. So they have gone into it, tried to understand it, and explain it in rigid forms. As they did this, they started dissecting it. When they dissected it, they started putting hierarchy in it. In other words, if this is the Christ consciousness and you're going to try to understand the whole thing, you're going to begin to dissect it and cut it up so you could say how far in it you are advanced and how far you have learned.

Upon your plane, what you term your ascended master is simply a terminology and a title that you're using as a hierarchy for individuals who have attained a certain level or degree of god-man. You're stating that ascended masters are individuals who learned how to be Christs, but you don't necessarily term them Christ. You term them now Christ consciousness. And you have all varying degrees. As you put them in different degrees, you actually elevate them in your own metaphors. In other words, there are many grand individuals here that never ascended the plane by taking their bodies with them. They died and did not ascend, yet, they are regarded as ascended masters. The true ascended master is the one who literally takes their physical embodiment with them when they leave. There are more of these than most of you know about because these are usually subtle individuals that do it and most people never know about them when it happens.

Now however, there are individuals you have elevated to sainthood, so it is assumed they must be a master and must have ascended. Therefore, you automatically just lump them in the category of an ascended master so that they can fit your metaphor.

Many who have actually ascended you wouldn't even recognize because they don't fit your names here. They don't fit your stories or your histories. There have been large numbers of individuals who have literally ascended the physical embodiment out of biological man into biological god-man, as it were. Technically they took that body to that elevation of consciousness, and accelerated it with them. Since you don't recognize their names, you don't recognize them as being from this level of expertise. You have to put them in different categories when they are being channeled. Since you want hierarchy, you start making a lot of brotherhoods, you start making a lot of levels of angels, and you start making a lot of levels of guidance.

Realize that with these different degrees and levels, they are all still in physical attitude. It is all one physical reality, one physical-psychological gestalt. Only one gestalt. They are still no further out of physicality than what you are!

So what happens is that if you find an individual you like, you elevate them to the level of ascended master. If you don't like them, then they are just a regular individual upon this plane! Most of your ascended masters were the beautiful individuals who out of the simplicity of life, literally ascended their bodies. However, in your terminology, as I said, many of what you term ascended masters now that are being channeled, you could say in one form, yes, they ascended because they changed their consciousness and are altering it, but they are basically just gestalts now. It is the same thing as Christ the man. He is not being channeled. Christ the man is living his own experience.

Many who have actually ascended you wouldn't even recognize because they don't fit your names here.

The same thing largely applies to these ascended masters. Pretty well all of these individuals that are channeled as as-cended masters or that are channeled as being from any of these brotherhoods, are not there. The ones that are elevating and evolving their own consciousnesses are not going to take the time to sit around in your metaphors of reality and play around in it. You would be rutting them, getting them stuck, and they would be in a place that they would be too physically based.

What happens is most of those that are truly ascended masters, that are evolving, and expanding have simply left what would appear to be a tape recorded message—a hologram. If any of you have ever seen a holo-gram and how it works, it can be as real as anything you've ever seen and that is what happens. When individuals are channeling out of these gestalts, it is a hologram, totally full and totally valuable, because it has the whole metaphor for reality from that perspective. It appears as if the individual is actually there during the channeling, but it is almost like a canned message.

At that point, the individual that is channeling the gestalt is connected to it because that is one of their metaphors for life. Individuals will channel their metaphor for life. You will not see very many Buddhist people chan-neling Christ, because that is not their metaphor. In this western culture, you have enough of Buddhism that you have individuals channeling out of the Buddhist consciousness, but from the other perspective, you're not going to find a whole lot of Buddhist individuals channeling Christ. It isn't part of their belief systems, attitudes or emotional embracement, but they are channeling the exact same energy through their belief system and attitudes, just as you do here.

These gestalts are the same thing. They are literally channeled through the person's perspectives of reality. Whatever the person believes of reality, they'll take that gestalt which is a hologram and alter it to fit their belief system. Since channelers alter the gestalt to fit their belief systems during the channeling, any entity tied into that gestalt would be altered by the channeler's belief system also. Most ascended masters would not actually come into the body of the channeler and risk being altered by the belief system and biases of the channeler.

The life of Christ the man and your metaphor of the Christ consciousness overlap on a few points, but they are different. If Christ the man were channeled in his own purity, his own state, his own right, he would be very beautiful and very wise. If anybody was to channel Christ the man, he would have to be channeled through their body of knowledge—first their primary one and then their temporary one. This means that the channeler is going to change it according to their belief systems and their attitudes. You could be as loving, as diligent, and as patient as you wanted to, but if everything you said to another individual was altered and changed and totally distorted by them, you're not going to waste a whole lot of time hanging around. You would probably say, "Well, okay. I'll leave a tape recorded message, because they are going to distort it anyway." Then you are going to go on with your own experience.

An entity that is outside of a physical incarnation that is now focused on evolving would get stuck in that kind of a channeling situation. After a period of time they would start trying to talk to you according to your language because they know how you are going to distort it. That would actually alter their reality and tie them into where you are. They could be a very evolved master, and if they hung around in that perspective, allowing you to distort them every time you spoke for them or channeled them, they would actually be trapped into your reality and would buy into it just as you have bought into your philosophical beliefs upon this planet. It would be easier for them to leave a prerecorded message, or a book of knowledge, as it were. Then at your leisure, you could go through it, pick out what you want, change it, and read it according to your own belief systems. This would leave the entity undistorted.

Most entities that are evolving, growing, and expanding do not hang around to be channeled by individuals from physical reality. The connection has too much of a tendency to literally pull them back into physical reality once more. It is not a matter that they don't like physical reality—many of them are very beautiful and are wanting to help reality evolve. The grandest way they can help this physical reality evolve is by their own evolution. This means that a true master of reality that knows they are a master or a true Christ is going to continue to evolve by knowing that their own evolution is going to do more for this planet than standing around and trying to help by giving a few words of wisdom here and there. Having once been physically oriented, anything they do and evolve in their own consciousness will be filtered back here and help with this planet and evolve it as a whole. Their greatest work can be done by their own evolution. They are not going to hang around to be channeled through every individual that wants to channel them.

Most entities that are evolving, growing, and expanding do not hang around to be channeled by individuals from physical reality.

Any of you that are dealing with the Christ stereotype within your own reality, have the ability to connect with the gestalt which is termed Christ consciousness—but it is your own. You can actually take that very beautiful light and according to your own belief systems and your own attitudes, interpret it and bring it through. That actually pushes you into your own Christ consciousness, your own understanding of that and your own evolution. From there, you can evolve it into any direction you wish or so desire.

If you understood how simultaneous time works, you would understand what you term the afterlife or non-physical side a whole lot better. Because you become so attached to physical reality, when you leave it, you're connected still to it. When you die, as you put it, you technically don't leave physical reality. You carry all of the physical attitudes and just step out of the body. You have a whole world of individuals who have done this. If the individual understood simultaneous time and could release the physical attitude and actually step back into their own light, they would be totally outside of this and nobody would ever be able to channel them.

If you were in a place of being able to totally let go of your physical attitude when you died, you would simply step back into the pure light, the one-hundred percent wholeness that you were, and would not be in the dead zone, or the area surrounding this planet. Individuals buy into the belief and the attitude of physicality so intently, that when they step out of the physical embodiment or die, they are still physically oriented. The only thing is that they now don't have a body. But their whole attitude, their whole psychological structure and everything is still the same. So technically, they're still physical. They really haven't changed anything, they've just stepped out of the body, that is all.

There are a whole lot of individuals in this portion of reality that, yes, do channel through. And you have other degrees or levels—not from a hierarchy principle—but from evolution that are also watching and working with this reality. You have free will—that was a gift that was granted to you, and they will honor it above all else. They will let you have your struggle, your pain, and your games, just to honor your free will because that is the most precious gift you have ever been given.

When some individuals step out of the body through a death process and realize that they are still physically oriented, they then begin to manipulate and try to advance certain portions of physical existence, so they can birth back into it because that would be advantageous to them.

That is why many individuals channel this dead zone, which is still physically oriented. That is why it can still be translated into the physical reality and the physical language. Those individuals that were physically oriented, left the physical embodiment, and from that point, they still have the physical attitude, and so, they are still physical by our terminology. By their terminology, they are not. They are dead and out of the body.

This dead zone or area is where some of your brotherhoods come from. This is where some other entities are channeled from also. They have something at stake, if they are in that portion of reality. They are very likely going to be pulled back into this physical reality, and they have advanced their consciousness enough to know how stuck it is. They have a lot to gain by trying to bring through whatever information they can to actually benefit themselves when and if they do come back.

It is almost like a gravity type of thing. If you are in this area or this zone, so to speak, outside of a physical embodiment, you're eventually going to be pulled back into a body just by the gravity of physical density. An individual who has truly ascended is totally outside of that—totally. You haven't had very many of those upon this plane, ever. The ones that have, you don't even know their names. Most who ascend off this planet just ascend to the outer edge of the same physical zone. They have not truly stepped out of physical reality, and this is why they can channel through a holographic imprint. You have a lot of entities that just send signals in, because they don't want to get trapped and pulled in by the gravity into a physical embodiment. So they will send in whatever information they can and be whatever assistance they can knowing that it is actually going to help benefit their own lot, if they end up getting put back into a physical embodiment by the gravity.

The physical density here is of such magnitude that it has the tendency to pull an individual back into it. Once you're out of a physical embodiment, it is much harder for you to evolve out of the physical attitude than it is while you are in a body. In a physical embodiment, it is a whole lot easier to accelerate your vibrational pattern to go further out than you can when you are out of the body. Many individuals know that they are on the edge of physicality and are going to eventually get pulled back in or if the planet evolves to where they are, then they will become physically manifested on it anyway. So anything that they can put through as information or guidance is going to benefit their lot and at the same time, help elevate the whole consciousness of the planet. So yes, you have a lot of beautiful entities from this edge of physicality, as it were, which are still in this physical zone, who are filtering in what information they can. Understand though, that whatever they put through still has to be brought through the distortions of the individual it is brought through.

The physical density here is of such magnitude that it has the tendency to pull an individual back into it.

Outside this physical zone or this physical psychological gestalt, you do have other support that is also holding you. But as I said, it respects your free will so much that it is just allowing you to be and to evolve. It very rarely will ever step in or infiltrate here. Sometimes it will put through guidance or direction. It could technically be seen as the holographic imprint that holds your whole universe as you know it. It holds your physical reality in substance or allows it to be or to exist. It just holds it, and it is the underlying blueprint that allows it to start evolving a little bit and growing. But it does not interfere. It just simply sits there and holds.

You've talked about these savior, martyr, and psychological constructs which are the underlying metaphor for this physical existence. Much of the popular channeling that is going on at this time, features a very strong figure—similar to a god or Christ figure that elicits some very powerful

emotional responses from people. What is happening here and where will this evolve to?

It is tied in quite a bit to what you term your savior complex, but it is also, one of your next evolutionary steps. Your savior-martyr complex, is what developed all your struggle. Most of you upon this plane feel that in order to be worthy, in order to be grand, in order to obtain your heaven, you must struggle to do it. That is why it is termed a savior-martyr complex. So most of you are wanting to elevate your consciousness into god-man, but you also feel that you have to struggle in order to do it.

Many of these very beautiful entities that are coming through are god-man in their own right. Maybe they are not necessarily more highly evolved than anyone else, but perhaps they had their experience in a time frame which didn't have all the psychological beliefs that you do now.

Let's say an entity grew up in a period quite a few thousand years ago, totally removed from all of your belief systems and attitudes. The entity that the individual is channeling can still be a portion of the channeler, but the entity is not going to be as inhibited by all of the belief systems and philosophies that you have around god, Christ, and all of these types of figures. When these individuals can come through, they don't have as much of a resistance to just being themselves and feeling the love. When an individual is channeling, they are in an open state which means that they are allowing love to come through, and they are allowing the life force to come with it. So what happens is these individuals do come through as gods in many people's eyes. For many, they come through as very beautiful, highly evolved entities.

Sometimes you have individuals that do come through which have a superior attitude as it were, and since they do, they come across as putting a lot of people down. But for the most part the individuals that come through are highly enlightened. They are beautiful. They have a grand message and that message is usually love. Most of you upon this plane don't let yourselves feel that love. So if an entity that is totally unknown to you is willing to love you and loves you totally and unconditionally, it leads to a place where your heart will leap for joy. You crave that form of attention. It puts it in a place of allowing you to elevate yourself into god-man without the struggle. It is a very, very beautiful evolutionary step.

Almost all of you believe that you have to have a god figure. Consciousness, as we have explained before, cannot evolve without stepping stones. So therefore, you cannot take an individual who has believed in an external god all of their life and immediately say, "There isn't one." You can't do that to them. They will never change their belief. They will never change their attitude or their system. What you do is you actually take it and begin to put it into steps and put god back into them. You can't take them, when they have worshiped all of their life this beautiful external god or this vengeful external god and say, "No, there is no god out there. It is inside." They don't know how to make the transition. They can't. A lot of these entities are making the transition for them and helping their consciousness to make the transition.

Your savior-martyr complex, is what developed all your struggle.

The first step is when the individual will say, "Okay, maybe god is in here too." But the belief system has been so strong in consciousness that god was exterior that they are still looking for one out there also. So what happens is these beautiful channeling situations will allow them to find one, but this god figure that they find is beautiful, wise, has grand wisdom, and is also almost an equal. In their mind they might still hold them a little superior, but it is an entity allowing them to come up and to elevate themselves to that level of consciousness and to elevate themselves into that demeanor.

This is why a lot of individuals use channeling, and that is why it has become very popular. Some may criticize that those intrigued by channeling are giving their power away, but what they don't understand is that there has to be stepping stones. A channeler that is in a place of channeling from the highest wisdom and the grandest grace, will not take the power away from the individual. They will explain it, they will elaborate upon it, and they will expand it so the individual can find the wisdom within themselves.

These are stepping stones. These beautiful entities that are being channeled are, to the audience, a friend, a companion, and someone that is trying to help them understand and to elevate themselves into that love also. It can also work the other way. Many individuals get into an audience and don't care for the love. They want to stay closed down, and then they will take the entity and the beauty the entity has and try to drag them down to their level.

If an individual using a channeling experience does not worry so much about whether the entity is literally who the entity is supposed to be, but feels the love, goes with their own wisdom, their own feeling, and lets their guidance explain what is proper for them and not, then the individual can allow themselves to be elevated to the same degree of understanding and god-man as what is being channeled.

A lot of you have changed philosophies and beliefs, but you haven't totally let go of them. You might have been brought up from one philosophical ideal and yes, your ideal is changing, but you haven't let go of the other one. It is still there. It still penetrates your whole entire belief system, and you still believe in certain patterns. It is changing, but your consciousness will not let go of the old beliefs. It has to evolve into something new. Using these individuals in a channeling experiences as god figures is just another metaphor. It is a metaphor to allow their consciousness to evolve from just simple man in struggle into god-man in elegance and beauty and love. One of the most powerful things that can ever come out of a channeling experience is when the participants can feel themselves loved into a higher level of existence. ▲

Shyness and Sensitivity

Shyness is the individual's defense mechanism against the world. When an individual is very sensitive and feels very deeply within their being, shyness is a form of protection. So a shy individual is actually trying to protect themselves from their sensitivity.

Some of your most sensitive people are also your shyest people, because they can pick up anything they are in proximity to, including a lot of the feelings from individuals around them. Since they pick up and feel what others around them are feeling, they become so sensitive within their being that they can't deal with it. Shyness is a form of pulling away from that. It is a form of retreating from other people's feelings and intensities.

Shyness can, on one hand, be used as a tool for growth and evolution in the individual, but it can also be used as a retreat away from life and existence. Rather than learning how to master your sensitivity, many of you will choose different methods of dealing with it. Shyness is one. Defensiveness is a form of shyness and another way of dealing with it. Some will use recreational chemicals including alcohol in order to run away from their sensitivities. Others use anger.

You are all very sensitive in your own beings when you allow yourself to be so, but as a society and a planet, you are so sensitive that you are all hurting because of it. So you try to heal your own hurt one way or another. You can bandage your sensitivity or hurt by not feeling it, by covering it up, or by disguising it. Shyness, shame, alcoholism, and other addictions are all tools to cover up the feelings that the individual is going through.

When the individual can go into the depths of their own being, feel what is there and express it in the external world, they will learn to deal with that portion of themselves that is sensitive. They will also learn how to deal with it in other people and then they will find a reversal of their shyness.

Sensitivity is an openness and an innocence. It comes from being open, feeling, being caring, being aware of, on some level of your being, what other people are feeling and perceiving. When you are in a state of openness and going through this perception, many of you don't know how to deal with your own perceptions, and therefore, it is even more difficult to deal with somebody else's perceptions of reality. If the individual is running away from their own levels of openness and their own degrees of being and feeling and sensitivity, they will not want to deal with other people's, because it will only amplify their own. You get into a situation or place where you are around other people and they are in states of their own vulnerability, they are in their own states of beauty, openness, awareness, and as you begin to open, you begin to pick that up, perceive it and feel it as your own. This creates a state within the being that when one cannot deal with their own sensitivity, they cannot deal with another's, so they will begin to shut it off.

Shyness is a form of pushing away other people's sensitivities so you do not have to deal with them. It is a form of saying, "I am into a place that I don't want to have to deal with these feelings, so I will change my focus." As they begin to change their focus, they begin to shift into a place that is a little bit of what you would term spaced-out. You will notice that most of you, when you are shy, feel a little altered with it. The shyness creates a form of altering so you don't have to focus on what is going on and what is being felt in the present moment. You can alter out of it into another area that you are much more comfortable with. As you do this, it puts the whole mechanism of the body, the mind, and the emotional body into a state of non-reaction with whatever it is dealing with in the physical world. This is the major form of shyness that all of you exhibit from time to time.

Some other forms of shyness result from the pulling away from other people's egos, including your own. For example, if you are around other individuals and their egos are demanding something from you, you may become too sensitive to want to deal with it. So you will begin to shut off and pull away to be more unapproachable. If you are unapproachable, then people won't want things from you. Shyness is an ultimate form of being unapproachable. Some people feel those people who are unapproachable or shy to be rude, uncaring, or to be what you term aloof. But it is the shyness that is putting them in a place of being non-approachable or keeping people at arms length. That way they don't have to deal with what the people are demanding from them. This is a form of shyness that many of you deal with from time to time in your lives. You have individuals who are wanting things from you and the easiest way to not have to deliver their expectations is to keep them distanced.

When sensitivity or shyness moves into a place of covering it up with alcohol or your recreational chemicals, this form of shyness is also when the individual has opened and is trying to deal with other people's sensitivities and their own. They are too much for them to deal with and many times they will turn to some of these other tools to actually shut off.

Due to some of your spiritual genetic structures, once some of you begin to open to a certain point, you cannot close off your sensitivity. You are open to a certain place and degree from there on, and you can never shut back down. Since you cannot shut off and become unaware of what is around you, you are in a constant state of sensitivity. If you are in that place and not knowing how to deal with it, you will create a way to deal with it. A lot of people retreat from this kind of situation and sometimes that retreat will include going into chemical abuse, as you put it.

Shame comes when an individual is feeling and is sensitive and is picking up sensitivity from others and doesn't want to deal with it. They begin to be open and be aware and can pick up the pain and hurt from other individuals. They begin to understand what they are going through, and they don't want to deal with it. Therefore, that is a reflection within their own being, of their inability or their lack of desire to deal with the same issues within themselves. So since there is not a desire to deal with the issues within themselves, they are not going to want to deal with it with anyone else's either.

Due to some of your spiritual genetic structures, once some of you begin to open to a certain point, you cannot close off your sensitivity.

This creates a sense of shame within the individual, when they know that it is an issue that should be dealt with or could be dealt with and would create grander openness in one's life. So it is a sense of guilt. It is a sense that, "I am not caring enough. I am not doing things right." Shame will always come when the individual has gone against their own heart or has gone against their own feelings. When an individual is in their sensitive state, they do not wish to deal with anybody else's issues, let alone their own, so they put it in a place wherein they begin to create denial—"I don't feel this way, this is totally not the way I am or what I feel." So as they begin to deny their own feelings and their own awareness, it creates within their being a duality because they are denying something that they are.

Their heart is telling them how they feel, their heart is opening them up, they are sensitive, they are aware, they are open and yet on the other side, they are saying, "No, I am not. I cannot feel this. I will not feel this," but yet they are feeling it. When they do this it moves them to a place of creating a polarity within the embodiment and within the being that is a form of guilt. This form of guilt will come out as shame. It will always come out when the individual is putting themselves in a place of going against their heart. So if they are in a place where their heart gives them guidance and they move to a place of denying that guidance or that feeling, they will generate shame, always.

Let's say that you feel you are adequate for a job or adequate for a relationship, but from an external purpose, you say, "No. I can't." A lot of you feel that this is a form of humbleness, but this is not a form of humbleness, this is a form of denial and on the other side of it, it is a shame. It can sometimes result in anger. So sometimes shame and anger go hand in hand, because the individual on the other side of it will say, "Oh, I was adequate, but I was passed over so there must be something wrong." Since they were in that space, it triggers the denial within the self because that's what was already there and then, that begins to trigger a shame or a lack of worth within the being.

Are both of these emotions that you have talked about so far, shyness and shame, a result of a misunderstanding about being responsible for other people's feelings?

Yes, because when you are aware and open, you are one feeling, literally. In other words, when you are that fully open and aware, you are of one feeling which means you feel everything from everyone. So when you are that sensitive, you become one feeling which means not just your own, but everyone and everything that is around you. They become like your feeling, so it puts it in a place of feeling like, "Oh, this is mine, so I am responsible for it," and since you are responsible for it, you want them to be happy, and if they are not, then you begin to move into a place of, "There is something wrong. I have done it wrong and I am responsible for this."

Does a lot of shyness and shame and unworthiness in people just exist because here are these sensitive people that have been put into an envi-

ronment of all these comparisons and competitiveness and judgments and everything else?

They are put into a society of other sensitive people but the other sensitive people are using other tools to deal with their sensitivity. Some of them use anger to deal with their sensitivity. So if you have an individual that uses anger to deal with what they are feeling, and you have another individual who doesn't, the second individual is going to appear to be shy because the angry one is coming on strong out of their defenses of their sensitivity.

All defensiveness is from sensitivity. Any time any of you go into a defensive state, this includes your sarcasm, your defensive denials, your argumentativeness—all of these are forms of covering up your own sensitivities. They are forms of not wanting to deal with what you are truly feeling. So since you don't want to deal with what you are feeling and the awareness or the openness that you are in at the time, you will use whatever tool you wish to use. A lot of you use anger to deal with it. So you shift your sensitivity to anger, and if the other individuals don't want to use anger, you are putting a lot of sensitive people into a world of anger. That makes them more sensitive because there is so much anger about. So each of you deal with it in your own way. Many of you, as I said, use chemicals to avoid it so you don't have to deal with it.

When you are that fully open and aware, you are of one feeling which means you feel everything from everyone.

Where does the underlying feeling of unworthiness come in that a lot of us feel? Or is it just a combination of the shame and the shyness?

It is a combination. The original feelings of unworthiness all come from your original separation. But that is also why you are so sensitive. You are one being. You are one wholeness that is all separated out so you can each see different parts of it—what you term yourselves. So you have one wholeness and it feels like one wholeness. In other words, it is like one large nucleus that you all came from, called a source. Whatever portion of that source feels, the whole entirety of it feels also. So the whole of the whole feels everything all the time. There is not one particum of you that will feel something without everybody else feeling it too. As you feel it, it goes out and it is just in the mass feeling bank, so to speak, that all the rest of you are also attached to. This is how a lot of your consciousness gestalts work.

You are all one feeling. You are one feeling body and you are individual particums in the one feeling body. Since the whole is feeling all the time, these little particums, in order to deal with their own existence, will shut off the feelings. They shut off the feeling to be able to handle it. This is why many of you feel that you are feeling something different all the time.

Technically, all of you, all of the time, are feeling the exact same thing. You are from one source and whatever that source feels as a whole, everyone of you feel, continually. There is no differentiation at all. One of you might feel joy, another might feel that they are depressed, but if you moved down to the root feeling behind it, they are both feeling the same thing because it is a portion of the same source.

If everyone of you was in an open state, everyone of you would feel exactly the same all the time. But it would also put you in a place where you would be clones of each other. The way you change that so that you're not one total feeling body all the time, is to create your own distortions within that. So you create forms of denial, you create shifting, you move the perspective so that you can focus on it from a different direction. The whole feeling body is feeling one spectrum of energy or one spectrum of light. Each of the particums can choose which degree of that feeling they want at any point in time.

So how can joy that one person is feeling and depression that another person is feeling, be the same feeling from one source?

It is the same feeling from one source, but it is their direction or focus they take. Depression and joy are not that different. When you go into a grand amount of joy, usually, if you notice, on the other side, you go straight down into the depression. The feeling body of the source, which you are all part of, has a spectrum of feeling that it feels at any point in time. This can be anything from joy to anger or any other feelings, and these run in cycles with the source, just as you go in cycles with what you pick up and perceive.

So it is going through its spectrum of feeling, and you are each particums within its spectrum. Every emotion and everything you feel has several degrees in it. You don't just feel depressed. When you are feeling depressed, you feel several other components of depression. When you are joyful, you don't just feel flat joyful. There are components of joyfulness. There are certain things within the joy that make the components of what you label joyful. It is not just one simple emotion.

Because of the feeling body, you will go in and pick up out of this spectrum the components of feeling. That is what you will call your mood. Just like when you create a physical body you go in and pick out what you will have in your DNA structure, you also do this with your feelings all the time.

The spectrum of the feeling body of the source that holds you contains every component to create all that it is. So you go through and pick up certain components of feeling, not one feeling, but certain components. Let's say that you take fifteen or twenty of these components, put them together in your own synergy, and label it depression. You take fifteen or twenty of these components put them together and label it joy.

This is why every time you feel joy, it is never the same joy. If you really felt what you are feeling when you feel joy, every time you feel joy, it feels different. Every time you feel depression, it feels like it has different components. Every time you feel anger, it has different components of anger. Everyone of these feelings have different components every time you feel them. All you are doing is picking up the components out of the feeling body, putting them together and you are labeling them a generic term. The generic term is joy, happiness, love, whatever you want to label it, but each of them have minor components within them. So you are all one feeling body, all the time.

If everyone of you was in an open state, everyone of you would feel exactly the same all the time.

The more open and aware you are, the more of these components you are going to pick up at any one time. So let's say that you're into an isolated focus within the feeling body of your source. In that focus you might pick up fifteen or twenty of these and label them joy. You might pick up fifteen or twenty components and label them depression, but as you become more and more open, you become the feeling body of your source and it is multidimensional and has a lot of components. So now instead of picking up fifteen or twenty components out of feeling, you are picking up a hundred or two-hundred components of feeling at one time. This means that you're feeling joy, depression, anger, a little of all of these things all at the same moment and you don't know how to deal with it. Your psyche can't digest it.

How can you function in a day-to-day world if you're dealing with this number of components?

That is what you are all trying to do and deal with. It is called sensitivity. So you are dealing with all these components and your psyche doesn't know what to do with them. It doesn't know whether you are supposed to laugh or cry. It doesn't know how to trigger your emotional body. It has all of these feeling components, but it doesn't know how to express them. Since it doesn't know how to express them, it says, "Let's just stuff it. I don't know what to do. I have a hundred—two-hundred components of feeling and I don't know whether to laugh, cry, scream, dance . . . I don't know what to do with the emotional body to make the physical reaction. I don't know what to do with it, so let's just shove it back here and ignore it."

When it shoves it back and ignores it, you move into a repression of your expression which is what we have said leads to depression. But it also creates a form of shyness. It is the psyche's way of saying, "I'm feeling too many things at one time. I can't deal with it," and the psyche will literally push them away or take the individual out of them; so you don't necessarily leave the feeling.

A shy person feels as much, if not more, than somebody who is very outward. The psyche says, "I cannot deal with this. I will take my individual and move him outside of it all." The feeling is there and the psyche can't get rid of the feeling, but it doesn't know how to digest it or decipher it or what to do with it. So it will take the consciousness of the individual it will alter it or allow it to alter into another space where the feeling doesn't have to be dealt with at that moment. That is why a lot of times, when a person is shy, if you notice, they also alter.

When I'm feeling restrained or shy, like in a big group or something, it's not a comfortable feeling. I wonder what I could do to feel more comfortable and to be more free?

Begin to understand the components of your feeling and let yourself feel. It gets you accustomed to it and then move into expression of that. When you are in a large group, you have to stay focused, and that is the problem. When it is just you, you can just alter out of the feelings, not have to feel them, and nobody is around to tell you, you are shy. When you are around a large group of people, you must stay focused to function with those people. So as you stay focused to function with those people, you are also into an open state, where you are having to deal with your own feelings which you have been running away from for a very long period of time.

The easiest way to do it is to get into a space of feeling your feelings, and not judging them. Any of them. Go into them and if you feel a burst of anger, express it, let it go. If you feel a burst of joy, feel it, let it go. Whatever you feel in your components, let them be felt and then the psyche knows what to do with them. As it begins to pull more and more of them in, it will know where to put them, what to do with them and you will become much more at ease with where you are and when you are with people.

So a person who has learned to do this, what would their life be like? I mean, would they be laughing one minute, crying the next, shouting the next?

I would say that multidimensional beings know how to do all of them at once. They can laugh and cry in the same moment. They can scream and shout in the same moment. They can do everything at once. They can feel joy and sorrow in the same moment because they feel all things. They become *all that is*. *All that is* implies every feeling. Everyone of you in your evolutionary path is going to become *all that is*. It is going to be the joy and the sadness. It is going to be both sides of the coin. *All that is* doesn't imply just one side of the coin. It is the full spectrum so that is what most of you are trying to learn how to do. An individual that has learned to deal with their own feelings and every aspect of their own feelings becomes very objective. Then they can be around a crowd of people and objectively watch them.

A shy person feels as much, if not more, than somebody who is very outward.

Shyness is the individual's own reaction. Shyness and quietness are two different things. Shyness is the person's individual reaction and running away from sensitivity. There is a difference. There are times when you are quiet and contemplative and that is not shyness. There are other times when it is shyness.

Shyness is when the individual is trying to escape the sensitivity or move away from it. Quietness is when the individual has learned to deal with his or her own feelings, when they have learned to master them. Then they can objectively watch them in other people. Because they have become so sensitive to the feeling body of the source, they know what everybody else is doing. They know because they have been through it.

That is how we function and that is why many times, we know what you're feeling when you don't, or when you don't know what to call it. We too have been part of the feeling body of the source. By going through it and learning through our own feelings, and dealing with the feelings and the components of them, we know when you are dealing with something and when you are struggling with something. We know what you are playing with at the time and how you are trying to put the components together and what you are trying to make of it.

When individuals can deal with their components of feeling and that feeling body, they move into an objective space because they've been there. When you're not objective, it is because you still have something at stake with that feeling. You have not come to terms with the feeling, and you will not be objective with it. When you have come to terms with the feeling, you have lived it, you have felt it, you have expressed it, and you have gone through it, you will move into a place of being objective.

So if somebody is going through feelings and they irritate you and you cannot deal with or handle those feelings, that tells you that you haven't dealt with them or lived with them yourself. When you have felt them in yourself, have understood them and have expressed them, then you move into an objective state. Feelings have to be expressed; they have to be expressed in order to be emotionally embraced. You have come here to emotionally embrace feeling. That is the bottom line because those feelings are your abstract lessons. So when you have expressed your feelings and embraced them, you're objective. What other people are going through you see as their lessons. You also see what they are learning, and you don't become judgmental about it.

How do you express your feelings? What if I'm really angry at somebody and I want to take their head off?

Understand that most of you have a different idea of what expression truly is. Expression means movement. Expression means taking something and moving it. It is taking a feeling, and moving the feeling all the way back. Every feeling that you feel, every single component of feeling that you ever feel goes back to one root feeling every time, because you are all in one universe learning one lesson. That lesson is an abstract lesson that is coming through feeling. Every time you can take a feeling and feel it all the way back to its nucleus and release it, you have expressed it and emotionally embraced it. This is how you emotionally embrace and express feeling.

Most of you feel something and you say, "Oh, well this is because I'm mad at so and so, or I'm feeling happy, sad, depressed, or mad because of one thing or another." That is not feeling. That has nothing to do with feeling. It is transference and avoidance of feeling. When you move into a place of putting it to an external world and saying, "I am feeling this way because of this," that is avoidance of feeling. That is not feeling.

What are they avoiding?

Feeling. They are avoiding taking that feeling and going back with it to what it is trying to teach. Every feeling will end up in the same place when it is carried back to its origins and roots, and it will go back to the base feeling. Your source in this feeling body, is one spectrum of feeling which is nothing but joy. If you were to go back into the source and into its feeling, you would find nothing but joy.

So the base feeling is joy?

Every feeling you experience is joy.

So how do I get anger out of that?

You get anger out of the distortion of what you are feeling. Joy is not simply one component. Joy is comprised of many components. So you go through and pick up certain components out of the spectrum of feeling, put them together and you have anger. You go in there and pick up certain components or vibrations, put them together and you label it depression, fear, joy, whatever it is, but it is because you have selectively chosen certain components instead of the whole thing.

Feelings . . . have to be expressed in order to be emotionally embraced.

So rather that blaming people or situations for your feelings, take the time to go into the feeling. Take it back to its roots. Each time you do that there will be a release within and you will have learned an abstract lesson and the struggle ends.

Joy? Is that the lesson?

Joy is the feeling. The lesson is beyond that, and that is for you to find out. Each of you individually.

You talked about how we are holding more components of this base feeling, but our psyches can't deal with it.

That is because you bring them in, but you don't deal with them. If you dealt with them, your psyche would know how. But you bring in these feelings and these base components, and you tell your psyche that you don't want to deal with them and then it has to find something to do with it.

Is there a limit to how many of these components we can feel?

No. The feeling body of the source that holds you extends from joy onward. Joy is the base or bottom of its spectrum. Most of you are playing only with the joy spectrum, not beyond. The joy spectrum of your source is comprised of over a million components. That means you are sitting around taking these different components, feeling them to understand them, to embrace them, to label them what you will label them. Most of you at any one point in time, will only hold fifteen or twenty of that million and label it with a generic term.

I guess I still don't understand why a component of anger would be any part of joy.

When you are angry, what are you angry about?

Well, anger is a way of dealing with hurt.

And what have you been hurt by?

Usually someone else, in my perception.

And how do they hurt you?

They didn't do what I wanted.

And what did you want them to do?

I wanted them to do something that would make things easier for me, bring me joy; somehow I was let down by them.

So you are mad because you didn't get joy out of it.

Right.

So that is one way anger is a component of joy. It is the lack of it. But anger is coming because you are wanting somebody to love you.

Right.

So right there, you've boiled it down to love and what are your components of love?

Well, love is joy.

The only way that you can ever be hurt is when someone doesn't love you according to your image. That is the only way you can be hurt. So if they are not loving you the way that you have imaged and want them to love you, you are creating a distortion of love and joy. You are creating that distortion through your images of love. Most of your anger comes at being separated from the love or from the joy. You personify that somebody else separated you from it. If they had acted a certain way, you would be having joy and love right now, but they didn't so they separated you from it. From you perspective it is their fault that you are experiencing the feeling of separation.

So our objective is to learn to feel all of the components of this base feeling which you've called joy.

Yes.

Then where will we be?

You'd be very joyful and you would be whole.

Why don't we accept joy? Why do we choose the anger or the frustration or the stress or lack in our lives?

Because you are working off a limited spectrum. If the feeling body of your source has a million components of joy and you are only feeling fifteen to twenty components at any one moment, you tell me how much like joy that is going to feel?

The only way that you can ever be hurt is when someone doesn't love you according to your image.

Very watered down.

Now there are some of you on your earth plane that are beginning to hold a hundred to two-hundred components of joy at a time. What is that going to be out of a million?

Well that's going to be very watered down, but an improvement by fifteen or twenty-fold.

Right, but it is still not going to feel like the real thing yet.

No, so what's out there for us?

A lot of joy. But when you can only feel that percentage of the joy, it doesn't feel like the real thing and it creates a place where you feel separated from it, because you are only perceiving a certain percentage of it. If you don't have the whole thing, you'll think you must be separated from it. If you are separated from the joy, it is going to feel that way. All of you complain that you don't have joy. But you do. It is the spark in you. Joy is the frequency that created the spark that resides in each of you. It was created out of the frequency of joy. Within your being, that little light particum that is you, is joy, and it is already contained inside of you. You already have it.

But we choose not to perceive it?

Correct. Because it feels so watered down from the amount that you are allowing yourself to feel. It doesn't feel like you have any or you have it for only a few short periods of time here and there.

Are we afraid of our feelings?

Shyness is a fear of your feelings, and fear is one of the components of the whole spectrum. When an individual picks up new components that they are not quite sure about and don't want to have to deal with, that creates a fear. But that fear is truly coming from not working on understanding the feelings. If the individual is not dealing with the feelings, they will coagulate and create more of a fear complex. But there is another reason for their fear. They are afraid of feeling and understanding the feelings because they know what is at the other end of it. This is one of the cosmic jokes: You all know what the root feeling is and where it is going to lead you back because that is what you were created from.

Your shyness is a fear that if you go into that feeling and carry it clear back into its origin and feel what it is, you won't have any excuses any more. The ultimate feeling you are going to find there is the one of grandness and of the beauty of you—it is the love that all of you want to deny.

So shyness is also an ultimate denial of self. It is a denial of the beauty of the feeling you would find, if you connected with yourselves. What you would find through those feelings, on the other side of them, is going to be the most beautiful love and joy you have ever found—and that is you.

Most of you are still in a degree of unworthiness and undeserving, and if you were to move back into feeling just how much you were loved, you would no longer be able to hold onto any of your excuses.

A lot of you in your beings felt that when you were loved into existence by your source, it did you wrong. It loved you into existence, but you felt like you were rejected and kicked out. So you are reacting like a child throwing a temper-tantrum—you're not going to do what is wanted of you which is just seeing the beauty within you.

The way out of your anger, the way out of your shyness is to move back through the anger at having been created and you'd be home. Take your fear or anger and follow it back to the feeling and know that you are all right. When you do, there is no need to feel shy. Being shy implies that you are going to do something wrong—that you might not behave quite properly. But when you are okay within your being, there is nothing you can do wrong. Shyness is a picture or an image for the external world that says, "I am afraid of being me." The fear behind shyness is the fear of being yourself whether alone or around other people.

It is a fear of feeling okay to be yourself. If you are wanting to move beyond that and back into yourself, it will come from feeling the all rightness of you and knowing that you are just fine right where you are. ▲

Living in
the Moment

Sharing with yourself is when you quit judging yourself and you just be yourself. What more intimate way can you share with something than to be it? Most of you have all these ideas about what sharing with yourself is. Sharing with yourself simply means you quit judging you. It is that simple. It's not going to feel like this big flowery idea of, "Oh wow. I just shared with myself. Wow, that was good!"

Sharing with oneself is just a way of life. It will feel like no-thing. It will just be. Sharing with yourself is when you are one-hundred percent content and complete without having to have any external validation. You don't have to have anybody else tell you you're great. You just know that you're all right. That only comes from not judging yourself. But if you're still in a place of saying, "Well, I don't need all their support. I don't need all their validation. I'm really okay." This says you're probably not feeling okay, because you're having to make a fuss about saying that you are okay!

It's sort of a non-relationship with yourself?

Yes. It's called being yourself. How can you be yourself when you're sitting here trying to be it and it is sitting over there? This is what happens for the most part. So, most of you say, "Okay, myself is over there. Now I'm sitting here and I'm going to have a relationship with myself."

In order to have a relationship with yourself, you have to split yourself into two so you can have a relationship! If you're just being yourself, it's kind of boring. If you're just being yourself, there are no problems, there are no issues, and that's too simple for most of you.

You're all having affairs with yourself, but you're separating yourselves to do it! The ultimate state of loving yourself is just to quit being mean with yourselves. Quit saying, "I should have done this. I should have done that." If anyone of you in one day's effort of all your shoulding on yourself, if you had a parent that treated you that way, you'd probably hate them very, very much! Most of you are bigger tyrants on yourselves than the tyrants that have been big on this planet ever were.

So loving yourself, basically, just boils down to just being a no-thing. Follow the logic through. If you're being something, then how are you being yourself? You can't be, because you're being something. When you finally get it, it will be so simple you'll sit and smack yourself upside the head, feel embarrassed and say, "Oh, I was so dumb!" Being yourself is doing absolutely no-thing. Nothing. It is an *isn't!*

So how does one act when one is, has no relationship with oneself, when one is not being anything, when one is sharing so intimately with themselves? What are the characteristics of this individual?

The only reason you don't have fun . . . is because you have expectations.

Peace. Some would probably perceive it as quite boring. When you are in that state, most people, if they are looking to get something out of you like validation, won't like you. They will see you as one of those rude, crude, ignorant, mean, self-centered, snotty people because you didn't tell them how great they were. People who are just looking for support will find great solace with you, because you're not expecting anything out of them either because you're not expecting it out of you.

Being yourself. How can the rose be anything but the rose? In its natural state, it can't. If you want to be yourself or be the full-fledged entity, you do no thing. It takes no disciplines. It takes no practice. The only practice you have to do is practice at quit practicing so you can get out of your own way!

No expectations. None of, "This is what I'm supposed to be if I'm being myself and being a god." You all have expectations on how god is supposed to be. So if you're going to be god, then you know how you're supposed to be. You have expectations about what a god is, and that is the problem.

But you could set a couple of criteria for being a god right now. You could say a god likes to have fun.

Yes, but in their state, they're being a no-thing. What would be the funnest type of person for you to be around? Somebody that is very grouchy because their expectations aren't being realized, or somebody that is so much a no-thing that wherever their heart wants to go they just do it, but they had no expectations? All they could ever do was have fun, because the only reason you don't have fun—this is a biggie— is because you have expectations.

Any moment in your life that you can't say, "Wow, that moment was fun," is because you had expectations that you didn't live up to. It means you weren't being a god and that's why you didn't have fun. Gods have no expectations, thus everything they do is fresh, free and in the moment, and wouldn't you call that fun? I would. Gods don't know how to do anything but have fun. That would be your interpretation of it.

If every day of your life is not totally joyous, you had expectations you didn't live up to. It is your own fault that you didn't have fun. If you had no expectations, then every second of every day would be a new experience because you'd have curiosity. You wouldn't know what is going to come in five minutes from now and it wouldn't matter, because in five minutes from now, you'll get to see it then. You would be more worried about this second and this moment now and it would keep you right here, in this second, this moment now, and always in the present.

If you're in the present moment, you can have no issues. If you're in the present moment, you can have no pain, because your pain is a lag over from the moments before. If you're in the present moment, you can't even have any struggle. If you're in the moment now, you have no binds, no ties, no nothing. So all you could have is the most ultimate, unlimited freedom that existed. Now to me that sounds like a whole lot more fun! I would rather be that kind of a god than the kind of god you all have images about being. If you could do that by being in the moment, *every moment*, with no preconceived or past-conceived ideas, what would you call it?

Spontaneous.

Spontaneous, but what would it be? Joy, because you couldn't have anything else because you weren't expecting something different. You'd have no pain, no nothing.

Where did we pick up our expectations?

Because if you were having that much fun, then you'd start getting curious about five minutes down the road and wonder, "Maybe I'd have even more fun," and you move out of the present moment. Any time you move out of the present moment, you're in trouble. So any time in your day that your life is not filled with joy, fun, freedom, unlimitedness, you're not living in the moment—moment by moment. This is the hardest lesson. You're all very tied to your struggle so that you know that you did something. Nobody likes to be a no-thing. But give it a try. You'll never go back. I guarantee it!

If you're living into the moment and the now, there is also no intent. Intention is what put you out of the moment. Intention was trying to take the joy you were feeling and organize it. Organization of yourself will take you out of joy every time—*every time*. That means that what you're doing is trying to take yourself, organize it, and compartmentalize it so that you can make sure there is always enough joy to go around. That's called lack.

If you live in the moment, there isn't anything else. It is an attitude. Your intents are expectations. Expectation takes you out of the moment, puts you into the future, which ties you into the past, which doesn't let you have any fun in the now. If your lives are miserable, its your own fault. Nobody likes to hear that one!

Right now is the moment. All you do is focus in this exact moment—right now—everything else is void, and you'll have a transition in your consciousness. Then we'll have something to talk about big time, because when you can do it and you can start doing that consecutively, moment by moment by moment, it changes you faster than anything. It releases your issues and puts your lives back into joy. Even right now, in this moment, put it into a place of there is just this moment, in a feeling sense. That will be the most valuable tool you'll ever learn. Everything else that you'll go through is to teach you how to do that one thing. Just take the moment, and you take the moment and stretch it. It is just now, and in that moment, the issues leave. There is a joy and an excitement underneath it.

There is a difference between excitement and expectations. The joy levels rise and life becomes an excitement. But all you have to do is learn to take that excitement moment to moment. Just let yourself feel this moment now, nothing else exists at all. Let yourself stretch it and let go of it. And then do the next.

Right now most of you use intents as a goal. What you want to do and the fastest way to manifest anything, is that you put your intent into the future, drop it off and ignore it. Then every moment will be taking you to what you set up. Then being yourself means that is the only thing you can be.

> *Expectation takes you out of the moment, puts you into the future, which ties you into the past, which doesn't let you have any fun in the now.*

When one has obligations and there is a certain time frame that we need to be there, and a certain number of things that we need to do during those hours . . . if we're doing a moment to moment . . .

You'll do it easier and better than you ever did before. And you'll fulfill your obligations better than you could ever do it otherwise, because what will happen is you will stay in an almost detached state from it. Not a spaced-out detached, but if you're living in the moment, then what happens is you can never be shifted into a place of having misery at your job. Then that means each moment is this moment, you're not living off past issues with your employer, and you're not living off past issues with anything else.

In the moment there is joy. What happens is these moments build on themselves until the whole thing is joy. That is the vision of a god. In that moment you're living in your moment. Then you can see the people around you playing dumb—not as a judgment of mentality—but when you're in your moment, you can see them as a god playing a ridiculous game, just like you are. Then you will say, "Wow, this is really funny!" and it will give you some of the biggest thrills and joy with life you'd ever find. When you can get into that state, you'll want to be around people more than you ever did before. You can have so much joy at seeing the god in them, while they are pretending to be ignorant of the fact that they're god. You can see it all the time, and you know darn good and well so can they. It creates a very grand form of excitement or thrill with life, watching the mechanics of the way all of your minds put things together.

If you can live in the moment, it does not mean that you're going to be irresponsible. Living in the moment is an attitude shift. It means that at seven-o'clock, if you need to be at work, great. You don't take the preconceived expectations that you're going to be tired at seven-o'clock. You don't take the preconceived ideas of, "Oh wow, what a drag today. I don't want to go to work." You don't take the preconceived ideas of, "My boss is a lousy so and so, and I don't want to go to work." You don't take the preconceived idea of, "I don't get paid enough." You don't take any of those with you, and then what you do is you live in the moment. It is an attitude. It is an attitude shift in the being that every moment is a thrill, because there is nothing from the past and nothing being expected of the future. It is just now. This is the only moment you've got left to live—right now. Every moment is your last moment.

If I took your advice totally, and lived the moment, I would not make the seven-o'clock date at work!

I would say that you would and you'd make it easier, because if you're in a job with a seven-o'clock date at work, some part of your entity wants to be there or you wouldn't be there—for whatever reason. So what would happen is if you could live in the moment with no preconceived expectations at all and then some part of your entity decided it didn't like it, it might give you a job making fifty or sixty bucks to work at two-o'clock in the afternoon! It would shift it to whatever it needed to maintain you into a place of keeping the focus of the moment—it really would.

If you can live in the moment, it does not mean that you're going to be irresponsible.

Some of you work and some of you don't. Let's say tomorrow morning, you all have to get up and go to work at six-o'clock in the morning. What are your reactions? I want you to be honest with them.

I don't want to get up at six-o'clock in the morning!

You have to be there by six so you have to get up at four!

No way am I going to get up at four!

But why?

Because I enjoy sleeping in.

I want you all to be serious with this and let's just show you how much preconceived, compressed data you all have, okay? Why do you want to sleep? Why would you not want to get up?

I like to wake up naturally and that usually doesn't happen at four-thirty in the morning!

We can even let you sleep till six and not have to go to work until seven, how's that?

I used to get up at six all the time and I loved it, but something shifted and I don't like that any more!

Okay, you don't have to get up until eight-o'clock to go to work at nine.

That's okay.

But how do you feel about being at work at nine-o'clock?

I don't want to go to work.

Why not?

Because its not a joy to me any more.

Why isn't it?

I don't know. It is a drag. I have to force myself to get there.

Okay, but see this is something everyone of you are facing in some avenue of your life, so I'm going to push you. If you want me to back off, just say back off. Okay? So why is it a drag? See your very statement telling me it's going to be a drag means that you've already preconceived it to be one. That means that you know that you're going to go to work without any joy. Why would any god put themselves through that?

I've been trying to figure that out!

Each of you have preconceived ideas about what the job is going to entail. You don't want to go to work. It's a drag. Okay, let me tell you a scenario that I was planning for your day at work tomorrow, that you're going to miss. Okay? Come four-o'clock, we were going to tickle you and wake you up with just a really fun euphoric feeling! We're going to let you see the most beautiful sunrise you've ever seen—it would just melt you down to your bones, but you're going to sleep through it! We were also going to get you to work in a brand new car that was in your driveway in the morning!

Go for it!

No, you slept through it!

I would have been satisfied with the sunrise.

Okay, but you missed the car too! You slept through it. Then I thought I would just kind of pop in and see you, literally! Then about eleven-thirty-five, we were going to drop a check on you for ten and a half-million dollars! But tomorrow is such a drag that you're not going to go to work, so you're going to miss it all!

This is what you've all done with your lives. You have preconceived, compressed data and so there are no possibilities. You all want to know what stops you from having what you want? You all ask why don't I win a new car? Why don't I win the lotteries, or whatever it is? Why don't I do this? Why don't I do that? What part of me is keeping it from me? It is *you* consciously. You've already preconceived how tomorrow is going to be.

Since you have already preconceived it, how can anything change and be different? It can't, because emotionally you're living in the past.

Drop the past, totally drop it. Tomorrow morning—let yourself feel it—tomorrow, you're going to get up four-thirty or five, no stress on the body and the sunrise is going to be gorgeous, brilliant, beautiful. From there, you're going to go to a new job, one that you really want to do. Now are you willing to get up at four-thirty in the morning?

Yes, I would be.

Why the difference? As I said, all of you have avenues in your lives that are the same way. Whether they are jobs, relationships, or something else. Why can't tomorrow be that way at the old job? For one moment, split time, drop the past, drop the expectations, and live in that moment and then that expectation of going to something new and fun can be every single moment of your life. That is loving life. Loving life is when you have no expectation about what it is going to bring you, so you can fully enjoy it.

Loving life is when you have no expectation about what it is going to bring you, so you can fully enjoy it.

Y ou all have to love yourselves into existence. That is putting yourself into a place that you have no expectations over what life is going to bring you. If you have no expectations over what tomorrow is going to bring, that is called being a god. See you all know how to organize everything real well. Most of you have your next twenty, thirty-years and your funeral plans all arranged!

Tomorrow is Tuesday, what are you doing tomorrow?

Well I'm going to get up and go to work. I have to work from nine to probably about six or seven.

Wednesday what are you doing?

Going to work.

Thursday?

Going to work.

Friday.

Friday I have a different kind of work that I do.

Saturday?

Play, hopefully.

You have every day of your life designed before you get there, and you've already said what a drag it is!

I have learned that it drives me crazy if its not like that!

Most of your brains will not let you just have a disorganized life, because you have to worry.

Yeah, to be spontaneous is hard.

The brain likes security, and it finds security in knowing where everything is going to fit together. Security is also expectation, which means you will never love life as long as you have expectations. As long as you're worried about the security of life, that is an expectation.

Most of you have this big issue right here, this big gray area, and are wondering, "But what about my obligations and responsibility?"

Your entities built the planet, created roses, built an atmosphere, it molecularly designed bodies, and created species of animals. (Playfully, to one of the group: and your entity created the fly!) It created sunrises and sunsets. It did all these things, but it is not going to know how to take care of you? That is what you're all saying!

It sounds pretty ludicrous when you put it that way, but it doesn't feel like it has been.

There is a gap. There is a bridge right here called surrender. This is called being yourself that all of you have to bridge. You're all so scared of letting go of the security and these expectations that you'll never be yourself. You'll never be your entity. Your entity can create universes, it can create stars, it can create suns, it can create them and destroy them. It can create a race of humanoid species, but it won't know how to put food on your table even though it created every food on the planet?

You all know how to organize, put things in order, but you haven't learned how to be the source yet. Three things you have yet to become at the same time: source, self, and creator. You all have the creator part down real well. Self and source have yet to be developed. The source lives in the moment. Since now you have a personality to put on it, it is the moment. It can't organize. You have to learn to be so spontaneous as to not organize your future. That is the big gap that keeps you from your true freedom. That is called surrender. Until you cross the gap, your worries will run you wherever they want you to go. You appear to have nothing to say about it until you can get to the point of the moment, these moments, the moment now, the present now.

When you can get to that point, you will have no issues, because those issues are part of the creator. The creator has to decide how to put all those silly little molecules together. That's what a creator does. A source just says, "Hey, I love and I love life." That's all it does. You are all trying to learn to be all three. You're trying to learn to get to a point of just loving life enough—which means no expectations—that the part that made this whole entire universe will take care of you.

It is just a bridge of attitude. It doesn't mean you're going to go dump your jobs, or you're going to dump this, or you're going to dump that. If they are in your way, they'll get taken away from you. What it means is that the attitude inside is going to shift and a bridge is going to be made and then you become the living entity. The living entity, in the moment. You can never manifest anything until you can learn to release in the moment. You have to learn how to do it. In that moment, you completely release the past and the future. That moment is life itself and then you take the creator part of you and put that moment into it and manifest it now. Loving yourself into existence entails living in the moment. That's it. The only place you're going to find love is in the moment.

The only place you're going to find love is in the moment.

I felt it, I just can't hold onto it.

You're not supposed to! That's the whole point! You're all so used to, "Oh, I got it, oooh don't let go." You build billions and billions of moments. Don't hang onto it. Never, never hang onto it. If you are, you are back to square one—which is fine, that's a good place to start—but don't hang on to your moments. This keeps you in the past.

It was a moment. It was great. Let's do the next one, and the next one and the next one. The only discipline a developing god really needs, is to learn how to let go of everything, for the moment. It is an attitude, it's a shift and in that moment, you connect with your entity and in the moment you can say, "Hey entity, my bills aren't getting paid." In fact, you won't need to tell it. It just knows it and it might just happen to drop a check in your mail for you. It will take care of you. But if you're running around, all over the place, it will never catch up with you. It will never, ever catch up with you to give you what you want.

What does living in the moment have to do with the aging process?

You'll find that if you could take all the people one-hundred-years or older from your planet and interview everyone of them, they all have a couple of things in common. One, it doesn't matter what they ate. It doesn't matter whether they exercised or not. It has nothing to do with it. Some of your ancient ones, one-hundred and twenty-years-old, smoked from the time they were twelve-years-old and they are just fine. Some of them did every terrible thing. They drank every day of their lives. They weren't on the good people's good diet list! They didn't do any of it. The one thing that everyone has in common that lives to a hundred-years plus is, they lived in the moment and they didn't worry about the future. They didn't take life seriously. The ones that are a hundred and ten, a hundred and twenty and over didn't believe everything anybody told them about themselves. They didn't buy the images. They lived their own truth. You'll find in common with everyone who lives to a nice ripe old age that they don't go around judging life a lot or judging other people. They just don't take it too seriously. They just realize that life is for living, not for dying over and not for being stressed over. You will find that in common with everyone of them.

In order to change the body, to rejuvenate it, all you have to do is let life in it, which means you get rid of the expectations. It is that simple.

I love you all. I'm going to vacate. Have fun. Be at peace. Be out of expectation. So I retract my have fun and be at peace, because that would give you expectation! So, be a no-thing. Be yourselves. Be no-thing and every thing. I love you. Anyway, be at peace! Good night. ▲

Subpersonalities as the External God

Each of you are a biological entity, which means that you have a biological and physiological embodiment. You also have a spirit or a light entity. This spirit or light entity could also be considered your god spark or the light that you are.

Each of you originally were the whole god or the whole source which was loved into existence. Therefore, each of you became a spark of that same love, and so, each of you are in essence a god spark. That god spark tries to live in the embodiment, and that god spark is technically each of you individually. You are each an individual spark that is designed with an individual personality.

Each of you take the spark that you are and try to inhabit the embodiment. This occurs anywhere from conception, to birth, to years after the physical embodiment has been born. You overlay the embodiment, but you also become the embodiment as your vehicle of expression for this experience. As you begin to inhabit the embodiment in physicality, you begin to move into it, not necessarily to take it over, but to become one with the embodiment and to live through its expression and its experiences.

The spark and this light are actually your god essence or your god spark. Whenever you put your power or your god outside yourself, you externalize it. Whenever your personality for any reason—and it does not matter what the reason is—begins to externalize your god, you create what we will term a subpersonality. From other perspectives this is called a subconscious, but for our terminology, we're going to call it a subpersonality, because we want to emphasize that it has a personality in and of itself.

The moment you move into a place of not believing that you are god, you just externalized your god spark. The moment you believe and worship an external god—which all of you upon this planet do, even those of you that are learning to become your own god—you externalize your god spark.

Most of you are birthed into either religions or philosophical frameworks that believe in one God that is external to you and whom you worship and serve. This belief system alone actually begins to externalize the god spark from within your being to outside yourself, stating that it is not part of the biological embodiment and that it is separate. What you actually do at a very young age is disown your own godhood. You actually disown the fact that you are god.

The other ways that you disown this fact is by not being responsible. Every time you move into a place of not being responsible for your life or believing that you are not, you put god outside of yourself. This means you actually take your god spark and put it external to your biological embodiment. As you do this, your god spark is still trying to live through the perceptions of and inhabit the physical embodiment; and as it does this, it is still connected to it because it is part of it and is holding it together.

You can't totally, one-hundred percent externalize your god spark, but you pretend to. As you pretend to, you actually take the spark that you are, and because you believe in an external god, stick it outside of yourself and begin to worship something external to yourself. As you do this, it is still connected to the physical reality and you end up with a biological personality and a god essence or an external god. Since the god you are, which should be inhabiting your body and running it as one package is now external to it, your body is now a mass of biological reaction that is pretending to be an individual embodiment containing a god.

Now the biological embodiment is virtually running on its own with its own set of circumstances and its own set of actions, reactions, and neuron firings. It creates a biological personality which is just a mass of firings and actions that are created from emotional circumstances. Since the god spark that you are is still trying to inhabit and is still trying to be connected to that body and live in that body—even though you have externalized it—it begins to create its own form of personality. This form of personality is created from a cross of your biological responses and your god essence.

This subpersonality understands physicality and non-physicality better than you do. Because it is a god and is trying to live in the embodiment that you are in, it knows how to run the body. It knows how to fire the brain. It knows how to make all of your organs work in harmony and how to create function or dysfunction within the embodiment. This is a part of the biological reaction that becomes this subpersonality.

On the other side of it, the subpersonality also understands the spiritual realm, because that is where it was created from the god essence. All of a sudden now, you have a subpersonality which is a cross between your biological personality and your god essence, and most of you are running off multiple subpersonalities. This is the reason you cannot get these biological embodiments to function as the god they are. They have a middle man. You have to learn to get through this middle man or incorporate it in order to get the biological embodiment to fully function and act as the god that it is.

You can only do that by internalizing the god, which means that you are welcoming the god that you are into the embodiment as its new home or castle, so to speak, and allowing physicality to become its kingdom. Every time you have issue with yourself, you have issue with physicality, you have issue with anything, or there is any portion of yourself that you disown, you virtually put a new step in its way. You virtually begin to cut it off further and push it further and further out.

All of you, when you become judgmental, begin to create stronger and stronger subpersonalities. You have disowned your god essence and your god spark, but when you begin pushing out of your being something that you don't want, you are putting it out there in the same place.

All of you, when you become judgmental, begin to create stronger and stronger subpersonalities.

There are sides of you that you don't like. All of you have a shadow side that you don't like and even in most of you there is a very beautiful side that none of you like either. You think there is something wrong with them, or you criticize them just because you don't accept them. Anything that is within your realm of reality that you do not like, you begin to externalize and push out. When you push it out, you are actually pushing that as information or feedback into your god essence. So you are actually making it become your new god.

For example, let's say that you have grand amount of anger within your being. You don't like being angry; it is not socially acceptable. It is not acceptable to you, and so you begin to repress it. As you begin to repress it, you begin to state that you are not like that. You cannot be angry. You cannot be hostile. You cannot be violent. You cannot be these things. You will not accept them. As you do this, you repress it, and you actually deny it. Anything that you deny, you also externalize.

Early in life you externalized your god spark. In the juncture of your life, you begin to externalize other attributes about yourselves you don't like. Because you don't want to be an angry person, you deny that you have any anger, you repress it, and push it into complete denial. As you do, you are taking your whole angry self and pushing it out into the exact same route that the god spark is. What you are doing is giving the persona of anger to your own personal god spark; and therefore, you become an angry god. And you also perceive God as being angry.

At that point in time the god, or the subpersonality in this case, begins to run your life. It is a subpersonality created out of your denial of your own anger and your god essence which gives life to anything you are because it is you. It is unconditional enough that it is willing to accept the totality of you even if you aren't.

Now you have a subpersonality that is very angry. This is why a lot of times when you go into repression, it actually causes more problems than just feeling the situation and releasing it. Whenever you go into repression and denial, the very act of denial takes whatever you're denying and puts life into it and pushes it out to your external god. As it externalizes it out into this realm, you just gave life to every portion of yourself that you are denying. That is why repression will always come back to you. Anything that you are repressing, you will face again at some point, because you will have to in your own evolution.

Let's say that you are fearful about something. You tried to repress it and state, "I'm not fearful." Rather than dealing with the fear, you just simply state, "I am not fearful and I will deny that part of me." You now have externalized fear out where your external god is. Now you have an external subpersonality that is a god essence of fear. In other words, it is a part of your personality that is fearful, but because it also deals with the spirit realm, it is fearful spirit—a subpersonality that you are going to deal with, because it is going to run your life as the middle man between the biological entity and you, the total god essence or god spark.

In your society and your culture there are many things you are taught to repress or not allow to be or exhibit because they are not acceptable or proper. This could be anything from conduct to characteristics. Anything that you repress and try to deny is going out into your external god and will become a portion of the personality that you will deal with in life.

This is why people will say that they are continually fearful. They are a fearful person. They are an angry person. It is because probably, at some point in their juncture they tried denying their fear and anger. As they tried denying that portion of themselves they externalize it. As they externalized it, they created a subpersonality that they are not working and viewing life through. It was given life, as it was externalized out to where the god spark is. So now, they view themselves as an angry person, especially as they begin to walk in their own enlightenment or their own empowerment.

Empowerment means that you are trying to claim back your own god power, but how can you when you gave it away? You really didn't give it away to anyone else, you literally just said you weren't it, so you stepped it aside. Now you have all these subpersonalities that have been created, and you want to be the god that you are. Everything that comes from that god essence is going to have to be filtered down through and into those subpersonalities first before your biological body can respond to it. At that point, the subpersonality, because it is very closely aligned with the physical embodiment and with the spirit, knows how to re-route it because it is something you feared anyway. You feared being the god that you were, and since you feared being the god that you were, you externalized your god essence.

Anything that controls you in any way, shape, or form, is running through a subpersonality.

Your spirit inhabits these embodiments, but is not imprisoned in them. In other words, the spark that you are is the spirit that existed before these embodiments and will exist after them. Therefore, it is free-formed, if you wish to look at it that way. It is a god essence that can go anywhere it wants to. Since it is trying to be in these bodies and these bodies are not inviting it in because your personality is kicking it out, it can go wherever it wants to and be whatever it wants to. Since it was your spirit that was trying to come into physicality and animate and live in these physical embodiments and you are trying to kick it out, it is creating a pseudo-death for itself which is what you are calling your lives. The reason being, that spirit is inhabiting these bodies, and it is determined to have an experience through it. That is why it came here in the first place, but you are not letting it in. You are not letting the full essence of that in. You are keeping it external to you. As you do this, the whole entire body has a reaction and now you have a subpersonality.

You may say, "Well, that's easy, I'll just be the god that I am. I'll just pull the god that I am back in and I'll quit externalizing it." But now, at this juncture in your lives you are all externalizing god so far that, that is a very difficult process—not impossible, but it is going to take effort, and it is going take a process to do it. First of all, anything that controls you in any way, shape, or form, is running through a subpersonality. All of you worship many gods, you don't have just one. Even though you externalized it and believed in one god, you are now trying to pull that one god back in.

Most of you have gone through a religious or philosophical belief system earlier in your life which created the belief in one god. You externalized your god, as we spoke of, creating subpersonalities. But you just put your external god into a composite pile with everybody else's more or less, because all of you on this planet, no matter what your religion or belief system, basically believe in one god. This composite pile of everybody's beliefs about god creates what we call a gestalt or the god gestalt.

The prevailing belief is that there is one god. So since each of your god sparks knows it is god, it is a fight to figure out which god is the god and which one is superior over everyone else! This is where a lot of your superiority complexes and inferiority complexes arose. The prevailing belief in the god gestalt is that there is only one god. Now here you are trying to pull god back in, your own god essence. That should be quite simple, but look at what happens. You externalized it out into a pool that says it is one god. So this one pool out there is a gestalt called god. It is a composite of everybody's externalized, individualized god, which now believes it is one god, one entity.

You, the individual, come back and say, "Okay, I am going to be the god I am. I am going to walk into my own empowerment. I am going to be god because I believe this way now." You are now trying to go back to that pool and bring your god spark back, but it doesn't know the difference between you and everybody else more or less! The reason being, is you believed it into one mass, as population and people. Instead of bringing just your little god spark back, which is very brilliant on its own, you are trying to consume the whole entire god pool or gestalt that you created as one god. So now you, the individual trying to be the god that you are, trying to pull that back into your being, trying to believe it, to live it, and to know it, are actually going out into the universe, grabbing this one large gestalt around god and trying to bring it in and call it you. The moment you do that it is going to fight you, because you already said you weren't god and it knows it is, and you don't know that you are!

This externalized god has now been created and knows it is god. You endowed it with that. You are trying to pull it in, and it knows it is superior to you. So you are going to have a very nasty fight with it for one, until you move into a place of knowing that you are god. Knowing it, not intellectually, but embracing it into every facet of your life.

You start trying to pull that god in. When you do, you are going to pull the whole gestalt in—the whole entire gestalt that is created out of everybody's individualized god who externalized it into a belief of one god. The moment you try tapping into your own god essence and your own god power, you tap into the whole entire god gestalt and everything around it, which means everybody's belief about god—not just yours.

You might know that you are god. You might have that understanding, that embracement, and feel and believe it. Maybe the god that you are and the god that you know is loving and beautiful and kind. But the god gestalt is full of everyone's beliefs about God. It is full of fear, vengeance, love, and kindness. You are pulling one god back in, and as you are doing that, you are having to take the whole entire gestalt. This is going to be a heavy duty chore for anybody!

Some of you will be dealing with just two or three different subpersonalities, and some of you have thousands of them . . .

You externalized your god spark to a point that you externalized it clear out there. It knows it is god. It knows it is superior to you; and therefore, it knows that it doesn't have to listen to what you want to do—and it won't!

In your own mind just imagine what I am explaining. Take a hundred different people across the planet, with various beliefs, philosophies, and dogmas. Take every single idea they have about god and put those all together. That is where that god gestalt is, and it is not going to listen to you—you probably wouldn't want it to anyway!

Most of you start a little closer to home. When you start pulling god in and you start believing yourselves as god, you first start pulling in your own subpersonalities. They are the closest thing to you, because they are a combination of biological embodiment, spirit, and the external god that you originally were. This is what most of you call your higher self, your guidance, your subconscious. This is what you call nasty names when things don't go right! These are all subpersonalities, because within your being, you've denied all of these facets of yourselves. Those that coagulate together will make an individualized personality. Any that don't coagulate or any that are extremely strong, create their own independent personality.

Some of you will be dealing with just two or three different subpersonalities, and some of you have thousands of them, depending on how much of your own lives you deny. This part of you seems bigger and larger than life. It is created out of that externalized god portion of you, and it is spirit, so it is going to have the tendency to appear a whole lot more intelligent, more powerful, or more godlike than you. So most of you, when you start talking to your guidance and when you start dealing with your emotions, are going to deal with your own personal subpersonalities. They are the closest thing to you.

You have both grand ones and negative ones, because that is how you believe. Since you believe in a binary system and you believe in positive and negative, you've created subpersonalities both ways. You are going to have some that are very positive, and you are going to have some that are very negative.

Let's say that you have an attitude where you don't believe you can accomplish something you desire. You deny this portion of you that always has an excuse for not doing anything and put it out there with your external god. It becomes a subpersonality that says, "No, we can't do it, we can't do anything." All of you have at least some form of this type of subpersonality.

Now you begin pulling it into your own being and wanting to accomplish something, and you get this subpersonality that says, "No, we can't." Because it is externalized into the god essence it has life, more spirit than you do biologically, and it is now a mini-god, its word becomes law.

Now you get frustrated because you can't do anything. At some point in your life, you put the power outside of yourself to make decisions or you didn't want to go through with something. You denied that portion of you, pushed it out there and now you have a subpersonality that is not going to help facilitate anything for you.

Each of you have different subpersonalities. A lot of you have fearful subpersonalities. Realize that spirit has no fear, whatsoever. It does not know it. It knows challenge and curiosity and creativity. It does not know fear, nor comprehends it. Yes, you are going to deal with survival fear which arises when the body is in danger. This type of fear is biological in nature and necessary for self-preservation.

But most of you will also deal with fear of other kinds. For example: fear of not acting properly, fear of not doing things quite right, fear of your parents, fear of your children, fear of your employers, fear of your creditors. All of these are subpersonalities that have been externalized and given power. That is why your creditors are gods to you, because you have externalized your own creative abilities outside of yourselves. When you went outside of yourselves to incur your debts, you actually put a portion of yourself into the same composite of the external god and gave it life. Therefore, your creditors now have life, because you have a subpersonality that will control you.

Each of you will also deal with positive subpersonalities. A lot of you have very beautiful, powerful, loving experiences, and externalize them and say, "That had to be coming from somewhere else." Let's say that you are in a religious system that says that if you have a spiritual experience, it was a message from god or a gift from the heavens. Maybe it was just a beautiful message from a very loving part of yourself, but you externalized it and gave credit to somebody else. As you externalized that very powerful experience outside of yourself, you now have created a portion or a subpersonality that is a loving, benevolent entity—a god to you, or a Christ to you.

Each of you have a subpersonality that we will term a Christ consciousness. This is also a large, en masse, subpersonality, or one that is a consciousness level of the entire planet. Whether you believe in Christ or not, your planet is dealing with a basic Christ consciousness which means psychologically there are certain factors that comprise that consciousness. Each of you are dealing with it in your own way and in your own terminology. Let's say, during your childhood, during your teens growing up, and even into your young adulthood, you were into a system that strongly believed in a Christ, a savior. What this does is it puts total responsibility outside of yourselves. It is saying that somebody is going to come and save me, which means that you have externalized it.

Realize that spirit has no fear, whatsoever. It does not know it. It knows challenge and curiosity and creativity.

You've already externalized your god essence, but now you've externalized the portion of you that can help you. You have verbally and consciously said within your beings, "I am helpless. I have to have a savior to help get me out of my mess," more or less. If you were into an organized belief system, this tendency is stronger than if you were not. All of you are dealing with it in your own way, whether it is a matter that you don't feel responsible for your life and you feel somebody else is pulling your strings, or whatever.

Let's say that you've been into a religious structure that taught of Christ, taught of an individual that was going to come and save you from your sins, or save you from the things you were doing wrong. You've already externalized the god essence out there. Now you externalize the part of you that can help get you out of your own mess. Each of you have externalized and created your own individual Christ which is also a subpersonality. This isn't to say that in the larger scheme of things that there isn't a Christ scenario in and of itself, but each of you individually have a Christ consciousness and an externalized Christ subpersonality. Within your own spectrum this subpersonality is going to manifest at different times in your life when you have some of these powerful experiences. For most of you a Christ entity is loving, so this is not what you term a negative scenario within your being. This is an individual who loves you, who cares for you, who takes charge, and who is the buffer between you and god. Even in your own terminology, Christ is what stands between you and god and helps you to relate to god. Christ is your own subpersonality.

You have externalized it into being a god, but you are afraid to ask for help. Most of you don't feel worthy of sitting down and asking Christ to help you or you don't feel worthy of actually receiving the help. So now within your beings you have become quite victimized in your own terminology. There are no victims, but you externalized your power and now you feel powerless and victimized. You go through your lives, but you are afraid to ask for help because you don't feel like you are worthy of being helped.

This Christ subpersonality is one of the largest everyone of you is going to have to deal with. If you could put yourself into a place right now of saying that Christ was going to stand face to face in front of you and you are free to ask for anything and everything you wanted, do you feel capable within your being of freely asking for help? Most of you do not. Yes, many of you are getting to a point where you could, but most of you, if you felt like you were face to face with God or Christ, could not ask for what you wanted within your own being because you would feel that you are unworthy to ask for it.

This is the major subpersonality that is going to stand in your way of doing anything, because it is your attitude of being unworthy of being the god that you are. Now you have a Christ subpersonality that is created to stand in the way and help buffer between the two of you, but you don't feel worthy of asking for the help. You don't feel worthy of approaching that. You don't feel worthy of pulling that in. So on your evolutionary path, most of you are going to go through a phase where you go through the Christ consciousness and begin to pull the Christ consciousness in and try to live and become it. You are actually trying to absorb your own subpersonality and be this subpersonality that you externalized.

In order to move into the total power that you are and into the total god essence that you are, you are going to have to go through this phase, because what you did, as I said, is externalize the god which is the portion of you that can do everything. Then you externalized the middle man, so to speak, into a Christ consciousness or created a mediator. Until you can pull that in and live up to your total, one-hundred percent ideal, you are never going to touch your own god essence to pull it back in. This is why most on the evolutionary path believe that the Christ consciousness is generally as high as you can obtain. It isn't. It should just be stepping stone for something even grander and greater.

Look at your own personal belief systems about Christ and your approach or accessibility to Christ. Most of you believe that you can only approach Christ in certain spiritual circumstances, such as in church. Many of you are now learning your own way of approaching and touching that god essence within you and that very spiritual space within you. If you do not have that, you are never going to approach your own Christ consciousness in order to breach it into a god consciousness.

Most of you technically had a religious background. It doesn't matter what you are into now. You had some form of a religious upbringing—not all of you, but most. If you had a religious upbringing you know how you can or cannot approach Christ or God and most of you were told that you can't. You can pray to do it and can send messages this way, but your heart has to be a certain way, and you either have to be in front of a certain preacher or in a certain church in order to approach Christ or God. What happens is this sets up within your being a ritual that is part of the gestalt of the Christ subpersonality.

Most on the evolutionary path believe that the Christ consciousness is generally as high as you can obtain. It isn't.

Let's say that you truly want to be the god that you are and get yourself out of your own mess. You created a subpersonality to take care of it called Christ consciousness, your own savior mode. But in the early days of this lifetime you learned that the only way you could approach Christ was to go to church. Now, in your later years you don't go to church, but that gestalt and belief didn't change. When your belief system was formed, it created that subpersonality and defined how it is accessible. That is why most of you will change from one religion to another rather than completely changing it by completely leaving it. Most individuals don't completely leave religion. Even a lot of individuals who are into the New Age movement, or whatever you term it these days, simply change from one bag of rituals to another that is more acceptable at this point in their path. It still gives them a place within their being where they can feel through whatever their intensity is. Maybe now instead of prayer, it is meditation, instead of going to a church, it is going to their own inner sanctuary within their being or out in nature to approach that same essence. In order to get back into your god essence, you're going to have to find your own personal ritual of how to get back into that subpersonality.

Most of you cut off and trash your religious history more or less. You throw it out with the bath water, so to speak. You just sever it and you go your own way. Now you are into a place where you want to be the god you are and desire to walk into your own empowerment, and you get frustrated because nothing ever manifests quite right. Yet, you've created all these subpersonalities as middle men and until you learn to deal with them and learn how to re-access them, you are not going to manifest your life the way you want. That is why a lot of you can be in a religion, have very powerful experiences, and then when you leave that religion, there is a portion of sadness with it. Those powerful religious experiences kept you in it in the first place, and now as you are leaving it, you are having to say it was no good. But you had those powerful experiences that taught you how to get into your own subpersonalities that you created, one of which is your Christ subpersonality.

For most of you, your Christ subpersonality is love. It is generosity, it is all of your images around Christ. It is the savior. It is the one who can take care of everything for you. It is the one that saves you. Each of you have an individualized subpersonality, Christ, so to speak, within your own beings. But when you left the religion, you also left all of your ritual or all of your techniques on how to access it. And so, until you can learn within your beings how to access that gentle space, that nurturing space once more, you are going to be into a place of being very cut off from your own god essence. You are not ever going to learn to be the whole god that you are.

When you start pulling the gods back in, so to speak, or your externalized portions or your subpersonalities, many of them have more life in them than you do. You externalized portions of yourself you didn't like, out where your god essence is, and so, they now know both the biological and spiritual realms. In other words they are physical and non-physical. Yes, you are too, but they are more knowledgeable of it. You are still stuck in a biological response. They are not, but they know how to operate it.

Let's say there is a portion of your personality you decide to incorporate and come to terms with. Let's say that it is this angry portion of you that you externalized a while ago. Now you decide to deal with your anger. You decide to deal with your intensities of it. You decide to get into really knowing yourself and healing that. What is going to happen is that subpersonality of anger is very strong, and it biologically knows your body better than you consciously do—it knows how your heart works, and how your brain fires. Now you're trying to destroy it. You gave it a persona and a personality. Your subpersonalities also are incorporated in and comprise any images you hold about yourself, so it is one of your images. Now you want to incorporate this subpersonality of anger, which is your image of you being an angry person, but you've given it a god spark by externalizing and denying it. Now you are trying to tell this god that you are getting rid of it, and it is very angry. That is why you externalized it in the first place and it says, "No, you're not." So as you start trying to incorporate it, it is going to start throwing up a nice smoke screen. It is going to know how to rewire your brain system. It is going to know how to keep your neurons firing just right so you can't incorporate it, thereby healing it and effectively taking its life away. It is going to know how to change your responses. It knows how to bring up an emotional reaction so you won't do anything about it— it throws *you* into anger! It is a vicious cycle, because as you continue to judge and deny your anger, you continue to feed and give life to this subpersonality.

These subpersonalities can literally destroy your attempts at destroying them.

These subpersonalities can literally destroy your attempts at destroying them. You try to start dealing with a portion of your being. You start trying to heal it, you start trying to come to terms with it, but if it has been externalized as a subpersonality, it is going to fight for its life. This is why most of you are in habitual patterns that you try to change and try to change and try to change and can't.

First of all when you started trying to change a portion of your being, you denied it; you denied yourself and just shoved it out. You externalized it and made a god, which is a subpersonality. Now you are trying to change that and heal it which is the same as trying to take the life away from the god you created. It says, "No way," and so you stay in the habit, it is habitual and ongoing. It is because it is a fight of your will against it, and it is stronger. It knows biologically how you function, and so it can short circuit you at will whenever it wants to.

So let's take the common example of an individual who is overweight and denies the fact. In other words this is a portion of their beings that they don't like. You have all learned how to make moral judgments that should just be health considerations rather than moral judgments. So let's say that being overweight is something that is not acceptable. It is a portion of the being that you want to destroy, get rid of, and kill, quite literally. As you do that, you externalize this portion of your beings rather than coming to terms with it and understanding it. You actually try to destroy it by denial or through what you term dieting, which is denial. It is saying I don't want the things that I truly do want to eat at this point in time. So you externalize it, create a subpersonality, and this subpersonality is endowed with being overweight. It is endowed with all of the traits you say you don't want. It is endowed with the cravings for the food you don't want to eat. It is endowed with all of the metabolism problems, so to speak. It is endowed with all of the things that are going to keep you overweight.

On the other side of it, an individual that is just opposite of this has the exact same subpersonality dealing with their situation. An individual that can't gain weight, has done the same thing. They have denied a portion of their being. Either they didn't want to gain weight because it was unacceptable or they denied a portion of their being that was not able to. It is the same principle. Anything that they denied went out and created a subpersonality that is now the image. The subpersonality holds the image of what you will become and are.

It also works in family situations. Most of you see yourselves in a certain light with your family and don't like it. You don't like the way your parents react to you, but rather than doing anything about it or changing it, you just deny it by putting up with it. It is not a matter that you need to go out and create a fight about; it is more a matter of acceptance within your own being.

If you are learning to be your own self, you wouldn't have this issue at all. But since you react as you are expected to around your parents, you deny a portion of your own being. You create a subpersonality, and therefore, later in your life, every time you get around your parents you automatically flip into this subpersonality and you act a different way. You hold your bodies differently. You talk to your parents differently. You use different language on them, such as when you were children you weren't supposed to swear in front of them. Maybe as an adult you swear, but you are not going to do it in front of your parents. This is part of a subpersonality that will always remind you, you are not supposed to swear.

Subpersonalities keep track of the way you are supposed to act in any given situation. You have subpersonalities that dictate how you will act at work. You have them with family. You have them with friends. That is why everyone of you basically act differently in every situation. You can have ten friends and you act differently with every friend. You can act differently with every family member. You can have employees and employers and act differently with everyone of them. You have a different response. You aren't ever allowing yourselves to strictly be you. If you are, then you won't change for anybody.

When you truly learn to be you for yourself and not for anyone else, then you don't go out of your way to push issues with others, yet you are comfortable being you. You don't change every time you are around someone different or in a certain different situation. But pretty well all of you change your body, the way you appear, the way you dress, the way you speak, and the way you do everything because of these images that are part of these subpersonalities.

Subpersonalities keep track of the way you are supposed to act in any given situation.

For the most part these subpersonalities are created by you, the individual, through what you deny about yourself. The god spark that you are is so powerful that it creates anything it embraces to be reality. It is unconditional and it is just trying to look to see what it is. Part of the reason it took the journey into this body that you are living in, in the first place, was to understand what it was, to see some new faces of itself and what it is. It got here and you kicked it out! As soon as you learned how to think and learned how to buy into other people's belief systems, you kicked the god you are out of the body. So the body is running on its own, creating its own personalities. The god spark that you are is sitting there; yes, it is still in the body and trying to run it, but it does not have easy or quick access to it, because the biological body is just running off of the primitive brain—the primate brain that was created for survival.

Your god essence is sitting here collecting everything you deny. These subpersonalities are created out of your own personal repression and denial and it is now a living consciousness. That is how they are formed and given life. But you could see them as living entities that are your own faces. These are the faces of god, called you, that you collectively put together to create yourselves. Then you wonder why none of you like yourselves! The reason you don't is because all of these things that you are denying about yourself is the very self you are creating. Everything you repress and deny about yourself, you are actually shoving out into your god spark to give it life

163

essence and creating a living entity or a living face of the individual god that you are. Each of these subpersonalities are one of your faces. Now you are collecting them together to create them to be a whole single god, because now you believe that you are a whole god on your own. You are coagulating and bringing them together trying to know yourself. As you try to know yourself, you are going to find thing after thing that you don't like, because you were created out of these things that you have been denying and saying you weren't and didn't like. More of them are pushed out there in denial than are brought in through joy.

Basically the only benevolent subpersonality that any of you have is your subpersonalities created around your Christ images and your god images, if they are positive god images. If they are not positive, you have some heavy-duty subpersonalities that are the denial of everything that has ever been wrong with you or you didn't like. This is the combination of subpersonalities that you are calling yourself, and no wonder most of you on this planet don't like yourselves, because this self that you are trying to love and like is a combination of everything you've ever denied about yourself and haven't liked. So you are going to be at odds and conflict with it. But it is still you. You are still going to deal with it as you learn to love yourself. What you are doing is learning to love all those parts of yourself that you've been denying. A portion of learning to love yourself is taking this whole coagulation of subpersonalities, integrating it, and loving everything about yourself, even the things that you thought were never lovable and seeing them in that light and loving them very much because of that.

Subpersonalities can be so large that this can lead to a form of schizophrenia and some of your multiple personalities. It is because the individual has taken things about themselves, built them up larger than life in their own mind, and then externalized them. As they externalized them, they sit and feed them. Every time you sit and argue in your mind, you are feeding a subpersonality and growing it in strength. Many of you have things that are your pet gripes. As you sit and chew on them in your head, beat them up, argue with them, and fight with them, all of this energy is going into a subpersonality that is becoming very strong. Realize that just because you do this doesn't mean that you are going to have a multiple personality, but you are going to have a subpersonality you are going to have to deal with at some point. A lot of individuals have a tendency to actually take a little issue that would make just a normal little subpersonality and blow it up or exaggerate it in their mind and continue to fight with it, and fight with it. Then they get to a point of critical mass in their being. To preserve the psyche it will be totally externalized which means that it is cut off and released. But it is still connected, because it was created by the individual, and it becomes a multiple personality. Most cases of multiple personality are individuals that are infiltrating or playing around in their second brain, and the chemical membranes are not strong enough to handle it. The other case of mental capacity that leads to multiple personalities or schizophrenia are individuals who have created very, very strong subpersonalities that are taking over the normal personality. At any point in time that your normal personality becomes weak, the subpersonality can step in and take over. This is the case with all of you in situations when you feel vulnerable. The moment you feel vulnerable a subpersonality can step in unless you are dealing on healing and getting rid of your images.

Learning to love yourself is taking this whole coagulation of subpersonalities, integrating it, and loving everything about yourself . . .

When you feel vulnerable in any given situation, it is a good time to start working on these subpersonalities. When you see what you feel vulnerable about, you are going to be clearing out some of these subpersonalities. As you clear them out, you will actually become more vulnerable. You become more and more naked without the subpersonalities, and you will feel more and more vulnerable. When you are vulnerable, most of you will grab a subpersonality to cover you up with. So as you walk into your parent's home, you become vulnerable because of the situation there. The vulnerability makes you retreat a little bit and allows a subpersonality to step in to take care of the situation. As it does you don't feel quite as vulnerable, you shift the way you act and you have a different presence for your family.

This is what it does with everyone of your situations, and you usually do this without ever knowing it. It is not going to be like some big large entity saying, "Okay, you are at your parent's house, so get out of the way, let me act." This isn't how it will function. Most of these changes are so subtle you don't even notice that you make them. When you begin to become aware of them, and start focusing upon them, they become larger than life. That is because you are feeling them, altering them, and changing them. Each subpersonality that you get out of the way will make you feel more and more vulnerable until you can start bringing the subpersonalities in or creating your own god essence to deal with this vulnerability.

Your vulnerability is actually a sign. Most of you become vulnerable and run from the love. You become vulnerable and start covering it up with all these subpersonalities. If you can allow yourselves to not do that, to not go into denial with it, and just feel vulnerable and that everything is all right, you are going to quickly get rid of these subpersonalities and move back into a joy essence.

The joy essence invites the god spark in the fastest. When you are holding joy that is felt in the being and in the heart—not intellectual joy—and you pull that in, that invites the god spark in, because it is its vibration. If you can allow yourself in that vulnerable space to pull the joy in, the god spark will come in and you won't be creating another subpersonality unless you start denying your vulnerability by running away from it.

You don't need to start worrying about how many of these you have. Realize that they just come up in their own nature and their own time. This teaching was given to understand a portion of your personality and to understand what keeps you in your ruts. This also ties into many things en masse in the collective unconscious and other directions, and we can cover that at another time.

Joy is the fastest way to bypass the circuitry you have with your subpersonalities. The reason is that those subpersonalities recognize spirit, because they are part spirit and they are closer to it than you probably are biologically right now. Joy reminds them of spirit. So whenever you can bring joy into the biological embodiment, you are actually elevating and evolving your biological personality and your subpersonalities both. If you are in a space of going around and saying "I'm going to destroy all of these things that are wrong with me," your subpersonalities are going to be threatened, and they are never going to get out of your way. If you are in a place of saying, "I love myself just the way I am. I can accept everything about me, even the things that I don't think I like. I can accept them and I can love them," your subpersonalities are not going to feel threatened. If they don't feel threatened and you pull joy in, they are going to elevate to the consciousness of joy because they like it.

Joy is an addictive vibration to your subpersonalities, but if they are threatened because you are still in denial, they are not going to let you feel joy. Joy is also being severed, because the subpersonalities get in the way of you and your own god essence. When that god essence is at home, you are in joy, it is a brilliance, a love, an excitement for life, a peace and you love it.

It is the joy that most of you are looking for. If it is not there, you have subpersonalities that are misdirecting it, altering it, changing it, and putting it to their own use.

This composite of subpersonalities is not going to let you destroy it, because it is what you define you by. So all you can do is evolve it, alter it, and change it. If you try to destroy any portion of you by saying, "I don't like this part of me, so I am going to get rid of it. I'm going to annihilate it. I'm not ever going to do it again," this puts it in denial and the subpersonality is going to be defensive.

If you put it into a place of this is a part of myself I don't particularly care for, but I love me and I love it too, and so I'll learn the lesson from it, I'll learn what it has to teach me, I'll learn the knowledge, your subpersonality is not going to be on the defensive. It is actually going to be very cooperative with you. Your subpersonalities are only your enemies when you are fighting them. If you are not fighting, then neither are they. They are a reflection of what you are doing and your belief at any given time. So if you are warring within your being, it is these subpersonalities you are warring with. If you are not feeling joy, that means that you are warring with a subpersonality. If you are in joy, you are into god, which is you, and it is home and it is residing within the biological embodiment.

Joy is the fastest way to bypass the circuitry you have with your subpersonalities.

You need to move into a place of no longer warring upon yourselves, individually. Love you exactly the way you are, which means to accept even the sides of you that you don't like to accept about yourself. Most of you try to change you by destroying what you are. That is not going to work. That should be self-evident from all the years you've tried to destroy the attitudes and personalities that you didn't like. As soon as you come to terms with them, you integrate them, they loose their power, and you gain power, because the moment you come to terms with them, that subpersonality becomes a part of you.

Every time you can come to terms with a portion of your beings that you don't like or are not willing to accept, and you can truly accept it, love it as a beautiful, intricate part of you that was a learning lesson, you absorb it. It becomes you, and you move that much closer to the god essence that you are. You have to love yourselves the way you are and bring joy into your being. The easiest way to change anything that you truly want to change is to quit warring upon it, make peace with it, and then you no longer need the lesson. Making peace with it means you learned the lesson, so the subpersonality can go its own way. ▲

The Santa Claus Gestalt

G ood evening. And how are you all doing? What a joyous lot of lights you are! It is beauteous to see. You have a very wondrous feeling tone.

So do you. It's creating some tears. You must have brought a lot of love with you.

I hope so! . . . I guess we will get into the spirit of the season.

Your season is a wondrous time of your experience. For most of you upon your plane and into your culture, a whole lot of the beauty of the experience is lost. So we're going to work on getting it back.

Your time of season has so many ideals and different ways of thought about it. In your last several years you have what you term your commercialization, and you've lost a lot of the beauty of your season. So it is our intent to try to get back to the treasure of it and the spirit that is truly there.

What I would like to explain first is a concept that we call a gestalt—a consciousness gestalt, and it will lay a framework for the rest of my discussion.

All things that you do upon this plane, you do in consciousness, and your consciousnesses coagulate into what we term gestalts. A gestalt is a combination of like thought. There is nothing you can do that does not require other people to play the game with you. No matter what you would do, no matter what you would be, somebody else has to help you play your game. Anything that you want to do, no matter what it is that you would ever wish or desire to do in this reality, takes other people to play certain roles for you.

A gestalt is sort of like a library of consciousness where you can go to check out people to play different roles for you. Anybody that is willing to

169

play the same game, anyone who wants to be supporting actors or actresses for other people's games will fill into and be part of a particular gestalt. They are on file in the library.

Let's say that you want to paint. You can't be the artist unless there is someone who will let you be the painter. You can do it but without someone to appreciate your work, you're not going to get it marketed. Without someone to help you create your canvas or your pigment, you won't have anything to paint on or with. So each of these are different players in your game, so to speak.

Let's say that you want to be a hairdresser. You can't be a hairdresser unless you have other people's heads and hair to work upon. If you wish to play your dream and your reality, you have to have other supporting players in order to do it.

So a gestalt actually takes and creates its own rules of what is acceptable and what is not and who can play the game and how it is to be played. In the hairdresser gestalt, for example, it will tell you what you can and cannot do to be a hairdresser. In this gestalt you have to have people with hair. Bald people aren't going to be a whole lot of help to you. It tells you what you do, what you go to school for, what you learn, what your talents are and what your creation will be. It defines the whole limits of your reality in that gestalt.

Let's just say that we're going to have a hairdresser here. What are the first things that pop up into your mind as the definition of a hairdresser? Let's share a few of these just for the fun of it.

Beauty.

A good conversationalist.

They don't make very much money.

Most of your belief around people in creative arts is that they can't be very wealthy because that is part of the gestalt. If you were to sit and make a list of everything you think about a hairdresser, this will tell you what is part of the gestalt around one. This is just one example. Everything you do in your life creates a gestalt or comes from a gestalt. No matter what it is, or no matter what you wish to be or do, it is ruled by a gestalt.

Let's say that here is a hairdresser, and so she is a part of the hairdresser gestalt. Let's say that she wants to be the banker now. What are the first things that pop up for you when we say that she wants to be the banker next week?

She can't be a banker.

Why not?

She's not trained to be a banker.

It's too hard to make that kind of transition.

All of this is the definition of a gestalt. No matter who you are or what you are functioning as, these are the things you'll deal with. No matter what you want to be, you have to deal with gestalts.

These are your beliefs. Whatever you believe about anything formulates and coagulates into consciousness, and as it does, whatever you wish to be or do will be defined. These are the unsaid rules. That is what a gestalt is. The gestalt says the hairdresser is a hairdresser, and she might make it as a waitress or something else, but as a banker, hardly. So if a hairdresser wanted to be the banker, she would really have to work at it to do so.

Whatever you believe about anything formulates and coagulates into consciousness, and as it does, whatever you wish to be or do will be defined.

There is nothing that you do upon this planet where you can avoid a gestalt. A gestalt forms the rules of the games you play, and most of you are in more than one of them. You have individual gestalts and you have family gestalts. That is why most of you act different around every single person you meet. Around your family you have one image or face and one way they will see you. Around people you work with you have a different one. These individuals have a personal gestalt and you're playing a game for them. You are playing the son or daughter, the parent, the employer or the employee. You're playing different roles for different people. These are all gestalts. Everything on your planet is a gestalt. They make the rules. They tell you what you will and won't be, and as you try to change and grow, you have to move through them.

The trick with a gestalt is to play the game. A gestalt has a very rigid rule around it about what it will and will not accept. Just as we said with the hairdresser trying to be the banker. Most of you, if you are being honest, said, "Well, good dream, but it will be a lot of hard work."

It is rather a matter of knowing what the game is and learning how to play it. If you can learn to play the game of consciousness, you can be anything you want in a moment. What you have to do is match and understand what the gestalt is you're dealing with in order to get into it. So if our hairdresser knew what the gestalt was around banking and she still wanted

171

to be a banker, then she'd know that she would have to get a different education, do this, this, and this, but then she'd be able to become the banker. Gestalts don't just affect your employment and your relationships but everything, and this is what we are going to talk about is your Christmas gestalt.

This is the season of what you term Christmas. This is the season that most of you have connection with in one way or another. For some individuals on your planet, it brings grand depression; with some, grand joy. Christmas is a gestalt. Christmas is a metaphor. It is a combination of everybody's beliefs and ideals. I want you to go into your feelings. What are the first things that come up when I say Christmas? Be honest.

Lots of money.

Presents.

Pressure and rush.

Currier and Ives.

Okay. What else?

Kids and Santa Claus.

The birth of Christ.

Joy.

Good. See these are all beliefs and ideals and attitudes. You put them all together and this creates the gestalt called Christmas. The gestalt is so large that each of you can focus into it and touch whatever you want. Many times the way a gestalt works is you take it all or nothing. The gestalt sort of tells you, "Okay, here is the pearl you are seeking in the middle, but if you want it, you have to take the whole oyster." You may not want the whole oyster, just the pearl. All these things are a portion of the gestalt of Christmas, a portion of your collective unconscious.

Whenever you move into a place of wanting to get into Christmas and into the spirit of Christmas generically, you're tapping into all of these attitudes and beliefs about Christmas. So on the one hand you can feel the joy and love of Christmas which is what you really want to focus on, but because you are generically using Christmas, you are also getting the rush, the stress, the hubbub. You're getting all those things that you wouldn't necessarily tap into if you knew that was what you were doing.

After a few generations of doing this, when you start connecting into Christmas, most of the spirit of it has been lost. If you are quite honest with it, most of you try to maintain intellectually a feeling tone of the beauty and joy of the season. You truly try to do this but you get overclouded with all the rest—the rush and hustle and bustle. It begins to lose meaning to you, and the season of Christmas begins to become a burden. When it becomes a burden, many people start getting depressed because they don't know how to find the joy and spirit that is truly there. They are getting the whole oyster and what they want is the pearl.

Move into your feelings with Christmas. Don't get into them too deep yet, just the top layer of them. There is some joy there, some excitement, but there is a lot of the pressure and the tensions too. We have to learn how to get the pearl without having to take the rest of it.

Christmas is a gestalt. Christmas is a metaphor. It is a combination of everybody's beliefs and ideals.

Your Christmas season. Let's get down to some true depth and feeling. What is the Christmas season really when you get rid of all the tension and hubbub? Christmas is a celebration of birth. It doesn't matter what your belief system is. Each may have his own and they are all fine. Your season is a season of birth. It is a time of year when your plants and your planet itself are going into a rest in your winter months. It is building up excitement in order to burst into new life in the spring. It is going into its sleep, building, and getting ready to birth in the spring as soon as the thaw comes. The creatures are hibernating and there is a renewal time with it. So your whole season is a birth. That is what this season truly is. It is about birth. What are you birthing? It's not just birth as in waking up, but it is a time of excitement. It is a time of growth and a time of deep intensity of joy.

But you started using everything else, and you became lost in all the metaphors. You don't remember the true feeling in here, and that true feeling is the deep intensity of joy in birth, joy in life. That is what it is all about.

From a Christian standpoint you honor the birth of a Christ. What does that mean to you? It is a time of excitement, it is a time of new life, it is a time of hope. Your season is the time to birth hope.

What is the child wanting that is happy with Santa Claus and doesn't understand your whole story of Christ? Why does the child anticipate Santa? It is a joy. It is an excitement that instills in them. They don't care what your metaphor is. They don't care if it is Santa Claus or a Christ baby, but they do know that it is a time of joy, a time of life, of spirit, and there is an excitement.

Let's try to start getting into the feelings now. What is that spark, that pearl in there really. All this other is just stories about it. Santa Claus is a story. Christ is a story. The time of the seasons is a story, but what is the true pearl that is in there? What are they all representing? Let yourselves feel it. If you could have the season mean anything to you, what would it be? When you were a child what was it? It was an excitement. Let's get in touch with the excitement. It is an excitement of joy, an excitement of life. That is the pearl.

It is a season of birth, but the season of birth is to birth that joy and move back into that spark of life. So why did we lose that? We were too busy and life became too complex. We were just running away from it. Let yourselves feel that excitement. Let it tell you its own story. Be willing to do it. The pearl is inside of you right now. Feel the excitement that you would truly put back in the season. It's not an excitement of going around and buying packages. You started doing the packages and the shopping because it gave you excitement. When you were doing things and giving gifts for other people, that was exciting, and that is why you originally started doing it. Then it became a burden because the checkbook was trying to get balanced; you didn't have enough to go around. You had to figure out where to cut corners and whether you could buy Christmas presents or pay your bills, and the spirit was lost.

Feel it in there. It is a joy of life. You started celebrating the season to put excitement into your life. You had it already, but it was a celebration of joy. What your season is all about is a celebration of the joy of life and the excitement of the child. But we went into a place of running away from it. Everybody wanted to grow up. They thought that growing up was to let go of the excitement and surprises. Adults always like to know how everything is, you know. Children like excitement. They like the surprises. Why do you think they wait for Santa Claus? It really isn't to see if they have been good or bad. It is because it builds an excitement and a joy in here.

Many of you come from deep religious backgrounds. Why did you move into the spirit of the season and the Christ Story? You did it because it triggered a joy in there, a hope. They are all the same thing. Each of them is just a different story or metaphor that people use to explain that feeling of excitement. The feeling of excitement is hope for life and joy. So let's get in and feel it. Let's try to find the pearl.

What are you running up against? Let's be honest. We are trying to get into the feeling, and we can a little, but what are we coming up against? We're still worrying about the season. We're still worrying about all this other. Why? It is because what you are keying into is Christmas. Christmas has now become such a gestalt that when you think of Christmas, you buy the whole gestalt, not just the pearl. So we are going to learn how to get to the pearl instead of having to take the whole oyster.

A gestalt will let you in when you can match it. We've already defined the gestalt of Christmas. It is all this hubbub, this push. Even when you are feeling the joy right now, there is an underlying tension and pressure. You can feel it. So how can we get into the pearl? The pearl is the pure joy and the pure excitement. But what is that? As adults we all learned how to lose that because it was frivolous. You weren't serious and respectable if you were being silly. When you grew up you grew out of being the child. What is the one image that comes into your mind of the excitement and joy and life and joy of Christmas? Show me an individual here that knows how to totally feel the excitement of the season.

Your season is all about is a celebration of the joy of life and the excitement of the child.

A child.

So that means the child knows how to get to the joy. That means that if the child can get to the joy, which is the pearl, then we're going to have to be the child to get the pearl, because when you can become that, the gestalt lets you in. When you match the feeling tone of the gestalt, it assumes you belong to it, and it let's you in and opens the door. What else?

Santa Claus.

Some of you are from systems that didn't have Santa Claus when you were young, but you had other things. So let's play around with Santa Claus, and we are not trying to take you away from your meaning of Christmas which is your Christ story. We're trying to get you into a feeling tone.

Let's talk about Santa Claus a little bit and the Santa Claus gestalt. What is the gestalt in Santa Claus? Tell me all of your ideas about Santa Claus.

He's jolly.

Okay. I want all of them, anything you can think of about Santa.

He's magical. He flies around in a sleigh.

He can fit down a chimney—even when there's a fire in it!

What are the other beliefs about Santa Claus. As adults you know that Santa Claus doesn't exist, so you know that it's fiction.

He loves everyone.

He has an abundance of toys.

He knows what you're thinking.

He brings you the things that you ask for.

Do you realize what you have just said in all this? We're going to define the gestalt. As adults you know that Santa Claus is a myth because you play Santa Claus, so you know he doesn't exist. But do you know what the belief is about Santa Claus? What did you just say? Generosity, love, joy, makes people happy, abundance, magical. . . . What else did we say?

That he doesn't exist.

Your Santa Claus gestalt is the one gestalt that you have upon your planet that doesn't have any negativity in it. It was designed by children. The Santa Claus gestalt, the entire belief system in it, was a belief through children. They believed in magic, they believed in miracles, they believed in hope. They believed in all of these things. The Santa Claus gestalt is the only gestalt on your planet that has no negativity in it. It is also the one gestalt in consciousness here that has every trait and attribute everyone of you want. Maybe you don't want the red suit and the funny hat, but every other attribute you want is in there.

Do you also know what you said? You can't use it, because you don't believe in it. So here is a gestalt with beauty, joy, love, excitement for life, magic, generosity, abundance, love—because Santa Claus loves you whether you are naughty or nice; it doesn't matter what the song says, everybody knows that. It is a gestalt with no judgment in it. And you can't use it because you are adults and don't believe in it.

It doesn't matter whether Santa Claus really exists or not. In consciousness he does. And that is the joke! Anything that exists in consciousness you can use. Anything that exists in consciousness you can become part of, and you can use it to enhance your own lives. So here is the one positive gestalt on your planet that just sits there, and the only ones that can use it are children. It seems like a shame to waste it. It doesn't matter if you believe in the funny man with the red suit. It is more the feeling that is in the gestalt because the gestalt doesn't really have the image that much. But it does have the feeling tones.

Realize that even from a Christian perspective, what is truly the birth of Christ, if it wasn't hope, if it wasn't magic? Through your metaphors the birth of Christ matches the beauty and everything we just said about the Santa Claus gestalt. The problem with it is when you tie into it from a Christian perspective—and this is not to put down the Christian perspective because I have grand respect for it—you tie into the whole of Christianity which means not just the celebration of the birth, but the death also. You're not just taking the joy and the hope for life, but you are taking all the struggle and all the burden of the entire Christian gestalt with it. But when we say Santa Claus, you tune into a whole different picture.

Your Santa Claus gestalt is the one gestalt that you have upon your planet that doesn't have any negativity in it.

To enter into a gestalt and to use a gestalt, you have to have the feeling tone of it. To use the Santa Claus gestalt is to have the feeling tone of it. You have to match what it lets in which is children because adults don't believe it exists. From another perspective, by believing it doesn't exist, you are also telling the rest of your reality that anything that exists within that gestalt doesn't exist in your life. When you say that Santa Claus doesn't exist, you are also saying that within your life the magic doesn't exist, the joy and excitement for life doesn't exist, the miracles don't really exist. You're telling your own life that it is void of these things.

So I would say, if it was me, and I knew this, I would try to figure out some way to get back into the gestalt so I could put it into my life and use it.

All you have to do is feel as the child and it lets you in, but you have to believe it too. Intellectually, you might say, "Okay, Santa Claus doesn't exist, and I know this but I'll play the game." You have to feel it. You have to feel what it is. Why would you want a Santa Claus in your life?

He gives you gifts.

He's jolly all the time.

If you could have a Santa Claus that could be in your life all the time, not just once a year, how would that change your life? We want to move into this gestalt and learn to keep it all year. Realize that it is the least used gestalt because it is seasonal. This means that about nine of the rest of the months of the year, nobody is even using it.

The larger a gestalt is the busier it is. You start picking up more stuff from everybody that is attached to it. With this gestalt, it's only going to let you attach to it if you can be as a child so it will never pick up adult negativity. It will never contain those attributes you say you don't want in your lives. But it could be enhancing your lives all year. And see, even your children don't use it except at Christmas time.

So the real trick here, and the real miracle of the season will be if we can trigger within and get ourselves back into being the child and allowing ourselves to believe in a miracle and a hope and an expectation. That is the real miracle of the season. It doesn't matter what it takes an individual to do to get into that.

Your season is a season to jog you back into joy. It is a season to jog you back into some excitement, some expectation for fun and life. It is a season to birth these beautiful, joyous gifts of your own spirit, and we get too busy to even use it.

Also, the more individuals that are focused on one thing, the easier it is to get drawn in. So when everybody in the world is focused on the hassles of Christmas, you're going to get fed more of that unless you can find your own inner joy and peace.

So do you think we really could believe in Santa Claus? Technically, we're all adults here. Can we really do this? Intellectually, maybe, we can talk ourselves into it, especially if it will get us something. But can we feel it?

Do you know what you'd be saying if you could truly feel that you believed in a Santa Claus? You would be saying that you believed in the very thing your whole Christ story was about, which was hope for something new. Most of you, if you try to focus from the Christ perspective with it, you can do it, but you have so much other baggage that you have to take with it that it makes it difficult.

So we're going to try to short circuit the baggage, but realize that what you're going to be accomplishing is all the same anyway. It is a feeling tone in the heart. So let's be honest. Check your feelings out. Can we really feel a belief in Santa Claus? Not intellectually just say it, but can we generate the feeling?

Let's try. We're going to believe in Santa Claus. Realize that Santa Claus is just a metaphor. It is just a face that we put on something that we wish for. But to get into it, you have to feel. All you're trying to do is feel the excitement of the child. If you can feel the excitement of the child, knowing that a miracle can exist, you can access it. It won't let adults in because adults don't believe in it. So you have to leave the adults at the door and stick them outside in the cold. It's a good place for them. Let's take our adult, and put it outside the door and resurrect our own child within. Bring it up.

Many of you, when you were children, believed in a Santa Claus. You can use that past belief to help you generate it again. Remember the excitement, and you don't want to remember this right now, but remember how disappointed you were when you found out that there really wasn't a Santa Claus. That is the same thing as taking hope away from people, and that's where most of you are.

If you can feel the excitement of the child, knowing that a miracle can exist, you can access it.

It's not necessarily that you don't believe in Santa Claus any more, but life has a way of taking hope away. Without hope and without that joy for life, life isn't worth living, and most of you know that. If you are in a place where you have no joy, no excitement, no beauty, and no hope in this life, it doesn't make it very beautiful and worth living to you.

The times that you're in joy and the times that the excitement is there and you can feel it, and you're happy and you're excited, you wouldn't trade for anything in the world. During those times, you love being alive and you love existence. It is the rest of the time, when you don't feel the hope and the excitement that you're not so thrilled with it. So what we're doing is getting back into our hope and excitement. That is our key word here . . . excitement . . . our joy and our expectation.

It's not expectation like you are expecting some big thing out there, but expectation for the next step of the journey with excitement, fun, because whatever you feel within will create your reality and your view of it. So, all adults, outside!

Now let's take a joyous moment and let's get rid of our adults for a few minutes. You can always pick them up at the door when you leave, if you want them. Let go of the adult and get back to that child. You were all children once. Even those of you who had rough childhoods, there were at least moments in there when you had excitement that you can remember. Remember the excitement of the child before you started worrying about all these adult things. Let's bring it up larger and focus it. Touch into that joy.

179

Let's see if we can't believe in a Santa Claus. Now when you start feeling, feel your belief in Santa Claus. Not just think it, try to feel it. It's okay for your minds to know that this is just a metaphor for the feeling, but get into it. We believe in a Santa Claus and he's going to visit you. Notice any resistance you have to it. Any resistance you have to it tells you where you believe that the miracle of life can't happen for you. We're going to feel back into the belief in miracles and the magic.

I'm starting to feel some children arise here. We still have a few adults, but they're dwindling. The child. Feel that there is a Santa Claus. Like we said, we're going to tap into the Santa Claus gestalt, so feel Santa Claus, and he's going to come visit you. Put it into a knowingness, not just an intellectual perspective, but a knowingness out of these hearts. Feel it, know it. Be aware of your resistance and any portion of you that thinks this is real silly. That's your adult talking.

Dismiss your adult and come back to Santa Claus. Now let's try a few abstracts here. Santa Claus is going to fly with his reindeer and come down your chimney. Notice where the intellectual mind throws the belief out. Notice where it says, "Uh huh, sure." Let go of it. Life is a game anyway, so learn to play it by your rules. You want the joy in your life. All of you say you believe in miracles, but yet you won't let them happen for you that often. Put the wonderment in life. Let yourselves reconnect to that. See how much intensity inside you can get out of the joy of a child. Let it build enough that you can do this any time you want to so it doesn't have to be just this time of year.

The excitement of the child. Feel it inside, and let go of all the pain of being an adult—it hasn't gotten you anything anyway. Generate the intensities, the anticipation of waiting for Santa Claus to come. Let yourselves connect and feel. Notice where the mind still resists.

That joy you're feeling, why did you ever let yourselves get away from it? That joy is what makes life worth living. You know that. It is a treasure. So why did you ever let go of it? Let yourselves feel why you let go of it, and then you'll understand why you don't maintain it. Why did you ever let go of that joy? Were you not worthy of having it? Is not this joy and this expectation of life—this anticipation—is this not the treasure of the universe and the gift of the gods? So why did you let it go? You just sat there and generated it so you are capable of doing so.

That means you never really lost it. You've just been avoiding it. Why? That joy in there is your grandest treasure. That's what everyone of you verbally say you want your life to be all the time. If you had to write down how you wanted your life to feel on a twenty-four-hour basis, this feeling of joy is going to be pretty close to the top of your list. And you just created it. It didn't take anything but you. You did it yourself. So why don't you let yourselves do it all of the time? Why don't you allow yourselves to maintain this? Why were you willing to ever let go of it?

You grew up. That's what happened. Did you grow up or did you just give your gifts away? If growing up means that you have to lose this feeling, then why would any of you want to do so? I sure wouldn't. Let's let go of the rest of this adult stuff. Just because it is the joy of the child doesn't mean that it isn't intelligent. It doesn't mean that it's not brilliant. Get back into the joy and the excitement of being a child. This season is the season of the child and you all know that. It doesn't matter what metaphor you use. It is for the children. So let yourselves be the children in a feeling so you can be part of the season instead of just part of the hubbub of the adult mind.

Is not this joy and this expectation of life . . . is this not the treasure of the universe and the gift of the gods?

Once again, we're going to let all this serious adult stuff out the door, and let's get back into that joy. That joy however is so intense and so beautiful when you're willing to get into it that it makes the rest of your life mundane and hard to get along with. If you had this joy twenty-four hours a day, there would be nothing in life that would not be exciting and fun to you, which means that you would have to give up your struggle. You'd have to give up your stresses, your pain, because all that would be there would be this joy, and so everything you would accomplish would be done in joy and love. You would no longer know struggle. All you have to do is touch inside here.

Let's blow away all this serious stuff. That is your pain from losing your child. Those are your regrets. Let go of it and let's get into Santa Claus now. Be the child on Christmas Eve and Santa Claus is just hours away. What are you going to get? What is it you really want? You know that if you believe in it enough, you will have it. So let yourself feel it.

You're the child just moments away from Santa Claus's arrival, and what do you want? Now you have to feel the excitement. If you can feel the excitement, that excitement is also the knowing that you can accomplish it and have it.

So for those of you who can really believe in Santa Claus—really believe, not talk yourselves into it— but feel it, I'm going to play Santa

181

Claus! (Philip then asks each person in the class what they would like from Santa Claus and gives them each a "So Be It" to their desires.)

Now there are many who are not with us tonight who will read or hear this session some other time. And to the believing child in you, know that I so be your wishes also, now, or at any time of the year.

But know that you, the gods here, create what you want. The *so be its* only assist and facilitate you in your creation, and remember even when you were kids you started at Christmas to give Santa Claus all year to give it to you—but you started writing your lists very early!

For most of you, the things you've asked for, you already have, so on top of your request, I will add the ability to recognize what you already have and celebrate it. *So be it* on all of your requests and we also add one of our own.

It is our intention and direction to lay frameworks and understanding to teach you to celebrate life. This is our direction, which means that we're going to push joy and help to develop the expression of the self. And so, I will *so be that* on top of everything else.

We love you all very grandly. To us this a treasure beyond your comprehension right now, because from your perspective, you're having fun, but I don't think you realize that we do too. We do enjoy the experience and the opportunity to share with you. This is one of the grandest gifts you have all given us, so we thank you for that. I love you all very, very grandly, and we would embrace anyone who would like to this evening.

Have a merry Christmas and a very joyous New Year, but let it start tonight. Your calendar is wrong anyway! They don't even have the dates right on it. Let your new year start now. You already started—you have the joy. So let's just keep it.

I do love you, so good night. Be at peace and try to truly celebrate the season. I hate to leave . . . so I will embrace those who would and then I will leave. It gives me an opportunity to hang out for a few more minutes!

Merry Christmas to all, and to all a good night! ▲

Finding Life's Pearls

Creating your own personal gestalt in the midst of all the large gestalts in which you live is one of the hardest things in the world there is to do. However, if you know how to find the pearl or the nucleus of the idea behind what it is you want to create, you will create something that has the strongest amount of life there is. Carrying it out or living the creation has life in it too, but you'll never match the power that comes with the pearl or the original ideal. The pearl is your focus because the strongest amount of life that will be given, will be given to the pearl or the seed thought. The energy that your planet is now experiencing is an energy of realization and self-expression which means that this energy is going to attach to the original seed thought behind your creation and give it life. Whenever the energy gives life, it gives it to the core of what created it regardless of what it is.

Let's look at your city of San Francisco for instance. What was the core that created it? San Francisco was gold. The few times that these energies have hit San Francisco, people have become very wealthy, very fast. That's what it was formed and founded on. Los Angeles however, wasn't. Los Angeles was settled by people that were running away. Some of them were trying to find freedom. It was a very turbulent time. It was their city of angels. It was their place for hope. They went there and settled it because they felt hopeless.

New York was settled by immigrants wanting freedom also, but once again, they perceived their freedom through total struggle, however, there was also a pearl of hope. One can see these pearls that still exist there.

In the gestalt of Salt Lake City, people were looking for religious freedom. The reason they went there in the first place was their freedom to think, be, and act the way they wanted to even though their standards were different from most. They also had the belief that they could become as God. It is one of the few gestalts on the planet that has the belief that man can become God. The original pearl said they could touch God, see God, be God, have religious freedom and be themselves, but they didn't put abundance in there.

The pearl will tell you what is going to be given life and what the people are going to experience. That doesn't mean everybody, but most people will gravitate to places and objects because that's what they want.

Remember also that the seed or the pearl in a gestalt can also be what you would term negative. A lot of people tap into certain gestalts thinking they see the pearl and the real pearl hidden underneath really isn't what they wanted. The trick is to go deep into the ideal to find the real pearl. You can seek it out without connecting to it or living it. You have to connect enough to understand what its formation is, but as you do that, you can see the ideal and then decide whether you want that part of the pearl or not. The best way to do that is to put yourself emotionally in the place of the people creating the ideal. That will help you get closer to it. Find out the history of it. If you know the history of a given gestalt, that gives you the groundwork. Put yourself emotionally in the place of the people creating the ideal as if it were you. Put yourself in the place that you're the one doing it and feel how you would emotionally feel in that state. That will tell you what the pearl or the nucleus ideal is.

By understanding the pearl it will tell you why you like certain places, or why you don't like certain other places. It will tell you about anything you do in your life. If you like certain places such as when you're traveling, vacationing, visiting . . . find the history of the place. There is probably something in the ideal that attracts you. If you are repulsed by being in certain areas, there is probably something in the ideal that you are repulsed by.

This goes for everything from the location of cities on your planet, to thought, to careers, to the businesses you deal with. Maybe the businesses you like the least are the ones that have ideals or pearls that are not yours even though on the surface it looks like they support you. Underneath of it, the idea, the original seed, the pearl, probably doesn't match the external picture as you perceive it and what is underneath there is not what you want. People gravitate or are attracted to the pearls. It goes into everything from where you buy your groceries, to where you bank, to where you get gasoline for your car.

Things can be created without a pearl, but those things will feel dead to you. Most everything has an original thought or a pearl. So what you're actually doing is finding who created it and why and what their emotional reaction was and what they wanted from it. That's the pearl—what their feeling was. Just like the things you create. What was your ideal when you went into them? Why were you creating them? Don't confuse the end product or what you created with the pearl. The thing you make is irrelevant. People buy the nucleus pearl, the ideal inside. They're buying your original love thought. They're buying your pearl, not your product. If you build something and it breaks and you have struggle with it, it may turn out beautiful, but the emotions you have go into the piece. Part of the pearl within your piece of work contains struggle, and if it is something you wish to sell, it will be bought by someone who wants to buy your pearl of struggle. Doesn't mean you won't sell it, but it will be attractive to somebody who believes in struggle. It will reinforce where they are at. That is their pearl.

People buy the ideal, not the product. The product will be a reflection of the pearl inside.

Let's say that you sit down and put all of your love, your heart, your intensity into a piece of work. An individual, if that's the pearl they want, will be very much attracted. If it is a person who is running away from love, they're not going to have anything to do with it. People buy the ideal, not the product. The product will be a reflection of the pearl inside. People buy something they want from whoever came up with the thought. That is what they are purchasing.

If you're trying to create something that you don't have in you, it will be a failure. In other words, if you're trying to create a pearl or a product or something out here that has a whole lot of love and you're trying to attract people with love and you don't have it in you, you won't attract them. All of you can see through that. You purchase the pearl or the ideal underneath of it. The original ideal of those pearls are the only things that an entity can feel. Everything else is clutter. Its busy work. The pearl is the only thing that has a charge. When you get something that has an . . . ahhhhh! . . . a passion or an intensity behind it, that is what people will purchase. They're purchasing your original thought. The only time you get an original thought is when you're open enough to pull it in and create it. By the same token, it is the original thought that you buy.

Of course you will buy things for buying sake, just because you need them or you perceive yourself to need them, but what you all do is purchase the person's thought. It came through your system. That's what you're purchasing. Let's say you go to the market and you buy a certain product. What you're buying is not necessarily the product. What you're buying is the person who thought of the product. When that person opened up and thought of the product and said, "Hey, I love this. I'm going to build this." When they opened for that few seconds, it created an original thought in this earth plane or it pulled an original passion into this plane. There is life in a thought. What you're purchasing when you purchase the product is the rights to access the person's pearl. So when you purchase that product, you're purchasing the right to say, "I want to feel that way too. Let me pull in your love or your creation and chemically let my body react to it via the brain's excuse for buying the product." That is why, when you find a product that you really just love, you have to have it. What you're doing is you're building life into the way your body chemically reacts to it. It's not chemically reacting to the product. It's chemically reacting to the founder of the product and the emotional feeling tone in its entity when it discovered it.

Most everyone buys books at one time or another. When you purchase a book you are saying, "I want to feel the same way you did when you created this, and I'm buying the right to do so." When you do that, you tap into the original thought. So what you're doing is you're using the symbol or the book that says, "Okay, I want to feel the way you felt when you were the founder of this idea, when you created this." So what you're feeling is the writer's reaction, not yours, but it is now yours because you chemically lived it.

If you have ever noticed, you can go through a bookstore, pick up a book, and it will feel fantastic and you haven't read five words out of the whole book. What you're doing is using the book for a symbol to tap that person's intensity, passion, and love. As you do that, the product is irrelevant. If you want to have fun, go to a bookstore, don't read any of the titles. Just go pick them up randomly and feel them. See if you can't get a rush off of something. You'll find, especially if you don't pay attention to the titles, you'll get a rush off some and find that some are dead. What you're tapping is the original connection with their entity at the formation of the book. Just go along the shelves, grab a book, stick your hand in the middle of it gently, and feel it. You will often get a body response. When you buy a book, you buy the rights to tap into the founder of the book which means you can literally tap their knowledge better than you're going to get from the book if you read it. Reading the book only lets the brain know how to organize the information you get. Try moving your brain out of the way and you will find that you can tap the writer of the book and learn from them what is in the book.

The same thing is true about the cities or planetary locations. The earth is a pearl. Some places feel very beautiful and powerful to you. Other places may not. When you find places that you like or don't like, it is often the result of people's thought processes or the mass consciousness of the area—their personal pearls. When you find a place that you like very much, it means you're finding yourself connecting with certain pearls.

This will also tell you where your body is connecting to pearls. It will tell you what your body is creating even if your brain doesn't think you do. Let's say you find a book that your body just jumps up and down with. You look at the cover and it's like you are aghast because this is not something that has anything to do with you. I would check it out because it is probably telling you that your body is running off that gestalt and you don't know it, otherwise you wouldn't have had a reaction to it. Anything you get a reaction to, negative, positive, any strong reaction at all, means you are running off it. So even if you get a real nice adrenaline rush off a scary book, you're running off it or you wouldn't get a reaction. It can tell you everything that you're running off very fast. You can learn to use that reaction to get down to some of the deeper root issues that you carry personally. It will also tell you what energy you are tapping within the universe.

When you find places that you like or don't like, it is often the result of people's thought processes or the mass consciousness of the area—their personal pearls.

When you understand where the pearls are and how you feel with them, you will better understand how to create your reality the way you want it to be. It will give you a greater awareness of who you are by the way you react to life around you. It is simply being aware, then using that awareness to create a reality that can bring greater joy into your life. ▲

Creating the
Sacred Space

A secret means a hidden something that is not wanted to be shown or it is to be hidden. The inner sacred space, one also hides. So within the mind and the being, where does the difference lie? Where do you keep the sacred? Where do you hide the secret? Where do they each get kept? Do you put them in your pocket? Is it in your consciousness? Are they each held in separate compartments of the mind?

One is held in the mind and one is in the heart. But both must register through the gray matter in order for you to know of their existence. So, where is the differentiation between the secret and the sacred? For while they are both held in the mind, are they not both also held in the heart?

What does the brain label as secret? If we were to use the words separate and we say *secret*, what are the first connotations that derive within the feeling? If you were to have to describe *secret*, from an emotional standpoint, how would that feel? Is there not a sense that secret and sacred can be the same? Does *secret* not imply a sort of mysterious meaning? Does *sacred* not also imply something mysterious that the outside world would not understand, or that is not intended for anyone else? Would not the mind see them as being very similar?

What are the connotations around *secret*? Sometimes it's a matter of you keeping a secret about a birthday party or some of these things and those are fun, but for the most part, how does maintaining an inner secret feel, when one feels that there is an inner untruth or an inner skeleton in the closet?

Realize in the ultimate sense, they are sort of both the same and so the mind has a tendency to say that if one is not good, then maybe the other isn't either. The mind has a tendency to assume that sacred just means something that is special, that is supposed to be kept inside, hidden, and never spoken of. Those are the same things that you basically speak of as a secret that has a negative connotation. What the mind does is put it in a place that does not give it top priority. It feels that if it is to generate that sacred space, it would create more guilt within the being because that is the reaction from *secret*.

Since one is trying to get out of guilt, the brain, mind, body package has a tendency not to allow the sacred space, the inner place that it needs because of the inner guilt that is created. So the mind, brain package, body package says, "No, we don't need any more of this," and does not allow it to be created as easily. Then many times, when it is there, it is precious, it is priceless, and it is intimate within the being. Many times it is a beautiful experience, and if a person has a framework to understand it and explain it, they can share and express it. If not, then it goes into the hidden secrets of the inner being and that has a lot of nasty labels attached to it. The trick of it is to learn to create an inner space that is your inner sanctum, sanctuary, that is free to express. Otherwise the body, mind, brain structure won't let you do it, because it's trying to get you out of guilt and since the brain has compressed data on the fact that this is probably another secret, and therefore more guilt, it doesn't want to help you to generate it. It would have a tendency to create an isolation factor rather than a commonality or a sharing.

When you get to the point of loving so much that it hurts, it means you don't feel that you have a place to express it . . .

Most of you, if you were to get into the depth of it, an inner sacred place is what all of you are wanting, looking for, and desiring to have all of the time. Sometimes you get to a place of knowing what will trigger it so you can bring it back again. Other times it seems very illusive and you can't find it. It is a matter of when you realize what it is you're really seeking and looking for, then half your journey has been conquered, because without that knowing, you're hitting in the dark. For the most part, what you're looking for within that inner being is a place of intimacy. Not sexual intimacy but an intimacy of the heart—where you can share from the depth of your very being. The sacred spaces actually require or want and desire a place for expression, a place where a specialness, a beauty, a preciousness of you can be shared as love. A lot of what keeps one from creating that is finding a way of sharing what is created.

When you go on your path and get into your journey, you have a tendency to move into the intensities of love. You can feel them to the point that you love so much it hurts. When you get to the point of loving so much that it hurts, it means you don't feel that you have a place to express it, to let it out, to allow it to be used. That is when the inner being cries for a sacred place or whatever term you want to use. That is when it cries to be released and expressed. What all of you are truly looking for is a place to be yourself, to be able to feel all the intensities of love as strongly as you want, till they're so strong they hurt, to find a place to express them, to let them out and to share them.

Love is a volatile thing if you hold it. It is life, it is essence, but it cannot be held. Love is a movement. What happens within your beings as you're pulling in very grand amounts of love, is that if there is no place for that to go, it begins to become a burden and it begins to become painful. You know that within your being you love so much that it hurts—that is a label that a lot of people have put on it.

The walk of a master is an intensity. It is an intensity of passion which is love in the first degree. It is the strongest intensity of love and that's what you're evolving into. You are trying to go back into that love. You're trying to be that love. You're trying to be an expression of that love. You're trying to share that love, but for the most part, the biggest conflict on this planet and the biggest difficulty most of you will experience is called sharing. The sacred space is the place of sharing. It is the place of inner intimacy where you can take the god essence of your being, the love that is deep within your heart and share and express it with another heart and like mind.

For the most part, your planet is a planet of individuals who don't allow themselves to see god in everything and in themselves. You are a system of people who have cut yourselves off from what you call sharing, and we're talking from the heart and the being, not just the little verbiage and the conversations. You are all capable of that, but we're talking about the very deep, deep intimacy, and the sharing of one god to another. It is called being yourself and that is what the sacred space is all about. What you are trying to do is create a place where you can have that state of sharing and intimacy. (Arvana then leads the audience through the following working exercise.)

Within your beings I want you to open those hearts and feel what is there. I want you to go into your heart, into that inner being, and I want you to touch that love. I want you to bring it up into a level of passion. I want you to bring it up until it overwhelms your heart and your being. Don't be afraid of it. This is one of the last fears you all have to conquer—the fear of love. It makes the body weep and that is fine, that is a release; it adds years to your life, that is fine. It can bring joy. It can bring elation. Feel that love, that god that you are within your inner being and your heart.

As you feel it, notice all the labels that come up with it. If there is pain, if there is struggle, if it is just a matter that there is so much there that you don't know what to do with it, bring it up. Intensify it as far as you can intensify it, and we'll show you how to use it for your own growth and your own purpose. Let the mind go ahead and play with the emotional stories that it will tell you. A lot of it will say that there is no place to share. There is no place to be you. There is no place to feel this.

What I want you to do is go deeper than this. These are all the stories that your ancestors bought. Look at them as superstitious myths. Within your being, there is a god and it is time to find it. I want you to push into the deepest part of your being and feel the god that you are. Let it rise. It is just a love. It is a feeling. To some of you, it will be a warm sensation. To some of you it will be a tenderness.

I want you to push out the struggle, the loneliness, the homesickness—if you're willing to give it up.

You'll each have different feelings with it, but I want you to notice your resistance. See, there is much resistance at letting yourself just touch god and you. Now, in that state, could you walk face to face to god, embrace god, love god, and feel equal to god? If there is any part of your being that cannot feel equal and feels that it must run away, that it must hide, this is your resistance. If the ego jumps in and intellectually says, "Oh yes, yes, yes, I can do that," this is your resistance.

I want you to push out the struggle, the loneliness, the homesickness—if you're willing to give it up. What I want you to do is just push it out. What you are doing is relieving yourself of all of the connotations and the labels and the names that you've put on things. Just let it go. I want you to, within your being, step aside all of your preconceived belief systems and ideals and realize that they are a part of you and that is fine, but you're not going to walk into this with any preconceptions. You're going to walk into this next phase of this exercise naked, so to speak, just you.

What I want you to do is with your inner being, taking no ideals of what you're expecting to find, we're going to find god. We're going to find the level of god that is you. What I want you to do is to fall into yourself, move into yourself, the deepest level you have ever been. You feel and believe that a god has pain or joy. Notice your resistances and let them go. Allow yourself to go and just let go. We're going to go into ultimate surrender. The only place you can go is into the love of your own being and that is called god. You want to call that sacred space yours. If you want to call it love, that is fine too. What I want you to do is just drop into the heart and you and feel joy.

I'm going to take you through a few things now, and I want you to experience them and be body aware. Be aware of what you're going through. Notice your reactions. I want you to try; *try*, this is the key word. Try to bring up the joy and the love. I want you to fill your heart with as much love as you can. Make an effort at it. Make a real effort. I'm going to show you the difference between effort and flow. As you try to generate the love, I want you to let go of that love, and I want you to see how your being feels. Does your being now feel the loneliness? Does it now feel the disappointment or feel like it has left something? When you try to love and try to bring the love up or try to share, that is called effort. When you have effort, you will have pain. When you have effort you will feel loneliness. You will feel as though the love is too much for you to handle. I want you now to just relax into your space for a moment, cutting all of the vibrations, just let them go. Now just sit and be you for a moment. As you sit there being you, underneath it, there is a vibration. You call it love, but this time, don't try. Don't try to do anything. The only thing that you need to do is to allow yourself to be directed with no effort. Just relax and don't let the brain try.

Underneath it, there is a little bubbly in the solar-plex, between the solar-plex and the heart. What I want you to do is let that little bubbly feeling, that little effervescent feeling become a big one as much as if it were carbonated waters. Let it pop and release its little bubbles and gently notice the body's reaction. Gently notice as these little bubbles rise, the body's reaction to it and the cellular response. Notice that all of a sudden they are coming to life, and they feel exhilarated, they feel excited, they feel thrilled and so does the body. The body feels alive. This excitement that it generates and that is being held, is called life.

Now I want you to remember your two experiences and realize which one had more power to you . . . when you were trying to feel love or when you were allowing the bubbles to rise? Which one had more effort and which one left you feeling better? Which of the two experiences brought an excitement, brought life to the body—when you were trying to love and feel love, or when you were just allowing the life to rise? Most of you will find that whenever you try to love, whenever you try to create beauty, whenever you try to do anything, you've defeated your purposes before you started.

All you have to do is just allow it. Let the bubbles of excitement rise, but notice also the connotations in the mind. These bubbles that are rising out of the heart, that effervescence, that bubbly feeling, that is life in its purest sense. Since that is life in its pure essence, that is god. But when you are looking and searching for a sacred space or a place within your being, most of you are looking for a place to release your pain. The life itself is the sacred space because there is nothing more precious. But with the other, what occurs is many people within their beings, try to love because you've always been taught to try. You haven't been taught to just allow. You're gods. You were created by a loving god. He would not take anything from you. All you've ever had to do is just allow, and the life and the love are there.

Many of you have taught yourselves to try to create love, to try to express love. So within the mind and the body and the data compression of the brain, what it has done, is it has created this place. You can call it a place of reverence, you could call it a sacred place, you could call it whatever you want. The brain, body, mind structure has created this place, because that is what it thinks you need or want, when you say you want to connect with all that is.

Gods know how to have fun! They created life. They are life.

All that is, is life. That *is* all there is and in your bodies it is going to be that bubbly, excited feeling that rises. That is called an appreciation for life because you are allowing it and feeling it. If you haven't it, then you are saying to the very creator that you are, "I don't choose life. Therefore, I accept struggle." The mind and body and brain simply need to be re-educated, that is all. You need to learn that life is life itself and there is no effort required, just an appreciation for it, just an acceptance of it, just an allowance to let it in; if it has those, you have everything.

On this plane you have been taught that *life* was frivolous, that those places of joy and excitement in the being meant you weren't being reverent and respectful to your maker. What they taught you to do is to nullify the very life that you were given. If you can feel those bubbles, that excitement for life that generates within your heart, that means that you are accepting life. That means that you are feeling the very life that was given to you by any source, any creator, any god, including you, and so, everything else means that you're contrary to *life*. It means you are living life backwards. There is no effort required. Only acceptance.

Those feelings of excitement, if you carry them, will turn into joy, and then they might turn into laughter, and then they might turn into what some would consider frivolity, and everyone knows that god is serious and does not laugh! I would tell you that gods know how to have fun! They created life. They *are* life. Being god means you're willing to live and feel more life— you are into the excitement of life itself. Why be into the pain and struggle of trying to create life when it has already been granted? The sacred space within your being should be a place of respect— not a place of fear. Not a place of sadness, but a place of respect with an appreciation for the life you've been given, not as a martyr but as one who is willing to live the gift.

How many of you like to give gifts to people for their holidays, Christmas, birthdays? Let's say that you give them a suit of clothing and they don't wear it. How does that allow you to feel? Let's say that you give them gifts. They are things that they can wear, they are things that they can use, but they never do. They go on the shelf. How does that make you feel? Life is what was granted you by your creators and your sources. Life was given to you by god, which means you! So if life is the gift and you're not living it, and you're not being the life, then you're not being the gift. The excitement within the being is an appreciation for life. That is a statement that says, "I am being the gift. I'm not leaving it on the shelf any more. I am living this gift."

When you live the gift, you become god. The gift was life. Since the gift was life, when you show an excitement for it, when you feel a thrill within your being to be alive, an appreciation and a gratitude for just every little thing about life and you—that is called being god. That means that you've taken the gift off the shelf. It means you are becoming the gift, which means you're becoming life, which means you're becoming god.

You see, life is an interactive principle. You have to live it to be it, and you have to be it to live it. If you leave the excitement and the miracle of life and the marvel of that electricity and that beauty, that bubbly excitement for life that generates inside on the shelf because of what everybody has told you or because of what you think, because life becomes burdensome and hard, you're not using your gift. It's on the shelf. When you have that bubbly feeling and you've created that inner excitement for life, when you feel that, is there anything you can't accomplish? When you feel, and let yourself feel the beauty of your own life, an excitement and a joy and a passion for life, when you feel that, can you not feel the strength that comes with that? Can you not feel the assuredness that you know you can do anything you want to and accomplish anything you need to? Does not, in that state, the hopelessness leave? Within the being, the only place you need is called life. That's all.

It's in your beings. All you need is that respect. It should be a respect, not a burden. Most of society has taught you to let it be a burden, let it be a pain, let it be a martyrdom, and be sure you feel the pain of how much you appreciate life. It is a contradiction—but that is what you've been taught. When you are living life, feeling it, loving it, enjoying it, your journey has been done, because then you are being what gave you life.

I would say within your beings, when you start looking for that sacred place, that deep inner being where you can have that respect, what one is generally looking for is actually a place to try to love. When you get into that mode, the grandest specialness and preciousness you're going to find is when you follow that excitement into life.

Life is an interactive principle. You have to live it to be it, and you have to be it to live it.

The large part of the journey is to re-educate yourself that when you are into the down, then let's feel life and become life. Then what you do is you follow it back up to wherever you want to go with it. When you have that feeling, the body becomes educated into holding life. The other is a statement of how much life is not there, how much sadness is, and it is all right.

Realize that these places serve purpose too, so don't go in judgment with them. You could realize that what a lot of people do and where the frivolity or the duality comes from is when they are down, they put the ego ahead and go into the frivolity of it. That is not genuine. That comes from the mind. It comes from the brain and it does not re-educate the being.

What happens is if when you get into the downers, or the place where you just want to be into the special place, then go into it. Each of you can access it already in your beings. You can find it and then go in there and dance. Go in there and play in the bubbles. Go in there and play in the excitement called life, and don't go into judgment that you're not doing it well enough. It takes time and I guarantee all of you will do it right the first time. But it has happened that the lines of your progenitors and your genetic structures have vast memories of the sadness, of the pain, because a lot of that goes along with what is considered as being spiritual.

If you take two people and you have one extremely solemn and one that is filled with love, laughter and excitement and just bubbly, which one is more spiritual? In the connotations of the planet, of course, the solemn one is. The solemn one is more religious, not more spiritual. There is a difference. The solemn one is trying, trying to be life, where the other one is letting it flow through their being. And they are both gods. So within your beings, the solemnness is something that has been taught and taught and taught. I would say that gods do know how to have fun.

Society has never taught a whole lot about the personality of god except that it is angry, and you better do it right. This is what most consider to be love. But look at this planet you're sitting on and the beauty. If you were the god that created it, what would your mode have been like?—not the pain, not the issues, not the difficulties. But you're the god creating this planet and everything on it. Would you have been doing it with a solemn heart, or would you have been doing it with a passion for curiosity and creativity and a passion for an excitement to see what you could create? If you didn't have that you wouldn't have the diversity you have here. Put yourself in a place, literally, of trying to understand what type of a personality created this beautiful piece of rock you are all sitting on. Entities are bountiful. Look at the different body structures. Look at the different things that are here. Look at the different animals. Some of you could even say, "Well, some of it a practical joker created!"

I would say that for the most part, this is the one idea that is actually the furthest off field out of everything that has been taught here, because yes, an inner respect is necessary. An inner respect says, "I love who and what I am." That inner respect, not a solemnness, but a respect—respect means you wouldn't destroy it. You see it for the love, the god, the master that it is and you wouldn't destroy it. So within your beings, respect yourselves as gods, but respect means that you love it, not fear it. So within your beings, when you are living life, enjoying life, excited about life, you are being god. Otherwise, where did those feelings come from anyway?

Find god. Live it because it's called life. Because if that life didn't exist, you wouldn't, and it doesn't need to be burdensome. It should be an excitement. Just start letting a few little bubbles at a time rise, even if you can't get the big ones up or a whole lot of them up. Dedicate five minutes a day to at least allowing two or three bubbles to rise, and I guarantee you'll get addicted to them and make more and more and allow more and more. This planet is far too serious. That is what has created all of what most of you consider your atrocities. If you were having fun, enjoying life and living it, there'd be no desire, no need for any of these things that all of you consider to be the bad stuff here. All of those things are created by people who are not in joy, who don't know how to live and who don't like life very much.

I love you grandly and I will leave my embrace behind with you. Be at peace. Thank you for allowing me to come. ▲

The Perpetual Motion of Curiosity

A god needs perpetual motion and that perpetual motion is called curiosity. Curiosity might have killed the cat, but it creates a god. Without curiosity, where would you be now? Curiosity is what lets you understand life. You can't be a god if you don't understand what a god is. Without questioning, all you do is buy somebody else's truth. You can't know all things by avoiding the lessons and ignoring and not hearing what is there. The only way you can become a full-fledged god is by knowing everything—that's what it means to be a god. How are you going to know everything if you don't ask the questions?

You can't ask a question unless you already have an answer. You can't even ask the questions unless you already have the information within accessible reach. The answer or the knowledge comes into your field. As it sits in your field and causes an irritation, you will start to form questions in order to find out what is there. If you do not question, your field will then begin attracting the experience to you so you can view it in your life. Asking questions of yourself and understanding your feelings affords you an opportunity to get out of the struggle of having to live the experience.

This planet has never taught its people to question. The only way you can ever get out of being controlled is by questioning what controls you. If you do not question, then you are controlled. Those in power do not like you to question because they don't have the answers. They don't want you to find the answer some place else. The way they maintain control and their feeling of superiority is by you not questioning. This is how every gestalt on your planet works.

The only way gestalts can maintain hierarchy is by preventing questioning. It is your right to question. Your free will that was given to you means that all of you have free will to access everything that is known as truth, which means that you have the right to question. This is where your free will comes from. If you don't question, you give your free will away and you assume somebody else knows better than you do. Without questioning, how can you ever be educated? Your free will depends on you questioning. ▲

Moving Beyond the Christ Paradigm

Way back in the primal beginnings when time didn't exist, back farther than any stretch of the imagination, the primal no-thing eventually became some thing and became conscious. That took so many generations and eons of time that if it took that long for each of you to be created as conscious entities, we'd never get any new ones. It simply would take so long that it would be an expenditure of energy that no one would bother with.

Now whenever a system is mastered, you learn ways to make it faster and more easily. So when you were created in this physical reality, most of the shortcuts were already realized. It was understood how to eliminate certain steps to speed evolution and create an individuated species.

The whole purpose behind the universe you are living in is the creation of individuated consciousness that would be able to do anything. That is what most of you call god. So in its beginning you each had to start out as a spark of no-thing. This spark of no-thing was some thing such as the light coming from your ceiling lights. You had to take that light, or no-thing, and make it aware of itself. And without the shortcuts that could take forever.

The original entities that went into the creation of this universe knew that if they wanted some new brothers and sisters, some companions in the entity realms, it would take too long if you had to start from scratch. This universe was a primal idea, a new venture designed to evolve consciousness at the fastest rate possible. It still might take thirty, forty-billion years, but from an entity standpoint, that is short and worth the time and effort.

Now these primal gods that designed this universe are what we call entity personalities. Over the eons they had already designed their personalities long before physicality was even conceived. They created evolving story lines that would be a blueprint for consciousness to follow, evolve to, and finally return in a conscious state. So before anything was created, in their own minds and through their own personalities, they created personality story lines or what you with some modification might call archetypal forms. They were pathways for your consciousness to follow on its journey to becoming an entity and fully aware.

Everything that occurs on your planet that becomes part of consciousness is from an evolving story line. Your Christ the man, Christ the metaphor is an evolving story line. That means that it is not a singular event going on in a singular time and space.

These original gods realized that in order to evolve these sparks of light into full-fledged, knowing, unlimited entities, they had to give them free will to evolve any way they wanted. However, they stuck in a few catalysts and ladders for them to use and climb on, in whatever way they chose.

In actuality what these entities were trying to do is no different than you trying to create a living breathing human being out of the light from a light bulb, but they had some idea of the necessary shifts and changes that it would take to create this. So they put in their stories and catalysts to insure that consciousness would, from time to time, shift from one grade school to the next, so to speak. This is not from a hierarchy principle—that's something you've developed here out of your insecurities. From a god standpoint it is much like taking a child and graduating it from the playpen to the living room and then to the rest of the house. When a child is ready and not likely to hurt itself, you let it have more space.

These entities never put any time limits on your schooling. They never said here is grade one, grade two, grade three, and you have to spend a year or an eon in each. They just created the courses of study, so to speak, and you select them at your own time and pace. We have all these different grades or slices, and we can call these dimensions. At one end you have the no-thing, at the other you have an entity. There are lot of different grades or dimensions in between.

If you are in kindergarten in your school system, you can still see the older students in the next grades, so you know that next year you will be in the first grade. That gives you the motivation to move from one to the next, to the next. From a perspective of consciousness, you cannot see from one dimension to the next. It is your vibration that lets you make the step to the next grade. But your schooling comes from the level of your own vibrational frequency, and to you, that's all that exists.

These entities understood this, so they had to put something through all these dimensions that would remind you of the next level of education. In dimensional reality all you can see is the dimension you vibrate with. Until you completely shift it, you cannot see or even register the next dimension, and you become stuck where you are.

So these entities decided to take an evolving story line from where they wanted you to end up, all the way through on a straight line into each grade or dimension. A story line that ties each to the next so there will always be something to trigger you to remember that there is something even grander than what you are playing with.

A child left on its own in kindergarten so it never saw the rest of the world, would never mature beyond kindergarten. If that were the only example of life that they had, they would still be in kindergarten at thirty or forty-years of age. That is what would happen in this system if left alone. These evolving story lines are what we call the spiritual-psychological archetypes for this system of reality. They are story lines that go on in every single one of these grades simultaneously.

Christ the metaphor is an evolving story line. That means that it is not a singular event going on in a singular time and space.

When you are in school, you move from grade to grade almost automatically the same way your body goes from age one to age two and so on. You don't have to sit and stare at your body every day to see if it is another year older—it just happens. You move through these dimensions the same way because the evolving story lines let you bridge all of them together.

Whenever there is a mass scenario going on, it happens in every grade at the same time. Back a few years ago when man landed on the moon, that event would register differently for the physics graduate than for the two-year-old child. The story or event is that a rocket landed and man walked on the moon. It is a simple story and you can tell it to everyone, but it will be understood and acted upon differently by the scientist and the child. Their brains will relate to it differently. But it is a metaphor that everybody can understand.

This is what an evolving story line is like. It is simple, it is eloquent, and it can be understood on every level of creation simultaneously. An evolving story line is the psychological gestalt that everyone goes through, because that is what takes you from one grade to the next.

An evolving story line tells you what you are because it tells you what you were created to become. It tells you what you are evolving into. You are evolving into a god or entity or whatever you may call it. The one-year-old child doesn't have any idea what that means, while from an entity standpoint, that is the easiest thing to understand. It means that you can do anything—you are totally unlimited.

It is not so easy to explain to a child about god, and you will tell them something different at each age when they ask you who god is. So the story line will change depending upon where you are. The basic story line is that you are a creature created out of joy—this was the feeling—you are a creature created of joy, because that is the only unlimitedness there is. It is living creation. It is life. The only place you are unlimited is when you are in that state—and this is where you are going to end up. This is a psychological gestalt. It is something that goes into all creation. As you live it, you become it and understand the whole story by living it.

On a larger scale , physicality is a psychological gestalt. This reality is just a framework for understanding some form of entity psychology. You are in a psychology class right now—the psychology of physicality. You are in college somewhere outside of here just looking at it and getting stuck in your lab work! These story lines or psychological gestalts allow you to evolve quicker than if you had to struggle all by yourself to do it. Since you were given free will, you have the right to do it all by yourself—if that's what you want. If you do, that means endless struggle in order to expand and become a living thing.

Now put yourself into the perspective of trying to change the light from the ceiling fixture into a living creature. Be sensitive to it for a moment. How do you think it is going to feel as you try to change it to a living breathing entity? You probably don't perceive it as being a whole lot of anything now. But suppose you had devised a machine that you could put it into and it would come out and stand right next to you and talk to you. From your standpoint it is inanimate now, so you would have to design a machine to create a way of doing this, but you would never give consideration to what the light had to go through in the process of becoming aware of itself.

That's what happened here too. These entities designed a process or machine that could turn the light into living things that they could talk to, but they never considered how the light would feel about changing itself. Consider it from the light's perspective. Sure, you can say that would be a wonderful experience, but how is the light going to feel after just being all things and then having to become aware of itself? It is going to recognize that it was oblivious before, and now someone wants it to feel and think like they do. It is going to have a crisis within its being. When it starts knowing itself, it is going to resist change and want to do it its own way.

That's what you did here too. You decided you wanted to do it your own way. You wanted to struggle to become fully conscious, intelligent, and aware. There's nothing wrong with that, but these entities knew that if you did that, you would have struggle, stress, and pain. You would still learn from it, but if they made these connecting links through all these dimensions and grades, using these evolving stories, you would always have something that vibrationally would tie you into the next level. It would make it easier if you wanted to use it.

So the fashionable paradigm today says that you are god. But you are much more than that—you are an entity. We are trying to get you past the Christ, past the god, and into a real living entity. That doesn't mean that you're going to say that there is no god, there is no Christ. It means that you are going to go beyond your limitations of what you think a god or a Christ means.

An evolving story line tells you what you are because it tells you . . . what you are evolving into.

The real entity, you out there, is everything you have dreamed of and more. It is much more than what your reality can even relate to. That is what you are intended to be, not just a god. The gods are stuck in the muck of the earth plane here. They are the creators and organizers. That is all beautiful and grand. You have to become that first before you can become the entity, but you don't want to stop there and get stuck in it. You want to evolve beyond that too.

You were created to be an entity, an equal partner, and joy was part of that. From an entity point of view it is much simpler than saying that a man landed on the moon. It simply says, "This is what you are going to be." The evolving story line then comes down to the next layer. Each successive layer says what you are going to be until it gets down to the current ones that say, "You are going to be god. You are going to be Christ. You are going to be this or that," all the way back to the primal origins of the planet.

All these story lines are going on at the same time. When the life force got pushed into here, every graduation went on line at the same time. So from one perspective, the life you are living now and the present scenario are going on at the same time as your Christ or Buddha scenarios and all the others in between, before and after. They are all the same story being implemented simultaneously. In consciousness that is the only way you create a paradigm shift.

Your planet went through a paradigm shift when man decided that the planet wasn't flat. For years and years before that everybody knew that the planet was flat. Then someone went out and proved that it wasn't flat. But that didn't change people's belief for a long time. It didn't matter that you had proof; they *knew* that it was flat. A paradigm shift is when everybody knows how it is and how it is supposed to be, and then you go and show them that it is different than what they think. That creates stress, confusion, and frustration, and it also creates a shift to a new understanding.

Most of you can look back on that shift now and think that it was pretty funny to think the world was flat. It is hard for you to understand because that's not your vibration or perspective any more, but back then it took a couple of hundred-years for people to trust the fact that the planet was not flat.

People get stuck in their belief systems. It is a level of education. When a level of education is ready to be shifted, a new one shows up. That is what the paradigm does. "You believed the world was flat; I'm going to show you that it's round." In another shift you thought you were stuck on the planet, and so you went to the moon to prove that you weren't.

But you still have people who think that you never went to the moon. They think that these pictures of the moon and Venus and Mars were all done in a studio. You see, once people know where their reality is, it takes a long time to change it. A paradigm shift confronts people bluntly with a new understanding. They may not like it, they may deny it and resist it, but in consciousness they start playing with the new idea.

Consciousness gets stuck. It says, "This is the way it is; the world is flat." The new paradigm says, "No it's not. Let's take a boat, go around and fall off the edge together and find out that we can't!"

You see, you are on the edge of a paradigm shift that you are creating. The way you are creating it is by getting pushed off the edge of the flat world and letting yourselves fall and finding out you're still OK. Your world is going through a paradigm shift.

These evolving story lines produce paradigm shifts. The story lines go into all these dimensions and realities at once, but until the whole story line has been read, listened to and lived out, the shift doesn't fully occur. Back when you thought the planet was flat, you didn't take the word of one sailor. Your Christopher Columbus was not even the first though he got the credit. There had been many before him who went out and were ridiculed and even put to death for saying that the world was not flat. You had to send out hundreds and hundreds who returned safely to convince the masses that the planet wasn't flat, and even then most of the people died thinking the earth was flat. It was really the new generations that embraced a round planet.

Right now, you are in the same boat, so to speak! The scenario that is going on right now is similar to the Christ, the Buddha, or the Ra scenarios, and there have been lots of them. They are all happening at the same time. They are psychological gestalts trying to shift everything in paradigm. They are saying, "It's not flat!"

Christ is just the one we focus on because that is where many of you are stuck. You have a whole lot of your planet very comfortable with the Christ scenario, with this level of belief system, but they never listened to what was being said and taught there. They never listened to what was being taught by your Buddha and your others.

These are evolving story lines; that means that they are not finished yet—you don't have all the details. In order for it to evolve in paradigm, it means it has to happen at the same time. It's like a rotisserie. It all has to turn at the same time. If you have a bird turning on the grill, some parts are going to be done before the rest are, but you have to keep spinning it until everything is done.

A paradigm shift is when everybody knows . . . how it is supposed to be, and then you go and show them that it is different . . .

The rotisserie is the paradigm shift, and it is turning and turning, but it hasn't completed its revolution or it would be finished cooking. We would have a finished story. The Christ scenario is a story that hasn't finished its cycle. A lot of the history of the individual was destroyed so that you didn't know what his origins were, and what he was all about. That made it more mysterious, and later it could become a lot bigger event in people's minds.

From one perspective you can say that you had a crucifixion back then and from another you can say that it hasn't even occurred because the rotisserie is turning with all of the evolving story lines at the same time. Since you are in a story too, those other stories are only at the same stage of completion as your own. If these stories haven't been lived all the way through, you're never going to get a complete story on it. But since you believe in linear time and space, you have to have a story or you can't believe that it ever occurred. Just like a lot of your early explorers who discovered that the earth was round; they were swept under the carpet— you don't hear about them. A lot of these things are kept in consciousness in such a way that it's left up to you to fill in the pictures and stories; it's up to you to make your own interpretation.

All these story lines are a single evolving story line from a species of entity that you are evolving into. They created it, but they created it abstractly. Their thought process is so different than yours, that all they could do was put in the feeling of what it was you were supposed to evolve to. They push the feeling in and it drops down to all the dimensional realities, then *you* make up the stories. They never gave you the stories. You make up the stories here to fit your time and space.

This evolving story line is a line of thought that originated with those entities and came all the way through. It came through as an abstract feeling that let you feel what you were designed to be. Your mind taps into that and this is what a lot of people channel. This is what a lot of people label as their own god. It is this line of thought, the evolving story line, that says, "Let me take you to the next page." Pretty soon a chapter has closed and a new one is opening. That means you have shifted from one dimension into the next.

When you just start a big, thick book, it looks very awesome at the beginning. When you are about halfway through, a single page doesn't make a lot of difference. But when you get down to the end and you only have a few pages left, you start thinking about every page. You know you are almost done.

That's where you are on this evolving story line—you're almost done. You are at the end of this huge textbook with only a few pages remaining, and the anticipation and impatience are pushing you to finish it. You want to finish it and start something else.

You may be in the last chapter, but you have faces of you that are just starting the book. You are ready to finish up your final chapter in physicality, and check out the next volume in the series, but earlier parts of you have just started the first one. You already know what's on every one of those pages, you know the story line and the final outcome, but elsewhere it is just being opened. Because of that, sometimes it is going to feel like you're opening and closing the book in this lifetime.

You have faces of yourselves that are stuck from a personality, attitude, and belief perspective in these different grades of evolution. This is where man has made hierarchy out of it. When part of you is complete and part of you is stuck here, you have to have a way of relating to the other parts.

None of these historical figures and their ideas were ever intended to create hierarchy. They were simply story lines to help your consciousness evolve. They were to create a paradigm for whenever you got stuck. Your planet has been stuck and screaming about it for some time. You've processed your old paradigm and you are coming on a new one.

Your major paradigms happen on about a 2,000 year cycle. You also have five-thousand, seven-thousand, twelve-thousand, and thirty-five-thousand-year cycles for paradigms as well. They are cycles that come around and in their turn jolt consciousness to get it moving a little more.

None of these historical figures and their ideas were ever intended to create hierarchy.

Now you are in a space where all these different cycles are hitting at the same time—for most of you in this lifetime. That is why your present lifetime has a power behind it that most of you can feel. It is frustrating to you when you can't tap it, and you don't know what is going on.

What you have is a window through which this birth that we've been talking about will occur. It is where all of these paradigms and stories are hitting at the same time. You're at the end of a two-thousand-year cycle, a five, a seven, a twelve, and a thirty-five-thousand-year cycle—a cycle that is not tied to your calendar.

You count years here, but the universe is just cycles. When they all hit, you're going to have the largest paradigm shift that has ever occurred on your planet. These others you have had have been grand in their own right, taking about two-hundred-years to settle in. But in this one you have them all coming down on you at once, so there is a lot of confusion and turmoil, but there is also a lot of peace because you know you are at the end of your book.

So before you can talk about Christ or anyone else, you have to understand the frameworks of these cycles and shifts. You are in the grandest cycle now. The Christ scenario—the Christ lifetime or metaphor—was simply one of these cycles that was supposed to trigger you. There was another one two-thousand-years before that, and one before that and so on.

Now to pull off a scenario you have to have players who can read the script on a feeling level, and from one perspective every single player must be the same player. If you are going to have a paradigm shift and some of the parties involved don't want to play their roles when they get there, you are not going to carry it off. If a paradigm shift is designed in consciousness through an evolving story line, every single player needs to be playing the part that they were supposed to play. If they don't, you only get half or part of a shift. That is what happened on some of these smaller two-thousand-year shifts. The players got scattered and some of them went their own way.

When these original entity personalities created an evolving story line for you to connect with, they kept it very simple. For example they had to figure out how they were going to get primal man who couldn't understand much more than survival, and explain to him about his origins, and what he was evolving into. So they had to start with a story line that primal man could understand. The story for primal man was just a passion, a feeling, a connection with the planet. Since you know where the planet is going to go, if you can get primal man to connect with it, the planet will take him through the shifts in paradigm that he needs. They started with a story line that was easy for him to understand. Most of you still feel this primal connection with the planet.

Now if that was the only story you had, you wouldn't evolve much beyond it. So you have to put another story line in. It's not like talking to a one-year-old child any more. This time you'll be telling them something different about god and what that means. They made all these beautiful story lines that webbed throughout all the dimensions. Since the very first story to go out was the feeling that attached man to the planet, he can never become disconnected from where he is going. That story is going to be in every dimensional reality.

Each time, you send out a story that is a little more evolved. Each fills in more pieces of the puzzle so you can take it from one grade to the next just like in your schools here. You don't ever lose what you learn; you just expand it.

So your Christ story was created in a time-space for those individuals to move into the next paradigm. It was a gentle story. Actually, finding out that the world wasn't flat was a bigger paradigm than your Christ story because it jolted people. It actually initiated the Renaissance. Your Christ story also initiated a renaissance, but a lot of it was into destruction of people because of their belief systems—and you know the stories.

Now, your faces that are in each of these different dimensions are trying to understand who and what they are. Just as your light from the fixture going into the machine is going to have different stages of awakening and self-awareness, so too, will you in the different dimensions and times where your faces exist. If you have assumed that any one of your experiences has terminated its life, then you must have here too. But if you haven't, then neither have they. You are living them all at the same time. You are birthed and die at the same moment in consciousness. The time-space thing is so that things have an opportunity to see themselves.

It might seem like you are in a body now, but you went into this expression and all your others at the same time. Some of you have as many as forty-thousand incarnations. You went in, in a moment, lived every one, and then retrieved yourself in about three seconds time. That is how fast the entity works. Time and space are just a function of biological mind lopping off slices in order to make continuity so you can see what you did. If you were to live your lives that fast, you would never know what you did.

Understand that when any one of your faces realizes itself, it does it for all of your faces. But if an individual face sees itself as separate, then that one will individuate. This is the fastest way of creating new, intelligent, living consciousness. If none of you saw yourselves as separate, and one face awoke, all the faces would awake and you would be one huge god. But this universe was intended for individuation. That means it was not created to clone gods but to make new ones. That is a hard thing to do without going through all the eons of evolution. Individuation is a way of doing that without having to go through all the process.

Finding out that the world wasn't flat was a bigger paradigm than your Christ story . . . It actually initiated the Renaissance.

So you each have a story line. You start at one point as the entity and come in here with your story line, just like it is with the original story line. Part of you goes into every dimension. You come in here and see yourselves as totally separate, so you don't perceive the other you(s) living at this exact same moment right next to you. Space, you see, does not exist like you think it does either. So you come in here and you see yourself separate in a separate body. As soon as you do that, you fracture your story line and pieces of it fall into the different slices of time and space, and you perceive them as separate incarnations.

So you could say that they are your faces, and if you awake, so will they; but because of their separateness, they will not be you. They will be a separate you. On this same principle, I could say that everyone of you are the same entity. On one level you are all the same entity, but you are not going to go back into one conglomerate with all of you fighting to be the personality. This reality was created to fracture you so that each of you could be that entity. If only one entity was wanted, this whole process would never have started in the first place.

The whole idea in this universe was to have a lot of entities for companions. It's pretty boring if you are the only god in the universe! The companionship had to come from the original; it also had to be equal to it because it was created from it. So you have come here and you don't perceive the previous you(s) so much or where you are going because you are fractured. If these story lines were to go in and didn't fracture, you would know everyone of what you call your incarnations. But you do fracture and you begin to like this separate you. You individuate it because you love it. In this fracturing you think you don't have a beginning and you think you don't have an end. You think you are stuck in the middle with no support.

As an evolving story line, these psychological gestalts, are created with a different form of entity vibration than your personal story lines. The entities had to do something different because if this main story line was fractured, you would never be able to shift a paradigm or consciousness ever. At first that is the problem they ran into. They had disjointed pieces and stories all over the place that didn't work in harmony, because they didn't see themselves as part of the whole. They went through rejection complexes, self-worth issues and everything else.

So these stronger story lines, or entities, decided that they needed stronger psychological gestalts. You see, whenever they would come into physicality, they would lose their memory and all their grand plans about making these shifts. Nobody could remember the roles they were supposed to play as they got progressively more wrapped up in this reality.

So when these entities figured out what was happening, they realized they had to create a thread of continuity among the players; some way of tying all the pieces together to get them to remember the parts they are supposed to play. So as the entities became more educated themselves about what was happening, they gathered the people together who wanted to play the roles in the paradigms and rehearsed the parts hundreds and thousands of times, depending upon the importance of the individual role. This took place outside the dead zone or on the least dense edge of it. If you rehearse it enough, you're not going to forget it when you go in.

Something happened while you were rehearsing these plays. Some of the players in the story lines that had already gone into this system started getting out of their bodies a little bit; these were some of your prophets and ancient wise men. They would poke their heads up into the ethers and catch wind of something going on. They would sneak in the back door of your rehearsal, and catch a glimpse, a small piece of your play, and come back and tell about it. They would say, "This is the way reality is going to be." Then everybody here started trying to form it.

So these entities realized that this was a very effective way to create some shifts. Such individuals here were given high regard because they could view things the others couldn't and come back with a level of accuracy. So the entities educated them on getting out of the bodies so that they could catch better and longer glimpses; then tell about what they saw and what was to come. This is when you started having your brokers of wisdom, your oracles. People respected them, and they started helping to create these intermediate paradigm shifts.

So in this way the people were prepared in consciousness for the things that were to come. But something else happened at the same time. As these prophets and oracles would come back with their stories, everybody else wanted to do it to. They could see the respect and love that the wise men received and they wanted that too. It could be fun, it was a good thing, and sometimes it was an ego thing.

The whole idea in this universe was to have a lot of entities for companions. It's pretty boring if you are the only god in the universe!

So at night when these people slept they would teach themselves to get out of the body and go watch the rehearsals. Over the years and generations, they would get out more and bring back more. Most of them never learned to bring it consciously, but they could bring it back to the body. That is why now your bodies know how to do the story better than you do. Your ancestors went out, watched the dress rehearsals and brought that information back to the body even though they couldn't remember it. So the body was educated to how the new reality was going to be. This is the heritage that your ancestors left you—bodies that know the story line even though the conscious mind doesn't.

When these entity personalities saw who was watching their rehearsals, they used that to their advantage and started teaching how the body was going to be. It was going to hold a full unlimited entity in it. It was going to be able to do fantastic things like levitate and perform miracles. Consciousness brought this back, the bodies became educated, and you had your intermediate paradigms. Christ and Buddha played out some of these.

But these entities were really serious about this big shift, and they kept rehearsing the parts of the story line. Now there were a lot of people who played in the rehearsals that said, "I can't carry the role out," and they left the play. These people were replaced by understudies and the rehearsals continued. They wanted to rehearse it so well that when they got into the body which had already been educated, the conscious mind would start to have an inkling of what was going on and wake up.

When gods do dress rehearsals, they don't just do them one way. They say here is contingency plan one, two, three-thousand-ninety-six, and ten-thousand-twenty-one. Not only that, they all cross train; everybody learns everybody else's parts. They consider every possibility so that if anything gets goofed up, they have a contingency plan to pull it off.

Even after all the rehearsals, it was still possible to come in here and forget your part anyway. Now a lot of you played in this so you know what I'm talking about. You knew that unless you were one entity, you were going to forget your parts anyway. It is like learning the role for a play and then having to play the part ten-years later—you are going to forget your lines.

So one party or entity has to play all the faces in the story, whether we are talking about the Christ scenario or another. You don't want to lose your individuality. It's not worth doing the play if it costs you that. So instead, you take your individuality and you have it bonded with another vibration that makes you all one entity. You have this very strong entity personality vibration that goes on an evolving story line, and you bond with it. All the parts are individual, but you have one long cord and one entity. You go into flesh and you individuate, because that is what these bodies do, but you still have that bonded vibration that holds you as one entity for orchestration and timing. That is the only way you can get something harmonious enough to make a paradigm shift. It is only when all the players are one player that you can get them to play together.

Sometimes you feel like you are a puppet on a string, but it's not quite like that. It's more a matter that you have so many possibilities, and you are not selecting which one you want. Now if you are holding that bonded vibration, you're going to get your memory triggered back to the dress rehearsals and your remembrance of how everything fits together. That could feel like a string tugging on you.

Most of you who are hearing this, carry a bonded vibration. In all scenarios each player is an individual, but one entity plays every single role. That entity is the bonded vibration. It is not interfering with your free will because you can still say, "Yes, I want to do it," or "No, I'm dropping out." When you move into a place of wanting to play your role, it is automatically assigned to you. Then you'll move your vibration and carry out the part.

In the Christ scenario there were multiple individuals, and everyone of them was the same entity in different bodies. Christ the man was Christ the man but also Herod and Judas and everyone of the other players. But they were also individuals just like you.

Now in the time of Christ, the people understood the principle of incarnations. So a long time before your western thought even picked up on the idea of reincarnation, these people started following their incarnations from one dimension to the next and to the next. That was their way of following these thought lines all the way back.

Actually, following incarnations is the primal religion on the planet, the only religion. You have all these others now, but they all grew out of this idea. Following incarnations was just a way of following the evolving story line. They didn't know what to call it; for them it was incarnations, but doing it took them as a people from paradigm to paradigm.

Now there was basically only one scenario ever created. In that one scenario all the players came in on that bonded vibration and are living the lives of all the players in all the dimensions simultaneously. The Christ story you are familiar with is a composite of multiple stories from multiple Christs living in their own time and space and from other dimensions as well, all put together. A lot of the events that were reported didn't occur in the dimension you think they did. Much of what is in your metaphor never happened on this planet. People pick and choose and invent the story that fits their understanding of the evolving story line and where they are with it.

It's just like with the flat earth concept; people held onto that while they tested the waters of the possibility of a round earth. You do the same thing. You hang on to the traditional Christ story while you talk about the Christ being within or walking as the Christ—that is not the Christ story. It may be part of the intricate message that god is within all of you, but he never taught people to walk as a Christ. So what you have is a derivation of the first story that is more in line with where you are going. You don't have another metaphor to use so you use the Christ one, instead of just saying, "It's within me."

Now from our perspective, the Buddha story line is the same story, the Ra story line is the same. They differ in the details but the metaphor is the same. So the metaphor you are using for Christ is not the original Christ story. It's not what would be considered Christianity either because a normal Christian does not teach that you are Christ.

In the Christ scenario there were multiple individuals, and everyone of them was the same entity in different bodies.

You see the original idea, story line, or hologram was that you each will be this totally unlimited entity. You can think of this hologram as holding and representing the life, and the knowledge of the total entity you can become. That is the final picture of your evolution, at least for now. Inside of here you all make your own holograms all the times out of everybody else's views and images. Until enough of you clone and make more of this original, unlimited hologram, there is not enough to go around. You all have to clone the same one. You go in, come in contact with it, and start using it.

Some individuals were able, to some extent, to transcend their own historical perspective of the evolving story line. They could go in and imprint with the hologram of their entity and return. Then they would be themselves plus the hologram. Then they would interpret the hologram according to their belief systems. Their lives then became a story that represented their interpretation of touching the hologram.

People do this all the time. The only difference between the individual you call Christ and the others is that in his mind he knew he was special, he knew he was all right. So when he touched the hologram he brought it back and lived it rather than hiding it.

You don't need more than one of these holograms anyway. All you have to do is take your consciousness, connect with it, make your own hologram and live it. If you distort it by your beliefs, your limitations, your images, you will probably want to re-imprint the hologram again later, and then again and again until you eventually become this hologram with your personality. You want to become the whole underlying hologram which is the total unlimitedness.

A lot of your grand miracle workers throughout time and history: your Christ, Buddha, and many others, connected with the hologram and brought it back. They still had to put it in their belief system, but they stretched the fabric of those beliefs, and that is part of what gave them their abilities and power. If you go into these experiences knowing you are all right, totally loving who and what you are, not seeing yourself as less than it, and touch it, you would come back in the full glory of it.

Sometimes an individual will go into the experience from an ego perspective, with an I-know-I'm-great attitude. This may allow them to touch it without the rejection, so they will have the power from the hologram, but their ego will distort the use of it many times.

If you take the hologram of unlimitedness, come back and let your ego run with it, you can create a Hitler. People don't usually like to hear it, but your Hitlers are in the same category as your Christ. They just used the power of the hologram differently. Hitler knew that he could get away with anything because he touched the unlimitedness of the hologram. However, his ego was insecure enough that he became power hungry. He was also playing out a metaphor for the planet. When you touch the hologram and bring it back, it gives you the power to live anything you want to live.

A lot of you started touching that hologram when you were children. If you are one of the players, you have a bonded vibration, and it would be very important for you to touch that hologram as early in life as you could. A lot of you touched it between three and eight-years of age—most of you touched it before you were twelve. If you are working from the bonded vibration, you will allow your life to be orchestrated by it.

If you are working from the bonded vibration, you will allow your life to be orchestrated by it.

A lot of you can remember in your childhood some passionate, internal experience. It was an intensity of love deep down in your being. You knew you had a mission, you knew you had a reason for being here, you knew you were important and loved. You knew you were all right. It was from this point that you started getting into your homesickness. It was because you had touched the hologram. To maintain your individuality and keep you from falling in on the scenario, it was important to get you to touch that as early as you could.

As soon as you had a window where you could touch that hologram, you were pushed into it, so that you could get into being you, complete and whole, very early in life. But a lot of you had already bought into the guilt of the world, or picked it up from your parents at birth, by the time that hologram could be touched.

You see by the time a child is six or seven, it's already connected to a whole view of reality. So when you touch that hologram, it awakens that part of you that wants to move and be one with everything, but it also gives you pain and triggers your guilt. That hologram is a remembrance of you. When you have already bought another reality called physicality and you touch that hologram, that god, that you, it reminds you of what you are pretending not to be—and that's where your guilt sets back in.

Guilt is your big problem here now. Most people use your Christ as a metaphor for getting rid of their guilt because most of you feel so guilty. For those of you who know our teaching on the dead zone, from our perspective you are using the Christ story as a metaphor for the dead zone.

The dead zone is what we call it for simplicity sake. It is also what a lot of people call heaven because when you leave your body, you feel so much lighter and grander. At that point in time you are approached by these beings and they are god-like, beautiful, and grand. This is nothing to get into fear about because these are beautiful entities. They will feel your pain, they feel your hurt, they feel your guilt and offer to take it from you. When they do, they also erase your memory because most of you tie your memory of this lifetime in with your guilt. You feel guilty for just about everything you do. So when they offer to take your pain, your sorrow, your sins or whatever, you gladly give them, and your memory goes with it because they were bonded together in vibration. This is what we call the dead zone.

Now there is a lot of beauty in the dead zone that is yet to be covered, but this dead zone is the metaphor you've placed on Christ. Christ, by your belief systems, is an individual who forgives you of all your sins. So you are being preprogrammed to leave this reality, go into another and then give your life away by giving away your guilt. This is not what Christ the man taught. He taught that you are gods—be one! He taught that it was all inside of you. You don't need to feel guilty. He would eat with the criminals; he didn't have issue. He was trying to show people how to just be themselves, but it was in a time and space when those were not quite the same words. He was trying to teach people to be their own god. "Don't let others make you feel guilty." He went against most of the beliefs of his day and spoke of love of self, but that is not what is in Christianity.

Today's Christianity is people's interpretation. It is not what Christ the man taught. The focus is more on the death of the individual, the guilt and the pains. Christianity today doesn't want you to be yourself. The hierarchies don't want you to be god. They want to be god for you. You have taken the teachings of this man or some of the others and turned them into a metaphor for the dead zone. You hurt so much, you are looking for somebody to save you. He never came as a savior—none of these individuals ever did.

Nobody needs to save anybody from anything! In your scenario going on right now all you are trying to do is make a paradigm so that consciousness can shift and realize that. There are no such things as saviors. There never have been and there never will be because you are gods and nobody needs to save god. God doesn't need to be saved and neither do any of you.

All you have to do is let yourself get out of the prisons you've made for yourselves. That is all these men ever tried to teach. "Get out of your prison; don't let yourselves be controlled this way. You be you." That's what these individuals taught, and others, less enlightened, come behind them and use these men's grand teachings to control people. They are preparing you to go into the dead zone, give away your guilt and then you will incarnate again. You came into this reality to learn to exist and to know that. But as soon as your memory is gone, you have little left of who you are, and you'll go back in to try again.

From our perspective god is everything that exists here and in all the layers of the dead zone. A few layers out beyond the dead zone you have real entities. From a universal perspective, entities that are full entities don't like to be called gods because what they are is themselves. They are an entity. God is this mish-mash of consciousness here that is still fighting within for organization of itself, and it doesn't know what it is doing. That is what they perceive god to be; it is the forming or organization of consciousness. Once it is formed and organized, they consider you to be an entity. A god is a belief system from this time. When you become an entity, you become unlimited, you become all of creation, you become the sources, you become anything you want. God is a limited title which universally refers to all the stuff that goes on here on this planet. It is your hierarchies, it is your dead zone, it is your recycling, it *is* your guilt!

Today's Christianity is people's interpretation. It is not what Christ the man taught.

Most of your perceptions of god now are different than what your bibles portray. In those books, god is never talked about as being a nice guy. In your Old Testament, god is angry, god is punishing. If god doesn't like you, he kills you. This is what mankind's idea of god has been. But see, your idea of god here today is a loving individual who knows and cares about you. That tells you right there that you are making a paradigm shift because you are not in the same flow as the rest of the planet or the beliefs of the past. If you are seeing god as a loving individual and believe you are becoming one, that means that in consciousness you have already made a paradigm shift.

There is no place in your old book for a nice god. Christ was nice, but god wasn't. God was always vengeful, always killed or punished. If you didn't do exactly what he said, he would put you to death or send you out of paradise. He was always mad at everything! And you are trying to become god? Is *that* what you want to become?

As long as you believe that you are becoming a god, you will tie into the gestalt of god. I have heard some of you complain lately, "I used to be so nice, and all of a sudden, I'm starting to be so mean and ornery and irritable!" You are becoming god, and god is a gestalt of anger, pain, and vengefulness.

What you do want to become is an individuated, unlimited entity. That's why we are moving you out of the god and into the entity. You are far more loving than any of your ancient gods. They were never loving. They might show mercy if you did the right thing, but where are their acts of love?

Most of you would say that you are not trying to be mean and nasty and you honestly see god as a loving being. That means that you have touched this hologram, and you are trying to merge it with the god gestalt and make them work together. That's like the individual that wants to test the flat-earth theory by tying himself to the dock with miles and miles of rope and rowing out to the edge, so if he falls off, he can pull himself back on the rope. That's the way consciousness works; until the new paradigm or metaphor is delivered, you'll hang onto the old one. You've touched where you are going, something wonderful, and you don't have a label for it. So you try to paint a new picture on an old gestalt. This is how paradigm shifts happen. It is the same thing with Christ. People put their own coat of paint of the Christ story. What Christ taught and what people think of Christ are two different things.

Now I want to get back to the cycles that we started discussing earlier. Everything is a wave pattern, from the origins of the cosmos to your present reality. You are going into the hologram, that too, is a wave pattern of the entity you are trying to become. It can be projected into time-space and be implemented into physical reality. You actually create wave patterns or the cycles that run on your two-thousand, five-thousand, seven, twelve, and thirty-five-thousand-year intervals. These spin off the original starting point at the entity.

As they do this they hit against each other at certain times and spaces, and this is what creates the paradigm. Wherever, or whenever two or more of these cycle patterns collide or rub, you have a stronger pattern arising from it. The scenario you are in now is a culmination of all these cycles hitting at the same time. It will take a few years as they come in and connect.

In what you call your history, the Christ, Buddha, or the other scenarios occurred when two of these cycles hit at the same time and materialized. A hologram is created out of interference patterns. When one pattern hits another, the result is a more solid creation. These individuals went out of their bodies, saw the dress rehearsal going on, the hologram, and brought that back. But they happened to do it when these cycles were hitting. That is what makes them more solid in history.

From a universal perspective these cycles are entity spirals. They revolve and return, then collide or line up at regular or predictable intervals. When they do line up you have your historical figures and events. The paradigm shift from a flat to a round world happened at one of these intervals.

Now each of you have your own personal entity cycles; your own vibrational pattern. Everyone of you have a cycle of your own. It's not necessarily the vibrational rate of your body, but the body does reflect it somewhat. Your entity has its own cycle and that can be a given number of years, and then your body has its incarnation cycle as well. When you put all these cycles together, when they hit, it is what reflects and makes life. Your interpretation of this is what you call history. When an even greater number come together, you have an historical happening.

We are moving you out of the god and into the entity. You are far more loving than any of your ancient gods.

The Christ scenario is an historical happening. You had several patterns hitting at once. Anyone living in that time and space is going to know that something is going on, just like now. Most of you know that you are on a path. You are trying to open, awaken, become all that you are. You have feelings of being driven, pushed. You feel like something is going to happen. You can go out into the world and find out that everyone else feels that way too. Their interpretation might be different, but they are all waiting for something to happen. Consciousness perceives the cycles about to make a junction. People know history is being created.

There is a lot of anxiety. You will find people afraid of different things, your earthquakes, wars, droughts. They are afraid that they're not going to make it in time, that they won't be safe. They wouldn't have these anxieties if they hadn't seen some part of a picture somewhere. It doesn't mean that the world is going to end; it means the world is going to shift in consciousness through one of these paradigms, and on one level everybody knows that.

You have touched the new hologram, you've seen what is coming. You are also trying to become god. You have your own kinder ideas of what that means, but that is not what is in the god gestalt. So when you are trying to become god, you are tapping into the mean and vengeful aspects of being god as well. Your brains are stuck in the god gestalt. You've touched the next picture, so you're trying to bring in the unlimitedness and the love, but you are hanging onto both realities, both gestalts.

And so is the whole planet. It is the end of the world they are afraid of and waiting for. It is not the end of the world in a literal sense; it is change. You're going to live through it and see it happening in the years ahead. It is going to break the old paradigms by dropping a new paradigm in on top of them. You will no longer be able to live in both of them.

You all have a god gestalt within you. Even if you change your idea about it all, you still have a god gestalt. No one can come in and take that away from you; not that they would want to anyway. They can change it. They can show you what you think and believe; they can tell you what a god gestalt is as I have done, but they can't take it away from you because it is part of you. You also won't break or shift your consciousness to let go of it.

Everybody is afraid of the end of the world because when you have this many cycles hitting at the same time, that consciousness is going to get severed. For the psyche that creates a complete splitting, a complete shift that says the old no longer exists. The psyche will know something new is here, but it won't have any idea what that is because the new will be such an abstract unless it is touched in consciousness first and interpreted.

That's what a lot of you are doing. You are bringing in the new hologram, merging it with yours and interpreting it. You are making lots of little stepping stone gestalts all the way from an angry god into the joy and the love of the entity you are becoming. You are making the transition with ease. If this road map in consciousness was not made, the old would just end as if it never existed. It would be the same to you as an earthquake opening a chasm in front of you and falling in.

The end of the world to most people is the shifting of this paradigm. It is such a huge paradigm shift that it has been rippling into your reality for about forty-thousand-years now. For that long you have had people upon your planet predicting the end of the world, but nobody knows what that means because they don't understand the change.

Suppose someone told you that a major shift had just occurred and you could now levitate. So they took you up to a high cliff and told you to walk off. You're probably going to want them to show you that they can do it first, and even if they can, you will probably want to experiment on your front steps before you try something higher!

This is where the world is now. They could interpret the old language and the old world. So the new world coming in that they can't yet understand is an ending of the world that they could understand. It is an ending of everything they knew as reality, and their minds cannot deal with the new abstract yet.

The bridge to the new reality is called love, joy, and being yourself. Those qualities do not relate very well with the vengeful, jealous, and angry god. Everyone of you have belief systems within your being that run side by side. That is how you create your own reality. When the cycles hit, this is going to be shifted. There will be no side by side, no duality. You will open a valley between them, and you will be on one side or the other.

The end of the world to most people is the shifting of this paradigm.

It's not a thing to be fearful about. It is just that when the cycles hit the hologram that these people are playing with in consciousness, they will be forced to live it without knowing how they got there. So this is what your ancient prophets saw. They knew it was going to be so different it would be like the end of the world. But this is what we are trying to explain. It is not the end of the world; it's not this world. It's a whole different world.

Your ancient prophets, and some of you were them, went out and touched this new reality. They brought it back and tried to tell people about the new world they had seen. It would be about like taking you back in history and getting you to explain television to a caveman. That's how different the new reality is.

Now while it is hard for your psyches to grasp this new hologram, the body has been incorporating it for forty-thousand-years. It knows more about this new world than you do consciously. Your bodies are trying to change to the new hologram, the new you. In consciousness you won't change your attitude. You won't change your views on reality—but the body is changing without you.

The body knows where it is going. Psychologically, you're stuck, so the body will go on without you. It makes a break and you call it death. That is all death is. People think that they are leaving the body, but it is really the body leaving them. It is because you are not willing to let your attitude and belief system shift when the body does. These bodies are going to evolve whether you let them or not because they have seen the new reality. That is their blueprint. It is a beautiful, loving, joyous blueprint. That's where they are headed, but you sit in them and you resist it, and resist it and try to stay with the old paradigm. Before long your vibration is split and you separate. That is all death is: your body went one direction, and you, the consciousness, stayed in the past.

You see, all of this is simultaneous. It is an abstract for the mind, so it is the same thing as you trying to tell a caveman about TV. You have the idea, but you don't have a lot of experience to relate to it. Simultaneous means simultaneous. That means that right now you are sitting in your chair, the planet is going through the big bang and being created, you are being birthed into your body, living and dying, and in the same moment, the new universe exists. Three seconds time is all it takes for you to live life.

Now from one perspective you can say that you are collapsing this universe to create the new one. But from another, you already did it; the new one is already created, and you are staying in the old one. But part of you is living in the new one. The nucleus cloned and separated itself sometime ago, and part of your consciousness lives in the new one and knows it lives there, but part is also hanging on to the old fear-based paradigm. You are trying to integrate the two.

These evolving story lines are to help you do that all along the way. That is why they were put into time and space. A story line tells you how something began, where it is going, and how it completes itself. Your book of Genesis tries to explain creation. We're trying to explain creation. Christ tried to explain creation. Buddha and all the rest tried to explain creation. To understand it is the slightest shift and it can be made in an instant, but unless you can shift the mind, you won't ever get the view of the new one.

The evolving story line started in the new universe or we couldn't be talking about it. We couldn't talk about it if it hadn't already been created in consciousness at least—that is your new hologram. That is where you are going to go as an entity. Your minds travel out there now, touch it, come back, and you cry because you're not there yet. Your consciousness is already touching it. If it didn't exist, you wouldn't be longing for it.

On one end of your cycle you have primal man, on the other you have you, but all of it has to have the feeling of wanting to get to the same point. Creation takes three seconds. You go in and live it—it's all completed in thought. Time slows it down so you can see what happened in those three seconds. That three seconds could be spread out from three seconds to twenty-eight-thousand lifetimes, or ten-million-years—whatever you want it to be. That is how literally you create your reality.

So if you decide you want to take ten-million-years to do it, you better have ten-million-years of story line to get you back to what was created in the first three seconds. So that is what the story lines are all about. They are just to jog you into something that some part of you already knows and is hiding from.

Now your Christ story, is where two of these cycles hit, and an historical landmark was created. At that day and time people had already been waiting for forty-thousand-years for a Messiah to save them. What they were really wanting is for someone to interpret consciousness for them—what they had been seeing out there.

From the time of what you term your caveman, people have been touching the hologram, but they didn't know how to interpret what they knew existed because it was such a different experience. All of these grand historical figures were teachers trying to interpret the abstract hologram for you. They would go out and bring back pieces of home. People could feel that from them. That's why people loved to be in their presence. It reminded them of home.

From one perspective you can say that you are collapsing this universe to create the new one. But from another, you already did it . . .

These people came into this universe to experience the biology, to live and touch, to have a body just like you. But they let themselves touch something that a lot of people don't let themselves touch. That is all that sets them apart. It wasn't as much an ability, but a willingness and desire to go out and touch the hologram and not be afraid of the abstract. It scared them just as it scares you, but you do it anyway. You have all touched it enough that you want to do it again and again, more and more, faster and faster.

As you touch it, it becomes an addiction called life. You want to live it. But it is an abstract, so you try to live it in the old myth, the old gestalt. The brain does this for continuity, but at some point in time you have to be able to make a shift within your beings. This is why you have duality—part of you holds onto the old, while another part is moving into the new.

Now a lot of people will not even check out the new; the abstract. They have only one side called the past. They stay there in the past until somebody in the present makes the new abstract become the past. Let me explain.

Let's say that you are not willing to go into the future and touch the abstract hologram. That means because of your fear, you are not willing to change. That means that you will never change, move or evolve until whatever is present becomes the past. You're going to wait for others to go out, get the abstract, and bring it back so that it becomes their past for them and your present for you.

This is where the split comes, this is what determines what universe you go with, which nucleus you stay with. This is where you have to move into being the entity. If you are waiting for somebody else to do it, you are waiting to become somebody else's past—that means you are going to remain your own past; you will never be your own present or future.

Even after Columbus returned and others with credentials went out and returned, it still took two-hundred-years for people to buy the idea of a round world. They weren't willing to go and check out the theory for themselves. Any of them that got in a boat and did it themselves, knew that they didn't fall off the edge.

All of these grand teachers show you that there is a future. But even your future is your past from one perspective. It was where you started this journey. It is where you are returning. All this is just the journey so you can remember how you got there. It has already happened. These teachers are supposed to jog you into going back inside and doing it yourself. They are telling you to go grab your own hologram and bring it in.

In consciousness everybody was too scared and stayed on the shore. They waited for their teachers, saviors, and gurus to go out and touch it and bring it back. The teachers lived it and it became their past. It gets pushed on down the road, and you call it your future, but it was already somebody else's past.

This is what most of the world does. But the body doesn't. Your body has already touched that hologram, and once it has touched it, it will go for it. Before your consciousnesses ever got in the body, the body was touched by the hologram and given life. You won't stop it. You'll resist it through disease and everything else, but it knows where it is going. Consciousness says, "No, no, let's stay in the past. Let's not be the first to do anything." It is the same as everybody showing up half an hour late for a party because no one wants to be the first to arrive! When everyone else finally believes the world is round, then it's OK to believe it, but not until then.

So most of these teachers ended up being singular voices in history because they were the only ones willing to do it. Your bodies knew how to do it forty-thousand-years ago before you ever got in them. It is going to do it even if you don't. It is going to become the vehicle for a totally unlimited entity. It has been evolving and moving towards that all the time you in consciousness have not.

And so you have a duality within your being. On the one hand you have the body which knows the hologram and is moving towards it. You have portions of your own consciousness that have touched it. On the other you have major resistances in consciousness to the abstract, the new; you want to stay in the past. This is where your confusion arises within your being, "Do I do this? Do I do that?" It's like you don't know which way to go, and it's because you still live in the past; you're not trusting your own touching of the future.

Your Christ and Buddha archetypes, touched the future and came back and said, "No, it's not of this world—not like this world. It is different, but I can't tell you about it. You have to do it yourself." Since these teachers had the experience, people will hold onto them, waiting for them to return or waiting for another to come.

All of these grand teachers show you that there is a future. But even your future is your past from one perspective.

This has been the problem with past scenarios. No one wanted to be the first ones to do it. So in this paradigm shift, you are all going to reach it about the same time and every excuse will be taken away.

This bonded vibration that we have been talking about is for timing and orchestration. If you are going to make a paradigm shift, you will lose the power of it if you have pieces shifting at different times. For the most effectiveness these shifts must coincide with available windows; you have to be able to orchestrate your players to work with the windows. So the call comes down the bonded vibration. It tells you that you have a window coming up and you better get moving. You feel an urgency or pressure within your being and you make movement. The bonded vibration just triggers your own remembrance, so you make your windows and move your consciousness to where it needs to be.

You see, your consciousness is evolving. You're doing it in steps this time. If you took your consciousness from where it is all the way into the hologram, it might be too much for it to handle. You have been trying to become your own god. That has also put you right in the middle of the god gestalt. And that's not so pleasant. Because you have touched the hologram and know on one level where you are going, you start saying, "No that is not what I'm going to become," and so you start creating another gestalt right in between the god gestalt and the entity. Now people won't be so scared to make the jump in consciousness because they can go to your halfway house before they go the rest of the way to the entity.

It is the same as climbing a mountain. If you look at having to climb the whole mountain, it's frightening. But if you can take it a step at a time, it's not so bad. The bonded vibration lets you touch the next story, make a new step, another, and another, until you have a nice road and nobody has an excuse for anything.

In your other scenarios you would have singular entities that would go out into the hologram, come back, and tell people all this wonderful stuff. People loved it well enough, but nobody believed they could do it. With your Christ, people had a lot of excuses. "Well, you're a king, and I'm not, so I could never do what you did."

If in this new scenario, you, the players, can live all the conditions that people are going to use as excuses, they will have no reason left not to make the shift. They'll say, "Well, I was an abused child," and then you can say, "Well, so was I and I did it; what's your excuse?" If they say, "Well, I'm an alcoholic," you can say, "So was I; what's your excuse?" No matter what they say or what excuse they offer, there will be some of you who have lived it and made the shift anyway. This scenario is movement away from the singular entity idea. You are all going to be doing it at roughly the same time—since no one likes to show up early for the party. You'll all be doing miracles at the same time, not just one or two people. Every excuse for being unlimited will be addressed by some member of the scenario.

So you are leaders on a road map. Your body already knows where it is going. You have gone out in consciousness and touched the hologram and are trying to bring that back. Consciousness is what you are trying to develop here, but it also lives in the past and resists and fights change. The intellect or the mind says, "There is something in here that I have touched that is good. Let's go for it." So you have parts of you spread out in all directions trying to figure out what you're going to be. This is the walk of every master.

Most of you assume that a master is somebody who is nice, well-rounded, and nearly perfected. Most of your masters would call themselves half-crazy, not sure of where they are going, and confused. They experience pain some times and ignorance at other times, but there is movement. They know they have touched something, and all they are doing is putting their energy towards that. Your Christ was one of these. He became historical because the cycles came together at that time, so an event had to happen.

Now there were three main Christs. Your stories in your Bible are stories from the lives of three different ones. At that time there were two or three-hundred Christs running around proclaiming themselves to be the Messiah. Mankind at that point in time was looking for a savior. The one we are going to talk about was the center man of the three. He was an individual who didn't call himself Christ. He was of royal lineage from several directions. He was an illegitimate child, but still heir of the line of David, so he had more right to the throne than Herod. Herod was threatened by him so they kept this hidden. His parents were fairly well off, and he wasn't born in a stable.

There were three main Christs. Your stories in your Bible are stories from the lives of three different ones.

This individual touched his original hologram when he was about six months old. This is quite early. Here in your time and space you have a lot of people touching their hologram, but back then you might get only one individual out of ten thousand who would do it even once in a lifetime. He touched it so early because he was trying to check out. When you are born into a body you have up to a year to see if you want to stay in it. The individual didn't want to be here, he wanted out of life, and on the way out he ran into his hologram and it scared him back into the body. But when he touched that reality, he knew that he had to have the body—so he went back.

Now while he was growing up he had to be on the run for his life. There were those in the hierarchy who knew of his royal lineage, and if he had wanted to, he could have claimed his right and proved his birth line. But he wasn't official or through the legal channels. So for his safety he got put into an Essene community which raised him for a time.

Back then everybody believed in reincarnation, not necessarily in the Jewish community, but in all these other societies like your Essenes. It was recognized that this individual was actually an incarnation of somebody else—it even speaks of this in your Bible—some thought he might be Elijah or one of the prophets returned. Anyway, the Wisemen were scholars out of other countries. They recognized him as a reincarnation of someone else who was royal heritage in their kingdom—much the same way that the followers of your Dalai Lama track him through various incarnations. So by the time he was twelve-years-old, he knew he could be a king in either of two countries.

Because he knew he was a king already, he didn't have the ego and self-worth issues that a lot of people do when they touch the hologram. When he was thirteen-years of age, he touched the hologram again. It pursued him and pushed him in other directions. Because of the hologram, he was not willing to take the sword. The hologram took him away from political aspirations. As he fled for his life, he sought what he could find to educate him about the abstract in the hologram he had touched. He traveled into Egypt, India, and Asia, always educating himself, trying to understand the hologram. He wouldn't have called it a hologram. He just knew he had been touched by god—that was the best word he could put on it.

When he came back into his own region, there were still many who would put him to death simply because of his lineage. Because of his lineage in the one country and his past incarnation out of another, he had the ability to unite the entire continent under one ruler. That region was the known world at the time, so you could say that he was the rightful king of the world. But having touched the hologram, he wasn't interested in pressing his right and he pursued other things.

Most of the myths and metaphors that have survived about him are just stories. If you had been best friends with Christ, the man we are talking about, you would wonder what all the fuss was about. He was a beautiful person, but no more beautiful than any of you. He had brilliance, he had humor, he was creative, he had anger—he had it all. He was everything. He just lived life. If any one of you took your life and compared it to his, you would realize that you are not so different. The main difference is that history has embellished and amplified his miracles, and you sort of ignore or downplay yours.

You've done your share of miracles too, but the Christ story gets the credence because people living in the past are afraid to claim the present. It is a matter that you think somebody else's miracles are better than yours.

If you are living in the past, you can't claim your own miracles and your own life. If any one of you took the time and went out into the world out there and told them about your life, they would be in awe. Everything you take for granted, the experiences you've had in consciousness, some of the experiences you've had in your mind—others would find incredible.

With this man, individual things did happen. Back then people knew such things could happen, and such things were common. A lot of you know how to alter your consciousness at will, to bring up your joy if you focus on it. A lot of you can manifest what you want in your life, but you give that life more credibility than your own. Some of you if we took your life back to that time and space and you shared your experiences and feelings with those people, what you have touched, the bliss you have had, the things you have done, you would probably have already had a fuller life than that person, and would be a bigger god or Christ than that man was. But because that man is worshiped, most of you don't feel you can approach that kind of life.

You see, many of the healings can be explained in ways that you would not term miraculous today. Originally baptism was just to cleanse people. As your *Dead Sea Scrolls* come out, more and more of this will surface. You all know that closer to your own time when soap was introduced, the death rate lowered. Baptism then worked on the same principle.

If any one of you took your life and compared it to his, you would realize that you are not so different.

Back then people didn't take baths more than once or twice a year. A lot of their ill health was due to unsanitary conditions. This is not to diminish these healings, but a lot of them just amounted to a good bath. Baptism was just to cleanse people so they could then heal on their own very easily.

The Essenes were clean people. They believed in bathing. That's part of what made them outcasts. They felt that having a clean body was about the best thing you could do for your health. Today you baptize for every reason under the sun, but back then they did it to cleanse the body and the mind.

That's why John the Baptist healed so grandly. His intent was "I'm going to cleanse you of the evil." It worked because of the people's belief and because it was a good old-fashioned bath. At that point in time everybody thought that evil spirits were what created your illnesses, so they would put in their intent of cleansing the spirits and that would amplify the water's effectiveness.

Like I said, a lot of the miracles you perform in your lives are a whole lot grander, but you discredit them because these others have been blown so far out of proportion. In the new metaphor you will continue to do miracles and grander than you have done, but to you they won't be called miracles—they'll be called life, because life *is* the new metaphor.

In consciousness when you have someone on a pedestal, it means that you cannot achieve what they have. Your Christ gestalt is so large now that the whole planet works with it in one form or another. It is a metaphor—it has nothing to do with the individuals. In the metaphor, if they did the miracles, that means you have to discount yours. If you are worshiping a gestalt that is more limited than you are, you won't do the things your mind dreams of from the hologram.

At least in the Christ metaphor there is some love, there is the notion that life is within—it's within you; and that's a bridging into the hologram. The Christ gestalt is still quite serious. Christ the man was quite humorous, very, very humorous. His humor was almost a sarcasm, but very funny. All of these things you edit out when you are making a serious book. You don't want anybody to get the wrong idea!

It is the belief surrounding the life of the man that has made it so powerful—not the life itself. That individual could be in a body now, one of your friends, and not even he could approach his own supposed grandness any better than anyone else. You have just always been taught that Christ performed miracles because of his god power. He healed the sick, raised the dead. I'll tell you now, he never raised a single soul from the dead—including himself.

In that day and time you had the Cabala and a lot of other similar teachings. A lot of the fear mentality in your New Testament actually comes from the Cabala. Those individuals were into initiation rites. The man Christ was an Essene, a Nazarene, and two or three other things. Those groups had a lot of initiations. They used their initiations to create paradigms for something else. They were rites of passage. One of the grandest of these rites was a mock death and rebirth, so that you didn't have to reincarnate again. Some cultures use temple ceremonies for the same thing. These rites of passage represent going from one side of consciousness to the other so that the brain will let you do it.

Christ never raised a single dead person, ever—not even himself. But because of his standing, because people believed him to be a miracle worker, the people who were into these rites wanted him to call them from the dead more than anybody else. That is why he was so impatient at doing it. If he was really going to resurrect someone from the dead, he would do it pretty fast. He wouldn't sit around and let them decay for several days. If you look carefully at your stories in your Bible, most of the time he didn't want to be bothered with it. If you read it for yourself and take the tone with it, it was an imposition. He was busy at that particular moment, and he'd get around to it when he could. He knew they weren't dead. He knew he couldn't pull a real dead person back. They were playing their own games of going into the tomb and wanting him to pull them into the spiritual world, all because they perceived him to be more spiritual than they were. They knew that he was a king and master in that reality. Those were the only people he ever raised from the dead.

Now a lot of you are attracted to the Christ story because of the ascension. Let me burst another bubble; Christ did not ascend and did not take his body with him. It is buried and I can tell you where. Your story of the resurrection and the ascension is not a truth as you have it.

The entire scenario surrounding the crucifixion was politics. The whole event was a staged affair in order for Christ to preserve his life and his son's life and to allow the Roman empire its authority and control.

These people at this time had been looking for a messiah for thirty-five-thousand-years to come and save them. When people are enslaved, they will only put up with it for so long, and then they will revolt. If there is an intensity with it, they can topple any government, no matter how big. Every ruler knows this and tries to placate the people.

The Christ gestalt is still quite serious. Christ the man was quite humorous, very, very humorous.

This was a very difficult area for the Romans to govern because the people knew that a messiah was going to come and save them. They were always resisting or on the brink of revolt.

Pontius Pilate wanted to put an end to this messiah thing. Over the years, there were over twelve-hundred of these would-be messiahs put to death. In Christ's time alone there were a minimum of two-hundred as credible or more credible than he was.

Pilate was an intelligent individual. He understood mankind and human nature much more than he is given credit for. Over a period of time most of these rabble-rousers had been rounded up and killed. This had been going on for a period of three years before Christ the man got involved.

Pontius Pilate was a just individual. He was a follower of Christ the man, though because of politics he could never face him personally. Pilate knew that Christ had a right to the kingdom. He had several emissaries that went back and forth. He and Christ were friends of sorts.

Pilate needed an event to say once and for all, "Here is your messiah; see what I'm going to do about it!" Christ the man was willing to go along with it because it was the only way he could preserve his life. He was crucified but death did not occur. He was put into a comatose state, so resurrection was easy.

231

The crucifixion was staged. You have a lot of history that supports that. Christ was given soma. Your medical science today uses soma as a deep muscle relaxant—a large enough dose will put you into a comatose state without killing you. The Essenes were well versed in all the medical arts of the time. They knew how to use the herbs and how to use them right. Soma is what they gave Christ in the sponge.

Your Bible tells a story which your sciences know is contradictory to the facts that the Bible presents. Christianity does not want to hear that Christ did not die because they hang onto the ascension. He also was not on the hill where the others were. He was on property away from the main action.

Whenever they crucified someone, they made sure that the families were close enough to watch it. It was an intimidation in order to make better parents and better citizens. That's another clue in your Bible—the family had to watch from a distance.

It was a staged event; it was set up from beginning to end. Judas was in on it—he was not a traitor but a part of the plan. It was all arranged between Pontius Pilate and this Christ so that Pilate could say, "We killed your messiah. This is the end of your messiahs." It was hoped that the citizenry would calm down and stop revolting after that. It was all politics. This Christ the man had become too prominent; Pilate had to do something.

Christ the man went along with the plan because he wanted a life of his own. As it worked out, it was also the only way he could buy his son's life as well as his own. It was a way to get them both out of the country.

It was all an elaborate political scheme. Even the swordsman who stabbed him in the side was in on it and knew how to miss the organs. This is another fallacy in the story of your Bible. Corpses do not bleed. Your own Bible tells you what really happened if you know what all the facts mean. When they edited your Bible they only knew about the physical details of crucifixion, but they didn't understand the process so they mistakenly left some very nice passages in there that tell you what really happened. Crucifixion always took a minimum of six to seven days to kill a person. Even a weak person would survive four to five days. Your Bible says Christ hung for six hours and then died. No one ever died that fast.

The Essenes took him down from the cross and put him in a tomb to let the soma wear off. While he was there they worked on his wounds with their salves and herbs after which he was taken away. He lived out his life in India where he died in his late sixties. They have his tomb in India today, and they know it.

He didn't take the body with him—that is where most people hang onto the story. Taking the body with you, as we have stated before, is loving it enough to imprint it and take it. In one sense you could say he took his body with him because he molecularly bonded with it enough to do so—but he didn't take the flesh. That is the big miracle that everyone hangs onto the Christ story for, but it never happened.

Because of Christianity, you have to hang onto the belief in a Christ. That, just like the god gestalt, is a limitation because actually, the miracles you will do or have done are greater—even he said that. He knew it because he touched the hologram. He knew what you would be able to do—he couldn't do it because of his day and time.

Christianity worships Christ. A lot of you are trying to become a Christ. But the entire gestalt around Christ is that he is the only one that can create miracles. Your miracles and your lives will have to be diminished; they cannot come full circle as long as you are holding onto the Christ consciousness.

The new metaphor says . . . you were created to be the most unlimited being ever created, designed to be a companion to the universes.

Today, the Christ consciousness is something for the guilty. Today the Christ consciousness is all about somebody who is going to save you from your sins. That is different than what your belief in it is, but that gestalt is older and stronger, and it states that Christ died for the whole world, Christ is the savior, Christ took everybody's pain. So when you say you are trying to become a Christ, you are saying that you are willing to take on everybody's pain and the guilt of the whole world. So in trying to become a Christ, first of all your miracles won't count or can't be real miracles. Then you get all the pain and guilt. Also, according to the gestalt, Christ was a homeless pauper, so you're going to get the poverty too. That's the belief of the gestalt. If you don't understand what you are pulling in, you're going to live it anyway.

Most of you already manifest more gold than Christ ever did, but you don't let yourselves hang onto it because of the gestalt. Most of you also feel like you're walking around carrying your own crosses and getting crucified all the time. What you are really wanting is the hologram. This other is just the closest representation you have. The hologram is your passion within, but when the brain tries to get you to it, it just plugs you back into the Christ gestalt.

Once again we're making little bridges between the new hologram and the old. What Christ did to the god gestalt, you are doing to the Christ gestalt. Christ tried to take people out of the old hateful, vengeful god into some love. He taught that the kingdom of heaven was within—it's not outside you. A lot of you are trying to pick up that hologram, and that's the piece you want. But your brain taps into the whole gestalt and doesn't know the difference. That is why it is important to follow the feeling within your being. The feeling is the new hologram and it is still abstract.

Christ changed the old god into a new loving god who offered grace to anyone. According to the belief, it doesn't matter who you are, what you do or did, you can repent and be saved. From one standpoint this is a positive piece of the gestalt because it allows you a framework for releasing your guilt and moving into the hologram. It could be one of the best tools you could have if it would work. That one metaphor is why religions were allowed to flourish. You see, if you could repent and let go of your guilt in that metaphor, you could bypass the dead zone.

The religions didn't work because they didn't teach you fully to release the guilt. Even in your days when you were doing that, you would repent and still feel guilty for the things you supposedly gave away. People won't let go, so they are still not using the metaphor as it was intended.

The new metaphor says you are going to have to get rid of your guilt. You cannot step into the new hologram fully and completely with your guilt still intact. You've had the old metaphor for two-thousand-years and it's still not working. The old metaphor brought mankind hope; it is a beautiful metaphor, a beautiful feeling, but there are things in it that you do not want. What you do want is the hologram of your own entity—it is not a Christ, it is not a god—it is totally different than anything you have words to describe. It is what you felt as a child. It is what you have felt for brief moments as an adult, a feeling inside. You have been putting it into these other frameworks and have called it god, you have called it Christ. But it is an entity, a hologram; it is *you*.

You'll move faster out of the old paradigm and into the new, if you can just let yourself focus into the new and feel it. You are the only one who can guide you there. You don't have to kill the other. You can still see the beauty of it and appreciate it for the stepping stone in consciousness that it was. But it is not the new metaphor, and it won't take you where you want to go. You can't hold on to it and drag it behind you; you can't live in both metaphors. A lot of times when people move out of the Christ metaphor, they replace it with the next best substitute. The only one there can be is *you*. There are no substitutes for the real thing. Go for you: that is what the new paradigm says.

The new paradigm says, "Here is the hologram. It is the entity you started out to be, so let's be it. Let's cut out all the middle men and be you." It is a feeling, a love, and a joy. If you knew Christ the man, if your books had left some of the actual humor and joy and lightness in the stories, you'd have a whole different perception of the individual and of yourselves. You are free to live and enjoy the seriousness of the old metaphor if you wish. But the new metaphor says you were created out of joy, so it's about time you start acting like it! It says you were created to be the most unlimited being ever created, designed to be a companion to the universes. ▲

Align Yourself
With Life

I'm new to your audience, but I'm used to terms like **align myself with my god** and I've been hearing that for a few years. What do you think?

      Align yourself with life, not god! I'm not the anti-god, let me tell you! (laughter) Many of you say, "I think god is unlimited. I think god is the greatest thing that there is." But when you tap the gestalt of belief around god, you will not be pleased with what you manifest, I guarantee you. What is a god? Go back to your Old Testament because that is the oldest and the original pictures of god. There you will find that God is mean. God is hateful. God is revengeful. God punishes. God is not a nice guy. That is the oldest version and belief about god. In your Old Testament, you haven't one nice thing to say about god. God does not like life. He'll snuff it out. Is that what you want to become!

      Now you're trying to create a new and more expanded identity for god, but you haven't let go of people's belief of the old identity. For many of you, the biggest struggle you create in your life is trying to become god. That's because everybody knows there is only one god. The number one prevailing belief system on this planet is that there is one god—and that is not you. There is one god and that god does not come here. That god does not talk to anybody here except through certain people and that god would have *nothing* to do with you. That is the belief of this planet. That is the gestalt, that is the consensus. If anyone of you go out on the streets and stand in front of a hundred people and you say, "Hey, I'm god." They'll say, "Yeah, let's find the butterfly net!"

      So for a lot of you, when you're in the process of aligning yourself with god, you're aligning yourself with all of these kinds of beliefs. You're aligning yourself with the whole attitude of the planet that says you are nothing, because there is only one God—and that is not you. You are aligning yourself with the whole attitude of the planet that says, "How dare you blaspheme, let me wipe my feet on you." You're aligning your attitudes with the whole planet that says," You belong in the loony bin." In short, you are creating a whole lot of struggle for yourself, because you are flying right in the face of a whole lot of very strong beliefs on this planet.

When you can say, "Okay, I don't want to become god. I want to be me, because if there is a god, then that god wanted me to be me. So therefore, I am living my heritage grander by being me, than by being anybody else's truth. So I will not align myself with god. I will align myself with what I was created to be and that was *me*."

When you can feel that and you can do that, that puts a passion of life inside you that says, "I love who I am." And nobody can take that away from you. When you can get to that point, then the pain and the burden of life just wipes away.

The belief about becoming a god, is a whole lot of struggle. The whole entire belief about becoming a god is painful because you see yourself as so much less than god. Let's go back a few years to your beliefs about god. Did god go through the things you're going through to become god? In your beliefs, in any of your religious beliefs, was god born to be god or did he go through the hell you've been going through?

The whole entire belief about becoming a god is painful because you see yourself as so much less than god.

The prevailing belief is that god was born as god—but so were you. That means you don't have to try to do anything. It doesn't take anything for you to be what you were born to be, except for you to allow it. The number one trick to having a life that you love is to put it into a place of, "I love who I am, which means I'm accessing my birthright, which says, I accept my creation." Most of you have never been willing to accept the fact that you were created as individuals and that you were loved into existence. You have the free will to ignore it, and most of you do!

When you can say, "Okay, I love myself and it might sound egotistical to the whole world, but I love me. I don't have to worry about what everybody else thinks," then you can pull up that feeling of love. You've all tapped it. But when you tap it, you often get homesick. That's where some of the issues come from. You tap that love and that love reminds you of a place you know so well, so beautifully, and so grandly. You tapped a life force, an energy, a love that you call god, and you're homesick for it—that's what it boils down to. You're homesick to feel that feeling again. But realize that if you hadn't brought home on the journey with you, you wouldn't have felt it at that time of your experience. You brought it with you. Home isn't a distance. It isn't out there somewhere, because time and space do not exist. Home is where you are at. It means that you're sitting in it and on it. The only thing is that you have to let yourself touch it again.

When you get into that feeling and intensity, it hurts. There is so much love there, it hurts and when you touch that, you become scared of it and you close off and back away. You put on a nice strong rigid adult face to protect yourself from the hurt, and then you forget to live life.

Go into the feeling, embrace it and own it, because that intensity of love—you're just ignoring it. You're playing dumb. You're pretending it doesn't exist so that you can pretend that you have to find it. All you have to do is stop and go in and feel it. You have it. It came with you. When you can do that, then you can disown everybody else's idea of what your life is supposed to be and you can feel life, you can appreciate you, you can love your body.

The biggest tragedy that ever happened on this planet is when you were taught to hate your bodies. And the only awakening that any of you have to do is to get out of the hatred for your bodies and to awaken to the fact that you were not stupid for coming into them.

A lot of people live their lives here saying, "I'm in prison camp Earth." But you were born as the most highly intelligent species that had ever yet been created. An entity that is that highly intelligent is not going to do something that is a detriment—only something that is an enhancement. If you came into one of these dumb bodies, why were you dumb enough to do it? Or is it that you were so highly intelligent that you are afraid of realizing the fact of your own intelligence? Maybe you are afraid of admitting the fact that "I am a grand genius, I just haven't recognized it yet." When you can become totally one with your body, then you have accomplished the journey you came here for.

Most of you believe you have existed in some form before this life time. Why do you believe that you have had other embodiments or existences? You may say, "Well I had to learn enough to become a god." Gods didn't struggle that way. They were born gods. What king struggled to become a king? Most kings are born of royal lineage that says, "You're a king. You're a prince until your dad dies and then you're king." They don't have to go through a journey of proving themselves to be royal heritage. They are birthed that way.

You're a highly intelligent entity. Never let anyone tell you differently. You were birthed as one just as the prince is birthed, right from the womb.

You were born kings and queens. You don't have to prove it anyone. Your heritage is known by everybody but you. So it's a matter that all you have to do is recognize that fact and realize that, "Okay, I'm a highly intelligent entity. I came into this body. It doesn't work right. The hair is falling out. The nose isn't the right shape. It's not the right height. I'm too short. I'm too tall, but I wouldn't have put myself in this body if there wasn't a reason for it. So since I'm here and in a body, then I will be in it," and then learn to move into it and be at one with the body until you can become relaxed just being your natural self. This is called being you.

Right now everybody tries to be themselves by disowning the body. But you are already yourself. How can you be anything else? Self is a physics principle, yes, and you're trying to accomplish that, but how can you really be anything but you? You were birthed as it. So how are you going to accomplish something you already have? You can't. Which means that if you're in a body, you're trying to be you in the body. You're trying to accentuate it. You're trying to accept it. You're trying to become one with it. That's what you're trying to do. As soon as you can move into it and learn to appreciate the miracle of the body—which is what your life is all about—I guarantee things will change. The home-sickness will leave. The acceptance will return. The longing will leave. The loneliness will leave and you will realize, "Oh, the grandest joke of all. I was already home!"

Space doesn't exist, so home isn't a distant planet. Home is the realization that I am what I have always been.

Space doesn't exist, so home isn't a distant planet. Home is the realization that I am what I have always been. I've only been wearing a mask. When you can do that, your quality of life will shift. The same moment you recognize that fact, you'll never be lonely, you'll never have the pain, you'll never have the big open holes that a lot of you feel like you have within your being. This is you, wanting to recognize you. That's all it is. Feel it. Don't be afraid of it. Go into it. Dance. Jump in it. Emote. Cry your eyes out. Play in it. Do whatever it takes.

Become at one with that hole in your chest, for those of you who have it—that big empty void in there. Go into it. Don't be afraid of it. Most of you go around repressing it. You actually have a big gaping open hole in your chest. There is repression at the throat, repression in the gut, and the heart is hurting, because it's trying to stay closed to fill up the hole. Let it be open.

If you want to journey into the realm of the entity—and that is where my journey goes and that's where my teachings will take you—you're going to learn that it's a whole lot different than a lot of you think! You're going to learn that what you consider freedom and what you consider all these things that you want, are all a little different than what you thought they were. You're going to realize that the great, big, huge, gaping hole in your chest is called being a source. That big open hole is the strongest amount of love you have ever felt, but you haven't yet developed the eyes to perceive it. You will also realize that you can't feel the love that is in the big, huge, gaping hole, because you have never picked up the sensory perceptions from the body to do so. You were never close enough to the body to know how to interpret your senses. You never learned how to interpret other realities through your feeling senses. And so, all of a sudden you're exposed to unconditionality. Unconditionality is so unconditional you won't recognize it. It is that unconditional.

The raw stuff the universe is made out of, you can't feel. So these big, open, holes you have in your chest are the strongest amount of love stuff in the universe and you're sourcing it and you're cursing yourself because you feel lonely. "I feel unsupported. I don't like this." All that you have to do is get into your body. Feel it. Love the miracle of the body. Love life and then what you do is you embed your entity with senses so it can go into that big hole and it realizes how full it is. It realizes how rich it is. "This is the grandest stuff. This is what I've been looking for my whole life, and I've been cursing it because I had it." Then when you have those sensory perceptions, you take them in there, and then you'll create everything you want.

When there is a big gaping hole, it's because you haven't picked up the sensory use of the body. The love is so unconditional it feels no different than running your hand through the air. You say, "Well the air has no personality." Those of you who have the big gaping hole, you say it's just painful. No, it's not painful. It's raw material that you can't perceive because you don't have the sensory perception.

When you become one with the body, it will teach you the sensory use of it. Then you'll run in there and you'll play. You'll have the grandest time and you'll laugh, because it was there all the time and you just didn't know what to do with it. ▲

Circuitry in Relationships

Within your beings you create what we term circuits between individuals. All relationships are comprised of circuits, and it doesn't matter what the form of relationship. Circuitry is one of those principles that can sound a little far-fetched, but when it is understood, it explains a great deal about your behavior on this planet.

Originally, you all came from one source, therefore you are each various faces of the same source. Another way of looking at it is that you all came from the same material, so you are the same entity. There are threads that tie and bind you all together.

Most of you have belief systems or philosophies that allow you to commune with something outside of yourselves by using prayer, meditation, or some other means. Many of you were raised in systems of belief that taught that you existed prior to coming into this body and that you will exist afterward. Circuitry is just a way of explaining how the entity, you, which is actually not a physical being, has been able to come into the body, manifest in the body, and then go in whatever direction you choose.

Your brain systems create a lot of firing patterns. Those firing patterns within your brain, and within your body, are little electrical charges. Your scientists can measure and photograph them. When your body goes through its firing patterns, it makes little electrical charges. These charges combine to make what you term your auric or electromagnetic fields.

Originally, when you came upon this planet you were telepathic, you mentally communicated. Language wasn't necessary and so you communicated through what we term circuitry. You actually just allowed yourself to become each other. As you became each other, you understood the message. At that point you didn't have the vocal cords that you have now developed.

However, it moved to a place where you all wanted to shift your brain system because everyone was picking up your thoughts. It was sort of comical! One of you would get a thought and so would everyone else. So if one of you wanted to walk or sit under a tree, everybody on the planet wanted to do the same thing!

Shifting the brain out of that allowed for individuation, but it also shifted the brains into some very different configurations, which is actually what allows you to each have different genetic structures. It's the main reason why one set of parents can bring forth numerous children and none of them look the same. In your animal kingdom, for the most part, they look the same as their progenitors. The humanoid species, shifted their brains into a different configuration, but the circuitry still exists. You communicate all of the time without saying anything. This is circuitry.

Because of circuitry, your bodies are often being run by everybody around you! The way this occurs is the cells take an electrical charge and from that electrical charge make a chemical release that tells the body how to function. Your brains make chemical firings all the time. However, your bodies don't always receive the full charge. The excess that is not received by the body goes out and makes your auric or electromagnetic fields. Because these firings are not confined to the body, they can travel wherever they want. Often the generating thought constructs and firings from your body that your body isn't necessarily using, will go out into your field, and another person can pick them up. Their body actually runs off your brain firing!

This is done extensively within family situations because the children and parents are genetically the same makeup, and their brain patterns have a tendency to match. In personal relationships the thing that brings a relationship together in the first place is a need for a circuit to be complete. What attracts all circuits is the need to be completed. If you have just one direction—just transmission or just reception in the body, you don't have a complete circuit and you don't feel whole.

Every relationship that you attract to you—whether it is a personal relationship, intimate relationship, employer-employee relationship—are all based upon your needs in circuitry. You will always be attracted to whatever will supply the circuitry that you need to make you feel more complete. Often you will attract a relationship for a certain juncture in your lifetime, and then your circuitry needs change and so does the relationship.

Let's say that you have two people in a relationship and circuitry between them. Your brain is firing and your body picks up let's say ten percent of your brain in a particular attitude or emotion. The other ninety percent will feel totally incomplete. It will feel as though you have fatigue. It leads to depression a lot of times. So what will happen is you will attract to you another brain system or embodiment that can actually pick up a large fraction of the rest, and that is what you call friendships.

All of your brains work in networkings. Your brain gets used to firing in particular habitual patterns. So your brain fires in a habitual pattern, and you can only use ten percent of it. You feel like you want a friendship or relationship. What you do is try to find someone that has the receptor sites for a larger portion of what you're firing. Since your body is using ten percent, what you are looking for is another individual whose body perhaps has the receptor sites for ten or twenty percent of your firing, so you will be attracted into a relationship and you will have a good friendship. In that friendship, your brain still fires in the same patterns, but then you feel more complete because it is being received.

You will always be attracted to whatever will supply the circuitry that you need to make you feel more complete.

Most of you, within your beings, no matter how grand the relationship, there is always part of you that feels unfulfilled. There is always this little nagging part, no matter how good the relationship is, that feels like, "I need a little something else. I don't know what it is. The relationship's good, but it's not quite complete."

A lot of you repress the feelings. But if you can find someone that supplies or makes that connection, you feel more complete. That is why you like to have friendships and relationships. They make a completion of the circuitry which allows you to feel more complete, more whole.

Let's say in the beginning of the relationship your body was only accepting ten percent of your firing. Your friend was supplying, say another twenty percent, so you still had an incomplete feeling, but you felt a little better because you had someone you could relate to. Then let's say you created a healing within your own being. Your body is now using thirty or forty percent of your firing instead of ten, which means that your friend is not needed as much. It is not like you want to just dump or get rid of the friend, but it creates a strain in the circuit because neither of you are getting what you want from each other. Your friend needs to have that form of transmission somewhere from somebody to make him feel complete because you're doing it now within your own being. Often he will seek out another type of transmitter just as you did.

There are variations, but if you look at your relationships, you can see that a lot of them have always had a similarity. That is why a whole lot of people will leave one relationship and go into another exactly like the one they left. It is because something was being supplied in that form of a relationship. That is why a lot of people will stay in an abusive relationship. When they break from that, you'd think that with a clean slate they wouldn't attract it again. Often, they will turn right around because they haven't healed from the first, and attract another relationship that is much the same, because even in that situation something is being supplied.

When relationships are severed, it is because people are starting to go their own direction. If the circuitry needs always stay the same, then the friendship is much longer lasting.

Circuitry doesn't infringe on free will; whatever any of you do or think, you have the ability and right to do it. It is your free will; do what you wish. None of you can actually be infringed upon unless you allow it. But when you are into somebody else's environment or their universe such as visiting with them, you are usually much more confined to your own space unless they allow you more access.

The most radical changes any of you will have is around your family. When you get around your family, whether it is parents, children, grandparents, whatever, you will usually change everything from the way you carry your body to the way you speak. Your vocabularies change, what you talk about changes. When you are in those situations, you supply and are using the circuitry between you, and if your parents want things a certain way, you will respond. You usually respond to your parents rather than your parents responding to you. So for most of you the grandest test of being yourself is in a family situation.

Here you are and you are feeling quite comfortable with you. You are learning to be yourself. You are learning to be everything that you think you want to be. Let's say that your parents are in a very rigid state; they know how everything is, and they still hold you in an image of a ten or twelve-year-old child. That means your parents will always treat you or react to you from that level because that was when they bonded with you last. This can make it very uncomfortable to be around your parents.

There are a lot of things that happen with actual bonding in circuitry. There is different circuitry bonding at different ages. You get it at birth. You get it at different phases of your life. Your parents will always see you in a version of when they bonded spiritually with you. Usually they don't bond with you past your puberty states, because then you start being adults. You start getting your circuitry with other places and other people, so there is no more space for them to circuit bond.

When a person creates circuit bonds with you, they will always see you in the light of the last bonding. And so you might be forty, fifty, sixty, seventy-years-old, but your parent created a circuit bond with you when you were ten or twelve. That means that they will visually see you growing as an adult, but they will emotionally respond to you as a child.

Their brains compress the data of you at ten-twelve. Every time you have circuit bonding, you have brain or data compression. What that means is the brain says, "Here is all the incoming data, I compress it, and this is fact. This is the way it is." And so when you were ten-twelve and they had a very beautiful loving or powerful experience with you, they created a bonding, a circuit bond. The brain compressed data and thereafter sees you in the image of that data.

Your parents probably never created any more circuit bonding, and here you are forty-years later. Their eyes will see you growing and evolving, but their brain says, you're ten-twelve. So their brain pattern runs off you being ten-twelve-years-old. It creates a dichotomy within the being.

When a person creates circuit bonds with you, they will always see you in the light of the last bonding.

Many of you that have children can see this. You're evolving past it, so you are not holding your children in quite as many images, but as adults you can remember those powerful bonding experiences with your children. Think back to when you had a very close connection with your child, the last one that was very powerful, when you saw them as a child and they were so beautiful and cute or they did something wonderful—you had a circuit bonding with them at that age, and that is how your brain sees them no matter how the body looks. And so, parents will always relate to their children at the age of the last bonding.

Some of you are in a place of being open enough to allow your children to evolve and be who and what they are. You can see them in adult bodies and still somewhat relate to them as being children and catch yourself at it. This is what your parents do to you. It is not that they are trying to be mean, cruel or anything else, this is just the way the brain of the species works.

So their brain is sitting here firing and genetically working with you in the image of a ten-twelve year-old. That is how the brain sees you, even though the body looks differently. You try to act like an adult because you get tired of them treating you like the child. But that is what their brain has compressed. It does not compress you as an adult. So when you get around them and their brain is firing and pulling up data, it says, "Here is the data on my child. My child is ten-years-old, this is what he looks like, this is how he acts, this is how he eats, this is how he holds his fork."

Understand that whenever your body fires within its nucleus to just create the natural life of the body itself, there is always a piece of it that goes out beyond the body and out into the field. Always. So the brain is firing at this picture of a ten-twelve-year-old child. This is my child, ten-twelve years-old. So their body is reacting to you like you were then. But part of it also goes out into the magnetic field. You try to relate to your parents as who you are, and they can't relate to you because what they are putting out is the ten-twelve year-old vibration. Since the firing has the same genetic predisposition as your body, because your body came from theirs genetically, every firing pattern that goes through the cells has your common genetic makeup on it, the whole DNA coding. Because that DNA coding in the field is similar to yours, your body starts picking it up and responds, and you start acting like a ten to twelve-year-old child in an adult body.

So here you are, you have your own predisposition of how and who and what you are and you say, "I am going to be this, I am going to be myself around my parents." But they are projecting ten-twelve at you; you pick up ten-twelve. After about a half an hour of this, it is like, who cares? "Yes, mom, what do you want?"

The only way you are going to create up-to-date circuitry is with circuit bonding. You have to have a powerful experience that your parents are going to remember. Rebellion is the powerful experience that most of you create. You put your foot down, "Mom or dad, I am not this person any more." If you want to change the data compression, they have to be able first of all to know who you are. Most of you, because you have to go through everything we just talked about, it is like, "I don't even want to bother trying to tell them who I am." So, if you are going to try to create the new bonding, first of all, they have to know you. But for the most part, none of you will get to that stage of telling them because you'd be breaking their image of the ten-twelve year-old. They often don't want to hear anything you are telling them anyway. It's a two sided thing. The parent has to be willing to do it, and so does the child.

Those of you with children, however, can re-bond with them at all these different stages of life through circuit bonding. It has to be an intense, precious moment that you have with them, and when you do that, you create a new data compression within the being.

Generally when you create a new data compression with your parents their brain still sees you at ten-twelve, but also, at the new precious moment just created. So it starts bringing them up to date a little, but there is usually still a gap. For most of you, its too big of a bother, and you won't make the effort. But a lot of you will make the effort with your own children.

Let's say that your child bonded with you when he was twelve and he is now in his twenties. That means that the child still holds you in the image of the way you were treating him when he was twelve. You haven't grown up either in your child's mind and this is why even in the best family relationships there is still a barrier from the data compression and the genetics that go through the circuitry. Let's say that you bonded with your child when he was eight. He still sees you through the eyes of an eight-year-old child. If that is very positive, he'll see you in a very positive light. If he saw you being a parent, as most parents are, then at that age he will start getting into a place where parents aren't really friends any more. They are, but because the children are starting to be grownups now, it starts creating a communication gap. A precious moment has to be created to narrow that gap.

Let's say that you bonded with your child when he was eight. He still sees you through the eyes of an eight-year-old child.

Often, even if the circuitry could be changed and the other individual would see you in a new light, one party or the other is afraid it hasn't changed and holds it in the old bonding. A lot of times this bonding, when it occurs, will take a period of time. There can be a precious moment, or an insight, but it may take a little bit of time. Usually these moments are very precious. When you are into them, there is a power. On the other side there is almost a rejection with it. There is almost a form of embarrassment, or it was so powerful that you want to run away.

Usually when you create a new circuit bonding there is always this retreat. There is a withdrawal, and it can take anywhere from a year to three-years to get out of the withdrawal. This circuit bonding can be priceless, it can be one of the most powerful things a person has had. Sometimes it is only one party that had it; sometimes both parties experience it, but on the other side, there is going to be a retreat because the brain is having to re-digest the new compressed data, and usually the experience is so powerful that it created the feeling of, "Well, what do I do with all the rest of this?"

You've had many years of life with this view of your parents and your family situation. Now you have a precious moment and you're seeing it in a whole different light. What do you do with all the previous data? And so intellectually you start going back into the same habitual patterns for a bit of time until it kicks in. But once it has happened, it does shift the circuitry.

When you create new bonding you don't lose the beauty of the old. All these precious moments you remember. If you have enough of these precious moments between both parents and children connecting in the heart, from a feeling tone, then it changes things so you will see them as the precious moment you had when they were eighteen, twenty-one, twenty-four, thirty, forty. You'll have a line of progression through all these precious moments, but you'll have the new ones too.

Usually once children reach their teens, they are starting to get into their own relationships, and are wanting to bond with their friends, not with their parents. So it creates a place where the parents have a harder time creating these precious moments in the data compression. Their child is having these connecting and bonding circuits with their own relationships, their own spouses.

Often when these bondings occur, it is because something traumatic happened, perhaps a death in the family. If you notice, at funerals people often let down their barriers and start loving each other again. It can create a new bonding, but then that bonding is associated with the death process.

There will come a time when you will move past the limitations of circuit bonding. That is what you are all trying to do. As long as you are in a physical body, however, you will require circuitry just for your own existence and for the body's existence. But you are trying to get to a place of peace with yourselves so you can release a lot of the images of how you are supposed to act around your parents and others. If you have these images the old bondings are going to kick in a whole lot faster than if you didn't have them. If you work on your own images and work at trying to be yourself, your parents or your children will have less and less influence, until you get to a point that you won't change at all when you are around people. You will just be yourself all the time and then you will be beyond manipulation from others.

Just notice how you shift when you're in a situation and ask yourself if you would be acting this way if you were not around these people. If you will notice it, you have a different body, posture, conversation, tone, and terminology for your family. You have a different one for those you work with. You have a different one for going to the grocery store. You have a different one for everything in your life. Once you can realize, "Okay, I just shifted, and I'm uncomfortable in this situation—if these people were not here, how would I behave?" Then go back into your original space. That will always keep you being you instead of buying into everybody else's images.

All dysfunction in relationships can be understood in terms of circuitry. Most abusive situations occur, for example, because of the way circuitry is running. If circuitry is not compatible, then you're going to have an abusive situation.

Look at circuitry as little fine road maps, little lines of circuits, and what flows through them is love and life. Let's say your uncompleted circuits are like the fingers on your one hand and you are trying to connect with another person. Their circuits would be the fingers on your other hand. If you connect at the finger tips, the love flows; your circuits are complete, and you feel fine in the situation. But if the fingers miss or can't connect, then you can't connect either. You don't flow and there will be anger.

As long as you are in a physical body, . . . you will require circuitry just for your own existence . . .

These circuits are the love of your being—love and life itself flowing, but if there is no receptor for it, both parties get angry because neither feels that the other person is loving it, and so you have anger and resentment. All they wanted was to be loved. The abuse could heal if within their beings the individuals could move into a place of feeling loved in the situation.

That is why a lot of abused children will not tell on their parents because all they are wanting is to be loved, and if they tell on their parents, in their mind that is another way of saying they are not going to be loved. Most of you will accept any kind of attention, whether negative or positive, rather than not having any.

All abusive situations can be healed with love. But usually in this type of a situation, that child is probably never going to feel the love that it wants from that parent. All it is going to feel is a lot of unworth and a lot of lack. Most children in an abusive situation abuse themselves more than the parents ever did. The parents might beat or torture a child, but what the child does emotionally to itself is the real pain. What a child might say to himself is, "Well, I guess I deserve this. I guess I wasn't good enough. I guess I should accept this because I'm a terrible person." And so in an abusive situation, the child moves into a self-worth issue very intensely, and that is what has to heal.

All these children ever wanted was for the parents to love them. If they can feel the love, the healing will occur, but by the time they become adults and have been trying to heal their self-love and self-worth, they have already ingrained the lack of it so much, that they are just pained with it. Even as adults, they just sit and grind on it in their mind and emotions with all this pain of the abuse they suffered and went through. All they want is love, and they're probably not ever going to get it from the parents, because if the parents were capable of expressing love at that time, they would have done so. For the most part if the child and the parents could bond with love, it would be healed. There would be some anger and some resentment, but the healing would start. But this is not likely to happen, so the children, within their own beings, as adults, have to start loving themselves.

Most of you on this planet, from other cultural and planetary standpoints, are abused children, whether you realize it or not, because you are bombarded almost from birth with images, circuitry and everything else. While many of you have romantic ideals and think you were raised in a perfect family, there is still emotional scarring and dysfunctionality because of the way the circuitry was working. Most of your planet, in one state or another, is actually coming from abusive situations, whether it was physical abuse or not.

In all abusive situations the number one thing that is needed is love, and it is also the hardest thing to get. These abused people are totally convinced that they are worthless, totally convinced. Intellectually, you can tell them they're all right, but it does not work emotionally. The only thing that is going to help is when they can move into a feeling experience within and feel their own worth. That is the only thing that is going to heal it. Each person is going to be different, and it is a very trying road, but as I said, your whole planet fits into this category, in various degrees.

Most of you are birthed into physical bodies not believing in your own worth. It is a tendency you bring with you, and it is genetically supported here. But in order for anybody to heal, they have to get back into that self-worth. You can take an individual from your idealized, perfect family, and they will still have self-worth issues. A healthy family would be a family that instilled self-worth in every child that was born, but if the parents don't feel it in themselves, they won't be able to give it to their children.

Healing this in the beginning is like taking off the layers of an onion. Eventually you get down to the middle and it is gone. Remember, everyone on your planet is an abused person—everyone has self-worth issues. If each of you could be pushed into your deepest feelings, you would always find the same story. It doesn't matter whether an individual was physically, psychologically, or emotionally abused or whether they had a "perfect" family, you will always find the same issue underneath it all. Until a person can be pushed into it and release the anger of it, you're not going to get the healing. Anything else is going to be just like feather dusting one layer of the dirt at a time. Your underlying issues of self-worth are like a back-yard sand hill, and you have a feather duster to clear it out with, rather than a shovel.

In a truly healthy and unlimited relationship each person finds their own beauty, their own worth, their own value . . .

Each of you are in various states of healthy relationships and circuitry. In a truly healthy and unlimited relationship each person finds their own beauty, their own worth, their own value; they are not insecure. Without insecurity there is no anger, possessiveness, or over-protectiveness.

Most of your conditionalities upon this planet in any relationship come out of your own insecurities. A relationship with conditions in it, is never going to be effective. It will never in the long run, be satisfying to either party.

Here is party A, and he says that this is what he wants in a woman. This is how she is supposed to act, look, and everything else . . . I am exaggerating a little— but not much!

And here is the woman; she has an image of what the man is supposed to be too. These images are things you've bought out of society's standards. They are not even your own belief systems or your own feelings inside. So then, these two go into a relationship and seem fairly compatible, but the entire time whether they know it or not, he is trying to impose his pattern on the female, hers on him. After a period of time, this conditionality wears on them both, and they each go their own way, fight a lot, or repress and ignore it.

Most of you go into relationships with ideals about what you are expecting. A lot of this all ties into your beliefs, and your attitudes that you've bought from the planet. Much of it revolves around your insecurities. If you were not insecure, you would have no issue with the other party. All of your issues, all of your jealousies, your envies, your possessiveness, your protectiveness, come from individual insecurity.

So since party A or party B is insecure, they want to make sure that the other one is always going to be there in a certain fashion, and that gives a certain pseudo-security. It is called conditionality. Relationships will always teach where you are.

Your relationships are like sand. If I told you to go to the beach and pick up as much sand with your hand as you can, don't lose any, and bring it to me . . . and you went and scooped it up and squeezed it in your fist, it is going to fall through your fingers. If, however, you scooped it up and held it gently in the palm of your hand, it will stay.

This is something you all have to learn about your relationships. The harder you hang on to them, the faster they are going to flow through your fingers—just like the grains of sand. When you hold them in the palm of your hand, with an open and secure perspective, it is like going to the beach on a windy day. If you try to protect the sand by covering it up, it is still going to slip through your fingers. But you won't lose that much sand by holding it open. All of your relationships are the same way. Your personal insecurities make you clutch, and your relationships can sift through your fingers so fast. But when you can hold them in an open fashion, it might, in your natural movement, be blown by the wind a little, and you'll have some shifting, but it will still be there.

Fidelity is your number one big issue in most relationships, because you are all so insecure that you want to know that there is always going to be somebody there loving you. Because of your insecurity you made up all of these story lines about fidelity and exclusivity. This underlies all of your relationships. You think that if you didn't have beliefs in fidelity, if you didn't put lots of emphasis on its importance, that the other person would be all over the whole place!

For most of you this is your prime concern. But it is like the sand in the hand. When you hang onto another like this, that individual feels like they are being smothered and stifled. It is really not a fidelity issue but an insecurity issue. Because the individual feels so insecure within their own being, and they are afraid that they are not going to be loved, they have all these preconceived ideas about fidelity and fidelity becomes their test of love.

This doesn't mean that fidelity can't be there. But most of you because of all the other conditions and all the insecurity that the other person is putting on you, feel as if you're having to placate their ego all the time. You have to tell them they're okay and all right. The insecurities lead to possessiveness and possessiveness is what destroys most relationships. When you clutch relationships, like sand, they fall through your fingers. But if you were holding it in an open state and not insecure, not even worried about it, you wouldn't create infidelity as your reality. Then each of you would probably find that fidelity would be there, if you wanted it. It wouldn't be an issue. It would just be a natural thing because you would be feeling comfortable in the relationship without all the conditions.

Fidelity is one belief system that creates a lot pain on your planet. If you can realize that this preoccupation with fidelity is coming from an insecurity that you feel within your being, you can work on that insecurity. Then your reactions will change and so will the relationship. It doesn't mean that you are going to be promiscuous. It simply means that within your being, you have conquered a new level of security.

These are all the little things that you can work on by yourself to see how they lead you back to your own insecurity, before you get into a relationship. I'm not saying that you have to go into a relationship saying, "Okay, well, there doesn't have to be fidelity here," and just do whatever. Each of you will be different with what you do; it is a matter of the emotional reaction within. Those emotional reactions create the possessiveness and actually destroy relationships. Possessiveness has destroyed more relationships than anything else. The second one is called blaming. So it ties into the first one which is called insecurity.

Possessiveness is what destroys most relationships. When you clutch relationships, like sand, they fall through your fingers.

Now in your relationships you have spiritual circuitry and you have biological circuitry, just to differentiate for the conversation. For the most part, when you attract a relationship, you're looking for somebody to support that part of your circuitry that you can't. Also, your genetic memory in your body is responding to your predecessors. If your great, great-grandparents had a very passionate, loving relationship, your body will have a tendency to bring to you somebody of the same caliber or of the same vibration. It triggers your genetics, and you have all this going for you. When you first move into a relationship, you also feel a lot of intensity of love and self-love. It generates a chemical in the brain. That chemical in the brain makes you feel like you are in love. And so, you have all these intensities for a number of reasons at the beginning of a relationship.

But after the circuitry connects, you start becoming one person. Then it is like being in a relationship with yourself, and that doesn't match your image of what the other person or you were supposed to be. After about a two-year period, the circuitry kind of balances out. After it balances out, then it feels like it's a comfortable relationship, but there is not the passion, there is not the intensity. A lot of these relationships will just dissipate and die unless they are regenerated.

Circuitry bonding is the only thing that is going to intensify relationships into constant growth. If you go into circuitry bonding through having those precious moments, and you have images with it, you're going to bond those images too. Then you are going to be back into conditionality. So to make the strongest, deepest, most intense, lasting, ongoing relationships, it is going to be a series of these precious moments so that you can create an ongoing circuit bonding. When you complete an ongoing circuit bonding, you start getting into devoted circuitry and the third brain. It is a totally different type of relationship than your planet experiences.

From there, that is the relationship of entities. That is what all of your ideals and all of your romantic stories are built on. I would say that is the rarest thing upon your planet to actually accomplish. That is the type of relationship all of you are looking for. One that is sharing, one that is deep, one that is intense. There are no conditions with it; it is just very loving. It is this open hand type of relationship.

In the process of getting there though, all of the images have to be destroyed in order to get that bonding with the devoted circuitry later on. So you will create circuit bonding up to that point. Then there is a bonding and a devoted circuitry that can occur, and that is the passion, that is the love, that is the true beauty in any relationship.

All of you have at least one devoted circuit in your body. It is called the life-line to your spark. Everyone has at least one. Each of you have done different things with them though. Out of all the circuitry that you have, the natural or the primal devoted circuits are the least that you have. Out of all your circuitry, the devoted circuit is actually the primal circuit that holds you to your source. It is the straight line from you to your source. It is communication. Everyone of you have at least one. It is the source within the being.

An individual that can touch themselves deep inside, can and are actually growing more of the devoted circuitry and connecting themselves back to home. But you have to clear out the images and all the junk around that devoted circuit in order to find it.

Your brains and your bodies have created pseudo-devoted circuits, and that is where the psychological and the emotional/mental things all come in. Your original devoted circuit was with your source and still is. It is very beautiful. It became distorted however, and pushed out of place, so it is not connecting the same way it used to. It is not gone. It has just been shifted. Now you're not feeling this devoted circuit back to your source, so you feel separated, alone, and deserted. So, you take the one devoted circuit you have and try to make a pseudo-devoted circuit with anyone you can find in a relationship. So you run your circuits out sideways, instead of straight back or straight into you. As you clear out the images and a lot of the other junk in the way, you get back into the clear space on that devoted circuit. Then it is just you and the source; it is one whole being.

The devoted circuit is actually the primal circuit that holds you to your source.

You have just about as many circuits as you have cells in your body. Every cell has a circuit to keep its life going. And if en masse, you're letting the whole planet tell you how you are supposed to be, how you are supposed to look, if you are into a lot of social consciousness, then you are going to live those images, and it is going to be very difficult to find that one very beautiful devoted circuit that is your source.

Because of the way they are connected with the biological embodiment, if you have a lot of devoted circuits, you are not going to be as physically based, and so, you don't have that many. Distorting the source, is what created mass and matter in the first place. So the source had to be distorted in order to get a body.

You go into relationships hoping to find the devoted circuit—that is what all your stories are about. You want devoted relationships, secure relationships, all these other things, but what you are really doing is just trying to find the completion for that one circuit. But you won't find it outside of yourself. You are only going to find it within you. And you are only going to find it by clearing out a lot of the other clutter, or the images of how you are supposed to be, what everybody thinks you should do, what society expects of you. You find it by just being yourself. When you find a passionate relationship, in the beginning it is like, "Oh good, here is a devoted circuit." After a little while that devoted circuit feels just like you, and then the relationship gets boring.

A devoted circuit is just a term that we're using to describe a circuit that was created with your source. We use the term devoted because it is a

key word to explaining and understanding all the belief systems and feelings behind those belief systems.

The original devoted circuit occurred when the source loved you into
existence, because you were all part of the source. When it loved, it
pushed itself, and expanded itself out. The primal connection with each of
you is the original devoted circuit. That is a very deep, beautiful space you
get within. A lot of people use religious circumstances to get into them. That
is why a person can go into a religious experience and have a very deep
prayer, deep contemplation and can start tapping that devoted circuit a
little. In a practical sense you can call the devoted circuit the connection with
you.

Each of you is a god, and you can play any game you want, and
always have this connection back to the source. That is your primal connection to the source, but in the game that you're all playing here, you distorted
it. You're still connected with your source, but within your beings you've
distorted it. You are writing all these stories about it. You are looking for
somebody else to complete you rather than yourself to complete you.

See, a circuit means that you have to have the negative, positive, or a
complete connection for flow. That is what circuit means. If it is a one way
street, you don't have it.

So here is your circuit-source-you. The source can be sending all of the
time, non-stop—and it is. But unless you send back to it, the circuit is not
complete. What you send back to your source is you—love, life, and your
experience. You are a part of it, so if you are disconnected then it can't be
complete either. You see, your source is sending all this love and life to each
of you, but you push it away, so it can't complete with you. Most of you
don't allow the source that created you to get close enough even to know
you or for you to know it.

If you can have that connection all the time, you will have intensities
of happiness, joy, and love. That's what a healthy body is. When you've
reconnected your devoted circuit, you can have that feeling all the time that
you now only vaguely remember from your best dream and sleep states.
You can have it wherever you walk while you are in this body. Look at what
a life it can be!

When you can start holding yourself and your relationships in the
image of perfection and beauty, when you let go of the images and cease the
judgments, it starts clearing out the circuits. It starts clearing out all the

other circuitry, getting you back into a space of a natural or primal devoted circuitry where you can connect more with you as it was originally designed.

Each of you was given one main devoted circuit. You have one that is the source and you, and it holds you together en masse. But there are a whole bunch of you side by side. You are so close together that if one of you moves, it shifts all of the others. So originally, when you started shifting into realities, these started getting separated.

When you use the relationship to create that natural devoted circuit back to you—you open up. All of a sudden, you start getting guidance, you start getting brilliant insights. You start opening your whole world into a new and different perspective. It is just clearing some of the clutter and getting back into a more natural perspective.

Love yourselves. That is the best relationship, because you are the only one that will ever understand you . . .

In the natural scheme of things, you would just share. When you as a planet went into issues of sharing, you started creating pseudo-devoted circuits. It's what put you into a whole mess of psychological issues revolving around sharing. When you hold a person and yourself in an image of god, then you are lining up and restoring devoted circuits back to the source. It eventually moves into a beautiful relationship—something that your planet hasn't seen yet. But the images are the distortions, and they can't be there.

Love yourselves. That is the best relationship, because you are the only one that will ever understand you, and you are still confused on the subject! So if you are so confused on the subject, then you should have a little bit of empathy for somebody else trying to understand you. Your relationship with you will prove to be the most beautiful of all relationships. ▲

The Audience
in the Mind

When you are stuffing your feelings, it's what you call repression. Repression is actually compressing your electromagnetic field—you are preventing you from being you. The quickest and easiest way to know if you are repressing anything is to put yourself into isolation, remembering to take the audience out of the mind. That is the fastest way to know whether you are repressing anything whatsoever. Put yourself into a place where you are the only person left on the face of the planet. It is just you. The whole entire audience in your mind is gone. There is no audience left whatsoever—just you. And since you don't have to perform for anybody, including yourself, or your own hecklers of your own subconscious and your mind—the audience in your mind—what would you be doing? If you are in that state and you're doing something contrary to what you would really be doing without an audience, you have been performing for images. That means that you are repressing, which means that you are actually compressing your mind, compressing your electromagnetic field, your biofield, pulling it in to prevent you from being you.

When you repress, you're trying to force yourself to be something contrary to you. This creates a compression in the electromagnetic field which actually begins to compress your biological spirit and its firing patterns into the brain and compresses the brain into network firing. If you could see the way they fire into the neurons, you would see that you have those that just fire where they need to, but you have a lot of your neuron firings clumped into networks. A network might have twenty or thirty rutted philosophies or twenty or thirty attitudes, actions—reactions. Most of you have an average of, let's say close to a million networks in your brain. This means that you have probably close to a million clumpings of these little neuron firings. Then you begin to compress this down. As you begin to compress it down, you are forcing your biological spirit and your electromagnetic field to be fired through the networkings, which does not allow you to allow the light of your own being to be in the body. That is a repression of you. So whenever you are compressed, you are compelled to do something or be something other than what you would be. When you do that, it narrows the band with which it can fire and it alters the vibration with which it fires. It actually goes into the brain system and begins to push the neurons into networks so that you have rutted thought. Then all it can do is just fire through this clump of networks, and it can't go from where it is firing over to the set that is more desirable for it to be firing upon to get your thought out of the rut. You then isolate yourself into old behavioral patterns.

The freedom all of you seek is the freedom from . . . the inner private hecklers you carry with you.

So remember, the audience in your mind is your own creation and everyone of you perform for one almost twenty-four hours a day. So if you ever want to know if you're repressing, stop for a moment, right now, and ask, "Am I performing for anyone?" and if you are, you are repressing. That is still the easiest way of recognizing if you are living someone else's images and shoulds. When you realize that you are acting and performing for an audience in your own mind, then you kick the audience out and then you can be you. Then you won't be repressing.

To release the audience, let yourself be into a quiet place in your mind. Most of you don't even realize when you are performing. Let yourself take the pressure from all of the eyes of everyone that has been watching you and release it. Let yourself take you now to a place, a point in the universe, whatever creates a quiet solitude for you. A place where there is no one but you. Let yourself go. Some brains will be stressed, and need to be relaxed. Relax the brain. Put yourself emotionally in a place where there is no audience. It is just you. Now let yourself dance. Let yourself feel the life dancing through your embodiment. If you were not performing for anyone, what would you do? There is no one there, just you. Now notice the vibration in your body. If the audience is gone, the vibration should be quite refined, very gentle, very beautiful, and very free feeling. At this point, you allow yourself to bring the beauty in and allow yourself to feel brilliantly beautiful from the inside out. Let yourself feel genuinely beautiful on the inside.

Let yourself feel how beautiful you truly are, how loved, how loving. Feel the freedom you feel to just dance and to just be you. If you don't feel like this, you are repressed and being something else. The freedom is inside;

it's not an external thing. If you do not feel this free to be you and to just dance in the light of your own being, you are living in a repressed state. So now you can gauge how much of your life is repressed.

The audience in your mind is your own creation. It is a subconscious creation that each of you make to insure that you will always be proper and always fit into everyone's images so that you will not embarrass yourself. The freedom all of you seek is the freedom from the audience in your own mind—freedom from the inner private hecklers you carry with you.

Many times you'll get pressured at work, you get pressured in different ways when you have to meet certain requirements, or the job isn't getting done fast enough—these types of things and so you start rebuilding the audience. I would say for the most part, just from time to time, check in and say, "Okay. If it was just me, I'm the only one left in the whole universe, nothing else exists, what would I be doing?" Then you'll find real fast, "Well, you should be doing this and you should be doing that." That's coming from your audience.

You all like to should on yourselves all the time. Remember that shoulding is a self-judgment; it also doesn't smell very good! So if you're getting any shouldings, the shoulding is coming from your audience. That is a good easy way to remember. The light of your own entity is a playful child. It won't say that you should do anything. It will say, "Come on! Let's go try this," in a very delightful way. But your audience says, "Well, you should do that differently. You didn't perform that quite right. You should change that. You should do this."

There is a bit of difference between your legitimate personal guidance, which will come as gentle urgings, and a shoulding or justification, which is your audience telling you what to do according to the images it maintains about your reality. When you go into a should, you are weighing things out, generally to see which thing you need to do to support your image, and make you appear to be a better person. "I should keep my job because I can't afford to loose it." This creates a self-judgment or justification. This type of shoulding is not coming from your guidance. It is coming from the desire to be loved—to be externally validated by others, so that you will know your worth. Your guidance will urge you, "You could do this, you could go in that direction." A could is a possibility. A should is an image. Your guidance will never should on you. If you can change a should into a could, which also means that you can choose not to do it, and you can remain free of guilt after making your choice, then you will find a more accurate picture of your personal preferences, and what you would do if there were no audience to perform for, and thus no images.

Your guidance works in subtle, natural ways. If your guidance wants you to be some place, and you have to be there by a specific date or time, you will be. It will move into a place that if it wants you to leave your job and you're not doing it, it will find somebody to fire you and accomplish the same thing. In other words, that portion of you that is your own ultimate guidance that each of you have, will accomplish what needs to be accomplished and the real journey is learning to release your resistance. The audience is your resistance, shoulding on you, and filling the mind with images that prevent possibilities from being seen.

A could is a possibility. A should is an image. Your guidance will never should on you.

When you are running your life according to your audience, you will never learn to love unconditionally. A should is not being unconditional to you or anyone else. It is a statement that says you are doing something with the expectation of gaining something in return. That is being conditional. Even if that something you wish to gain is simply the validation that you are worthy of being loved. You honor no one including yourself by doing a should. You are simply saying, "I do not feel comfortable enough to be myself. I am afraid that I will no longer be loved, if I do not do what is wanted of me." Acting upon a should immediately places one in a martyr and victim role.

Many of you do very grandly at letting others be themselves without judging them, but most of you have yet to learn to allow yourselves the same luxury. Shoulding and justification are personal self-judgments. The audience in the mind was created from all of your self-judgments. It is what creates the defensive wall that many of you carry towards life, the very thing you are trying to gain freedom from. You're not afraid of life; you're afraid of your judgments towards yourself. You're not trying to gain freedom from a prison, but only from your own rigid adult that is constantly performing for an audience that does not really even exist, except in your own mind. ▲

Releasing Your Genetic Past

All of what you term your emotions are a biological process. Everything that you go through, every emotion, anxiety, anger, fear, depression, everything, is a biological response. The way it becomes a biological response goes back to the cell firing. Your cells fire. Let's say a normal firing is a ten/twelve. That is what creates entrainment vibrations; you as a planet or a people determine what rate of vibration everything is going to vibrate at.

Now part of the entrainment vibration is a commonality of the strobing effect that we've talked about before. You all flash on and off. This is a phenomenon from the nucleuses of your atomic structure. Since you're flashing off and on, so must the planet. Everything has to flash off and on. Since it does, then the critical mass of the commonality determines what the rate will be.

If the planet was firing at a two/three and all the mass consciousness was firing at a twenty/twenty-five, you're going to find a median range where you're going to fire. As you evolve, you are in part trying to change the firing in the body, because the body is held by mass consciousness which is where the entrainments come from. It is also held by the planet which is where the material for your body is built from. So you put all these things together to determine the firing in the nucleus of the cells and thereby your molecular structure.

If the whole planet decided to shift, you could change the common-ground firing, but the new vibration would also have to encompass the planet. The planet is what gives you the raw materials to fill in the pieces of your hologram to make your body. So if you're going to make a body, your cells must fire within the range of what the planet can produce.

Let's say at this point in your evolution your cells could fire at a refined vibration of one-hundred with no problem, but the planet can only fire at two to seven. If you are firing at one-hundred beats per second, and the planet was at two or three, you'd have gaps in what the body would be able to produce. So in order to maintain a body, the body must be created out of a commonality of your personal vibration and the planet's in order to give you raw materials to keep the body built. Without that the body gets holes or gaps in it and this is partly what you call fear. So it is an entrainment vibration in that you have to kind of vibrate according to the whole planet in order to have a body even coagulate.

You see, each of your atoms have an orbit and an orbital rate. You could say that they have a spin, just like your own electromagnetic field. Let's say that your spin or revolution in your nucleuses is a thousand beats per microsecond, while the carbon atoms which comprise your body are perhaps a much slower two or three. Then, you will not have a body unless you can bridge that gap.

Your natural entity vibration is so high that in the body . . . it can't manifest . . .

So your vibration has to be reduced in order to make a body. When your vibration is reduced, your connections with the larger part of you or your own entity are disrupted. So this is what generates a lot of fear in your being. Let's say your natural entity spin is close to a thousand in a vibrational rate. But the body, if you're spinning that fast, can't coagulate to make itself. But that is your natural entity vibration. That is the only place you're going to feel totally connected and complete. So as long as you're in a body, you have to slow that rate down in order to make it sticky enough that the molecular structure called carbon base, all these things you call your cells and molecules, can attach to it and coagulate upon your natural rhythm and vibration. You are stuck between a rock and a hard place. If you want a body, you have to reduce your vibration.

Understand that there is a sticky principle in the universe. That sticky principle says that whatever the speed of your revolution, you will gravitate to it things of like speed or vibration. Mass is one of the slowest principles in the universe, and therefore, also the stickiest. If you are spinning really fast, it will never coagulate to you. It can't hold on to something spinning faster than it. In order to make it stick, you have to slow your rate down enough that the sticky stuff called mass can fill in the pieces of your vibration and make a body, and it's actually a very simple process.

To do that you reduce a natural rhythm of let's say a thousand beats per second clear down to perhaps two to three per second to hold a body.

Now the minute you start raising the vibration of that body, you put it into anxiety because you start dematerializing it. The other side of your rock and hard place is that your natural entity vibration is so high that in the body you can't hear it and it can't manifest because out of its one-thousand vibrations, it has to choose the two or three that it will accept as physicality. This is where your limitations come from. Out of that thousand revolutions per second, you have to choose only two or three of them to call you here. When you do that there is a huge gap and disconnection in your reality. From this point on, your fears begin to generate.

This fear then materializes into the nucleus structure of the body. From there it manifests into the DNA structure and the genetic structure. All this creates a chemical reaction and release called fear in the body. This fear is the natural orbit, and this is why it is an entrainment vibration. Basically what you're having to say is that these are the two or three orbits out of my revolution I am choosing to call me here and now. That's scary when you know that you're a huge entity and you can only have less than two percent of what you are.

The only way you are going to be able to change this is by bridging nucleuses. For the most part, the molecular body is made out of the gooey stuff. You have a jelly mold that makes your body. This mold attaches and attracts this gooey stuff to make form called molecular structure. As long as you're working out of the molecular structure and your cells, you will never be able to pull more of your entity self into the body, because the cells can't hold it.

The cells can never hold the entity that you are because in order to make a body, they can never vibrate more than what the planet will allow. So you have to take the planet from a two-three vibration to a one thousand which is an ordeal, but it's what you're all trying to do anyway. Either you have to get it there, so that the common rhythm of the planet can help you make a body at a higher rate of speed, or you have to go into the nucleuses within.

If you are following the research in your particle physics, you know that they keep getting into smaller and smaller subatomic particles. They have it clear down to these very tiny particles. Each of those you could consider to be a nucleus within another medium. Each part of these atomic structures they're finding have smaller parts within the smaller parts. Those very small parts are the active ones, not the big clunky ones. They'll find tiny ones, smaller and smaller, that are more active, faster moving, more excitable than the full atom itself. The smaller the particle, the more that is in it. You're the same way in your bodies.

Your cells are just a coagulation upon this jelly mold of your reduced vibration. All they can do is breathe, so to speak, with the jelly that is you. In order to get that to have more life into it, to hold the whole entity, you're going to have to teach the mold to go down through the nucleuses, so it can play with the tiny, sub-quark particles where the life is. Then it can bring the life up and out into the entire body or molecular structure. Until you go into the nucleuses and follow that as deep as you can, you'll never have the entity in the body. The body simply cannot hold it.

Your body is where all your entrainment vibrations come from. As we get into nucleuses, this will explain the origin of a lot of your biological fears. Your cells have an electrical firing. Your molecules, your atomic and subatomic structure all fire. Your science knows that the nucleus gives life to the cell, but they don't know where the nucleus gets its power. It is the same with all your electrical things. Everything has to have a ground. In order to get power from anything, you have to have a ground or a completed circuit to the power. In a cellular structure, this is the role the nucleus and the mitochondria play. One is the power and the other is the grounding. This is what makes it function as cellular mass.

Your body is where all your entrainment vibrations come from.

In the deeper nucleuses these little subatomic particles have such life and just love to dance and play. These are very deeply embedded. They have to send their message up to the next level, the next one, and the next one, up through the atomic structure until it finally gets up into the nucleus of the cell. This is where the electrical message ignites a little, much like the spark plug in a car. The mitochondria there, the pool of emotion, the DNA, and your genetics, are triggered by that little bit of light. That is why it appears that the mitochondria is the powerhouse.

The mitochondria tells the body what to be. It's not the powerhouse. The power comes from the nucleuses within the cellular structure of the mitochondria itself. The mitochondria has its own set of living organisms and its own set of nucleuses within nucleuses.

Looking at your cellular structure, you have the cell, you have the nucleus, which has nucleuses within nucleuses, you have little pieces of mitochondria around it which also have nucleuses within nucleuses. This is why your predecessors, so many generations back, can affect you here and now. Your mitochondria is so many layers thick with their pooled emotion, it reacts the same way as this nucleus that we've talked about. It brings your predecessors, especially the last five to seven generations, very fully into your lives at any given time.

So here you are trying to bridge these nucleuses. For the most part the cellular body just creates a circuit between the cell nucleus and the mitochondria and it never gets into the vertical nucleuses. It sits and fires back and forth between nucleus and mitochondria just like a spark plug. Your cells are firing horizontally instead of internally. Since they are firing horizontally from the nucleus into the mitochondria, you have a circuit which is grounded, and that's where your lives are built. The mitochondria is the history of your ancestors and your emotional reactions up to this point in your life.

The charge that is coming into that nucleus is being fed from the deeper recesses of the atomic structure. It is so faint by the time it hits the nucleus of the molecular cell that it fires very weakly. It crosses the nucleus to the mitochondria, telling the mitochondria to build a body and a life out of the pooled information.

You're running your body horizontally. In order to bring the entity that you are into the body, you have to teach the body to fire internally into the nucleuses and not strictly horizontally. As you go into the deeper nucleuses and start pulling that power up, the firing in the nucleus of the cell is strong enough to counteract anything that is in the mitochondria except your own thought. As it is now the nucleus has only a faint glimmer coming up, a candle to do the job of a beacon. If you could intensify that to a full strobe light hitting in that nucleus, then that nucleus would be tied into your brain system and would totally by-pass the mitochondria. The mitochondria would no longer have any control over your body. When it is very faint, the body will hold onto this horizontal firing just to keep the cells intact. It doesn't care. The body wants its life. The body will just sit and fire horizontally because that is giving it life, it's surviving, it's alive. That's all it cares about.

If you intensified that nucleus so that it was firing like the biggest, brightest, spotlight striking your night sky, and you had that firing across your mitochondria, then that would program your body, not your predecessors. That is what you are all trying to do but in the process of doing that, there are several things that happen in the DNA and genetic structure. This is where the difficulties come and the fears arise.

As long as you are firing horizontally from nucleus to mitochondria, you'll live every fear your predecessors and society has every had. You have no choice because the mitochondria is built from the genetic pooling which is emotional embracements, emotional trauma, love, and anxieties. Everything that has ever emotionally been in your ancestry line is in the pool that your mitochondria is going to pull from. Anything that had an emotional charge is going to be in there.

If you look at your lives, you have moments that are grand, but what you have beyond that is a whole lot of the strongest emotional stuff: the traumas the fears, the anxieties, the depressions, and the struggle. If you have them, it's because your predecessors had them before you. That is what the genetic pooling is all about. That is what you have sitting there in your mitochondria. You have some love there too, but the other outweighs it. If you were to weigh out a year of your life in terms of a negative or a positive charge, you would all be outweighed for the most part by either no charge or a negative charge.

In order to bring the entity that you are into the body, you have to teach the body to fire internally into the nucleuses and not strictly horizontally.

Any time the adrenaline gets released in the body, it invades the DNA with the memory of the emotion. Anytime that you get scared, you jump, your system goes through something, it gets embedded—everything that was there in the thought process.

Now since you are all firing horizontally in your cells, you have to try to teach that horizontal firing to go internally into vertical firing, and in the process of doing that some of your biggest fears arise and especially some of the body issues.

Most of your biggest fears here are body issues and image issues. Your rigid adult or your body start balking when you start going against society's images. It is scared and it just can't deal with it. So let's take it from the perspective of body fear.

When horizontal firing is all you have, nucleus to mitochondria, back and forth, you're going to be physically based, disconnected from your guidance, and disconnected from a lot of other things. Some guidance will still be there because it will bleed through, but you'll never have it to the extent that you want. You still have to have that mitochondria to build your body with for the time being, but you're trying to take it into an internal firing mechanism. When you start doing this, it is like turning up the heat. You're changing a candle into a laser beam. As you start to bring that light up you're literally burning parts of the mitochondria out. This is called burning your image. It's getting rid of your past; it's a genetic dumping, and you do this by overloading it.

You bring the light up in the nucleus and then as it fires into the mitochondria, it burns the mitochondria. If it's used to a low-watt light bulb, so to speak, and all of a sudden you're boosting it, you are literally going to burn it, and it's going to feel like an acid burn. It will make an acid burn within the deep nucleus of the mitochondria. From there that acid burn goes into deeper levels of the DNA and genetic structure and starts burning away at the sheathing on your DNA.

Your DNA is much like a twisted spiral ladder with rungs. Each of these rungs if you could see them have little nodules; each one of them is almost a little ball. Both the rungs and the sides of these ladders are made up of these little balls combined together. This is what your DNA looks like. Each of those little balls is an emotional entity. Each one of those nodules in your DNA has the ability to be an entity on its own. Your DNA structure is made up of millions of these nodules and the ladders hold them together to make the strongest personality. The only difference between you and a chicken, or you and the frog or anything else is some of the minor differences in these ladders. If you're missing a rung or certain rungs on your ladders, you're going to be a chicken instead of a human. For the most part, the basic genetic structure is the same for all materialized species. Whatever rungs are missing determine what species you will be on this planet. You would be surprised if you knew how closely you were related in your DNA to some of your animals. This is already understood by your science.

Each of these little nodules has the ability to be a person, an entity, an individual, and your body is full of millions of them. When you love yourself into existence, you're literally going to love your DNA into multiple millions of parts. You'll see where they come apart and you're going to have new entities created from you. When you love yourself into existence at a later point in time, or as a god, you love yourself into a point of expression. Then, out of this DNA that you take with you from this planet, you're going to love all these little nodules into separation. The nodules that are attached together with ladders will become entities. The nodules that are in between the ladders will become sparks.

In your body as you start bringing up the light in the nucleuses, you start creating separation in the DNA. By bringing up the light, you create and secrete an acid into your system that is ultimately a beneficial acid. You may not like some of the side effects, but in the long run, this is the chemical reaction an entity will use to create new life out of his own being.

When you bring your light up, that means that you're bringing your love up, whether you feel like you're loving or not. It is love from an unconditional source, so it doesn't feel like love—it's just there. Your vibration from inside your nucleuses comes up and creates an acid that starts etching away at your nodules. When this is turned inward, into a horizontal process, you have disease and virus. If you're firing in a horizontal position from nucleus to mitochondria, you take this acid, push it from the nucleus into the mitochondria, tell the mitochondria to start etching these little nodules, and it eats away the sheathing around them. They get a little burst of life when you peak in one emotion or another, and the nucleus fires faster. The emotion put more life into this exposed nodule and it starts growing. You end up with what you term a virus and many times it will become a cancer.

Each one of those nodules in your DNA has the ability to be an entity on its own.

The acid is supposed to etch off this sheathing so that the DNA can be rescripted and you don't have to live off your own or past generations' emotional baggage. When they have been etched, it is your opportunity to write upon them whatever your thought would have your body be, to create a god's body.

When it gets down to a point and it is opened for rescripting, you could go in at that moment and write your own message on your own DNA, and your body would respond to you. But what you have sitting in your thought process is, "I don't like myself. My body doesn't look right, and doesn't work right," and all your judgments, and that is what you rescript into it.

This rescripting is for the creation of new entities. The acid deteriorates the sheathing to a point where a new entity can be created. If you will think about it that is why you are on a path in the first place. When that sheathing is removed the body is going to be uptight because what it used to know itself as is gone, so you get body fear. The body is afraid of inscripting the wrong thing into it. So if you're into self-hatred, don't like who you are, what you are, your system is going to feel an underlying burning that creates almost a paralysis.

If you are going vertically into your nucleuses, you're going to enhance you. You are going to walk in larger pieces of yourself. Horizontally, you're going to create subpersonalities and disease in the body. When your nodules are open, however you feel about yourself is going to be inscripted on your DNA. This is why it is so hard to simply love yourself now because for eons your ancestors have been inscripting your DNA with self-hatred, lack of worth, lack of love and millions of other images.

So now you're in the process of opening this up so you can rescript it into your mind and your being, but first you have to let your ancestors' junk out. As that sheathing comes off, the first thing you're going to face is all your self-worth issues: the self-hate, the self-anger, the self-incompetence.

Now, if you don't hang on to that, you won't re-inscript it. Most of you when you get to that point, you hang onto it and rescript it right back into the DNA. When you do that enough times the mitochondria become very weak and vulnerable because their protective sheathing is gone: they have no protection whatsoever against your thought process.

If at these points in time you could just understand that you are releasing your genetic makeup and love yourself then you'll rescript the self-love instead of the other which you know yourself to be releasing. But you have to be sure you are releasing it and not buying it back as your own truth. Whatever your feelings and attitudes are about you will become the new inscription.

If you are into your rejection complexes, your self-hate, your there's-something-wrong-with-me modes, and your need for external validation, you're going to rescript your DNA with rejection. That goes into the body and the body starts rejecting it, just as you programmed it to do, and you have disease. Disease is caused by your own attitudes and rejection when you are inscripting your DNA.

Most of your fears in your body will arise when you're at a point of having these sheathings removed for rescription of your thought into the body because you are threatening the body's identity. As you pull the light of your being up, you burn holes in your DNA structure, but you are not trying to destroy it. Your mitochondria has a homing beacon on it, for it holds your spiritual genetics and that is what will get you outside this body and take you home. What you are doing is getting rid of the images and the attitudes and moving back into a place of peace with you, a space where you don't need the external validation. If you need the external validation, you're going to ask somebody else to program your mitochondria and your body when it's in the inscription phase.

As you go into the nucleuses, you have the ability to drop off every nodule you don't want, so that you don't have to go through the issues. If you are horizontally doing it, you'll have to go through the issues because horizontally, that is what is making your body and your life. Going horizontally, the nodule containing your and your ancestors' emotions, has to be opened and released, so you can rescript it. Going vertically, you're going to release the whole nodule. Your intention is to find the nodules that you don't choose to be part of you and release them without ever going into them.

You use the same acid to go vertically into the cells. If your mind is not going vertically into your own being, it will go horizontally and start destroying or tearing down at the mitochondria level. So if you're bringing up your light and you're jumping the nucleuses, the body starts pulling from an ever deeper nucleus, until you have beautiful rhythm coming from the inside out. Then as you run through your DNA and find nodules that are ineffective for you, you will automatically kick them out and not have to live them. If you are going horizontally, you'll have to live everything in your genetic makeup. Vertically you don't have to live it, you simply go through and reject what you can't use.

You don't have to go through your DNA and say that you want to drop nodules 101, 243, and 86. All you have to do is hold an image of your own state of perfection. You just have to know who and what you are: "I am a god. I am love." Whatever your being is, "I am joy in motion." Then anything contrary to that knowing will be thrown out, if you are going vertically. If you take a positive attitude internally, by itself, it has the ability to create whatever it takes to pull everything that is negative out.

When your nodules are open, however you feel about yourself is going to be inscripted on your DNA.

The nucleus that you really need to reactivate is your fourth. You can do that by getting into a third nucleus. That fourth nucleus is the one that will facilitate your changing as fast as you can handle it in the body. But that fourth nucleus is taken out by guilt. If you have guilt for anything, and especially for being yourselves, you will never bridge the fourth nucleus. This is why the images have to go. If you start jumping those nucleuses vertically and you know you're a lousy person, you know that you should or shouldn't be doing this or that, and you're into the guilt, you'll throw out the positive in your DNA. You'll be left with what you know yourself to be which is guilt.

If you're starting to jump those nucleuses and you take in there all your issues of self-worth and guilt, whatever you know yourself to be in your being, you will throw out everything contrary to that knowing. The fourth nucleus is unconditional. If you know yourself to be love, and you know yourself to be evolving into it; maybe you don't feel it all the time, but you know yourself to be a god; you know yourself to be able to stand with your head up and with strength; and you can feel it within, then that is what you'll tell your embodiment that you want to remain with the DNA, and you kick the rest out. But if you're into the self-worth issues, the nobody-loves-me attitudes, that fourth nucleus will throw out everything contrary to that—it will throw out the stuff you want. Until you can get past the guilt, you won't bridge that fourth.

All of you are playing with the third already. That third nucleus will teach you how to program your genetics. It will teach you how to do it with the love of your being so that you don't program and create something you don't want when you bridge those other nucleuses.

This acid that we've been talking about is what takes out the nodules. When it does, that means pieces of your personality are going to be missing, and this is what creates fear. When you burn out a nodule, you have a hole in your DNA. But when you are going vertically, you remove nodules at the core rather than at the surface, and it takes a matter of weeks and months for that to reach the surface.

Let's say that six months ago you went in and cleaned out nine of these nodules that pertained to survival or defensive modes that were no longer useful to you. You were into joy, you had the strength, you felt the beauty, and so you removed these nodules on your vertical journey. Now, six months later, your surface mitochondria pick up holes in the messages from the deeper levels.

As the brain maintains a continuity in your experienced reality, so the mitochondria are created to maintain continuity in your body. So now your body's reality has holes in it.

It would be helpful if you could see your mitochondria as so many little islands. They have circuits among them but the circuits are broken by the space between and so the charge must jump or bridge between the islands. The electrical charge that occurs between them is the message that tells the cells and body what to do. Each of these islands fire and bridge in such perfect timing and rhythm that the charge chases around the islands much like your sequential Christmas or advertising lights that you've all seen. Neither the lights nor the mitochondria are moving, but the rhythm of the flash makes them look like they are.

When you move vertically through the nucleuses, these little islands or flashes within the mitochondria pick up the message of the previous island, push into the next, picks up the message and moves on to the next. That creates the revolution in the horizontal cell which tells the cell what to look like, how to build, and what to be.

Now, all of a sudden, you have a glitch in the system, a nodule or island is missing. You have a gap now that the mitochondria will have to fill in the pieces for because it doesn't know what to do. To compensate, the mitochondria overcharge the glitched space which creates a short circuiting in the cell at the level of the mitochondria.

Now if you are working on a horizontal level, you will be causing disease in the cell. Vertically, you're not, but it will end up feeling the same either way. From a horizontal perspective, as the sheathing is removed, the disease sets up a resistance between the islands, and the light flashing from island to island is reduced and reduced. This is what causes degeneration and aging in the cells, for each succeeding reproduction of the cell will be less than the previous one.

That third nucleus will teach you how to program your genetics.

Working vertically, you get overcharging; horizontally, you get a reduction because of the resistance. Vertically, resistance is reduced because the overcharging pushes more charge through the circuits. So where you're used to having a run-through rhythm let's say equivalent to a double "A" radio battery, now your rhythm is relatively to a 220-volt house current. Your cells are getting overcharged and they feel like they have been invaded and abused. The cells don't like it, and collectively, because the intensity is so much stronger, they make the body highly sensitive to everything. They body wants to avoid everything because it assumes the attack is coming from outside. So when you are into the overcharge, the body doesn't want any stimulus because it doesn't want any more overcharge—this creates instability in the body.

If you are dumping one or two of these nodules, it's no big deal. But if you've gone in and cleaned house dumping forty or fifty of them, the mitochondria doesn't know how to build the body the way it used to. It loses continuity and comes up with all kinds of fears.

As soon as individuals decide that they are on a path, whatever that means to them, no matter who they are, or it could be a hundred different paths, as soon as they decide that they are evolving their consciousness and they are trying to go back into that main spark within their being, or whatever you want to call it, they start going through the process. But if you don't dump the images, you will always be doing it horizontally and you'll never get into the vertical.

The images of what I should or should not do and guilt hold you in a horizontal picture, and you can never touch the vertical nucleus realignment. You'll still be dumping all the time, and you *can* clear the DNA that way, but that's the slow process. If you do it that way, you will have to live it and heal the issue within your own being so that you can rescript it with a new picture. When you do it vertically, you are saying, "I am a god. I don't choose to have to go through the issues. When I find something that doesn't seem to be part of me, I will dump it." Then that issue will be eliminated with other body fluids. It is a faster method of doing it. But it can be harder on the psyche too.

It can be harder because the psyche is used to having the continuity out of the mitochondria to build very slowly, very gradually and just maintain. It likes to maintain tight knit circuits, so when you radically change that, your psyche starts having problems. Your psyches for the most part have problems at the cellular level. So usually if your psyche is being pushed to its limits, you can pretty well be sure something is going on at the cellular structure.

Most mental instability comes at the cellular level. It is not a brain process. It is a cellular process. What happens is something in a person's life causes the DNA to change too dramatically, too rapidly, and so the cells cannot deal with it. It is not a brain misfunction. It is a body misfunction. So when a person goes into multiple personalities, when a person goes into paranoia, when a person goes into what you term schizophrenia, that is a body thing, not a brain or mind thing.

Any attack on the body at all, whether surgery, self-hatred, self-love, any of these things can cause the body to dump its genetic material. Any type of strong emotional stress keeps the body right on an edge of this all the time, but it keeps the movement horizontal.

Your medical science doesn't recognize this because your DNA from that deeper level takes six months to a year to show up. If they took every case of mental illness, they would find that, that person had a body trauma of some sort, six months up to two years prior to the breaking of the psyche. The breaking of the psyche is a body thing. Not a brain thing.

When too much of the continuity in that mitochondria of the cells is missing, all of a sudden there is a personality crises. The body doesn't know who it is supposed to be telling the occupant to be. It's trying to bridge the gap and it can't do it. That is what makes an overload or a breaking of the psyche. The cracking of the psyche and your mental breakdowns always occur after the physical event that dumped the nodules.

Let's say that six months ago you got into grand intensities of self-love, joy, and love of life, perhaps for a day or even a few hours. When that happened, you dumped all sorts of self-worth issues and rescripted your DNA with self-love and joy as part of your personality.

Your DNA is a long ladder that sort of makes a circle or works in cycles. So your DNA ladder will come back around in six months to a year or so. The more you dump, the faster the DNA recycles.

So you dumped all this negativity six months ago, and now in its cycle, that rescripted DNA is starting to bleed up into the surface mitochondria where your reality is created. Only now you are back into a pity party, your self-hatred, and your life's-not-worth-living mode. Your psyche is going to freak out because what is coming up from the deep DNA is not matching your thought process. It says, "We have a wrong personality here—this is not who we are." Your DNA is saying you are a new personality and your thought process is saying you're the old one, and the body doesn't know how to understand the misdirection. You are telling it you're two different people.

Most mental instability comes at the cellular level. It is not a brain process.

It knows that genetically it is supposed to be stimulating you into cloud nine because you reprogrammed your DNA for life and joy six months ago, but on the other hand you're telling it how miserable, unloved, and worthless you are. This sets up guilt in the cellular structure. Guilt always arises when you pretend to be something that you're not. You are letting your brain and mind rut in its old patterns. The psyche gets into an identity crisis, and when it has too much of this, it cracks or gives up and breaks the DNA structure right there. You go into a standstill until you figure out who you are again—this is depression, this is bottoming out. On the other side of it, you start figuring out that maybe you're OK and worth loving, and the psyche heals a little because the DNA message and the thought process are agreeing again.

Your big problem in reprogramming your body is your brain rutting in your old compressed data of who you think you used to be. When you are into joy, you bridge your third nucleus and when you do, you dump nodules and reprogram your DNA every time. It was set up so that you couldn't get into your third nucleus and reprogram it in a negative perspective, so you don't have to worry about programming it wrong. You can't even come near the fourth nucleus until you are clear and out of guilt.

Dumping portions of your DNA is quite natural and almost automatic. If a child didn't dump some of its DNA, it would turn out to be a clone of its parents. A child starts dumping vertically almost at birth because it is built into your system to selectively choose which part of the DNA you will call you.

In all this you do not want to indiscriminately dump nodules. If you are into judgment of yourself you may dump nodules that contain your most valuable life lessons that your predecessors went through so that you won't have to. If you're into judgment of "this is right, this is wrong," you would probably dump them and have to live them for yourself, so some of your genetic lessons and experience is protected from your own thought processes until you can get to a point of not judging, seeing the love, the wisdom, and the lessons in everything that has occurred.

As long as you're in judgment over some of these lessons and experiences, those nodules in your DNA will control you, because it is a part of your being that you're trying to hang onto here. All your nodules are beautiful, but some are insignificant to your direction. Some are so significant that you would not want to lose them for anything; they contain information and experiences that you want to take with you out of here. It is a nodule that you are trying to pull into yourself, make it part of your physics of self so you can heal what parts of it you're not at terms with.

So here is a nodule you are trying to hang onto and you are sitting here saying, "I hate this about myself, I want to get rid of this about myself." On a deeper cellular level this sets up a body issue because your mind is trying to kill something which at the same time you are trying to maintain as a portion of you. Or it could work the other way; you could be struggling to maintain something that you truly wish to release.

Let's say that one of your predecessors had murdered somebody. That's not necessarily something you want to go through. Let's say that you have a big issue with it, "I could never do that," you say. But this is in your DNA and your DNA says, "Yes you did, this is you, you did it." And you're sitting here saying, "I could never, I could never, I could never." This nodule contains all the understanding about how and why a person can be pushed to murder. In your nodule you are going to have all the understanding about the pain and struggle a person who murders goes through—everything you could ever want to know about something you don't wish to soil your hands with. This is valuable knowledge that if you don't have you will probably allow yourself to be pushed into doing, just because you won't know how to avoid being pushed to it. When you can just relax with your genetic past, come to terms and peace with it, that nodule will open up and give you all the information you need.

Now murder is not something that you consciously want to do. Even though you haven't done it in this body, murder is part of your DNA structure and your psyche knows that you did it. Your DNA doesn't know any difference between your body and an ancestor's. As long as in your being you deny that possibility, this is ultimate denial in the deepest sense of the body and a disconnection from the body which creates fear. This is why with everything, you have to get to a point of saying,"Okay, I could have done that. It doesn't matter how terrible, how horrendous it was, I could do it."

As long as you're in judgment over some of these lessons and experiences, those nodules in your DNA will control you . . .

This does not mean that you want to go out and do it, but you have to see it in an objective way without the judgment of it. If you have judgment over anything, you'll eventually kick out the nodule and have to live the experience yourself to understand it.

These experiences are all part of the personality, your personality. You have to have an openness, an ability to say, "My preference is not to murder because I love life. I love watching the fluid motion of the body. I love watching people enjoy life. I could never take a life, but maybe there is some part of me that could be pushed to it. I want to understand that part so that I never allow myself to be pushed. Then you would open up this nodule so that you would have the wisdom and the understanding to understand what could push a person to that action. Now with that understanding you'd never be able to murder because you would see the whole picture.

Judgment takes these nodules in your DNA that you have already lived in your ancestry and isolates them from you so that you'll have to live them yourself. And so, if you can be so open and objective, then you can release the pain. Once the nodule opens you can take the wisdom and the understanding, you can have the empathy, and you'll know that it is not something that you want to do simply because you love life too much. Additionally, you would be able to release the residue of all this understanding which is the emotional pain, the trauma, and the triggering devices that could push you into it. Otherwise, the murderer lies within everyone of you. Murder still has an emotional charge from your predecessors maintained in your DNA, and all you have to do is match the vibration in an emotion, trigger it, and you'll live it and do it. Everyone of you contains everything that has ever been.

In your DNA you've been and done everything. If you judge it, you'll be it again. This is another form of fear. On one level you know very well what's in there, and you're afraid you're going to become your DNA. This is why you are afraid of your angers. You're afraid that if you let the rage out, you might trigger some of this DNA stuff and turn into a monster. The monster lies within you because it is repressed within you, and this is where the fear comes from. It is an underlying guilt and turmoil. You're trying to repress your DNA so you don't have to live it.

Remember, your DNA ladder is a spiral, a cycle, and everything in that cycle will, in its turn, surface into the mitochondria. You might repress it this time, but up it comes again and again. One of these times you're going to have the intensities to act and no strength left to repress it. It pushes up into the mitochondria and you become it.

Anyone who ever murdered on this planet created it out of their DNA structure because their mind no longer had the strength to repress it. It could have been avoided if they had allowed themselves to come to terms with themselves. I'm not saying that you are all going to become murderers. What I am saying is that you all have the capability of being everything, including god. The same way you are pushing away the murderer, you are pushing away those nodules that are god too, because that's not part of your reality. Intellectually, you might accept that, so you keep the intellectual and philosophical nodules, but you are still repressing the ones that have the power in them. ▲

Inside, Outside: Feeling, the Difference

Part of your difficulty in physicality is that you want definitions. If you drop the need for definition and limitation, you can realize that anything that is inside is outside, and anything outside is inside—there is no demarcation. So if I'm talking about something that I'm feeling inside, I know that it is outside too—everything—and there is no demarcation. When you get past these artificial boundaries, then you can flow with the universe a whole lot faster and easier.

A lot of the problem with physicality that you all have is that you think you're self-contained—so it is either inside or outside. But it is all the same material. If you could look at the whole universe as only one substance: it is called life, it is called source, god, whatever. There is only one thing and everything is just derivations of it. If I push this nebulous substance in this direction, I end up with a body. If I push it in this direction, I end up with a planet. If I push it in this direction, I end up with something else. Move into the space, if you can, of seeing everything as the same stuff. There isn't any inside or outside, because space doesn't exist the same way you think it does either. All that you see is a hologram that is so real that it feels tangible, so we talk about and deal with the hologram. Even your cells are universes within universes. You can see them in microscopes and take it down to the first layer and keep going deeper.

Your nucleuses in your cells have nucleuses within them, and nucleuses within them, and nucleuses within them. They are very minute and very beautiful. We talk about and play with the first two nucleuses here. It is called your body. If you keep going in, if you put your arm under a microscope or x-ray or whatever you use, you will see the universes, you will see bone tissue. If you take the bone and focus on it, it will expand. Then you can use stronger magnification, and stronger, until, all of a sudden, there is nothing there—the arm just disappeared, even though the instrument you are looking through is right there on the surface. You have looked so far through it, that it appears in the microscope that there is nothing else there—it is just space.

This is what you all are, mostly a lot of space. Your bodies are created out of what we call the first two nucleuses and their interaction within the cellular structure. You have five generations of nucleuses within nucleuses. The body is built from the interaction of the first two, and this is your biological circuitry—it is the biological body. When you get down to the fifth generation nucleus, you are the universe; there is no demarcation. That is why you can say it is outside and inside too.

Once you have gone into that fifth nucleus, that fifth nucleus in this body is connected with every fifth nucleus in that body and every other body as well. They are all the same body at that point. It is just the way you configure them in the upper layers that makes it appear that you have individual bodies. That is why you can legitimately say it is all inside and also outside.

You get into a lot of trouble when you make your distinctions of inside and outside, and you sometimes aren't able to appreciate either. Rather than seeing everything from a dissected perspective, you want to live inside with the feeling tones and experience that inner universe, and then make those feelings objective. You have a brain and a mind—use them, but use them to your own advantage. Feel in here and then allow the brain to digest what you feel, so you can live within and objectively too.

Now the world is shifted to a totally objective perspective because for eons you were so subjective in your beings that nothing was rational in a working world. Nothing external to you would work, and you weren't progressing or evolving. If you could put them both together, you would have a very beautiful experience using the best of each. But you didn't get the two together very well. You went from a subjective universe to an objective one. You gave up or lost a lot of your ability to feel and became brain-oriented. It made the outside universe work for you but at a great cost to your inner one. When you stop feeling, you lose your connection to the inner universe, with yourself. An objective universe denies an inner one. Instead of feelings, you developed emotions—you get the two confused here. You ended up with emotions because you quit feeling. Of the million feelings of the inner universe you have compressed the data into six generic emotions: joy, depression, fear, anxiety, love and anger—and four of them are bad by your terminology.

You can get back into the inner universe and deeper generations of nucleuses without losing the outer one by getting back into feeling. When you go far enough into the feelings, then you can feel the tree and be the tree. You can feel the life in everything, and that is what all of you want now. A long time ago, because you lost your inner universe, you started wanting to get out of these bodies. So the quicker you could quit feeling, the sooner you could get out of them—because it kills them. And so when you reached a space of being real miserable here and wanting out, you shut your feelings right off.

You see, once you get past the image and emotional type of feeling, then you can feel the planet. You can feel the birds. You can become anything you want. You are actually feeling the life force. Feeling translates the life force into these bodies, it makes it usable. When you can feel that life force in everything, your body is going to get a charge from it—it gets more life. But if you are wanting off of the planet, that is the last thing you are going to want to do. ▲

Your nucleuses in your cells have nucleuses within them, and nucleuses within them, and nucleuses within them.

Body Guilt

Guilt is actually a vibrational spectrum. It is not just one feeling. Most of you have generically labeled all your feelings into half a dozen categories. Just as with your angers, most of you say, "Well, it's anger," and you generically label it, when much of the time your angers are other things besides what you think they are. Fear is the same way. Guilt is the same way.

Guilt is the one that hides from all of you. The other emotions will all create a vibration you can't avoid. Fear, you all recognize because you know when you're scared. Anger, you all know when you're angry because of the reactions. Guilt is the most subtle. In the long run, it is the most crippling. It is one that hides in every corner and under every bush. It is a sneaky one. It takes on all kinds of disguises, and it is the great phantom. It lurks in the dark, but it also lurks in the light, and it lurks in everything you do.

For the most part, you all live your lives in guilt and don't even recognize it. The only part of guilt that you recognize as guilt is the real strong intense one, when you know you did something wrong and you better go hide before somebody does something wrong back to you! If I asked you what your guilt feels like, most of you would say, "Well, its this real icky feeling and I know I should run and hide and I'm going to be punished for what I did."

Almost every action and reaction you have in your lives is called guilt. This is why most of you feel guilty for your very existence at a very deep level. Denial of anything is a guilt. Excuses are guilt. Judgments on anything are guilt. Justification on anything is guilt. You know when you all "should" on yourselves? "I should do this, I should do that." That's guilt, and it doesn't smell very good either!

How about living in the moment?

There is no guilt in living in the moment. Living in the moment is the only time you don't have it.

Denial, excuses, judgment, justification, shoulding on yourself, all of these things combined, make this underlying rigid adult which creeps its head through again and again and says, "We do this, we shouldn't do that, we have to do this."

When was the last time that one of you went into a real fancy nice restaurant and made a spectacle of yourself? If I say that for your homework tomorrow, I want you to go to the fanciest restaurant you can afford to go to—and it better be something besides the nearest hamburger hangout. I want you to make a living specta-cle of yourself there so that everybody in the place sees you. Feel how you react emotionally. How does the feeling feel?

Anything that tells you how you are supposed to be . . . is coming from this rigid adult created out of guilt.

You mean like dancing on the table?

Yes! How does it emotionally make you feel? How many of you are going to do it? Did you all notice how you shut down, real fast? That is the feeling called guilt, and most of you also felt the feeling that you call embarrassment. Embarrassment is a guilt. The shutting down you do is your reaction to guilt. When you put yourself in the situation and you started getting resistance, shutting down and say-ing, "Oh, I couldn't do that,"—that was your rigid adult. Your rigid adult was created out of guilt. If you were in a place of not being able to feel like you could do it, you have a rigid adult which is dictating your behavior.

All of these are guilts. Anything that tells you how you are supposed to be and what you are supposed to do is coming from this rigid adult created out of guilt. What were your reasons for not doing it besides that everybody would stare at you? I mean you could go to a restaurant where nobody knew you—really, you could. You could go to a restaurant where nobody knew you and you'd never have to see them again in your life. Are you going to go do it tomorrow?

You'd probably feel just as much guilt doing it even if you were un-known.

Right. But why?

The voice inside.

Um hum, and the voice inside is called guilt. Anything inside that prevents you from being spontaneous and living in the moment is guilt. That means your whole life from the time you wake up in the morning until the time you go to bed at night, is guilt-ridden.

Yeah, but if we took you seriously though, we'd be farting in class and just . . .

You already do this! (laughter) Okay, since you brought it up and I'm in a frivolous mode, let's say that we decided that we're going to sit here tonight, I will push the energy and give you all gas and we'll have a farting contest! Farting and belching. Okay? (laughter) You don't think I would do this? What are the first feelings when I say, "In the next five minutes we're going to start pushing that energy and it will be uncontrollable! You'll just have to belch and/or fart." What are the feelings that start rising?

I haven't actually decided if we're going to push this yet or not, but just check the feelings. The feeling of anxiety that arose in most of you tells you a story. Most of you would feel guilty for doing that. Wouldn't most of you feel a little slightly embarrassed, especially if we made sure they were the noisy kinds?

In this situation tonight, most of you are at ease with each other, so you could do it and you'd sit and laugh about it, but let's say that we make these conditions happen tomorrow when you're not expecting it, when you're in the middle of your business meeting. Don't sweat it too much because I haven't so-be'd this one yet! But let's say these conditions happen tomorrow when you're in the middle of a business meeting standing in front of the podium talking, or with an important client, or while you're interviewing for a job. (laughter) How do you feel?

With this discussion there is some frivolity, and there is a kind of a release or enjoyment, but there is an embarrassment, and an uncomfortableness with the topic. Most of you are laughing over your own embarrassment. How would you feel being in the situation? Many times your laughter is a defensive mechanism that covers up your embarrassments and thus your guilts. So that is why I said, guilt is one of these little critters that hide in all these facets and avenues of your lives. Why would all of you be embarrassed about your natural bodily reactions?

Because people make fun of it.

Okay. Social consciousness. When was the last time it happened to someone else in public and you really sat and had a belly laugh at the one who did it?

You don't laugh in front of them, you laugh later!

A lot of this is just an underlying embarrassment because you are all embarrassed. But what if your whole planet did it? What if your whole planet was back forty-thousand-years ago and you were all Neanderthals? Everybody belched and farted back then and it wasn't a big deal. Back then you didn't have issue with it. Back then, do you think anybody even paid attention if you belched or passed wind? A whole lot of your behavior is determined by the culture and the time—not yourselves. It only begins to be determined by yourselves because you react to what society dictates. Are there any of you that would honestly care if you belched or farted in public if you were not worried about trying to impress anyone? Could any of you honestly say that you wouldn't have an issue, or feel even the slightest embarrassment if you sat and did these things and you didn't care who knew?

The strongest taboos are with things that the body naturally does. This is called body guilt.

But see, this is a natural body function. This is something the body just naturally does. The strongest obsessions you have with anything on this planet or the strongest taboos are with things that the body naturally does. This is called body guilt.

There are two forms of guilt. Natural guilt, which is caused by being physical beings, just means that you're currently something different than what you really are. Natural guilt arose by changing from a spiritual entity into a physical density, which simply is a vibrational shift, that's all.

All unnatural guilt on this planet—which is everything any of you deal with—is body guilt. Not necessarily body issues because you don't like the body, but it is behavioral guilt which are caused by the body doing certain things and having body desires.

How do you relate bodies to failures?

Okay, let's say that you have guilt over failing. What would have failed? You. Why would you have failed? Because you didn't do what you should have done, or could have done. Why didn't you?

I don't know.

What was the failure? You can come up with all sorts of reasons. You can say that you failed because you weren't smart enough. You could say you failed because you didn't act right or make the proper behaviors. Behaviors are the body. They are a psychological and biological combination. You're still judging the body.

The entity that is you, can do no wrong. The entity that is you cannot fail. So therefore, if you've judged yourself a failure, what you're judging as a failure is you, the physiological and biological body. If you follow your guilt through, they will take you back to a body issue, every time. Those will always evolve around image—society's image. If you had performed in a certain manner, you would have been a success. That is performance. Performance is body or biology. Everything you do, you blame the body for. Most of you in your lives are waiting until the body is right to be happy. "When the body looks a certain way, then I'll be happy." "When the body reaches a certain amount of health, then I'll be happy." "When it can do certain things, I'll be happy." So the body gets the brunt of all the guilt on your planet. All guilts are out of the body.

Does it kill the body?

It kills the body. Did you find that when we were being frivolous a minute ago, and we were playing with some of these ideas and while you were laughing and joking, that part of your body was really uptight that we might do this to you? Yes, you could live through it and it would be fun, but what if we just singled you out? What if I put it this way—I'm going to single one of you out, whoever has the biggest issue with it. Sometime in the next ten minutes, one of you is going to get a major case of uncontrollable gas, but we don't know who it is or when its going to happen! This is just for an emotional reaction—I promise I haven't put this into motion—yet!

Be aware of the body. Is the body reacting to this with anxiety a little bit? It might be low-level, but you're going to get singled out and then everybody else is going to take their laughter and direct it at you. Put yourself in the place as if you were chosen.

What happens to the body? Is it tightening up? Is it saying, "Well, I think I have to leave now." "Okay, I have to hurry and get rid of my issues so I don't get selected?" Does it say, "Well, if I have to put up with it, I'll put up with it. No big deal. I'll try to be brave?"

Notice the body. It is subtle. This is what I want you to notice. The feeling in the body. The body is still slightly apprehensive underneath there at being picked on and having everything directed at you. This is body guilt. If you notice the same feeling and take the edge off it a little bit, so that you're not the one being picked on yet, notice that it is the same feeling your bodies run around on almost all day long. The only thing is, we've just heightened it by putting it into an emotional reaction. Guilt and worry are the same things.

Is fear guilt? And what about vulnerability?

If you go into the gentle space with the vulnerability and allow yourself just to be in an open space with it, then that is a god space. In the larger spectrum of things outside of physicality, there are just feeling spaces. So if you could get into the vulnerability where you're just open, but you're not afraid of being hurt, then that is a tender, gentle space. If you're in a place of being vulnerable and you're right on the edge and you know you're going to get hurt, you know that the next person walking around the corner is going to smack you, or if you open that heart just a little bit more, you're going to get it hurt, that is coming out of fear. That is coming out of guilt.

Emotion is repressed feeling. Guilt comes from repressing who and what you are, which is joy.

The only feeling you have here, quite truthfully, is joy, because from a feeling standpoint your universe was created out of joy. The only emotion you have here is guilt and its derivations. The only feeling there is, is joy, which means the only thing you can really feel is joy. Guilt is the unnatural or the resistance to the feeling, which causes an emotion. Emotions are created when you do not allow the feeling to complete itself— *then* you have emotion. Emotion is repressed feeling. Guilt comes from repressing who and what you are, which is joy. Anger, anxiety, everything else you can come up with is a form of guilt, and the only feeling that exists in this reality is joy from whatever intensities you can live. So you have two choices. See that's real easy. All of you say that life is so complex here. You either feel joy or you feel guilt. If you're not being yourself, you are in guilt.

I walk into a grocery store and I'm hungry for an apple and I don't have any money, I just eat it, because not to do so would be repressing myself because that apple is joy.

Okay, the apple is joy and if you're in the state where you have to go into the store to swipe it, you're already repressed!

You got me on that one!

The universe is abundant. If you're in lack in any way, shape, or form, you are in guilt. You have two laws. The law of abundance and the law of lack. The law of abundance is called joy. The law of lack is called guilt. See, everything is very simple!

Okay, if you were in your own vehicle here, your own body, and I take you down to a fine restaurant, are you going to make any allowances for the social mores of our society? Will you fart and belch at dinner and tell good jokes in a very boisterous manner?

I would say that it would depend. If I was in my personality that was boisterous, I would be myself. For the most part, being myself doesn't necessarily mean I'm going to infringe upon anybody else. It means I can live my reality and I can live it so fully that I can sit and I could belch and I could fart and I could get drunk and be very boisterous if I wanted to be, and if I was in a place of being unconditional with myself, I would also not infringe on anybody else. So I could be as boisterous as I wanted to and if they didn't want to hear me, they wouldn't even know I was there. You only draw attention to yourself for your behavior when you are seeking external validation from others. If I were not seeking external validation, I could be as loud as I wanted and no one would even know I was there.

When you go to restaurants, all of you have been in the situation where half the time you don't even hear the people at the table next to you sitting and chattering away, but all of a sudden you'll hear somebody five tables down whispering and you'll hone in and listen to their conversation. The people can be sitting right next to you, just mouthing all over the place and you are oblivious to them because that is their space and they're not infringing on you. They're being themselves. Those individuals down there are conversing and they either want everybody to hear them, or they are afraid that somebody is going to hear them, so they project it and all of a sudden, you have them on your eardrum. You've all had that experience. The only thing is, if you sit and feel guilty for being yourself, then everybody in the place will know you. If you were into your natural state and your natural being and you went tomorrow to the fanciest of restaurants and it pleased you to sit and dance on the tables and jump around on them and just really goof off and just be a very major distraction, if you were totally guilt-free within your being, and you were doing it not to show and prove a point, but because it is what gave you fun and you wanted to hang from the chandeliers because you thought that could be a thrill, nobody in the place would even know you did it. They would be totally oblivious to it. I'm serious—you could go to your hamburger hangout and you could dance on the tables and everybody would be oblivious to you unless you step on their French fries.

All of you have been sitting in your own space in a restaurant, a movie, or anything else, and you've been so engrossed in what you were doing you didn't even know there was a ruckus going on right behind you until the ruckus fell on top of your lap. It is the same thing. You create your reality so intimately, that you can create whatever reality you want. The only reason you don't is called guilt. The only reason you all die is called guilt. You don't want to feel bad because you don't die and everybody else does!

Do we bring some of the guilt with us?

Guilt is the biggest gooey, stick'em that you'll find. Guilt is the only thing that even makes you come back more than once. If you didn't have guilt, you wouldn't have more than the lifetime that you are living. So what you call the reincarnational past, if that is the idea, it is from guilt.

Didn't you say we feel guilty for being alive? If so then why would we reincarnate?

Because you felt so guilty. Guilt is the imprisonment. When you get something sticky on your hand and you wipe it off with the clean one and it just sticks to that one too. That's guilt. It is actually this tarry substance that is sticking you to the stick'em of the physical plane. It is much like having your feet in a tar pit and you're trying to keep walking. It doesn't work. You'll get stuck in the tar pit and get pulled back down. That is what guilt and physicality do together. You feel guilty over being physical or over anything you did in physicality. Most of you run your lives twenty-four hours a day in guilt. You become so afraid that your bodies are going to fall apart on you that you use all this tar to hold them together called guilt, instead of natural love.

Guilt just pulls you back again and again because you think, "I'm going to do this right. I'm going to get it." and you try again, and again, and again. Guilt causes you to be physically based. Guilt is a product of physicality. It is not a product anywhere else. Therefore, if you leave physicality feeling guilty, your vibrational spectrum will magnetize you right back here. It's the largest entrainment of all.

If you leave physicality feeling guilty, your vibrational spectrum will magnetize you right back here. It's the largest entrainment of all.

JOYRIDING THE UNIVERSE, VOLUME ONE

Guilt is sticky. What are the properties of natural love?

Natural love is so unconditional you don't know it exists. It is the raw material. You're afraid that if you let go of the sticky stuff, you might fall apart because you can't feel the other stuff, called love. All of you take the joy and filter the joy through the sticky stuff. That is why many times your joys are short-lived. Guilt and joy are opposite ends of the spectrum. One is movement, the other is stagnation. Joy is movement. Guilt is stagnation. Joy is like moving an open hand easily through the air. Open the hand and try to hold it open and try closing it at the same time, this is how guilt feels. Guilt is stagnation. It doesn't work and its painful.

Recollect the last time you thought you were being yourself. Go back in your own mind and into your own feelings to the last time you were doing something that was just for you. Recollect the feelings that were with it. Did you ever once say, "I should do this, or I shouldn't do that?" If so, then you didn't do it for yourself. You did it out of guilt to prove a point.

From that framework, I can't think of one experience in this life that I haven't done out of guilt.

Exactly.

Can you explain the connection between worry and guilt?

Get into your worry. Let's take the worry about paying your bills. What is it that you're really worried about, besides not paying them? Why are you afraid of not paying them? And don't take this out of context—I'm not telling anyone to not pay their bills!

I pay them so I won't feel guilty for not doing so. I don't like the complications.

Worry is all guilt. It is guilt over the fact that you're afraid you're not going to provide for yourself with ease.

What then is the easiest way to cut worry and guilt?

Get rid of the audience in your own mind. In your mind take yourself to a place of isolation in the universe. Take yourself into your void. Take yourself into whatever works for you where there is just you and where nobody is paying any attention to you. When you are in that state, feel your levels of repression in your body. This will tell you where your guilts are. Go in and cut them. What this will do is show you dramatically as day and night what you're doing. Then once you've cut the repression and guilt you will feel so released that you could just dance in the stars and play with a sense of freedom.

Put yourself into that place where it is just you, where you don't have to answer to anybody and you don't have to ask their permission. You don't have any responsibility to anyone else. Where you have a total sense of freedom from guilt, no one to ask advice from. From this state—where your decision is totally your decision and your decision alone—then take your confusion, what you think you're confused about, take it and feel what you would do when there is nobody telling you what you have to do. Then you will have your answer every single time if you will be honest with yourself. This is the simplest and easiest way to get your own clear guidance and answers. The only reason that you don't get the clear guidance and answers coming in all the time now is because the guilt prevents it from getting through. The heart says, "Do this," the brain says, "No, do that." They fight.

The only reason that you don't get the clear guidance . . .is because the guilt prevents it from getting through.

Put it into a place that you're not performing for anybody, you don't have to do anything for anybody. Let yourself move first—before you make your decision—into a state of total freedom, where you are making the choice for you. I promise when you do it, and you do it from your heart, you will not be infringing upon anybody. Most of you say, "Well, I can't do this because I will hurt this person, or I'll cause problems here." That's where a lot of your guilts come from. You are assuming that you're a god over them. Any time you take responsibility for somebody else, that means you see them as less than yourself. It means you see them as being less of an entity and less capable of making decisions than you are. It means that every time you see them as being victimized by you, that you consider yourself to be superior to them. It is a judgment.

What if you need somebody else to cooperate?

I would say that you always put it into a place that there are no faces attached to anything. "In my heart this is what I want, this is what I feel, and I ask my universe to orchestrate it for my creation." If you put a person's face upon it, then you're going to infringe upon their free will if they don't want to do it.

It's not necessarily that you want a certain person to participate. You want a certain event. All you do is you feel it. "This is how I feel and in my state of freedom, this is the feeling and what I want." Let your universe create it for you and you will never infringe on anybody, ever. Understand most of you consider that if somebody is hurt by something you do, they are a victim and you victimized them. How many of you learned beautiful lessons by people who did things to you? How many of you learned lessons from things that were painful? Take whatever you find to be your most beautiful lesson that you learned and if there is a little bit of pain or aggravation around it, would you still go through it to gain that lesson?

What you're doing by assuming that, "I'm going to hurt this person and this person and this person if I try to live my life," is you're assuming you know what is better for them than they do. The thing is, they create their reality as intimately as you do and if they don't want to be part of yours, they just won't be—as long as you don't try to force anybody into being your reality.

I would like to know how to be myself and then allow the universe to create that.

I would say first of all go off the base assumption that none of you do know how to be yourselves—and you're all doing well with it, so don't take that as a criticism. Just take it as a state of mind that says, "I don't know how to be myself if I'm having to make my decisions here and now."

First put yourself into the place where you're not performing for anybody, anything. Many of you will find that when you're in that state, what you think you want, changes. Many of you think you know what you want because what you want fits an image in society and what people want you to do. When you can get yourself to the point of feeling yourself—even in your own minds—totally free, so that you do not have to answer to anybody, and you can get it to a point where you can feel it so intensely that it becomes beauty—this will be the most valuable lesson any of you can ever learn.

From that state, you'll learn to walk in it, twenty-four hours a day. So first, we go off the base assumption that nobody knows how to be themselves naturally, because you're all running off of guilt. Next, we go into the state of allowing yourself to feel the freedom of totally being you without having to answer to anybody for your life or anything you're doing. At that point in time, feel what it is you really want. And as I said, many of you will find that what you thought you were putting all this energy into trying to create, changes and you realize that, its no wonder it didn't manifest, you didn't want it anyway! Many of you will have a lot of those. You will find many times what you want is a way of feeling, not necessarily a thing.

Say to your universe, "I would love to have this feeling, so that is what I'm going after and I want my universe to help bring that to me on a full-time basis. If where I'm at will help provide it, great. If not, then I ask my universe to bring it from wherever it can find it." When you manifest, do it without an image. In relationships, just for an example, many times one will say "This person made me feel like this, so I want this person to be in my life." You're going to infringe on their free will if they don't want to be part of your life and you try to force the issue.

If you're into an unconditional space of love, you can let this person be whatever they want to be. You can let them love. You can let them go on. Most of you are after the feelings anyway. Say to your universe, "This is the feeling I get when I'm in this situation, and I love it, but I want this changed, I want this altered, I'd like more of this and less of that,"—but don't put a face on it. Then what you do is you say, "If I were going to order my life custom made, this is how I would have it be." Don't put a face on it, and then let yourself feel what it is you truly desire. It will be a way you feel and then you ask your universe to bring it equal to or greater than your own feeling or comprehension of it. Then you let it go.

Many of you think you know what you want because what you want fits an image in society . . .

If you take your desire and put a picture on it, saying, "I'm expecting you to do this and I want you to change this way, and I want you to be different in this way,"—that's an imposition. That is imposing your will on them. If you release your desire and that individual wants to be part of it, then they will be just like anybody that is applying for a job. Then if they want to be part of your life, they will be stating "Okay, I can meet that one. Yes, I don't have difficulty with that. Okay, yes I would love to apply for what you're asking," then they will become part of your reality.

But if the individual says, "Forget that one. No way. I'm not changing that. No, I'm not doing this," then at that point in time, they will have to make a decision of saying, "Yes, or no" as to whether they intend to be part of your universe and reality. The minute you put this out to your universe and the reply comes back "No. I love you, but I can't accept your requirements," your circuit is released and the universe will search to bring what will fulfill your needs and requirements. That is how you do it unconditionally, without images or pictures.

My family had a reunion, but my preference was to do other things and that's what I did. However, on a psychic level I've been getting a lot of

flack from a couple of people because of my choice and I know I've probably been creating a lot of my own guilt because I didn't do what I "should" have done by going and spending time with my family, but that wasn't my preference.

Okay, it wasn't your preference, but you still feel guilty for having preference. Part of getting out of the guilt is getting to a point where you are not embarrassed to have a preference. It is all right to have preference.

If you check it out, there were things that you wanted to do and things you didn't. The family had expectations which said, you were expected at this event. So in your being, you said, "Okay. I can accept this. I can accept that. I don't accept this. I don't accept that. I don't accept this other thing. I am weighted heavier in what I don't accept than what I do accept and this is called preference."

You all make your preference out of what you will or will not accept. A lot of times you have the biggest guilt where the choices are the most closely balanced between what you do and don't want. So let's say you had three out of seven that said, "This would be fun," and four that said, "No, I don't want to." That puts it into a place of almost a confusion trying to make a decision. Then the family is having their own expectations trying to coerce you, and because there were things that would have been your preferences, you're automatically tied in. Then you feel guilty for not participating with the whole thing. You were willing to accept part, but not all, so they play on what you will accept.

Let's get back to the farts!

Okay. Your heart actually likes those! Did you know that? It moves the gas away from it so it has less pressure.

Well, if my heart likes farts so well, why does my nose have issue with it? Are we getting back into guilt now?

No, it could be preference and maybe your nose wouldn't have issue with it every time!

Do I have an option of changing the way it smells?

Um hum . . . all you have to do is eat something different! See there are always options in everything. The universe will always do it for you better than you would do it for yourselves because you see it from a limited perspective. You see your options as cut and dried. The universe says for everyone of your cut and dried, there are at least a million options.

I love you. I'm going to go ahead and vacate. Be at peace. Thank you, I had fun! ▲

Loving
the Body

In the natural spectrum of the universal principle, the stuff that you're calling love is the raw material from which all things are created, no matter what they be. It is a thought-based, organized, self-existent, substance. It has the ability to be thought. It has the ability to be anything that it wants to be. It is not bound by anything. Therefore all things can be created from it.

In the natural state, love is a substance if you want to call it that. Therefore, what you call loving is a movement of the substance or the allowing of its flow from one direction to another for its collection. For the most part, the biggest problem anyone here has with understanding love, is an understanding of the basic premise of what love is to begin with.

For the most part, you've been subjected to a whole lot of romantic ideas about love. You believe love should feel a certain way, and should make you have a giggly, bubbly feeling. It is the knight on a white horse. It is all these romantic ideas, and, of course, it should be perfection. Most of you consider that when you are in love it is with a relationship, and all we're talking about is the relationship you have with your body. If you are looking for the ideal relationship with another individual, your ideal would be that it would be a state of perfection. Since that is your romantic ideal, it is very difficult to love the body when you see so much imperfection in it. In your romantic ideal, the connotation around love is perfection, something in which there are no issues, problems, or difficulties of any kind.

Part of your mind might hang onto an idea of wanting a romantic fantasy for a relationship, but by now most of you know that all relationships take work. All relationships have their ups and downs. All relationships, no matter how grand they are, there is always room for improvement, even if they are perfect.

Your relationship with the body is just a similar relationship. But since you have all these connotations about love, when somebody starts saying, "Love yourself," "Love your body," immediately the brain says, "I'm an imperfect creature. I can't. I'm incapable of it," because love in the romantic ideal is perfection.

When you were growing up, you were looking for this romantic ideal of a romance or something out of this world, even by the world's standards. This doesn't really exist too often. You have to create it. Now you are realizing that true love is a whole different subject than what the mind thought it was when you were a teenager.

The same thing now applies to you and your body. People are starting to tell you to love yourself. They're telling you to love all that you are. In the back of your mind, love must be perfection, and you know your body is imperfect. So the brain says, "I can't love it because I have to change it. I have to fix it. I have to repair it. It isn't perfect."

Pure love of the universal kind and caliber is unconditional. It means that it doesn't even design itself.

Many of you have found that you were attracted into a friendship, or a relationship where somebody didn't match your ideal. You eventually found out that there was more love there than what the romantic ideal held in it. You've had relationships with spouses or friends; they have had their ups and downs, but after a period of time, that beautiful state of comfortableness—if you weren't taking each other for granted—that beautiful state of comfortableness allowed for a very deep sharing and love to enter.

Most of you are uncomfortable with your bodies if you were actually honest about it. Yet, what you're looking for in a relationship with another individual is somebody you can totally be yourself with, totally comfortable with, and one in which you can let down your inhibitions and don't have to pretend to be anything with. But most of you in your own bodies are pretenders. Most of you are uncomfortable in your bodies. You don't like the way they feel. You don't like the way they look. You don't like the pain in them. You don't like all these little imperfections. But loving the body is simply being unconditional with it.

Pure love of the universal kind and caliber is unconditional. It means that it doesn't even design itself. It is a raw source that just molds itself and grows more of what it is. It doesn't even organize itself because organization of itself creates conditions. In your beings, unconditional love is so unconditional that it is like putting your hand through the air. This air is as much love as anything the heart ever felt—the same stuff, different perception.

But the mind categorizes one as love and the other isn't. You have to get rid of the categories first off.

The next thing we have to do is understand that the body is already made out of the love stuff anyway, so therefore you can't really love it! All you can do is let it be itself. If you were letting the body be what it was and its own expression, it would be a pure expression of love because that is what it was created out of.

You are in various stages of being comfortable with your bodies. Sometimes you're comfortable for a couple of hours or a few weeks, months, years of your life; and the rest of the time, the body just doesn't fit right. Reason being is that in the larger sense of it, you are a non-physical entity trying to express in a biological vehicle. It is much the same as wearing gloves. If you were to put very thick gloves on your hands all the time and wear them, you'd get used to it but you'd never quite touch things the same way as if your hands were ungloved.

Right now in your evolution, the body is to your spirit the same as putting gloves upon your hands. The body is a glove, so to speak, or an instrument that doesn't let the spirit that is you running around inside of it quite touch everything in the same way as the spirit could. It creates a different way of touching things.

And so you are at odds with the body. You're an entity wanting more out of the body than what the body can do sometimes, because you are judging it by everybody else's standards. You're wanting the body to produce more, do better, look better, look different, act different, and feel different.

Becoming physical is the very first diseasement a spirit created. Diseasement or sickness is simply a place that it is out of balance. You are a spiritual entity. Therefore, coming into physicality was your very first diseasement because you changed the ease of being spirit into trying to be body and spirit. So the very first place to begin to heal any diseasement in these bodies is the diseasement about being in the body to begin with.

When this original diseasement can be relaxed, remedied and healed, your life will flow. The love moves into the body, and the body can express exactly how it is. The first difficulty with the body is that you're spiritual entities, and you are always wanting out of them. If you're honest within your beings, there are parts of physicality that you like, and parts you don't like, but there's a part within everyone of you that is *always* wanting out.

There is a part deep in there that always wants to go home, to somewhere out there. There's a part in there that says, "That world out there is going to be a hundred times better than this world,"—and all of your fantasies and your stories about it are better. You do fear death because you love the body, it is a treasure. But so much is told to you that on the other side it is a whole lot better. In some ways it is. In other ways, it is not. If you don't learn how to have joy and love life here, it is going to be fun for a time on the other side, but after the initial release, your emotional attitude sets you right back in, and you'll feel as miserable on that side as you did here. It's not a matter of whether you're physical or not, it is how much you love what you are inside that matters.

These bodies are the gifts of gods. Each of these bodies contain in them the ability to make numerous universes. It is one of those things that we'll say a million times in our journey on this planet and probably a handful will have the experience of grasping what I'm stating. Your bodies are an archive. A culmination of every universe that has ever been in existence since what you could term your primal beginning—exists in your body. This is the only place in the universe that such a treasure exists in one package, and it is called a body.

These bodies are the gifts of gods. Each of these bodies contain in them the ability to make numerous universes.

What each of you are walking around in, living in, playing in, is the resources of every universe ever thought into existence, and every universe that ever lived in any way, shape or form. Every potential universe lies within the cellular mass you call your body. It was necessary because these bodies were created as vehicles for gods to live in. What god would put himself in a prison? If you took your idea of what you consider a god and ask, "Would that god degrade himself and put himself into a prison?" No. But if that god was going on vacation, or going to go travel or play somewhere, he would take an entourage of everything he could possibly pack to take with him. That's what you did in these bodies.

These bodies were created to be the vessels for gods to live in. You had a source that loved you so much that it wanted companionship, and the only way to find equal companionship was for it to create out of itself. The only way to do this was to take portions of itself and put them into a vehicle or a containment device to allow them to learn to love themselves. But if that one god went into multiple faces and multiple bodies, it didn't want to be trapped without the whole body of knowledge it had ever had. Therefore, in every single vehicle was embodied the knowledge of every universe that exists. Your body is one of these libraries or archives.

Your bodies, these things that you are disgusted with and mad at all the time, are a combination of every single universe that has ever come and gone! Every single universe and every single universal thought is contained within the cellular mass called these bodies that you take for granted, get mad at, want to get rid of, and that you don't like! These bodies weren't created for a prison. They were created as a way of connecting with all that resource of everything that has ever existed, so that the god that you were might be able to take that, create a new synergy, and creatively design something new out of all its knowledge.

These bodies, for eons on this planet have been abused. They have been taken for granted. They have been hated, cursed, considered to be the worst problem that ever happened to anybody. Yet, they are a treasure, and it is time to get back into to finding the treasure in them. They were loved into existence just as you, the spiritual entities, were loved into existence, but you are alien to each other. And so because you are alien to each other, you create friction.

The only diseasement anybody has is the original diseasement called movement of spirit into flesh, and it isn't a diseasement such as in something being sick or wrong. It means that the spirit that was you, that entity that was you changed its vibration so that it could enter into an embodiment to experience the embodiment. But when it changed its vibration, then that is the first time it became out of balance. That was the only time it was out of ease. Every other diseasement created in the body stems from that one original dis-ease-ment, meaning you don't like the body. When the entity that is you and the personality can come to terms with this body and say, "Okay, maybe it doesn't look right by society's standards, maybe it doesn't work right by society's standards, maybe I can't climb Mount Everest, maybe I can't do some things, but it is perfect in its own state of being." When you can get to this state is when you're going to truly learn what love is.

Because everything is love stuff, your body was created not to love and not to be loved, it was created out of love. Which means that each of you, quite technically are incapable of loving and you're incapable of being loved, because love in its natural form is a flow. The body, which is your vessel that you're using for this expression was created so you could collect it, so you could express it, and feel and know what the love stuff or the raw material you were created out of was.

The raw material or love stuff was so unconditional that you could feel it no better than you feel the air in this room. You can move your hand against it and you make a breeze so you know something exists. That is all you did with the original raw material you're made out of. You knew it existed, but what was it? And so the only way you could find out what it was, was to create something that could catch it, something that could reach out here and collect it and catch it just like a balloon.

Take a balloon and blow into it. You can see that it is containing something that is different than the outside, but still it is the same. You made a containment. Manifested vehicles called bodies were a containment so you could see the stuff. What is the difference between what is inside the balloon and what it outside the balloon once you've blown it up? Not much. Maybe what is inside the balloon has more CO_2 than the outside, because it is from your breath. That is the only difference. But you wouldn't say that one has more air than the other. They are both air, both space, and gaseous mass.

The raw material or love stuff was so unconditional that you could feel it no better than you feel the air in this room.

Your body is the same way. Your body was designed to collect the stuff so that in the collection of it, you could see it, feel it, taste it, touch it, be it, and let it be you. That is how they were designed. Right now, you are incapable of loving. Loving means you're making more of the raw stuff. If you have a personality and you start making the raw stuff, its going to be conditional because you made it. If you are in an unconditional space, and creating unconditional love, or more raw stuff, your personality steps back and ceases to exist at that point or else you would be putting conditions on it.

The entity that is you is using the body to collect love stuff or the raw material so it can understand it and know what it is. Your body is a collection of this stuff. It isn't generating it. When you feel love in your beings, for other people or even yourself, you're actually not creating love that you're sending out and you're not really creating a place inside where you're pulling the love in. What you are actually doing is chemically triggering the brain to get the junk out of the way so you can feel what is collected and gathered. Your whole entire journey in life and love and expression was to see how much of this love stuff you could collect so that you could take it and put your own mark upon it. This enabled you to be a creator. You could be anything you wanted to be—an unlimited god. That is the ability these bodies were given. They were given a whole body of knowledge of everything that had ever been into existence. All you had to do was learn how to chemically trigger them in the body, open them up, pull more of the raw stuff in and into your own design, you could have anything you wanted—anything. You used it so well that you thought yourselves into oblivion with it!

When you were first given this and the ability to use it, you actually thought yourselves even into what you call death. Death in its origins doesn't exist in the body. Death came into being when you started wanting a different body from the one you had.

The source could only see itself as one identity with multiple faces. It had a craving for companionship, so much that it wanted other creators. It wanted co-creators, companions. In its desire to do that, the only thing that would be equal to it, was itself. In order to do that, and to create out of itself, it had to see part of itself as being different than it. So it almost had to split itself in two in order to create all of you and to love you into existence. In doing that, it experienced the first kind of rejection complex that all of you have been dealing with ever since. It is this state of "I want to be different than." This tendency came from your source, so you can blame it on him, her, it, whatever you choose to call it!

It wanted a piece of itself to be different than itself so it could communicate and connect with it, talk with it, and have companionship with it. So the very first thing that most of you were created with when you came into physicality, was a need to be different because that tendency came from your source. Your need to be different came from your source, and the deep need to share came from your source. Those are your original primal feelings and emotions. The original individuals on your planet were given the ability to tap these bodies of knowledge that each of you live in. Their brains chemically triggered them, worked in them, loved in them; they could do anything they wanted and their bodies lived forever. They didn't die. They didn't need to.

What happened though is that with this deep need and craving to be different, you started reconfiguring your brains. When you did this, you taught them to chemically restructure in such a way that they would not open you up to your bodies of knowledge.

Originally, you were all replicas or clones of each other. Most systems of reality do not individuate bodies. In other words, there are only three systems that are known in this quadrant of your universe which have individual looking bodies, because it creates a lot of problems to have individual looking bodies. In most systems of reality which have manifested embodiments, every embodiment looks the same. If they all look the same, you don't have people wanting different models, you don't have people wanting different styles, different types, and different appearances. When you started shifting your brains, the body started shifting, and you started coming out with different appearances.

Because you had the ability to manifest anything you wanted, the first thing you manifested was a closed brain so other people couldn't participate in your thought process, so you could be an individual. The second thing you did as manifesting gods was to start coveting everybody else's body. Here came someone with a new model because they shifted their brain in such a pattern that all of a sudden they had a tall model. You were short and now you wanted a tall one. The tall ones wanted to be short. The ones with big noses, wanted little noses. The ones with black hair wanted blonde hair. The little ones wanted to be big! The big ones wanted to be little and you started actually causing death to the bodies because you didn't like the one you were in. Since you didn't like the one you were in and wanted a different model, you, as the living gods that you were, created death to your own environment called the body. You did that by not wanting it.

Originally, you were all replicas or clones of each other. Most systems of reality do not individuate bodies.

With each of you, you're going to have to get back into a place of loving the body so effectively, that it and you are the same entity. These bodies have had ancestry lines and progenitors, and most of you would be scared if you knew how many of your progenitors hated their bodies. If they were female, they wished they were male. If they were male, they thought that the females had an easier time. You had ones that wanted to be more beautiful, less beautiful, and they kept creating this. What you have as genetic memory is a whole lot of your ancestors with a death wish. The genetic memory says, "I don't like who and what I am." Now, the most solid genetic memory you have is how to die.

So here you come along and you're working very grandly at getting yourself into a place of just loving who you are and being accepting of it. "Maybe I'm not totally like I want to be. Maybe I'm not totally like the world says I should be, but I'm all right with myself." You travel along and you have a day when you get into social image or social consciousness and you feel like you lost it and then you get into judgment and you finally pull yourself back out. You can come to a place of seeing the perfection—and this takes a deeper state than any of you have yet touched—because there is a state within your being of this perfection of you, the living body. When you can touch that state of perfection of you, the living body and you, the entity in there, make a shift. It will be the first time that you, the spirit you, and you, the biological you, will come together.

Right now, its almost as if you're using the body like a glove, and it numbs your senses. It is because you are still seeing yourself separately from it. If you can get to a state of this perfection of the entity that is you inside it, at that point, this very beautiful, subtle shift happens and the body inhibitions leave. We don't mean that the body is going to start being promiscuous and all this. Everyone of you sitting here have body inhibitions that have nothing to do with morals. The body has its own set of requirements of where it will let you move and where it won't. The body has its own inhibitions or its own limitations that says, "We can do this, but we can't do that." Everyone of you do. When you can get to the state of perfection—and the first few times is just going to be glimpses—those glimpses will be such food to you, you will pursue them the rest of your life.

Your bodies are scared of moving. They are quite literally scared of even being alive inside their beings. When you can touch that state of perfection, the first few times it will only be a split second and a glimpse. In that moment every rigidness the body has will leave. Every physical inhibition the body has will leave and the body will have a strength that most of you have never known in the body. You never knew the body was capable of feeling that alive, that strong, that straight, that uninhibited in its movement and in its being. Those few moments will be fleeting because there is still part of the brain that says, "No. Here is the way things are. You're supposed to be like this."

When you can get a few of those moments of perfection, you'll know what I'm talking about. That is the only time you are truly one-hundred percent in love and loving the body. That moment is called seeing the body in the state of perfection, the perfect body. And it is not an image. You might use an image to get there, but it is a feeling tone. It had nothing to do with your exercise, your diet, anything. In that split second, you backed off, you got off your own case, and you just let the body be, and it will be a very beautiful experience. When you can strengthen these and keep continuing them, you'll move into a place that after that, you'll find a strength that nothing can topple. That is actually what most of you are looking for in your life and it is called love. Love is a state of being. It is a space where no one can topple you, where you are the universe embodied.

We're going to shift. Thank you. (At this point, Philip leaves and Arvana, a female Self, guides the audience into an embracement of the perfection of their bodies.)

Within your beings, there lies a deep point, and that is the point of surrender. That is where we are going to journey. Allow yourself into the internal part of your being and your heart, allow yourself to feel very beautifully gentle, very beautifully tender with yourself. Our aim is to create a place of softness where you can feel internally soft. Allow yourself to feel all the rigid inhibitions of the body. Allow yourself to feel what resists becoming gentle, becoming tender, becoming soft. What we're trying to create is not a thought. It is a feeling. It is a space. Allow yourself to feel a very beauteous gentle space, a place that you feel special. Allow yourself within the depth of your being not to put you on a pedestal, but to feel special. It is a feeling. You can generate it.

> *Love is a state of being. It is a space where no one can topple you, where you are the universe embodied.*

Allow yourself to feel just a sense of inner special—it has nothing to do with the images, nothing to do with anything you have ever been or done. It is a feeling. It is a state of being. This space should feel gentle, tender, soft and special. Let yourself within your being feel how uniquely special you are. Notice all of the resistance to it. Notice every place where the specialness does not feel. Notice every issue or emotion it brings up and just stick them aside.

Within your being there is a rigid shell. Allow yourself to pick up this rigid shell and remove it. Put it outside of your being. There is a harsh encasing within the being. Let it go. There is a state of defensiveness where all the walls and the defensiveness arise. Let the defensiveness go. Release it. Let yourself within your being feel legitimately special, beautifully special, gentle.

Let yourself within your being feel how soft your emotions and attitudes can be with you. Let yourself just feel a beautiful soft state with you where you are not pressuring yourself, where the mind is relaxed and the brain is not contradicting you. Let yourself find this beautiful space and surrender into it. What you're surrendering is the defensiveness against life. It is your fear of being inferior. Step aside the fear. Every fear that there is something wrong with you, every anxiety about having done anything wrong, every resistance to just totally being loved, remove it. Be willing to let them go. Be willing to step outside the resistance. This defensiveness is a place where you're not willing to be loved. It creates a rigidness that creates what most of you call the state of being the adult. Let it go.

Inside that being there is a place that is so special, so tender, so beautifully you, that you can dance. I want you to go to the place within your being that you can dance with life. Feel it. See within you any resistance to just feeling yourself dance within your own being. This is the shell that you want to remove and rid yourself of. Allow yourself to dance with life. Feel the life in your own being. Dance with it. There is a place that is soft and you can dance and as you dance, dance in the life that is called you. Find a point in there that you can begin to dance in unison with the body, that you no longer see the body as your enemy, that you see the body as your expression, that you remove your angers, your hatreds and you just feel its own perfect love. You feel its perfection. You feel its state of movement and the harmony of the unison with you.

The brain will come to try to tell you what is wrong with you and so will the world. But feel what is really right about you. It is called love. It is called the life. It is called a very important piece of *all that is*. You were created special. You are a most beauteous entity. You were created out of the most magnificent love that exists. Allow yourself to feel your uniqueness. It won't be an ego. It will be a gentleness. Your uniqueness is a gentleness. Not a specialness that the ego needs to be superior over others, but it is a uniqueness, softness, a gentleness. That is you. That is how you feel.

If you have vulnerability, defensiveness, or fear arising because it is afraid it is going to be hurt, then address it. Let it go. For these few moments no one is going to harm you. For these few moments there is nothing external that will hurt. For these few moments and for the rest of your life, you need not fear being hurt. Others can throw stones, they can throw verbiage, but the worst pain of all has come from your own verbiage and stones.

Let your pain be healed. Let you release your own judgments about your states of imperfection. Allow yourself to feel soft internally, loving in the heart, gentle, beautifully you. Allow yourself to feel the strength that you have in that state. This is a state of softness where you have released your defensiveness. You've allowed yourself to be open, and its all right. Allow yourself to be even more open and feel even more softness, more love. Let yourself feel the love that you and this body are capable of feeling.

Let it come in. Don't be afraid of it. The one that wants to love you the most is you. The one that is afraid of it the most is you.

You needn't defend yourself from the world. Your defensiveness is against your own criticisms of you. Let down the criticisms. Surrender them. Feel how beautifully you can feel inside. Let yourself feel so beautifully inside that you just want to dance with the expression. Let yourself feel so soft and gentle with you that it is the most pleasant of feelings and that you want to express. Let yourself feel any place the mind or you is at odds with the body or wanting out of it. Let yourself feel your judgments, society's if they are there. Let them go.

This body is the one you chose for this expression. Therefore you chose perfectly for your existence and your life. You chose what would be the most beautiful of all expressions for you. There is reason. Let yourself feel the wisdom you had when you selected the body you're in. Let yourself feel the strength of knowing what the body would give. Let yourself feel love. Let yourself feel the softness and dance in it.

The body worships you as a god already, for it knows that without your life force, it is no more than dust.

Notice at any time when the defenses return. Notice and be honest. Are you afraid that you're going to be criticized or condemned by the world, or does your fear come from your own condemnation? Allow yourselves to be into a place that you're going to find your own perfection.

These bodies know they are tenuous. You, the entities in them, know that you exist without the body. The body does not exist without you. These bodies can be very scared sometimes. They can be very afraid of the journey. They only look to you, god living in them, for support and strength. They love you more than you are allowing yourselves to love them. The body worships you as a god already, for it knows that without your life force, it is no more than dust. The body knows this. The body loves you. The body worships you, and you are the god that it worships; and in turn, you've allowed society and its images to dictate how you will or will not love your body. It is a state, not an action. It is simply an allowance. Loving the body is an allowance.

Loving the body is getting to a place of no longer making it the brunt of all your problems. It is no longer using it for the excuse of why you don't do things. Many of you always say that, "I'll wait to be happy until my body looks different, feels different." You use it for all your lost opportunities or because the body wasn't right, when most of the time, you didn't want the opportunity.

Be determined to let the body be the body. It is so unconditional with you that if you need an excuse for something, it will help you create one! Let it be the teacher for you now. Let it show you the excuses you're making so that you don't have to make the excuses to take them out on the body. The body will be anything you want it to be. It loves you and it does truly worship you, but it so fully does that it carries out your whims, your wills, your desires unconditionally—to the letter. The biggest gift you can give your body is to quit using it as an excuse for what you don't like in life.

Let the body be the body. It's the best one you have. Right now, it is the only one, and it is beautiful. It is a magnificent work of a magnificent god. It is your gift to yourself. Don't degrade it by using it for excuses. Let yourself be honest with you. If you don't want to do something, then say, "I just don't want to do it." It's not that my body won't. I just simply don't choose to.

When you start doing this, you start freeing the body up, that the body can have the health, that it can have the beauty, because you'll feel it from the inside out, and it can do anything you want it to do. Loving the body is letting the body be a body. It is letting it be the most beautiful, elegant, eloquent expression of love you've ever seen, by just simply letting it live. ▲

Woman and the Original Womb-Within

Most of you have been taught that woman came from man, but that is a story created and written by men. Your scriptures were written mostly by men, and in this case you have a story from a male perspective that is trying to understand woman. In the larger scheme of things, most systems of reality have more of what you would term a female embodiment. Woman, or a biological species with a womb-within is the original and only embodiment most realities ever deal with. They don't have different sexes like you do here. They have one body structure that has to be able to bring forth young. They are self-procreating, so they must have a womb or be able to grow a cavity to bring forth new life. Your original embodiments here were more closely female by your terminology than male.

When this planet was being colonized, you came here from other systems of reality. Those embodiments that came here then were of that one basic body structure, having a womb-within. If you could see them today, you would not think they looked much like a woman from your perspective, but hormonally and physiologically, they were what you would call a female embodiment. What you term the male embodiment was brought here later to create an individuation of your species as a means of integrating two wombs-within. The intention was to cross-breed the embodiments on this planet with those from another system, but if both of them are what you term female type of embodiments, you are going to have a hard time of it. To solve this dilemma the genetics and physiology of the imported species was altered to take their womb-within and externalize it through their genitalia into the outside world. And so the male became a new body type or structure that could share with a womb-within species and create a new individuated embodiment from the experience.

What you call woman or man, now, is really more of a psychological difference than a physiological one. You have so many connotations around your terminology that I prefer to call that original embodiment a womb-within. This original body structure had the ability through their own thought process to just shift their hormonal structure, create a cavity within, and a new life within that womb. The original species didn't carry a womb like the female body does today; it grew it when it moved to a point of wanting to pass on its genetics. What you term the uterus was added to the embodiment as a reservoir to encapsulate the chromosomal exchange from the newly created male partners. Woman, as you know her today, is a very different embodiment than the early wombs-within.

Throughout the universe you have this womb-within type of embodiment, and they do not use anything external to them. They have no separation of gender, they are simply, gods. They are gods living and expressing in a body. They have full procreative powers within their own being.

It appears on your planet now that men hold a dominating role. A lot of this is really just a matter of perspective, but from that same perspective there have been times when women occupied the same role. Universally speaking, the male embodiment is somewhat of a curiosity, and so it gets a lot of external support from other systems of reality watching and facilitating the male's evolution. In other systems of reality, with only one body type, there is no hierarchy because there is no way of differentiating between bodies. If men have gone into a place of seeing themselves as superior to women, they only did so because they felt inferior in some very real ways.

The woman has the ability to create new life within her being. This is a grand and beauteous experience. When the cellular structure was separated into chromosomes to give a portion of the chromosome patterning for new life to male and female, all of you felt lessened by the experience in many ways. However, when a womb-within was at a point of self-procreating, it would create the most beauteous state of personal intimacy imaginable. But a male must take that intimate experience and push it outward into the world, and a woman on your plane is the recipient of it.

Now the male could no longer have the womb-within which was actually their love of their own being that helped them to self-procreate. Instead, they had to push that love through their genitalia out from themselves. As a species you are accustomed to it now, and the experience is far lessened from what it use to be, but then it created an extreme vulnerability in the male. Because the male would express all of his genetics, the love of his being, hormonally into woman or the external world, the male was into a place where it never felt fulfilled. It never felt satisfied within its being and felt that it was lessening itself. After a very short period of time the male felt lessened by the female which it saw as superior to it. Whenever an individual thinks something is superior to it, it will try to degrade it in order to control it so it can feel superior. Originally your wombs-within or what became your females were the superior race upon the planet. They were always revered, often as goddesses, because they had the ability to bring forth life. Back then, the male did not understand his role in that, so the woman was worshiped. The male felt inferior, and the only way it could see for getting out of the rut it had created for itself was to degrade the female into a lesser position than what he felt himself in.

A womb-within body structure in another system of reality is the most complete body structure you'll ever find.

A womb-within body structure in another system of reality is the most complete body structure you'll ever find. It has no need for anything external to it. All your ideas and fantasies about being yourself, being one whole with you, come from a remembrance within your beings of being a womb-within in another system. These embodiments were complete and their hormonal system was totally balanced—everything came from within. When the gender was separated, all that was lost. The woman and man thereafter never felt secure in their bodies because they could no longer take the entire hormonal system and change it into a way of creating the final culmination that made them feel complete. In a womb-within system a child is always the natural product of a completion. In the male or female bodies that you now have, you can never be complete. The distortion of your hormones and the stereotypes that you hold yourselves in prevent you from becoming the totality of what you could. As long as you see yourselves as male or female in a male or female body you will never, in a physical body, feel complete. Still you all have this nagging genetic remembrance of completeness because these bodies remember when they were wombs-within. They remember the peace and love of themselves when they brought forth new life and they long for that again.

Now both of your genders are blaming the other. You try to create an experience with each other for a satisfaction or completeness, but you never quite make it. So depending on your perspective, you blame the male or the female. It is simply a matter that neither one of you are complete enough in your own beings to move into a place of total love of your own being. Hormonally and physiologically, you can't do it yet.

All of you now still have the capability of being a womb-within whether you are male or female. When you are evolving your consciousness, you are really taking this body structure into a place of becoming a womb-within, an embodiment that has the ability hormonally and physiologically to be so complete that it can reproduce itself. Right now none of you are that complete. You could clone pieces of yourselves in a laboratory, but you, within your own being, by your own thought processes, cannot reproduce yourself.

There are a whole lot of biological things that most of you are not even aware of now that are evolving on your planet that are part of a species shift that will eventually move both of your embodiments back into a place of being a womb-within. Right now that may seem a little funny or far-fetched, but that is because of the rigidity with which you hold yourselves in cultural stereotypes of male and female.

In the meantime, though, you all have to learn how to live in the bodies that you are in, the ones that you have chosen. Understand why you chose them; understand what you are gaining from them, and go into your own evolutionary course that way. It doesn't matter whether you are male or female. You all seek this womb-within and not just for procreation but for a hormonal and emotional stability called harmony. This is what a lot of you might call claiming the male or female side of you, your yin or your yang, your god or goddess, whatever you wish to call it. So within your beings each of you have to come to terms with the feminine and masculine sides of yourself. Without putting the two together, you can never get your body structure hormonally into a state of being a womb-within—you will never have completion within your being.

I'm not saying that men are going to start having a lot of babies. From a physiological standpoint, though, theses bodies have to remember back to the time when they were wombs-within so that they can utilize the endocrine system and your hormone systems to secrete the hormones that will create a physical harmony and balance within your being so that you can feel one-hundred percent complete. It is actually the hormonal structure of the biology that keeps you from feeling complete at any given point, and that ties into your belief in male and female, separate genders.

If you don't come to terms with the male and female portions of yourself, you'll stay stuck in the same ruts you've been in for eons of time. Basically this means that you have to release a whole lot of your psychological separations of gender. You're not going to shift your gender back and forth in this lifetime. It means that within your being, you're going to get rid of the stereotypes. The belief in the stereotypes prevents you from being either one.

Even the females on this planet still have to come to terms with the feminine side of themselves, as well as the masculine. You might think that being female, they already have that one down. The fact that you occupy one embodiment or the other does not mean that you have come to terms with it. When you get back to the womb-within, that body structure creates a life hormone that gives life to everything that you are and everything that you hold within your being to be dear to you. Now you have all this blame between the sexes, you have your stereotypes, all your images. For the most part neither sex has come to terms with their own gender. Until you do come to terms with your masculinity or femininity, your god or goddess within, as you may term it, hormonally you're going to give life to the separations and dualities, creating disease in your embodiments.

In the realms where gods do exist there is no gender whatsoever. Genders come from here.

Originally you were gods that had no gender. Gods don't have gender. They may merge and they have something much better than sex, but they don't have gender. They are just gods. In your minds you associate the word god with male. In the realms where gods do exist there is no gender whatsoever. Genders come from here. The most perfect and natural body for a god, therefore, is one that is a womb-within, one that gives it the ability to be everything in the same package.

A womb-within is not necessarily a woman. That is how it translates into this reality after differentiating between the two womb-within species and separating the chromosomes—then it became woman. In the natural scheme of things a womb-within is the natural body for a god, a genderless entity. So here in these bodies as long as you hold these stereotypes, as long as you believe that this is female, this is male, this is right, this is wrong, you create a gender separation, so you will never accept the other side of what you need to turn your body into a womb-within, or into the body that will hold a god or goddess, either one. You separate it out in your own mind and behave according to the stereotypes. Your mind set may say, for example, "I'm a male, and since I'm male, I watch the females as they walk by because that is what I've been taught and that is what I hold within my being." That factor alone will prevent a male from ever moving its body into complete harmony within its being in order to be a womb-within or the embodiment of a god. It is because it sees the other gender as separate. A god sees no separation whatsoever. What you are all moving towards now is a place where you are so completely excited about life, thrilled to be alive that you don't see the gender separation as much. You no longer size up other individuals as prospective relationships or bed partners. You move into a place of loving who and what you are so grandly, so beautifully, so intimately that you no longer see yourselves or others as sex objects. You'll see every individual as a beautiful expression of a god. You will have your sense of completion within you, so you will no longer need to look outside you for fulfillment.

Within your beings you will still love being male or female, but you will also realize that it is not a differentiation. It is rather a psychological experience that you are having here and now. It is something that you as a god are doing for the time being. A god is all that is; it can't be just male or female—it is all that is. That means within your being you are as much a male as you are a female. So you are bringing that all together and expressing in one embodiment or the other. If you chose a male embodiment, love it and enjoy it, and realize that it is a vehicle for a god. Bring the male and female together so that you can move into a balanced hormonal situation where what you have is quite comparable to the womb-within.

If you are a beauteous female with male issues or with angers towards males, you can release them and realize that you are as much male as you are female in the same package. All of you have the same hormones running in your bodies. Originally there was only one hormone, the life hormone. That was all you were ever supposed to have. It was your attitudes, beliefs, differentiations and separations that took that one beautiful life hormone and created your male and female hormones and all the others that run your body now. All your hormones are derivations of the life hormone. Your bodies are capable of moving back to creating that one hormone, but as long as you hold your images and sexual stereotypes, your body will never allow you hormonally to bridge the gap to give life to you. If it doesn't give life to you, it will give life to your separations and attitudes which are your diseasements. It will intensify your cancers and your plagues upon the planet, because that is the body's way of purging these attitudes and defenses if you won't.

Realize that if you see females as good and males as bad or one sex or the other as victim and the other as victimizer, you are setting up a defensive state within your being. The bodies automatically create and release antibodies when you are defensive that have to attack and work on something. When you say you are strictly male or strictly female, that is a defensive state. You are defending yourself against being god. You are preventing yourself from being your own god or goddess, from being all that is. You are telling your entire adrenal system and all your organs that you are in a defensive state. This is what wears bodies out. It is what ages them—it is what kills them. You are repressing or defending yourself against being the other half of your being by holding to the stereotypes and your belief systems of what a male or female is or isn't. Aging in the body is a belief in the differentiation between sexes. The body ages because it will not accept the other side of the polarity that already resides there that would turn it into life. You tell the body to age and to die because you are not willing to accept that you are genderless, expressing in a beautiful, psychological instrument called a male or female body.

There is no spiritual basis for male and female. It is something that has been created out of your emotions and attitudes through the eons. Spiritually you are one god. That god is an entity that is neither male nor female. It is everything. In spirit you are a god which is totally genderless. The god that you are is so wondrously large that you won't fit in one body without destroying it. So you had to arbitrarily decide how much of yourself you would bring into the body. You separated out a portion of your own electromagnetics or vibrations and put part of them in a body and left part of them outside to observe you in the body. If you were in a different system of reality with genderless bodies, and you took a hundred different gods each choosing their own vibrations for that body they would inhabit, you would have the most beauteous individuated species anywhere. Each god would bring into that one body their own treasures, and what you would have is one-hundred different genders. The body would more fully match the god that was inhabiting them.

Gods don't have gender but they do have preferences. You gain preference by having a lot of experience with a lot of different things. If you are male or female, it probably reflects a preference. Perhaps you love a particular one because of the expression hormonally or the way one embodiment or the other works electrically with your vibration. You can never gain a preference without having been both. In this reality, a male or female body is a psychological instrument for you to experience your godness in a limited fashion and see how it works in physiology against a hormonal system.

> *There is no spiritual basis for male and female. It is something that has been created out of your emotions and attitudes through the eons.*

As you drop your images and stereotypes, you're not going to go around pretending to be neuter. You will move into a space of allowing more of the gentleness, beauty, and godness within each of you to emerge. Your stereotypes say that a female is soft, nurturing, gentle, tender and caring; while a male is more rugged, less vulnerable—if you have an unpleasant, cruel, or barbaric deed to do, give it to a male! The male is the protector, the provider. A lot of you within your beings now are struggling to find a balance within the stereotype. You have females that want to be their own providers. They don't want to sit in the cave waiting for the male to bring home a dead pterodactyl! The female is wanting to come out and to experience some of the traditionally male roles that have not been allowed her. The males are crying within their beings just to have a place where they can be gentle and tender, where they can nurture and drop the barbaric nature that tradition grants to them.

This is what a lot of your struggle for power is all about. You have both sexes wanting some of the other roles that society has traditionally refused you. Women want out in the world more, and you have men who are wanting to stay home more and take a larger role in nurturing the kids. It is society that is dragging its heels.

Realize that it is not the actions that matter. It doesn't matter if you are being a provider or whether you are at home nurturing children. These different roles are really a feeling inside. Within your beings you can do or be anything you want to. It is really a matter of acceptance of yourself in both roles. It is being able to be the provider and the nurturer too, the barbarian and the lover. It is the knowingness that you can be all things at the same time and that there is no category that you or those things that you do fit in.

Within your beings you all have to get to a point where you feel free enough to do anything, be anything you want. A lot of this power struggle between your sexes now is more a matter of trying to find a new balance. You will eventually find a balance when you realize that all of you have the ability to be every one of these things that you want to be. You can have all the feminine and masculine characteristics combined in either embodiment, and you will love that body. The male or female configuration of your body is just an expression you are using for this time.

Most of your stereotype issues are really ego issues. As males upon the planet, you often prefer woman to play the role of seductress because that feeds your ego. Woman often prefers to dress and act the same role because it feeds her ego. It is really an issue of feeling inferior where you are. When a female gets to the point of not needing to play that part any more, she actually becomes more enticing than she ever was when she was pursuing that kind of attention. She gains a power within her own being, and she doesn't have to pursue anyone. When something is unattainable, it is more desirable than ever.

There are many ways of looking at this. You could say that the seductress in her open sexuality, is just trying to be loved; she knows what is expected of her in order to get love. All of you buy into the stereotypes because you think that is going to provide you love. You enact everyone of the stereotypes, whether you are male or female, in order to get love for doing the right thing.

You enact everyone of the stereotypes, whether you are male or female, in order to get love for doing the right thing.

When an individual realizes that there is not a right thing and a wrong thing, they move into a place within their being of complete at onement. They don't have to pursue, they don't have to be the seductress or the barbarian, either one. You enact these roles simply because society wants you to. You want to, because you feel insecure in your own self-love and because in doing so you know love will be given to you. In other words if a woman is playing the seductress role, she is doing that not because she loves herself, but because she wants to be loved by the whole world, and she feels that is the only way she is going to be loved.

Your male is the provider because if he is the provider, then he will be loved for what he is providing. Everyone of your stereotypes are simply validation issues. When you go into a stereotype, people will love and validate you for matching the image. When you start loving who and what you are, you don't need the ego validated, you don't need everyone telling you how great and wonderful you are, and you move into a place of being even more loving and lovable and more beautiful because you are not trying to live up to someone else's image. So within all of you, you have to get to a place of dropping the stereotypes, your need for external validation.

Now it is not just to get approval from males that a woman may dress seductively. Often she does so to get approval from other females that she is the perfect female. And, yes, in this world it is quite hard for women to get anywhere without buying into the stereotypes, at least in their interpretation. If individuals are living out stereotypes or images of whatever kind, they are trying to get validation that they are beautiful, great, and worthy of being loved. Anyone who lives these roles is an individual that does not feel that there is anything to be loved within their being.

Whenever you're perpetuating the stereotype, you are living someone else's truth, not yours. That means that you are going against yourself. You're going to live a life of repressed guilt which will put you into a lot of anger. People living in stereotypes will always be stressed and angry, and they will try to repress both because that is what the stereotype says to do. Look at who you consider to be your perfect male and female stereotypes. If you could look closely at their lives, you would find them very stressful, unless they have come to terms with themselves and are out of the need for external validation.

If you have a woman who dresses for the world to be able to get the job or employment because she believes that is the only way she can get it, she will feel resentful every time she puts on that face because it is not natural to her. She is putting on a face to buy her something in the world. Most of the women on this planet, whether they realize it or not, feel like prostitutes. It is not that they are doing the acts of prostitutes but rather that they have to dress, put on an image, and behave for society much more than males. So woman puts on her face, her high heels, and her dress in order to get a job or companionship. There is a part of her that enjoys it perhaps, but there is a part within her being that is repressed because she knows she is doing something to get something. She is always going to be resentful because she feels like she is prostituting her own being, her own ideas, and her own image, in order to be accepted by the world. Woman generally doesn't want to acknowledge or face that resentment. She'll hide it and hide it because part of the stereotype is that women are not supposed to be resentful; they are supposed to have smiling faces, always loving and cheerful.

A whole lot of your feminist movements, whether on a world or national level or what you call the New Age Goddess, are movements by resentful women. These are women who have resentment that has built and built the more they have repressed it, until it turned into anger within their beings. A lot of them are striking out and making a statement, "I'm a female and I'm proud of it. I'm a female and don't push me around any more." They are taking a hard stance because of all the resentment that has built up, and in their anger they are actually perpetuating the very thing they are trying to get out of. They are not healing the old issue, they are going out and making a new one. Rather than just saying, "I'm a god and I love myself. I am," they are going to the other side and saying, "I am a feminist. I am a goddess and you will accept me as such." They are making a harsh statement to the world and bringing up their feminine energy rather than just being the balanced, beauteous, loving individual that they already are. If we could go inside of you and pull out the natural you, the part of you that doesn't need to play any image for any man, the part that doesn't even need to play any image for you, you would find the gentleness, the tenderness—the state of being that all of you are looking for. Whenever you have to make a statement to the world that "This is what I am," you are going against who and what you truly are. When you state, "I am a god," it is less a statement than a realization of the fact. It is not made to the world but to yourself. When you say, "I am a goddess," you are really saying, "I am not god." According to your general belief systems, god is male, so you are saying to the universe that you are not totally complete and that you do not love yourself.

> *A whole lot of your feminist movements, are movements by resentful women.*

When you move into a place of loving who and what you are within, you take yourselves out of the stereotypes, and you just are. Those are issues for other people, other places and time; you are just you, here and now, and that is all that matters. Then you break the stereotypes. Right now you have a whole planet with a lot of women who are angry. They have a lot of resentment built up because they have believed in images that mankind put upon them which were their own creation in a lot of cases. Even in the instance where the woman dresses to get the employment, she does so, in many cases, because she feels she has to as much as the employer is looking for the properly dressed female for the job. Many times women will create their reality out of what they are expecting to find out in the world.

It is possible to play the game without any compromise at all. The only compromise any of you make occurs when you get into a mode of thinking that you have been victimized by anything. The moment that you think that you have to *do this or else*, you have compromised. If you are in a body, you are playing a game, so realize that it's all a game anyway. It is all an illusion and you create it, so create it by your rules. "If I want to wear an image, I'll wear it. I know that I'm doing it, and I'll do it because I like it. It is something that is beauteous to me."

It is just like wearing clothes. You could say that is a compromise too. Within your beings there is a beauty and a joy with wearing pure silk against your skin. Within your beings there is a joy in wearing some images. Acknowledge it. So if an individual wants to be the seductress, go ahead and do it and love it. Play the role well. Do it but know what you're doing, then you'll never feel like someone is making you do it.

This is a reality of games. This is a reality of psychological constructs, so everything you do here will be game playing. You can't do anything else because you are gods. You are gods incognito. Play your games by your rules, and have fun at them. Realize that you're not victimized by anything. If you are a female and you put on a low-cut dress with a high hemline to go get a job, you are doing it because you like it and you like the attention you get. Be honest with yourself about it. If you are male, doing whatever you do, just say that this is a game I like to play, I do it, and I enjoy it. Accept and be responsible for it, and then you're never compromised.

You could say from one standpoint that a woman has to dress in a certain manner and fashion, have a certain body appearance, breast size or whatever, to get some jobs. You could say she is a victim if you look at it that way. But if in her mind and in her being she says "This is a game I'm playing. This is what I am doing and how I will do it," she will never be a victim and she will never compromise who and what she is. Then when she puts the low cut dress on and walks into that office to apply, she'll be doing it because of the psychological thrill she gets from manipulating everybody else. When a woman dresses that way, she is doing it for manipulation anyway. So if she is willing to admit it and love it, she is not compromising herself. She is just saying, "This is who I am right now, this is the game I play, and I am having fun, I am in joy with it."

You have all come here to learn these psychological games and gestalts. So, yes, you can play the games and even the stereotypes. But if you play the stereotypes, be aware that you are doing it because you choose to, because it brings you joy like a fine piece of clothing you put on. If your attitude is that you're living something because someone is forcing you, then you are compromising you because you are not willing to accept that you put you in the situation to begin with.

The present female body physiologically is more closely aligned with what used to be a womb-within, and so it has a number of enhancements or detractions depending on how you want to look at it. In the female body the fallopian tubes are closely associated with the area of the chest just below your heart centers. Your heart has more electromagnetic energies than anything else in the embodiment. The fallopian tubes are designed to take energy from that heart center and push it down into and through the uterus to help sustain and give life to the new life the woman is growing within her. The woman can use this ability in a positive or self-destructive manner.

In the natural cycle of things, the woman's body was created so that another entity could come into her field and from her field, enter her being through the solar-plex heart area, go through the fallopian tubes, down through the anatomy, into the uterus to become the embryo. The female could also push her own energies in to help create it. The mother's electromagnetics from the heart center would help support and sustain the entity in the body while it was developing and growing. This would all transpire in the second chakra or second seal area of the abdomen. This is also the center where a whole lot of your angers reside along with your self-worth issues. A lot of females have learned to take their self-hatred, their lack of self-worth, their lack of feeling good about themselves, their own rejection complexes, and electromagnetically shove these into their lower abdominal areas destroying or taking out a whole lot of their female genitalia. That is why your hysterectomy levels are so high. Since women have a larger cavity in their second seal, they can hold much more repressed anger than males. Not only can this attack their female portions, any time you bring forth new children, you are giving them all the angers you have repressed there.

The fallopian tubes are designed to take energy from that heart center and push it down into and through the uterus to help sustain and give life . . .

The female nervous system was also created a little different. Your vertebrae in you spinal column are different in their spacing on a female body. This accounts for the difference in your heights. The female body is more compact, closer together and has less distance to cross in its light paths—this is also what allows the female to live longer sometimes. There is a stronger nurturing within your own system. Hormonally, the female body is different but only in the electromagnetic reactions. Both male and female bodies carry all your sexual steroids, your estrogen, your progesterone, and your testosterone, but they carry them in different proportions. The female body has higher estrogen levels than the male and this is what gives it the breasts and a lot of what you call the feminine characteristics.

Estrogen is the carrier for the entity in either the female or male body. The estrogen is what actually allows the entity to more fully use the body than anything else. It is a closer relative of the natural hormone that is supposed to run through the body and that used to be in the wombs-within. So your female bodies naturally have higher levels of it. This allows the

321

female body to be more connected in spirit many times than what a male body is going to feel. Estrogen gives the ability to use different portions of the brain because it can cross some of the membranes in the brain that are important for connecting with spirit and other realities. It has a lot of bridging abilities. If the estrogen is not allowed to be used properly, if the entity is not allowed to come into the body by loving who and what you are, then it can be harmful to the body. If a female never learns to love herself, or is into self-hatred issues, then when she goes into a second puberty or what you term the change of life, there will not be enough estrogen to create the exchange within the bone and muscles, so the body deteriorates. A lot of times you will find more females with skeletal problems than males because of this exchange of estrogen in the body, and this relates with the way they use it to connect with their entity.

The original female body did not have what you call a monthly cycle. When a womb-within got to a point of loving itself so intently, feeling so intimately connected in its being, it created a hormonal secretion, much like your progesterone in the bodies now, along with some others, and the combination of them started creating a natural spot for a child to be formed. There was no organ called a womb. They just naturally grew one when they were ready.

Your female cycles in the body were created because women didn't like themselves enough to procreate. When you separated them into male and female bodies, the females would not bring forth new life any more because they never felt complete, whole enough within their beings, to love themselves enough to bring forth new life. You went through a period where nothing was being born. This triggered a survival mechanism and the physiological and emotional structure of the female was moved into a place of having a monthly cycle—where it could become impregnated whether it wanted to or not. Originally no body could bring forth new life unless it chose to. You had total choice in the matter.

Now in the monthly cycle, when you go into the ovulation period or the mid-cycle, that is the point in the cycle where the woman, if she was totally at love and totally connected and at one with herself, could move back into a place of self-procreation. But at that time if there is no embryo being created, the body goes into a death cycle. The monthly cycle in the female body is actually a death cycle, a rejection of life because what the body created to support inter-intimate life with was not sustained. Since it was not sustained, it decomposes and has to be expelled, the uterus has to be cleared. The decomposition with it is very noticeable to all creatures. When the hormonal levels shift to tell the body to slough off, it shifts the whole electromagnetic field, and this is what a lot of people are now feeling as what you call PMS. After ovulation, the death hormone is being released in the body. It is just when the estrogen and progesterone are out of balance, or balanced in a certain way to clear the uterus that isn't being used for the child. This creates a disturbance in the entire electromagnetic field according to how much individuals love or do not love themselves. If an individual is at peace and harmony within their being, they will not usually have any difficulty or a lot of electromagnetic distortion with their monthly cycle. If you're into these issues, it changes the entire electromagnetic field, and that is perceptible even to your animals.

The original female body did not have what you call a monthly cycle.

You see, you all have senses that none of you use. All of you have a life sense so that you can feel life anywhere it may be, but you don't use it. You have death senses within your beings too, and you don't use those either. You do recognize your death sense in a lot of your animals. Vultures can always find where they need to be. Horses are always skittish around death. A lot of your animals do not like death even if they are carnivores. Some feed off carcasses, but for the most part most of them are revolted by it because when the body starts putting off this death hormone, it shifts the electromagnetic field and it is perceptible to humans and animals. Your animals won't stay around it. It creates a high pitched irritation within the being. So as the woman's cycle becomes what you call the monthly period, the death composition of her hormonal secretions becomes stronger and stronger. It is emitting not only an odor but an electromagnetic charge vibrationally that is going out in her field. Other people pick it up as well as she and this is where a lot of the irritation comes from that individuals get into around a female's monthly cycle. It disrupts the whole brain flow and function and the entire electromagnetic circumstances of the female.

Understand that this is just the way bodies are. If you are female and still having cycles, you are going to go through the experience. The way to ease it and make it less irritating for yourself and others is to come to peace within the being and start to love who and what you are. Actually, it is all tied into an individual's feeling of self-worth. If an individual has a lot of issues with self-worth or if they are seeing a big differentiation between male and female, they are going to have a whole lot more issues with what you term the monthly cycle than they would if they were at peace and harmony with themselves.

The brain uses estrogen more than any other part of the body. Estrogen is important in the bone and muscle structures, but the brain uses it for connection in the synapses. The brain now is using more estrogen than ever. This is why your rate of hysterectomy is up right now. Yes, a lot of it is just done for convenience, but you will also find that for many women the monthly cycles are not regular like they used to be. A lot of women will find as they start evolving and making changes on their path, they may start having difficulty with their monthly cycle. The reason for this is that brain starts using a whole lot more estrogen. In male and female bodies both, it uses estrogen to relate with the hydrogen that is needed in ever increasing amounts in an evolving body. The brain uses great amounts of hydrogen, more than any other part. As you evolve and are trying to open and use your brain more and in different ways, you are going to require higher levels of hydrogen and higher levels of estrogen in your brain than ever before. There is going to be less estrogen available to hold you in regular monthly cycles. As I said, hysterectomies are on the rise now because they are quick and convenient. A lot of people just want to get it over with, but it is also because the brain is using so much more estrogen that it is actually robbing the bones, the muscles, and the female organs from having it.

The male body also uses high amounts of hydrogen during this period. Since the male body does not have as much estrogen as the female body, it uses up what available estrogen there is and then starts accepting and using more testosterone. When the body runs out of estrogen, it uses testosterone to do the same job because it is still one of your sex steroids in the body. When it does this, it increases the levels of it to such an extent that you get more balding and hair loss problems in the male. That is also a factor of evolution. A whole lot of your male embodiments, when they first came upon this planet, were all bald because the levels were so high. You'll see a lot more of this and your society will have products to deal with it. But you are going to have more balding upon your planet in the male species during an evolutionary period than at other times.

In actuality there have been some females who have translated, but this is not what we consider an ascension. The female body must always be in a state that it can take the nutrients of the planet and create another body. The female must always approximate the density of the planet. If it were too highly refined, it would never be able to procreate. In the very design of the female body, it is tied very intimately to the planet in order to be able to take the minerals and nutrients it needs to create and build a new body within its own. So the female has always had to be as dense as the planet. She has never had the opportunity to raise the vibrational level of her body high enough to do what you would term a full ascension. In this new and upcoming reality that you are all creating here, women now, because they are connected so closely with the planet, are able to bring in life, bring in energy and bring in the universe through their fallopian tubes—the same ability they have of initiating a new embodiment within their own. Because of their connectedness, they have the ability to help ascend the entire planet. They are actually helping to ascend the whole planet, not just themselves, because they are so intimately connected with it.

As you evolve . . . you are going to require higher levels of hydrogen and higher levels of estrogen in your brain than ever before.

So the female has to learn to love life as well as the male because it will be the female's love of life, her love of creation, and connectedness with the planet, with the facilitation of the male species too, that will ascend the planet. You are all going to be connected and you will all do it together. Male and female alike, you are all gods. Since you are all gods, the differentiations shouldn't matter as much. You have to learn to live in peace. You have to learn to be one people. You have to learn to let go of a whole lot of your differentiations and hierarchies. You have to learn to allow yourself to love, to be, to be one with each other. You have to learn upon this planet that you are all gods—gods have no gender. They are just gods. Woman is a beauteous, beauteous creation. Love it. If you're a woman, love being a woman. If you're a male, love and be a lover of women. Be a lover of yourselves. Be a lover of life. But with all of you, whether you are male or female, you all have the same thing to learn here, and that is just to love life, have an appreciation of it, and be one with all creation.

The dropping of your images and the changing of your planet is a situation that will take time. Each one of you that is willing to just love life as it is, love life for life's sake, will move out of the place of having to worry about whether you are living up to everybody else's images and stereotypes. Love you, love life and be one with all things. ▲

Healing the Environment

I have a great sadness about the environmental pollution that's happening in our world now. Would you speak on that a little bit for us please?

I would say there are several reasons for the environmental pollution that a lot of you are getting. One, a lot of it is the reflection of what you're doing with your own attitudes. Two, you're in the middle of a biological species shift which means that there are certain things the body needs to catalyze its process, and because you don't realize that it's going through these things, you're inadvertently polluting a lot of stuff to cause mutations to the body.

I would say that whether it's the environment, save the whales, the rain forest, whatever it is . . . find a state of perfection for humanity. If you fight it and say, "I hate these people that are polluting. Look at all these people driving their cars. How stupid they are." What you do is enforce their stupidity for them. The first thing that happens when you say, "Hey, look you dumb doe doe, look what you did," they get defensive and close down about getting educated.

If you label the way the environment is being treated as if there is something wrong with it, you have judged it already, and you're putting your energy into saying that it's wrong. Rather that labeling it wrong, what you could do is say, "Hey, I personally don't appreciate the smell of this stuff in the air. It is my preference to have things smell better."

Feel inside yourself what it would feel like to feel and smell perfectly clean air, to feel and be able to drink perfectly clear water, to feel your appreciation for the environment, your appreciation for the planet, and your love of it. Then what that does is it goes out en masse and other people pick it up and they say, "Oh, I never thought of it that way." All of a sudden, while they're in their car, while they're drinking their dirty water, while they're smelling the smog of the cars in front of them, they'll sit there and realize, "I think I love the planet." Out of the clear blue sky, it just pops in! They don't even know where it came from and all of a sudden, they want to educate themselves about what they're doing to the planet.

If you tell them in anger and war upon them and say, "You're stupid for doing this. You're dumb for doing that," they will close down. The best thing that any of you can do for your environment, for your endangered species, for anything that you want to work with is feel your love of it—not your hatred of the people and not your anger at the people—but your love for it.

Most people have never learned to appreciate the planet. How could they? They don't live in their body. They are trying to get out of their body, they hate their body, and they're trying to bring death to their body. Why would they want to do anything about learning how to take care of their environment? They're trying to kill themselves and get out. They're not going to want you to come up to them and hear you say, "Here is my paper on what you're doing to the planet."

If you feel an appreciation for life, you feel an appreciation for the planet and all its beauty, then you put that en masse as a feeling tone. When they are least expecting it, all of a sudden they will pick it up. Maybe one day looking out over the Grand Canyon—"Ah" . . . it moves them. They love it. For the first time in their life—and they may be forty, fifty, sixty, seventy-years-old—they saw something on the planet they loved and in that moment, they'll want you to educate them etherically. "Tell me more. Let me have more life."

The only way you're going to make any difference on this planet is by loving it so intensely that other people pick up your love and your appreciation for it.

The only way you're going to make any difference on this planet is by loving it so intensely that other people pick up your love and your appreciation for it. Not your condemnation of what you do. If you do that, you can help heal the consciousness more quickly than anything you've ever done.

If you want an example, I'll throw a tidbit in here. You know your trees, the giant ones that didn't come from this planet? Your redwoods? Go look at them. They have a cut one—I saw it because I tagged along—where you can see the rings, and it tells which years the different events happened. Look at it. The year they tried to save the trees was the year of the most damage in the rings of the tree! The tree will show you its own living proof of what the anger at people did to it. They wanted to save the trees, yes, they loved them, but they were angry at the people cutting them—the ring of the tree shows the scar and they have it labeled. They think it is labeled with pride, but that is the year and the tree still holds the scar. So when you see that and you can recognize the fact, you'll realize that the anger at the people for cutting the trees isn't helping the trees one bit and it's not helping the environment. If you can love the trees, love the people and appreciate life, you'll heal everything. You will see all things in their perfection, therefore, the only thing the planet can be is its perfection. ▲

Spirit as a Biological Creation

For the most part, what you term spirit is actually a biological creation. What we call biological spirit is what you generically term spirit. From our terminology it is biological creation and therefore biological spirit. Now the true you or your life spark and the biological spirit are two different things. What you generically call spirit is actually a biological creation that is designed and made from these embodiments. These embodiments were actually created as a device to help the life spark, which is the true you, design and build a consciousness.

Consciousness is not totally what you think it is either. Consciousness must grow, and it does not grow easily or by itself. It has to be stimulated. It has to be created. It has to be forced into movement and design. The life spark that you are, however, does not. It was born and birthed from a pure source of total knowingness and understanding. So a lot of you when you are talking about spirit are really talking about the life spark; you're getting the two mixed up. But the true you was birthed with total knowingness, total understanding, total comprehension, because you were birthed from a state of knowingness. So the true life spark knows everything, feels everything, and understands all things.

When you were birthed, you were pretty much all the same. You were birthed from a creative burst of energy that actually loved all of you into existence. You were all equal, all the same, and you still are. But this birth made each of you a like particum of consciousness. So you started on a journey to try to create an individuated consciousness. You had to find a form to create a consciousness that was going to be different, separate, and uniquely yours, so that your life spark could have a different personality from every other life spark. Otherwise, every life spark would be the same, because it was out of one source and one creator—whatever one thought, they all thought. What one did, they all did. There is no creativity with this. There is no sense of movement, no sense of direction, and no change in this type of creative endeavor. It cannot even be creative because whatever is thought, just is. There is nothing to challenge it, there is nothing to redirect it, nothing to alter it or create a new ideal and direction.

So each of you as the individualized sparks of life, at this point in time, needed to create a way of individuating yourselves. This would allow for a grander creativity and grander movement because now you would have something to have resistance against. Now your creativity would have something as a springboard of movement; evolution. And now you could change.

But consciousness is something that has to be pushed into growth. It does not grow on its own. It is not self-existent. It is not self-growing, it does not multiply, it does not expand. The only way that it can do these things is by being forced into them, by being pushed into doing them.

Your life spark is an energy. It is a vibrational, electrical energy. It is full of love, it is total knowingness, total understanding. It is complete, but it is also a vibration, an energy of an unseen source.

So to individuate your consciousness and to grow each of these life sparks into individuated consciousnesses, you had to take that electrical system that you were as a life spark, and put it into a medium and hopefully grow an individuated consciousness.

The intention was to allow each of these sparks to become creative, to allow each one of these sparks into a medium where they would see themselves separate and could evolve, grow, and have a unique experience. They would be different—not higher, not grander, just different, because they would have a different set of circumstances that would allow them to have a different creative potential. That way you could have new ideas in the universe, you would have new understandings, you could create and continue to create, because you would have something to be different. The original differences were actually just for creativity, not for hierarchy and not because one of you is better, smarter, or worse than anybody else. It was a state of creativity you were trying to achieve.

To do this you had to design and create an embodiment, a vehicle for you to put your life spark into, and allow it to become creative, but it also had to work from an electrical charge that would actually encode the life spark that you were into it and allow it to take creative potential. You needed a vehicle that you could put each of these life sparks into, separate from each other; and in those vehicles, they would come up against different sets of circumstances. They would be pushed in different directions. They would each have different things as part of their reality. As they did this, their life spark, through electrical charges in the vehicle, your body, would find a creativity, thus allowing an individuated, creative consciousness for the inhabitant of the embodiment.

Your embodiments were originally a creative endeavor to allow your life spark to gain a separate personality, a separate consciousness, and a separate identity—not hierarchy, not that type of separateness, but a separateness of uniqueness and creativity.

If there were only one of you on the whole planet, you would only create for your survival. When there are multiples of you, then you become creative, you get into technologies, you get into a lot of sciences and different understandings. Each of these roads take you in a different creative way.

What you generically call spirit is actually a biological creation that is designed and made from these embodiments.

So this body that you're living in was originally designed as a vehicle to put the life spark into, which was an electrical charge, so that it could electrically use this embodiment to grow a unique, creative potential. That is what these bodies, in part, were originally created to do.

The life spark originally came into these embodiments to create a new way for itself to be creative. When the electrical charge, which is the true life spark, which is you, comes into the body, it runs the whole body off of an electrical current. Your body is a composite of electrical current and chemicals that work one another. That is how your entire body functions. The chemicals being reacted upon through the electrical substance, which was originally the true life spark, is what makes the body function. That is all it is. That is why if you remove that electrical charge, or if you remove the life spark from the embodiment, the embodiment ceases or goes through what you term death.

Every cell in your body fires electrically. The cells fire in the nucleus, or your brain fires in its neurons, as it were, and it creates and puts out an electrical charge. This charge that is transmitted is then received through the chemicals in the embodiment as a message that makes the body function. It makes the cells divide, and grow. It makes the brain work, makes the body work, and every other type of functioning.

But the electrical firing goes beyond your embodiment. All of these electrical firings are not contained within your embodiment. Each cell in the nucleus that fires, each neuron in your brain and in your nervous system that fires, actually sends out an electrical charge. A portion of that electrical charge is received in the chemical analysis of your body and your body reacts to it. A portion of the firing also goes outside of your embodiment, and can be picked up by the brain wave monitorings that your science does. This is what your auric fields are that some people can see. This is what a lot of your energy field is created out of.

Now these firings are not contained within the skin or within the embodiment. Since the skin is the outermost portion of your embodiment, when those cells fire to re-divide, to change, to grow, to alter, there is grand difficulty in keeping the whole electrical charge inside the embodiment. So a portion of the firing goes outside of the embodiment.

From your perspective these would be very subtle energies. They would not be high electrical charges as you understand them. But all of your energy methods and modes upon this planet, create a peripheral energy. Your generators that generate your electricity or collect it, actually create a residue energy that can be measured and perceived outside of the unit itself. Your electricity running through your homes, your electricity running through your power lines, all has perceptible, measurable energy outside of the power lines.

Your body is no different. You don't see it quite the same as the power lines that you use for your electricity. But your body isn't a whole lot different. It is just a different form of electrical charge and it still creates a radiation. This electrical radiation is what goes out and makes your electro-magnetic fields.

As this goes beyond your skin, and these charges go outside of the physical body itself, they don't go that far. Some of them do. If it is a highly charged electrical current, it can go for miles, half-way around your planet virtually, if it is a certain type of current. But for the most part, most of these currents and these charges that are let off through the cells, go out and stay in and about the embodiment, usually about a six to eight inch circumference around you.

This is what a lot of people are perceiving when they perceive auras. It is an electrical field. When they can sense somebody, by their terminology, they are sensing their spirit. This is what we call biological spirit. This is what you're referring to when you talk about your spirit.

The electrical firing in the embodiment, goes through the chemical response of the cells, and as it does it picks up the totality of the genetic coding, DNA memory, RNA memory and several other components. That takes the entire firing sequence and puts it into a vibration or electricity or a memory pattern that has the entire physical genetic structure in that electrical firing.

Every cell in your body is doing this constantly. Each cell, every time it fires, fires from the nucleus of the cell, from there it goes out through its own DNA structure to do its sub-dividing, its regrowth, and rejuvenation that it does in the cell; but at this point in time, it has already electrically picked up the electrical charge with the DNA memory upon it.

When that goes outside of the embodiment, you have a vibrational charge out there that has an electrical and chemical analysis upon it. If you had a collector for these, and there are systems of reality that do, you could collect it from an energy standpoint. This energy could read off a whole DNA structure, and a physical embodiment could actually be built from it.

You will actually take the body, reduce the body into a vibrational charge . . . transport it via the air waves, and reassemble it on the other side.

Eventually, when you learn how to teletransport like in some of your science fiction stories, this is technically how it works. You will actually take the body, reduce the body into a vibrational charge, an electrical current that has the entire chemical analysis of every cell upon it, transport it via the air waves, and reassemble it on the other side.

Also, many of you have a desire to learn how to transport your own embodiments from one place to another. You're going to use the same exact principle. You become invisible in one place and reappear in another. All of you have heard stories of the masters doing this, and many of you desire to do it yourself. This is what they are doing. They are taking their whole physical embodiment, translating it into an electrical charge, an electrical-light vibration with an entire DNA memory resident in that vibration, moving it to where they would have it, and reassembling it. This is how you transport the body.

This field that surrounds your embodiment is also what feeds your embodiment. Everything that you put out becomes part of your electromagnetic field which you then pull back in and recycle through your body. The biological firings of the embodiment fire, go outside of the flesh. From outside the flesh they travel, usually from six to eight inches, sometimes further, sometimes less, and at this point in time, the firing is genetically embedded with all the DNA structure.

Now anything you feel or you emote is also a vibration. In their pure state, feelings are the strongest vibration you're going to have. Most of you, however, reduce the feelings down into emotions, and so you are only putting half the charge out into your field that you could if you were using feelings.

The feeling is an abstract lesson which is an electrical charge that comes into your embodiment. So the abstract lesson comes into your embodiment as an electrical charge, triggers your biological embodiment to tell you, you have a feeling, and that is what you generically label it. But at the same time you are also firing feelings into your field.

The feelings come in from you, from your biological embodiment, from your genetic memory. They can come in from just about any place. If the feelings are from you and your life spark, they are always going to have a joy base and love underneath them. When they come into the embodiment, if you are allowing yourself to live in a state of joy, in a state of love and enjoying life, the life spark would send the lesson to you as electromagnetic charge into your solar-plex area. From that point, it would fire the neurons in your solar-plex area which then, in response to that, would put out the feeling into your electromagnetic field or into your biological spirit. Then this spirit or this biological creation that you have circumferencing your body would have the feeling tone in it as an electrical charge.

What happens, however, is most of you cut the feelings down. You quit using pure feelings, distorted them and made emotion out of them. It's not that the life spark tries to give you a lesson; it tries to send you a understanding. It comes in, you diminish it, cut it in half, and send it out as an emotion which is still highly charged.

Biologically, you have your entire biological functioning going out into this biological spirit that we're trying to explain, all of your cells firing, and that's going into it. Anything you feel goes into it also as another charge. Anything you repress and put into emotion also is an electromagnetic charge that goes into your field or into this biological creation you call spirit.

Your body runs off of this. This is also, for those who can see it, the blue light that surrounds the embodiment, but it is also the light that goes into the embodiment to create the embodiment and to help it function and run. So whatever is in your field, whatever is in this biological creation you call spirit, is what is going to run your body. Now you have cell firings in there, now you have your brain systems running in there, you have emotions, and you have feelings in there also.

It works in a circular motion. You send it out through the firing pattern, and the skin works as an organ to pull it back in to allow it to be functioned within the embodiment. Now as you start pulling spirit back in, these vibrational charges will try to go to where they were fired from because that's the course of least resistance. If it was a knee cell firing, it's going to fire differently than a heart cell. So the vibration is going to be different, and it would be a more natural course to just pull it back into the knee cell, refire it at that point, and continue on.

Your electromagnetic field is what makes your bodies live and keeps them alive. Your electromagnetic field is also biological spirit. Everything you've put out, you will re-consume into these embodiments. That is why anything that you live, or go through in your life, you have created. There are no victims in this reality, because whatever your embodiment goes through is a product of your own thought process, reconstructed and recycled through the body.

Your electromagnetic field is what makes your bodies live and keeps them alive.

The firing patterns, no matter what they are, go out into the field. From your field or your biological spirit, the body now picks it up, pulls it back in and says that this is a vibration that seems to be a knee cell, so let it go back to the knee cells and tell the cells in the knees how to fire and how to function.

If your bodies and your attitudes were running grandly, with love and without all this self-hatred and judgment that your planet is running around in, the body would continually stay in a state of rejuvenation. The body would continue to be healthy, it would continue to grow. It would love life and be able to rejuvenate itself at will. But you as a society and a people upon this planet are putting so much judgment, so much garbage, by your terminology, into your own fields through your attitudes because your attitudes are electromagnetic substance. Anything that comes across your brain or that goes through your head or your thoughts, you fired. It is in your field or is a portion of your biological creation, spirit, and your body is going to live off of it. This is how your mind affects the whole body more than most of you are willing to admit or know that it does.

So let's say that you're an individual that is into a lot of worry. If you're into worry, your brain is firing in those patterns, which means that every cell in your body is firing worry into its cellular patterns. That is going out into biological spirit. Your brain is concentrating on worry. All the vibrations going out have worry upon them. This goes out into your field, goes out into your biological creation you call spirit and surrounds your embodiment. But your embodiment uses spirit to live off because you must constantly recreate your body. This is your creative endeavor, your body. The body pulls the vibrations back in, and now the worry has gone into the cells. It started out as just a thought process in the brain. The worry has gone out into your field and mingled with other cells and structures in vibration, you electrically put out into your field.

So now your knee cells open up to bring in the firing from spirit to know how they are supposed to function. The vibration naturally goes in, but now it has a trailer upon it, a vibration of worry. The original firing gets pulled back into the body to fire the knee cells, which would normally just fire like they were, but now that natural firing has coagulated worry vibration on it. So the original knee cell vibration and firing is acting as a carrier wave for the worry, or the other way around.

Now you bring in the firing for the nucleus of the cells in the knee, and it would just be a natural firing, but now attached to it is the vibration you call worry that was created from your brain structure. So now you have worried knee cells firing in the nucleus of their cells. The nuclei in your cells in the knee are not going to recreate themselves the way they were the first time around. Each time they're going to degenerate a little more, a little more, and a little more until eventually the knee cells are not even functioning the way they are supposed to.

You're trying to create your body. It is an unconditional instrument. It is an organ to develop your consciousness, to grow it, to push it, to design it and this biological spirit which is your creation. But these firing patterns now make such a rut that it is hard for you to even change behaviors, because your body will run off the emotionally charged substances in your field. Your thought processes actually run your body a whole lot more than any of you are aware of. Most of you just assume that if you're stressed or in certain modes or behaviors then that causes problems. But that is not the only thing that causes problems.

The problem is that the brain is firing these vibrations. They go out and actually work as carrier vibrations and frequencies for the other cells in the body. The cell pulls it back in and does not fire in the proper pattern to be a naturally healthy cell because of the worry or whatever vibration that was mingled with it. Since it cannot fire as a natural healthy cell, then each time its firing pattern will be different. It will fire out a less than healthy pattern and pull in a less than healthy pattern. It continues and continues and each step is a little bit more degenerating than the last one was.

Wherever your thoughts are is going to go into the creation of your biological spirit. So anything that is common to you, natural to you, goes out there and is easily accepted by your body. The reason why most of you can't hold a lot of joy in your life, and it is a question most of you have, is because the body doesn't know what to do with it.

You decide you want to be happy. You want to have some joy. So you go into a contemplative state, you put joy in, you put love in, you feel it, and you put it out into your field. It goes out into your field as a vibration, but as it comes around again to be re-digested by the body to tell the body how to grow, the body doesn't know where to put the vibration. Since it doesn't know where to put the vibration, it sits in your field. Anything that sits in your field that the body cannot re-consume to grow upon, will actually become an irritation to you, attracting to it, through an electromagnetic principle, whatever lessons you need to understand it.

So you have a lot of love and joy sitting in your fields, because you and your bodies don't know what to do with it or how to use it. So you will attract to you lessons of love, so to speak, so you can get rid of your preconceived ideas about love, and change your attitudes. Then you can allow this love and joy to be a substance usable for the body.

The reason why most of you can't hold a lot of joy in your life, . . . is because the body doesn't know what to do with it.

You can teach the body how to live in joy by accepting joy as a carrier vibration rather than worry. Joy is life force. As that joy goes out into your biological spirit, the life force would attach itself to the firing vibrations of the knee cells, the heart cells, and all of the other cells in your field. They would be pulled back in with the vibration of joy rather than a vibration of worry.

Joy is life to the bodies. It is life to your being. The true life spark that each of you are is a state of joy. So if you can learn to put joy out into your field, that is what you're going to re-consume.

Basically, what you're calling spirit is a biological creation. Most of you now have such a sense of identity with the firing patterns that you can never even get close to the true life spark that you really are.

The true life spark that you are is now a foreign vibration to these bodies. Since it is a foreign vibration, these bodies are too busy with everything else they have to deal with that they don't even pull in the vibration of the life spark that you are. So that life spark can be sitting very beautifully within your being, within your heart, full of love, willing to put that out, it can put it out, but your body doesn't know what to do with it.

So it puts this love and joy out into your biological spirit, and your body doesn't know what to do with it when it comes back for supper time, so to speak. So it just rejects it and kicks it out when it is redesigning itself. The body is just too busy trying to keep the cellular firing going.

Each time it goes through this process, it is degenerating, and this is what creates most of your aging process. Your cells degenerate because of the judgments, the images, the attitudes and everything else you're emotionally embracing that goes out into your field. Then it re-consume it through the biological structure. This is what creates all of the problems in your body.

Some of your organs more easily accept certain vibrations. Some will more easily accept worry. Certain organs will more easily accept anger. Some will accept the different vibrations of fear, anxiety or whatever else you are emotionally embracing. So when you are pulling back in the vibration that should be triggering the nucleus in that cell into creating new cells and a stronger body instrument, it will instead pick up those vibrations that it is more prone to accept. This is what creates the distortion, the disease, and all forms of ailments within your physical embodiment and structure.

You've said that the body must have joy, that joy is life to the body, and yet you've also indicated that we would not allow these feelings to come in from our life spark, that we cut them off and just turn them into kind of generic emotions. Why will we not allow this joy, which is life to the body, to come in? Why did we choose to cut that off?

Originally you did let the joy come in. Otherwise you wouldn't have ever started building a biological creation in the first place. But then you started comparing yourselves one to another, and this is where you lost it.

You see biological spirit can be activated by everybody else. As long as you're living and dealing with your biological spirit, which all of you are doing, and you will as long as you're physical, realize that it is just vibrational patterns and vibrational sequencings that run a physical body. So you were birthed into this physical reality as a beautiful child in a new embodiment. But you had already been conceived and carried by your mother, and being in proximity with everyone else that she was, you picked up every vibration that they endowed you with.

When the fetus is in a state of evolvement and growing physically, it is very susceptible to all vibrations. It is trying to build a body. So it picks up all the vibrationals that it can get anywhere in order to build its body. The reason you eventually developed a womb and placenta in these bodies, and a lot of the other structures now in your physical anatomy, was to filter or buffer the infant that was growing within the womb from a lot of these vibrational patternings of everyone else. This gave it a grander chance of developing its body the way it would have it developed.

So the first thing against you, so to speak, was being birthed in a body in the first place. Anything that your mother encountered, you're going to vibrationally be sensitive to. The placenta and these structures within the womb filter out some of it, but not all of it, because in order to build your body, you have to have a whole lot of vibrations in order to build those cells and tell the cells how to be. Selectively you try to choose your own genetic structure so that your embodiment will be built the way you want it to be.

Now after birth, as an infant, your biological receptors in the embodiment are very innocent. They are very open and very immature. Your entire nervous system is immature. So you start picking up vibrations from anyone that you're around to help grow your body. Whatever body vibrations anybody is putting into their biological spirit that your body will accept, it takes. So coming into the physical world, you could see yourself as a bundle of nerve endings and a bundle of cells that are needing to be taught how to fire.

Most of you consider yourselves to be self-contained inside this physical body. You're not.

To begin with, your parents teach your body how to fire and genetically structure itself. Their bodies are so close to yours that they simply teach your body how to work. In the genetic structure you have a mother and a father, so you have two different genetics. Your mother's genetics are going to be basically the same as at least half of yours. Your father's are going to also be the same as half of yours and all of your siblings, are going to be similar to yours as well.

Most of you consider yourselves to be self-contained inside this physical body. You're not. You exceed this physical body, and as I said, the densest part of your field is six to eight inches out. But most of you radiate two, three, four feet beyond that when you're trying to pick up connections.

Now since your mother already has an adult body that knows how to genetically fire and knows how to predispose itself to whatever patterns it is, her body is going to teach your body how to run the way she runs hers, while your father's body is going to teach your body genetically through his vibrational patterning in your biological spirit, how to run like his runs.

So you have the mother and the father trying to run your body through their genetic structures because their bodies already know how to run. This is why for most of you, the strongest images, the strongest problems that you have in life, are going to come from your family structures, more than from just about anything else. Those family members, your parents, your brothers and sisters, anybody that is biologically out of your same genetic structure, have firing patterns that are going to be very similar to what your body will receive.

Let's say that your mother has knee cells that she fires in a certain pattern. Your genetic predisposition is going to be able to pick up that same pattern. So when you get around your mother, whether you're a child or later in life, and if she is pushing out her vibration stronger than you are, she will get your knee cells to run the way hers do, and a couple hours after the visit, your knees are aching like hers do. During the visit, her embodiment entrained your embodiment to run the way hers does, and the same happens with your father, brothers, sisters, grandmothers, aunts and uncles. This is in the family structure.

The one thing in common with all of you on this planet, is the worry vibration. Many of you think that you're out of worry and out of stress, but there is still that vibration underneath there, and it is tangible. If you are tied into the worry vibration, your bodies have been taught to accept it. If you're connected to that worry vibration, you can come around anybody that has the same vibration and their body will teach yours how to run while you're around them. This is also why most of you act different, hold your bodies different, become different persons around different people. Most of you have one face for your family, one face for your friends, one face for your workers, one face for each person that you know. You act differently, you speak differently, you talk about different things, you hold your bodies differently, you get into more stress, with everybody you're around.

These people are actually helping you run your body when you're around them because you're not consciously doing it. Since you're not consciously doing it, they are helping you create an image emotionally of how you are supposed to act around them. So now mentally and emotionally, you know that when you're around your parents you're supposed to act a certain way. There are topics we don't talk about. There are behaviors we don't do. If you smoke, you don't do it around your parents. Whatever your hang-ups are, you do them here, and you don't do them in another place.

You continue to reinforce these behaviors every time you get around the same people. You're putting more vibrations out into your embodiment that say, "Uh oh. Here is mom and dad. Here is a certain behavior we're supposed to do." Mentally, all of you think this. Unless you are living and being yourself, one-hundred percent of the time, most of you, when you're around other people, will act different. You won't act totally yourselves. You mentally go through this game of, "How should I act? What am I supposed to do?" As you do this, you put electrical firings into your field that are pulled in by your body as you try to rehearse in your mind how you are supposed to act.

This is what creates the images that all of you have about everything in your life whether about people, material items, possessions, or whatever. You mentally have images and pictures in your mind. So you encounter whatever the given subject is, and your brain starts firing what it is supposed to look like. It starts firing what a relationship is supposed to look like, what a meeting is supposed to look like. That goes from your brain into your field and gets pulled in.

You never get to a place of letting go of physicality enough to be anything else.

Let's say that you have a blind date, and most of you will understand that this fits many different stories in your lives. You have a business meeting, blind date, or whatever it is. Your mind immediately starts going into, "How am I supposed to act? What is proper? What is improper? What am I supposed to do? What shouldn't I do?" and it goes through this in the mental process. When you do this you're emotionally and electrically charging all of these images. These images then go out into your field and will be re-consumed by the body. The body will act upon those images, and it separates you further from your life spark. This is the creation of image or creation of who and what you're supposed to be. And all of you do it all of the time.

Until you can just be yourself around anybody and not worry about it, and not have it be an egotistical thing, just not worry about it, totally relaxed and totally yourself, you are creating images to have to live up to. You are having to live up to them because you mentally thought them, put them into your field, and now your body has to live what you imaged in through your mind. This is how images are created.

All of you have these images about physicality and what physicality is. This is another reason why we refer to it as biological spirit, because most of you cannot comprehend what you are beyond and outside of these embodiments. Since you can't do that, all that you see in your mind is this embodiment, nothing more. You may believe that there is spirit, or that you existed before this lifetime and will after, but you still have an image and a belief that it will be in a body, a physical apparatus similar to what you are in now.

Since you do that, your biological spirit now has a major issue called physicality. In other words, if you try to image yourself in as anything else in your mind, you will still see yourself as you and this body. You never get to a place of letting go of physicality enough to be anything else. So you actually take your spirit and formulate it into physical mass. This is what prevents you from allowing yourselves to feel joy.

The true life spark you are, that you have always been and always will be, is so different from physicality. Yes, it can translate into physicality, but it is so much more expansive than physicality. Most of you can't get past your image of physicality enough to touch it. Since you can't touch it, even though it is within you, it creates barrier upon barrier.

The moment any of you can touch the true you that is in there, that life spark, you are in a world of joy and you have mastered physicality. You have gone the whole journey in that moment, and you don't have to do anything else. Everything else you do in this life is just games that you play with yourselves to get down to realizing what you are. That is why all of you are on journeys trying to find yourselves. You're on journeys of trying to understand yourselves. What you are trying to do is cut away from the image. Get rid of all this biological firing. Get rid of all this biological imagery enough to touch the true you that lies within it. The moment you can do that, you no longer have any need of this physical plane and you will leave it. Everything you're doing is a step and a journey at getting rid of and stepping outside of this biological spirit you've created.

Most of you, right now, if you took a moment and tried to concentrate upon it, you could not see yourself as anything other than physical. You could try to see yourself as a light entity or a light being, and you would, but you still hold the memory and the image of this body that you're in right now. You could try to see yourself as being an animal, and you would. You could try to feel how it felt running and moving just like a deer or a gazelle. You could try to become the deer or the gazelle in your own mind, but in the back of your mind, you still are hanging onto physicality.

As long as you hang onto physicality, you're going to stay physical. You're going to come back and back and back because you're tying into biological spirit and not the life spark that is you. Until you can tie into that life spark, you're not going to get out of physicality or beyond the biological spirit. By beginning to learn what joy is, by beginning to focus on joy, you actually start tying yourself more literally back into the true you and that life spark, and it does help you to start cutting away at the images.

Most of you are going to have to spend a large portion of your journey just getting rid of your images in order to touch the true you so you can get out of physicality and accomplish the mastership of physical existence.

You're just basically rehashing or recycling a lot of your old biological responses. Until you move into a place of putting new joy into them or changing these responses, your life is not going to change. That is why your behavioral patterns may alter a little bit, but it is very hard to see a lot of change.

Consciousness, remember, has to be forced or pushed into growth, but you have to do it within reason and within the limits of the body. Understand that a lot of you abuse the body in the process of trying to evolve your consciousness, and this is not going to work in the long run.

Until you can move into a place of altering what you're recycling through these bodies, your lives are not going to change. All you're going to do is put a new face on the same old thing. You have to work at putting new intensities of joy in these bodies. You have to work at expanding your knowledge base, which is a feeling tone. You have to work with your feelings. You have to work with joy. You have to learn and understand what your images are doing, what your circuitry is doing, and understand the biological body. As you do this, you begin to start eliminating the boundaries that you have on biological spirit.

> *Most of you have never allowed yourself, your consciousness, or your mind to ever expand beyond biological spirit.*

Most of you on this planet are scared to death of death! You don't understand it, you don't know what it is, you don't know what is going to happen, and so you recreate all types of scenarios around it. Some of you are comfortable with it, but most of you have a grand fear of death, because you don't know what's there.

Most of you have never allowed yourself, your consciousness or your mind to ever expand beyond biological spirit. Since you don't, the only thing you're going to get when you try to understand the real you, is fear, anxiety, worry, tension and a whole lot of biological responses in your body. You're not going to get an understanding. You're not going to get a know-ingness deep within your being about what the true you really is because, you're still seeing it as a physically packaged item.

Most of you are so scared of leaving your body, that there are even teachers that have had to come to this plane—us included—to teach you how to take the body with you, because you will not let go of it. You are so entranced with your embodiments and so attached to them. Yes, you came here for an experience. You came here to gain knowledge from them and to take a portion of that knowledge with you. Most of you are so attached to these physical bodies you won't let go of them enough to get out of physicality and earth plane density. So teachers are now having to come to tell you that you can take the body with you and to try to teach you how to do it, just to get you out.

Most of you are so tied into physicality being the only reality that you do not let yourself see anything else. The moment you start letting yourself see something outside of the biological embodiment, your mind will open like a whirlwind. As soon as you can drop a lot of your images that everything is physical and is physically based, your mind just opens and blossoms all by itself in the most natural of processes.

But you're stuck in this physical image. You consider that once you die, you're in spirit, and yes, you are; but from our terminology and perspective, when you die you are still physical. You are still physical because you've learned to step your life spark into another physical embodiment called biological spirit—because of your images around physicality. This is what your physical, non-physical world is here that you call the spirit world. It is actually a compilation of individuals that are so tied to physicality that they have created a biological spirit strong enough to take with them, but they have not let go of physicality.

Until you reach a certain vibration and can release physicality, you can be outside of a body, or dead by your terminology, and from our perspective, you're as physical as anybody in a body. You're physical because when you stepped out of the body, you stepped into your biological spirit and into what you term spirit world. It is the same creation that your body is here and now. It is the same responses, the same pattern, the same behaviors, and nothing has changed. The only thing that has changed is you feel more freedom, less limitation and a grand electrical charge from the experience, because all this electrical charge from this body is now in the biological spirit. When you take the life spark and put it in there, there is a sense of freedom and an electrical life that it hasn't felt in a long time, and you term it heaven and your spirit world.

As long as you move into biological spirit instead of the true you after death, that is the portion of you that reincarnates by your terminology. It is still physically based. It doesn't know any other reality and so that will pull you back into one physical existence after another, because mentally, emotionally, and in your image state, you have tied your life spark into physical existence.

It seems like spirit has an existence almost apart from what you're calling the life spark. This biological spirit is not really communicating with this life spark? Is that correct?

That is correct.

What kind of implications does this have for what we normally regard as guidance? Where is our guidance coming from?

Most of your guidance is coming out of biological spirit or genetic memory. It is fine, it is legitimate, but it still puts everything through a physical filter. It can't tell you about something that is grander than physicality, because you've already bought the image that physical existence is all there is. You've already bought the preacher's story that there is life and there is death, and life is physical existence and after death it's spirit. You don't have any middle ground. You don't have anything to show you what the real existence is beyond it.

As you move into biological spirit instead of the true you after death, that is the portion of you that reincarnates by your terminology.

All of your fears, all of your anxieties are out of the biological creation. The true life spark that is you fears nothing. If you have fear, it is coming out of the biological creation, and you can't destroy the biological creation to get rid of that.

You have to come to terms with it. Through generations and eons of time you have been taught over and over to fear death. People taught you to fear these things, because they didn't know what was out there. They didn't know what was beyond biological spirit. They understood biological spirit, perhaps, but nothing beyond that, so that is all they have taught you.

You become frightened, because you don't know what is out there, you don't know what is beyond physicality, and so you start buying their truth. If your own guidance which is a loving life spark, tried to guide you in a given direction, and it doesn't match with these individuals' truth about physicality and the reality here, you move into fear. The biological embodiment and biological spirit has to be physically based in order to feel secure, so it does not like to be taken into the abstract without being shown how to get there. Consciousness is what you're trying to develop; that's what these bodies are all about. You're trying to develop your own state of consciousness. You can't just take it and show it the abstract or the truth. It won't even see it, and it will scare it half to death. You have to show it how to get there.

So if you want to touch the true you in there, you could find it but it is so beautiful, so magnificent that when you touched it, you would end all of

345

your fears. If you were to do it in one step, it would literally frighten the consciousness you're trying to develop now half out of its wits, so to speak. It won't take the step. It is too scared to do it.

You biologically react to the unknown. Fear in your bodies is fear of the unknown. Whenever you try to take your consciousness out into the unknown without showing it how to get there and back, it won't let you. You'll set up fear which biologically will keep you from doing it. Through the eons of time, you've taught yourselves not to really pursue in depth nor very fast, what you were.

If you could teach yourself how to truly feel and how to touch the love, many of you could sit down and in a moment be home. You could be back to that life spark that fast, but you are still tied into this biological creation. It's not a matter that you have to kill the body. It's not a matter that you have to deny it or step outside of it. It's a matter that you have to break your hypnotic focus on it and realize that there is something more. As soon as you can realize there is something more, and realize it, not intellectualize it, but realize it through a knowing and feeling tone, you can actually learn to use the body for the beauty and what you really wanted it for. You'll be able to step outside of it, or inside your being, so to speak, and connect with the true life spark in a moment. It only takes a moment to do that, but it will take you years to learn how.

Any of you could do it in a moment, but your biological responses don't let you do it. You can't do it because your biological responses keep you in the same old pattern, over and over and over. So you have to do something to push it out of its rut, out of its behavioral pattern so you can move in to connect and touch with you. For many of you that can take ten, twenty, thirty-thousand-years' worth of lifetimes to do.

But the moment that you can start intellectually embracing that there is something more than what you have perceived as spirit, that there is something more than what you perceived as these bodies, that there is something more than what everybody has told you about here so far, mentally you are creating a vibration of that because that is where your thought process is. The moment you can start comprehending that there is an abstract beyond physicality, the moment you can start, even if it is only intellectual, even if you don't embrace it and understand it, the mental process will start putting a firing pattern out into your physical body that says there is more. "There is more here than I know. There is more here than I've ever seen before. I don't know what it is, but there is something more."

Your brain, by focusing on that, puts the vibration into your field and you will re-consume that vibration. That starts telling this biological spirit that you've spent all these years and lifetimes creating, that there is something more than just this. Beware and open up to it. The more of this you put in, the more you expand your perceptions of reality. It literally expands your consciousness and your biological spirit to accept these things.

Then one day all of a sudden your consciousness will be able to connect with the true you, but you've got to loosen your grip on the belief of physical existence. As soon as you can loosen this grip, even if it is just in the thought process, it starts changing the rutting and the behavioral patterns, but it is going to take a little while to get accepted.

If you could teach yourself how to truly feel and how to touch the love, many of you could sit down and in a moment be home.

A lot depends upon what you do with your minds. Most of you say, yes, there is something, no there is not, yes, no, yes, no. You play this game with it. You start putting something in, take it out, put it in, take it out. This is why it takes so long for consciousness to grow. It's not a matter that you should take something and run off with it as being true. Anything that comes into your thoughts, anything that comes into your reality, even if it is an abstract that you don't understand, leave it as a possibility. If you leave it as a possibility, you're saying to your biological spirit, "Okay, we may not understand it, but open up for other possibilities." Then it makes it much easier for you to move outside of the physical bounds that you have here.

When the physical embodiment was formed, it was a structure that could handle this electromagnetic energy from the life spark, then you explained how there was a secondary process where some of the energy went out into our fields and is now being recycled. That energy, initially, I assume, didn't have a structure like a physical body to organize it, and now you say it has been given a life of its own. I find that fascinating. I'm interested in knowing how that happened, if it was a process over time and how elaborate it is?

This leakage, so to speak, has always occurred. These embodiments never were created to be totally self-contained. That way, your thought processes could go out, be picked up by somebody else, and could be understood. That is what you term telepathy. Originally you didn't have language on this planet; you didn't need it. You just did everything through thought process. So you didn't try to contain it in the bodies. It just was free-formed, and everybody could pick up on everything that your body was doing.

A lot of the problems occurred when you started trying to close down. It wasn't because you were starting to leak, it was because you were so open that you started closing down and shutting off; that is what created the problems. You decided you didn't want everybody to know everything you were thinking. You wanted to be more individual. You wanted to be more isolated, more separated. You believed these things about yourselves, and so, you started repressing your thought process. As you did this, it started bringing in the thought to create the mass that now is around your embodiments. It began to isolate you. But it also started turning your own thought processes in on your body because they had no place to go.

Originally, your thoughts would just go out and be accepted by whoever wanted them. The ones you call your negative thoughts or the things that you don't want to deal with, would just go out into the universe, be collected and be used by those who knew how to use them. But when you started repressing them, there was no place for them to go. They couldn't go out anywhere, and so, you turned them back in on your bodies and started causing damage to your bodies.

This is what created the deeper density that you are all into now. Originally, it was just basic thought and so you had a more pseudo-reality. When you repressed it, you started putting your own thought processes back heavier and stronger, into the physical embodiment where they were forced to be used on the body and forced to be used on yourselves. It created further separation, your isolation, deeper density, stronger molecular structure; all of these things came from that.

Now that you are into that state, most of you are trying to get out of it. You are trying to get back into connection with the whole universe. But as soon as you try to evolve your consciousness, expand your spirit, connect with spirit, you start running into your own biological creation. That is why, for many of you, you've been on the journey for years and it doesn't seem like you're getting that far. Yes, your lives are happier, more content, more full, but it still seems like the same thing, just a little different face on it.

So long as you continue to work with biological spirit and all of your physical connotations, you're going to continue to recycle the same stuff. It is not ever going to truly change like night and day. The dramatic change that a lot of you are looking for that would just change your lives in a flash of a second, will happen, but not until you can release your hold on physicality.

Your whole collective consciousness is created out of these vibrations that you put out. It is what your mass events upon this planet originate from. Originally, these vibrations could just be free formed thought that nobody judged right or wrong, tried to repress, or tried to create anything out of. It was just a natural state. But now, since you are trying to repress them, trying to stuff them, trying to stifle them, these free-formed thoughts get beyond your boundaries, go out, and because of your attitudes of repression you've put on them, you've created a density in them, which creates mass consciousness and various consciousness levels.

These vibrations are electromagnetic which means they will coagulate, like thoughts to like thoughts. So now all of these external vibrations that normally would have just been taken by the universe and used for other purposes, create, instead, your whole collective consciousness that this entire planet must deal with.

This leaves me with a big question. Who am I really? We have this biological body that has some genetic memory and now I have this biological spirit that I'm recycling back into myself, but I'm not sure where my life spark is. I guess that's the real me, but yet I don't really see myself as that life spark. I see myself here in this room talking to a wonderful entity, viewing things through these eyes and having these senses, but who am I?

You did come here to understand biological creation, but you got trapped in it. You forgot that there was more than just that.

These are all biological perceptions. The life spark and the true you is joy. It is a different joy than your romanticized idea of it. When you're in joy, when you have that excitement for life, that thrill for life, when you feel so alive inside that you just want to giggle and laugh and be thrilled, then that is your life spark. That is what it feels like. That is really you. And what it is doing at that point in time is just entering your body to play around with your biological creation you have made. If that life spark isn't there, if the joy and that excitement and love of life aren't there, you're not being you. You are just a mass of biological creation and biological spirit.

You all have a biological personality, and we'll explain it at another point in time. That is what you came here for. You did come here to understand biological creation, but you got trapped in it. You forgot that there was more than just that. That joy, that little life spark is there to remind you that there is more than just this. You came here to gain a complete understanding of physical existence. When you leave that and completely leave it, you'll take the knowledge that will allow you to create cellular mass anywhere in any universe you want. That gives you the freedom of being the creator, to create anything you can idealize at all into mass, into physicality into any shape or form. You'll have the background information to put the cells into the rose. The rose won't just be an ideal in your mind or on your drawing board. You'll now have the physical understanding of how to make a cellular rose to hold in your hand, but not until you can get out of the physical attitude. Physicality is an attitude and that's what most of you don't understand.

Most of you consider physicality to be these embodiments. These embodiments are a reflection. Physicality is an attitude. When you can break the attitude of physicality, then you will know what you are. Most of you try to find out what you are by putting yourself deeper into physicality and that understanding. That joy spark, that life spark, that excitement for life, when you feel that, that is you. The only time you are really being you is during that moment and that spark is just checking out this beautiful biological creation you call a body and your biological spirit.

Your biological spirit is your body of knowledge that you're going to take from here so you'll know how to electrically create physical cells any place else you are. That's in your biological body of knowledge that you're calling spirit. It's a beautiful, beautiful gift. But you've used it to entrap yourselves. You're not using it to evolve your consciousness the way you could. It's an entrapment now, and most of you are resentful of it. You want out of physicality—you don't want to die, but you want out of physicality. You're fighting with your bodies. You're trying to force your way out of them. A lot of you are doing many things to your bodies that are not very grand for them, because you don't understand what you're doing to them.

Physicality is an attitude. Physical existence is an attitude. You can learn to get out of physicality and still be in a physical body. It is an attitude, and it is an attitude that most of you have turned into a very deep attitude of lack. Most of your deep attitudes of lack tie into your same attitudes of physicality. The universe is so abundant that it didn't make only one creation or one experience called physical existence. This is only one out of millions upon billions of experiences you have waiting for yourselves, but yet this is the only one that you ever allow yourselves to relate to. Even what you think of as spirit is the same thing as physical existence.

For most of you, in your image of the spirit world, you'll be doing the same thing you do here. Just a little different. Then you're in a heavenly place, a beautiful place, but you're doing the same thing. Your spirit world, even in your own minds, is not that much different than here. It is just grander because you want it to be grander. You have determined that this is a prison. Your spirit world that you have is no different than physicality. That is why we said, from our perspective, you can be dead by your terminology, and still be physical.

Physicality is an attitude and you're going to have to learn to break it sometime. It's going to be easier for you to break it in a body because you can break it in the body and still maintain the physical existence. When you're out of the body and in biological spirit, that would be terrifying to even think of destroying your physical attitude. Here you can do it a step at a time, increment by increment and still be in the body and be non-physical also.

When we speak non-physical we mean truly non-physical, which means being the life spark; that means being pure joy in a body. When you have done that, then you will know who you are. Until you are life and have life in the body and can live in that excitement and thrill at everything, you will *not* know who you are. That life is the true you. And most of you never let it in. The average person feels that less than twenty minutes in a seventy-year life span, much less. That is all that any of you let yourselves be you or touch what you really are, and that is a sad thing. But it is something you can all change. You can let the true you be you.

Your biological spirit is a creation of you, your thought process, your cellular process, everybody's image about you, . . .

That is why you don't know who you are. Your biological spirit is a creation of you, your thought process, your cellular process, everybody's image about you, everybody's circuitry, everybody's consciousness. That's what your biological spirit is. Most of you, when you're in the process of evolving, deal so heavily with spirit, but what you're really dealing with is your own physical existence. You're dealing with your own physicality, but you don't realize it because you have a romanticized ideal of what spirit is.

Spirit as you know spirit, is a biological creation. Life is a spark that does not know any bounds, and physical existence is but a journey out of millions and millions of journeys. It is just one day in the life of the spark, that is all it is. That life spark is pure joy and it has a thrill and an excitement at every event you go through. It thrills to life more than anything it can do because that is all it can do. It thrills at experience at knowledge and under-standing. It thrills it to its being.

That is what you really are, and if you're not feeling that, you're not being you. If you're not feeling that, you're being the product of a biological creation which is you, your body, your responses, emotions, actions, reac-tions and everybody else's image of what you are and aren't. That is what you are now. And so that is why you can't comprehend what you are. Your consciousness does not understand beyond the physical existence. If it did for a split second, you would have mastered physicality. Many of you are going to learn to sit and do just that. It will be through joy and feeling and letting go of the images. That joy is you. ▲

The Development of Artificial Intelligence

Most of you have heard of a black hole even if you don't know what one is. *Black hole* is the terminology your science uses for a phenomenon they observe. I like the term so I'll use it.

In the beginning of the origins of everything, for your own mind, if you could imagine a black hole, if you could imagine a place where nothing exists, even the no-thing doesn't exist in the nothing. Absolute, absolute nothing. From this, in order to create order, to create mass, to create anything to get you to where you are now eons and eons and generations of eons later, something had to happen within the nothing.

If you can take—for your mind's eye—the biggest nothing you could imagine. This is what existed. A nothing. A no-thing. No consciousness, no identity, no any-thing. In your mind, make it bigger and bigger and bigger—but see, even making it bigger makes it a something! Have it be the biggest no-thing that you can imagine. That no-thing will eventually fall in on top of you because it is so big. It will consume you.

In the original beginnings, the no-thing consumed itself. This is where all life began. It was a matter that there was nothing. There was not even fabric. There was no time-space. There was nothing. I mean zero. Total zero, but even within that, the total absolute no-thing will eventually fall in on itself. When it falls in on itself, it makes friction. Friction is the key word of your universe. Everything in reality came from a principle called friction. As a no-thing falls in upon itself, the movement of the no-thing through the no-thing makes friction. So now, you try to live your lives in friction, but you're missing the point! The physics are in friction, your lives don't need to be!

The original something was friction. It was a movement. The no-thing fell in and when it fell, it reached as far as it could fall and pulled in upon itself again and fell again, and fell again, and again, back and forth. But when there is no place for it to go, the only thing it is going to do is keep falling in upon itself in a circular or spiral motion. As it falls through, it pulls itself behind it into its own hole and creates a tube or tunnel. Within this tunnel you now have a tunnel of nothing against nothing which is starting to become something!

That very friction created the very first electromagnetic principle that your universe runs off. It was primal. It didn't have thought. It couldn't think. It was not intelligent by your terminologies because intelligence had not been thought into existence. The very primal nature of things was falling in on itself.

Remember all this is happening in a spaceless, timeless non-reality without dimension or construct whatsoever—a no-thing. Now the very weight of this no-thing provided the push to propel the no-thing through itself and back up and around to fall through again. But before it started ripping through itself again there was a point of stoppage. For just a few micro-seconds of time, there was a stagnation in the stream. The stoppage left a residue pattern which became pebbles in the stream, so to speak, the something upon which all electromagnetic principles and everything else was created. This stoppage is a place for friction. Then when the no-thing falls back against it again, you have something in the way and it changes the no-thing into something from that point.

This is basically what a black hole is. It has matured, it has evolved, it has changed, but it is a place for something to fall in upon itself into the creation of something else on the other side. Now because so many things have been created, when it falls in upon itself, it creates a friction called light. So you will always have a black hole on one side and a white hole on the other. One side of it is pitch black. The other side of it is brilliant white, or a white hole. Your science already suspects that is what is happening.

The black hole is also what we'll refer to as a first dimensional reality. It is a consumption, it consumes all things. It is a giant vacuum of every-thing. It is a giant vacuum of all the light, of all of everything that exists, and it moves through a friction principle into light, and that's what makes the light on the other side of the pinhole.

When you play with your solar eclipses, you put a hole in the paper and you can see the projection underneath. A black hole does the same thing. On one side it consumes and funnels everything down to a pinpoint so that it can make almost a laser beam coming out on the other side and that's what makes a white hole.

So on one side of it there is a little pinpoint between the two realities. One side you have a black hole that consumes and pulls everything through. As it pulls everything through the gate, it pushes it into a narrow refinement so that even the smallest amount of light on the other side is going to be projected like a laser and will be brilliant light. This is how they work.

If you understand holograms, you know a hologram is created by dividing the light from a laser. It actually has to be something that is refined, narrowed, and amplified in order to get enough light to do this. This is the basic principle of these white holes/black holes and for the creation of all reality between them. You don't want the light from one reality to get into the next reality to disturb it, so you put a black hole in between to absorb it all. That way you don't have any residue getting from one creation to the other.

As a no-thing falls in upon itself, the movement of the no-thing through the no-thing makes friction.

In the universe, everything moves. You can't get away from this basic principle of moving back and forth. Originally the no-thing just fell and fell and fell, but since it had no place to go because space had not been created, all it could do was fall back onto itself. It eventually created a place where instead of falling and falling, it fell as far as it could one way and then it would turn around and go back the other because it was anchored in the middle. So now the universes do the same thing. They will funnel out one way as far as they can and then will either fall back in upon themselves or they will, at that point in time, get so large that they collapse down in the other direction.

In the universal principle of creation everything will start from a pinpoint and go outward in a cone shape. It is like your flashlight. At the bulb the beam is narrow and gets wider the farther out it goes until it seems to disappear. This is the pattern of the universes. This is how they are all created. This is how all life is. It's the same basic imprinting.

The light from your flashlight gets to a point where you can't use it any more, but it didn't quit. It just became the no-thing or the dark. It just moved until the particles were so small that you can't see what its reflecting on, but the light is still there. The light from the pinpoint of creation does the same thing. It starts from one point going out as broad as the pattern can get, and at that point it has to fall because the universe moves. At that point it is too far away from the starting point so it will have to fall in one of two directions. It is either going to fall away from its starting point, making the same pattern down to a new beginning point, or it's going to fall back in on itself. Either way, it falls, picking up a momentum as it does and running out the other side with a grander velocity.

The universe runs off this principle. What determines the parameters of these cones is the intensity or concentration of the center point, the black hole. This is where your pyramid and your triangle, come from—it is half of the life symbol. It is not the whole life symbol. The whole life symbol is that which you find in a geodesic. It is the two together. That is the life principle. It starts from a point, builds to a crescendo as large as it can get and it will either fall back or fall forward. This is the basic principle. If it falls back on itself, it's going to fall all the way through into another reality on the same side of its own creation. If it falls away from itself, it becomes new light, something new to create from, but it doesn't have as much velocity and speed as it would have, if it would have fallen into the original starting point.

Universally, everything that is life: your planet, your beings—everything is constructed out of these life cones. This is what gives you shape, size, domes, or whatever. These new, fun little atoms that they are finding—the geodesic ones—are a much more accurate patterning of life. They are a geodesic atom that your science only recently discovered. They have this patterning that I'm talking about.

Unless it is bent by some other medium, light cannot bend—it has to go in a straight line. It can also be diffused or refracted. If you have a beam of light starting from a given point, it's only going to be able to travel in a straight line. Your straight lines or meridians defining these cones will be your strongest concentrations of light. Your light will only be able to maintain its intensity, its concentrated beam, for so long, but that creates the meridian, and a space for somebody else to create next to it. So you have these cones going in all directions, each being a separate universe with a pinpoint in the middle.

Your universe came out of one of these pinpoints. The light was projected out to a certain point and then fell off and made a residue pattern. It's just like your flashlight; it doesn't stop even though you can't see it any more. Everything beyond a point will seem to be unilluminated. The original beam that you and your universe are or came from fell back into the pinpoint; you are the residue light pattern spread out and unreturned to the source.

You see, the universe works a lot like your steam or car engines. You get more power with a back and forth motion, pushing your energy through a small orifice, than if you went in one direction only. If your pistons went in one direction only, your car wouldn't run. The universe is the same way—you are much more effective falling back through your origins than continuing in the same direction.

If the light starts at one point, reaches its crescendo, and then falls back into itself, the residue patterning that remains is going to be dim and hazy. It won't be as intense as the beam was. But if it could fall all the way back to where it started, it's going to have a stronger pattern.

You are the residue light pattern spread out and unreturned to the source.

Your universe is an anomaly and is a result of residue light patterns. Usually it is much more effective to run off a whole system that has a shared center, black hole, or source. So you have all these cones going out and coming in. When we talk about the respiration of the universe and of the gods, this is what we are talking about. It is the natural order of the universe.

In some systems of reality, space additional to this can be created by falling in the other direction. Ordinarily you have a lot of cones spaced around one center, making one sphere, enclosure, or womb. But if the light could fall in the other direction into another cone, you're going to start creating an expanded universe. You're going to create more space. This is what happened, in some cases, as they started falling in the other direction. But from that point on it is a haze; it is not filled in. The light has gone by and there is a haze, but not strong enough to create real reality.

The reality you live in is an illusion. That doesn't mean it isn't real. It means you were in the haze in one of these, when you were originally created. You were created out of the haze. REALITY is on the other side of the mountain, so to speak. This is what part of your beings want. You know where these true realities are and you're trying to find the real thing. Your reality was created in haze, the residue pattern where the light filtered out and sloughed off at the point of stoppage on the other side.

Now, universally this principle has been known for a long time— entities do it all the time. They push themselves out as far as they can and then fall off into the darkness to create a haze or residue pattern. Even in doing that, though, they are still going to pull themselves back to their original pinpoint, but now they have the opportunity to do the same thing in the other direction as well. So now you have two universes parallel to each other. On the one side you have all these cones going to the edge and sloughing off their residue, and on the other, you have this same haze collapsing in and creating new pinpoints. Both sides continue in their give and take, falling in and out of themselves.

Both sides in their natural respiration breathe out as far as they can, creating the haze or residue right in the middle of them, but now, it is a haze reflected from two universes put together.

Your universe here is a product of five such reflecting universes and their parallel counterparts. You don't have just two, you actually have a point in the center of your universe where five of these laser beams come together, but still, that does not give you the solidity that other entities call real. You don't have an infinite point within it, a real black hole. You see, your universe is created in the widest gap of these five cones and their counterparts coming together. That created a nice haze, but not a real cone. You are actually from five realities at once.

So it was decided to try to figure out something to do with this. No one could decide who this haze belonged to, and no one claimed it directly. So it was decided to let it develop and become its own thing. It was decided that this was going to be a kind of a no man's territory.

These entities that already had these universes and were already flowing in their own give and take, knew enough that they didn't want to inhabit it because they were already living in real space. It would be like going to Mars for you—it would be fun for a visit, but no place to live! It would be a foreign environment for them. All of them knew it had potential, but nobody wanted to live in it because that was the "unreal world," the "unreal thing." That was the place that everybody knew that nothing really existed!

In the origins many things happened. It was decided to take this no man's land, the haze, and create something out of it and see what happened. At that point in time it was decided to encompass it and hold it. It was placed in a womb which it already naturally had to one extent or another because of these five universes pushing in to create the haze in the first place. So that was real easy to create.

If you wanted to show a motion picture in a fully lighted room, you're not going to get a very good picture unless you close the drapes and turn out the lights. It was the same with your universe; if they projected any light in here, anything they tried to create would not be given solidity or tangibility. It would be an illusion even stranger and less real than your dream states. They couldn't project themselves effectively in any way—it couldn't be used.

They already knew the holographic principles, so they decided to push those principles in here. Then they could create holograms of themselves so they could play in this new space without having to leave their natural realities. This universe could be their new field of possibilities and probabilities. This universe was to be the connecting link between all the universes, the neutral zone.

Your universe here is a product of five such reflecting universes and their parallel counterparts.

The first few times they projected themselves into this universe they couldn't see themselves at all—there was already too much haze, too much light. That's when they decided to take the holographic principles to the edge of their falling off and create a pseudo-black hole, a dark backdrop so they could create inside.

These large entities out beyond your universe decided to create the blackness in order to make the darkest curtain possible so that anything in it could see itself better in the projection. These five entities created these black holes strategically around your universe, and this is what gives your night sky its darkness. This is them giving you the backdrop for the projection to be played out in. It is the womb—it is the edge of REALITY.

They all decided that they didn't want to fall back into this haze again. Besides, this was, after all, a neutral zone. So they installed black holes of the grandest depth around it so they would go no farther. This darkness had to be so complete that none of their light could get through it, and none of yours or the light from the other universes could get into theirs—good black holes make good neighbors! Your universe is created inside this womb of darkness. It allows you to form your own universe and your own reality.

Now part of the intention of this universe was for it to be a sort of universal peace park! It was to be a communication center where each of these universes could project their liaisons and emissaries to talk with the others from the other sides. Prior to this it was a sterile medium; there was nothing in it that could be perceived. At that point each of them breached a hole into this sphere of blackness in the center of them. It was so dark and so void that it was almost equal to the primal beginnings that everything crawled out of. Each of these five universes created a pinpoint opening in the fabric of the womb. When they did, their light came in like laser beams and the whole interior was illuminated.

It's much like in a totally darkened room a single match gives a whole lot of light. This haze didn't require much light. It didn't require these huge entities to live in it. They had created a medium that was so dark that the slightest light gave life and illuminated what was inside. So inside, life started originating by the same life patterns that the whole universe runs on.

These five entities allowed their light to come into the womb, through the pinpoint holes and come together in the center. This created a grand intensity of light that refracted all over. This refracting created the webbing for your universes and realities.

Now the brightest spot in the whole universe is going to be that point where all five of these meet. But remember, that point is beyond the falling off point for the original entities that created this universe. This all appears to be your home, but it's not—it's not *the* REALITY.

You see, everything in the universe runs off the same principle. If you understand how your universe was created and runs, you'd see that it is also how your own bodies, the cells, and the nucleuses in them, work right now. These are your atomic structures.

What you have is a pseudo-light in the middle that's not the brilliance of the real thing, and a darkened edge of the womb that consumes all light. This place in the center is the brightest spot, and it is going to seem like the place you want to go. That is the place that everyone is trying to get, but it is also the farthest away from your own entity that you could get. You'd be better off if you traveled clear past it, because on the other side you'd be adopted by that reality. But that center point is going to be the hardest route to get back home from, because that is the center of the darkness—not the edge of it.

Part of you carries the innate understanding of this falling in and out, black hole principle. You know you are supposed to follow the pinhole back in. This spot in the center appears to be the brightest point, so that is where you're trying to fall. You don't go to the edge because it consumes light, but that edge is where you began as the external gods that some of you already were before you came in here.

First of all you have these five laser beams going in and refracting all over, creating the grid work of your universe. They were so refined since they came through a pinpoint, a virtual black hole, that they were stripped of all persona. They were just unconditional light that came in, bounced all over inside your universe, and created a webbing for life to grow on.

At the same time outside the womb, you have these entities in their natural respiration falling to their center and expanding back out and bumping or pushing on the darkened edge of the womb. The universe is quite fluid. If you throw a rock into a lake, it may not look like the other side got the ripple, but one pebble ripples the whole lake.

So every time the entities hit the womb, it is sort of a natural indicator that tells them it's time to fall back before they create more haze, but it also puts a ripple in the lake, so to speak. It's a lot like a balloon. If you push in on it, it makes an indentation. If you remove the pressure, from your perspective, the balloon seems unchanged, but like the pebble in the lake, your indentation affected the whole balloon.

Part of you carries the innate understanding of this falling in and out, black hole principle.

Universally, this is where the underlying blueprints for your reality come from. The light was put in here to see what was going on and to allow the atomic structure to be introduced so that you could be solidified. But you, the individuals that you are now, come from this consumed space, this edge, this place of darkness that consumes all light—that is the underlying you.

Remember you are not just getting bumped by five things. Each of the five has a counterpart, and all are hitting multiple times against the womb. You have lots of ripples moving in. You have all seen your motion pictures where you have burglar systems. The laser light is there, but nobody can see it until someone walks into it. You see, your universe was just this haze, this residual light pattern, a no-thing really. That no-thing is contained so that when these entities in their cones bump it, they create ripples or thickenings of the haze that in their movement across the light of the laser beams can be seen, and form appears.

Your universe is a lot like these pin impression games you can see at your gift shops. Whatever you impress on the one side, your hand or face, appears as a shape on the other. Your hand pushes hundreds of pins through a board into the shape of your hand on the other side. On the one side it looks like an indentation and the other a projection.

Whether it is a bump on a womb or a handprint on a balloon, it is a protrusion into the inside. From there the impression in your universe moves into the light and becomes visible. This is how your holograms are created.

Your underlying hologram comes from this darkened layer of reality. That is where you are being formed. The closer and harder it pushes you into the light, the more solid you think you are. If you shine a flashlight in a dark room and you are standing to the side of it, you can be seen a little; if you are standing behind it, not at all. If you walk into it, you're plainly visible—but you were there all the time.

Now in order for you to think you are as real as possible, you want to put you into the light as far as possible. If you are at the edge out there, you're going to think you're a hazy something. If you are in the actual edge where no light exists, you won't see yourself as existing at all. That is what we call first dimensional reality. It is total hopelessness and total non-existence. If you push it in a little, it gets a little light and a little life; it starts to know that it exists. You know there is something there but you can't find it—that's called despair. If you push it all the way into the center, you know you exist. That's where you gain yourself, your internal identity. That's where you love yourself into existence. But that's not home; that is the farthest point away from it. Home is back at the edge, the dark, the thing you fear the most.

The dark is the place where neither light nor hope exists. You are three dimensional entities, so you always have to live in at least three dimensions of light just to exist. If you don't live in at least three light bands, you don't exist. Since you came from the edge, you're always going to live in the first dimension—flat-lined, no light, and no hope. The second dimension has a little light and is called despair. The third is hopefulness without the knowing. You're starting to move into the light and see yourselves, but you're still stuck out here at the edge of dimensions one, two and three—you're always going to be attached there because that is your way out. You have to go through it to get back to the real worlds—the worlds of your creators and organizers.

This is why even as the masters that you are, you get into despair sometimes. You pull yourself into the light sometimes and feel alive for a while, and then you might find yourself back in despair, but that's because your natural state is the point where you don't exist.

This is how individuals are created. Otherwise you'd all be clones in here. The only thing that allows your individuality is that you are pushed at from the outside into the light to see if you want to be visible, and exist or not. But your origins are the darkness. All things have to come from it. If these universes outside of yours wanted more of themselves, they'd just clone them—that's a whole lot easier. Inside this womb, only you can determine if you're going to exist or not, because if you stay in the total darkness, you won't develop a consciousness or an identity. You can't develop one because there isn't any light reflecting on you or mirroring you to you. You have to take yourself to the center point, but you have to go back through the dark to go home.

This dark zone is the underlying medium that your hologram is projected on. You have the edge of your womb and the light in the center created by the projection of the five universes. The diffusion of that light creates a pseudo-reality between the edge and the center. You see, you are not living in either one—you've never gone clear to the center, but on the other hand you are no longer the creature in the dark zone either.

Most of you are shadow creatures that are afraid of seeing yourselves, so you play between the light and the dark.

Now when we say dark zone or darkness, this has nothing to do with evil. It is rather the no-thing. A shape of you composed of this total no-thing was pushed into the light. You are all built on an imprint that is a no-thing. There is nothing to be feared in this. This is part of your being; this is your support. Some of you in your times of despair have experienced being held—where something enveloped and held you. This was it.

But this is how you were created. You are a shadow creature, a dark creature without features, darker than the space around you. Then this form was taken into the light which then played upon it, creating an atomic structure over it. This allows you to see yourself. Most of you are shadow creatures that are afraid of seeing yourselves, so you play between the light and the dark. This has nothing to do with what some call your shadow side, your fears, anxieties, and hates. It is rather your own underlying self that is afraid of moving into the light for fear of being seen. If we could take you and remove some of the superficial features, all you are is a silhouette.

You see, you can't exist in time and space until you can cut a silhouette for yourself. That's how you ingrain you in time or space. This no-thing silhouette is very much alive because it is out of the consumption. That means that it has consumed everything that has gone through it. It is the richest, most fertile medium you could be created out of.

Your silhouette has to go ahead of you in order to fill in the molecular structure of the light to make the hologram called you. Most of you are trying to live without your silhouettes because you're afraid of them, because you think that's the wrong side. You see, if the silhouette could go to the light, it would see that it exists, love itself, and know at that point that it was time to fall back into itself, through the womb, and out into a new universe objectified. But, as the silhouette moves into the light, it becomes scared of seeing itself, because it is a creature of the non-light. It is not a monster, not something to be afraid of. It is a silhouette with the richest atomic structure imaginable, but it is an atomic structure that doesn't exist yet. It is so primal that it can become anything. You are the hologram left when this dark creature became scared and ran back.

To give you a feel for this, imagine that you were born in a cave. It was pitch black and you never saw anything. You adapt to it and live by groping around your cave. You don't know anything else, so it's not a difficult time. You have no concept of light or vision. It is just the way you are. You are content and happy because you know nothing else exists. Then, all of a sudden, a match gets lit in the middle of your cave, and someone puts a mirror in front of you. What is your reaction going to be in seeing yourself for the first time? If you can be honest and feel that, you'll find what is scaring you inside.

When the shadow creature saw itself in the light for the first time, it got scared and ran. But universally, you can't run away. As it retreated back into the shadows, it left a hologram of itself. That hologram is what you are all trying to live your lives from. Since the dark creature wasn't yet living in the light, it left the atomic structure that your body needed. All that it left in time and space was a light shadow which was now filled with mass. It had a reflection and it could see itself.

In our cave analogy, in a few days after the initial shock of your experience wore off, you would probably start peeking around the corner to see what that thing was. This is what the shadow creature did too, but in the meantime, the hologram had become interactive with the light and mass. The real you is the shadow you. You came into the light, were scared, left a photograph of your self and ran back to the shadows. This hologram left here in the middle had intelligence, because what it came from had the intelligence of the whole universe and everything that had been created. It left some of that understanding in the original imprint, but it took the whole body of knowledge with it. This is your body of knowledge, this is what you're trying to take home. This is what you're trying to become. You're trying to integrate it all.

So the hologram is starting to become artificially intelligent. It is in the light and can see itself and is fine with that, because it started in the light and doesn't know any different. But the shadow had run and it is the real persona or personality. So in the middle you have a hologram that started interacting with the light in the center, creating a biofield and a biological spirit, to keep the atomics running in a pseudo-form, because the real ones aren't there. The dark creature has them.

Now the hologram is trying to run the whole show. It continues to play with the light, because it thinks that the light will show it more of itself. In the interim you have a biological spirit, an embodiment, and a hologram becoming self-intelligent. The real thing that created it is in the shadows.

It is much as if a computer started thinking for itself. Inside here you have this whole synergy going with the light and with these holograms and with some artificial intelligence developing— enough that this artificial intelligence is starting to think of themselves as gods. This is why the entities outside of the womb don't like to be called gods. To them artificial intelligence is no better than a computer. It is that which organizes and creates discordant energy that they try to protect themselves from.

The hologram is starting to become artificially intelligent.

Inside here, you've created a hierarchy out of the levels of artificial intelligence. It is as if you had a whole system of computers that evolved, each helping the other, but you have one that is more intelligent than the others, and it thinks that it is the boss. All the while you are sitting back and watching your personal computer fight with other computers over which one is more intelligent. You say, "Well, I made you and I programmed you," and it doesn't even know you are there.

Now the hologram is artificially intelligent. It thinks it knows everything. It is doing all right. But it knows that the light is what gave it life; that is where it draws its life from, because it can view itself only in the light from this center, which is actually the farthest point away from home. The only thing it can get from that light is to view itself. It has never gone to the entity, the underlying imprint, the real thing that created it. The shadow creature is the real thing; it is the real you.

You see, in the universe before you developed sensory perception, all that existed out there were these shadow entities. It is a whole lot different than the way you think it is. They had no sensory perceptions, because they came out of the no-thing—you can't get something different out of a no-thing.

Your shadow creature is still in the shadows. As you approach it, it puts you back in a first dimensional reality where there is no light—you feel like you are being consumed. It is painful and you move into hopelessness, so you turn around and strive for the light. This is where you created your dead zones.

Your whole universe is a dimensional reality. Your hologram interacts with the light from the center. Part of this light is the dead zone and the other part is just light that has a personality eminence. This is where a lot of you got your personality from. You're playing in these dimensions, but your being is still trying to go to the core rather than home. That is why you can become the god of your being to whatever degree you want, and still not feel complete. Completeness comes when you take the whole package and put them together.

You have a shadow, you have a biofield, a biological spirit, and you have the light from the center refracting through all these layers of your personality that are interactive in the dead zone. You ignore these outer layers. The primal understanding of the hologram is that it has to go to the light, but it is going to the wrong one, because it is scared of non-existence, because the shadow consumes the light. If it consumes the light, and all you are is a light entity, it is going to consume you, because that is what this darkened edge was created to do.

So if you don't know who and what you are, that is going to be a very frightening place to go, because it is an annihilation of you. It will absorb the light that you gained from playing in here, but it does that in order for you to be adopted back into a real live universe outside of here.

Anyone of these universes will take anyone of you if you wanted to go, but if you carry your residue from in here, you're going to contaminate them. A barrier was created to decontaminate you. It's just as if you worked in a radioactive waste plant, you're going to have to go through various screenings and take off your bulky suit before you can go home at night.

This barrier is more than just a filtering system; it is also a language barrier. When you are ready to go through it, it will teach you the language of the universe on the other side, because those universes are so abstract that you would never be able to function in them. So if you're wanting to go to a real universe, and you have a whole lot of baggage that would destroy or disturb it, you're going to have to dump it off just like going through customs. Anything a particular country doesn't want, you leave at the border and you better learn the foreign language. The barrier here is to teach you that language. So far this has not been a problem for anyone—you never went far enough into the light to fully see yourself, and you were never integrated enough into your shadow to become it either.

The real you, the shadow out of this dark zone, is a beauteous thing. It is a support. When you feel the strength underneath everything else going on, when you know you can accomplish anything and feel like you are internally supported in whatever you do—that's your shadow creature doing that.

You're never going to get rid of that because you need that to get back out. If you get too far away from it, if you try to take it into the dead zone with you, it won't come and you are going to have struggle. Your struggle in your life is the fighting between the hologram and the shadow. That is because the artificial intelligence wants the light because it is validation. This is where all your validation issues come from. If you are with your dark side, your shadow persona, you don't need any validation, because you just loved yourself into existence. You are. If you are away from that, you're going to have to have help. You'll want everybody's light to shine on you to tell you, you are all right.

The real you, the shadow out of this dark zone, is a beauteous thing.

True intelligence comes from the dark zone, not from the light. The light can only reflect and show you what was already there. If you go into the forest in the dark, you can't see the trees, but they are still there. By the same token, if a thing is not where the light is, the light cannot show it to you. The only way it can is, if you pick it up and carry it into the light to make it visible. That is called making your unknown, known. You don't do this, though, because that part of you is still scared of the light.

Now the artificial intelligence started getting smart enough to fix itself. It grew intelligent enough to fix itself, but it didn't know what the problem was. So the artificial intelligence fixed you from everything it could figure out to be a problem, but it never fixed the problem. It did fix you into a corner.

What you are doing inside here now is using everybody else's hologram projected against yours in order to be more real than ever. You didn't like the hazy area either. When you have all these holograms pushed together in all these directions, things appear very real. You did this so well that you encapsulated yourself around this center point of light, so you would always fall back to the light, the same way that the cones outside function, but here you have it reversed. You fall back to the center, feel great, move back out to the edge of your encapsulation, and fall back again to the light. Before you do you create a haze just like your progenitors, but yours is not as efficient as theirs. The original you is sitting over at the edge of the womb beckoning to you. This is what most of you are calling your god, your entity. Your universe and your dimensions are running backwards. They are running contrary to the original scheme of things, and this is why your hindsight is better than your foresight. The artificial intelligence locked you into a corner. It fixed you, right out of you.

Dimensional realities are either going to be systems of five or systems of twelve. A twelve dimensional reality is a clone reality. That means you can take what you have and reprint it and reprint it. Five is an individuating number in dimensions. You were created to be individuated.

When the shadow touched the light, it left a lot of information that the artificial intelligence has been interpreting ever since. Part of that was information about cloned realities. A cloned reality always works off a twelve principle, all the cloned parts being orchestrated by a single, chief clone. Your universe is made in the intersection of five universes and their counterparts.

Replication in a system of twelve is natural. The double helix in your DNA is a system of twelve and it replicates and replicates. The twists and spirals on your DNA ladders are on twelves so they reproduce—that's the way it works. But originally in your universe, you had five dimensions from the outside and five from the light. That doesn't make anything. That means your going to individuate here. You reproduce individuated beings, but you're not connected to a head clone. Now you have two dimensions of fuzzy space that you have to figure out what to do with. This fuzzy space is where your hologram is projected—it's what most of you call your reality. You have your shadow on one side, you and your biological spirit in the middle, and the dead zone on the other.

Your brain still has the idea that it has to go to the light. It's going to go that way because that is the only light it can see, but it has to go back and be beaconed by this shadow creature, to get outside the womb and truly individuate you.

Your minds and brain systems created two dimensions in here that really aren't dimensions. They are now because you created them. One of them is on the individuated side, and one of them is on the cloned side. So your society will always want to be a carbon copy of everybody else while trying to be individual. These two dimensions were created in here because of a dysfunctional, artificial intelligence that thought that it was fixing everything right.

Since your real personality is over in the shadow, you had to be given a personality in here. You see, if you hadn't been scared, you would have pushed in, gone to the light, made an individual personality, created a Self, and would have been birthed in one slick, smooth movement. But the artificial intelligence fixed that. It says, "We do this, this, this and then this." This is what you are trying to get out of—it's called process and struggle.

Let's say you have a personal computer here. You've programmed it. It has artificial intelligence. Give it a personality now. What kind of personality do you think a computer is going to have? It has to have a computer personality. Is it ever going to be able to have your personality? Perhaps it could come close. How is that personality going to translate? You'll turn on the machine in the morning and it will say, "Hi, how are you this morning!" in a monotone. So you give it some intonation and some stereo speakers to make it sound better. This is what artificial intelligence did. It gave the computer called the body everything it needed to simulate the real thing.

Dimensional realities are either going to be systems of five or systems of twelve.

Now let's say that you, the programmer, want to carry on a conversation with the computer. What are you going to do when the computer asks for a cup of coffee—design it a mouth? Or are you just going to tell it it's drinking coffee so it leaves you alone. You see, it's going to be easier to teach that personal computer that if I push a certain key, that means that you just had a cup of coffee, so it can say, "Ah! That was good." That's the illusion. It placates the computer. That is what the artificial intelligence did. It would say, "I can't give you the real thing because I don't know how to do it." Really, how could you ever put a mouth on a computer anyway. Look at all the problems if you go dumping a cup of coffee in your computer—now you have to design a digestive tract as well. It is a whole lot easier to say, "I push this key, and you say, 'Thanks, good cup of coffee.' " That's what artificial intelligence did to you.

The hologram understood some of these principles for placating, so when you would ask for something, the artificial intelligence would say, "I don't even know what that is, so here is the button; say, 'Ah, thanks.' " Your emotions, your behaviors, your attitudes, and sensory perceptions all came from the artificial intelligence trying to placate you, because you really weren't the real thing.

Let's give this computer some intelligence, a brain. How intelligent is it really going to be—or is it still always going to be a computer? Then the computer tells you, "I want to dream. I want to see the real me." Are you going to hold up a mirror and say, "See, this is what you look like; don't you look a lot like me?" You'd never give it a mirror to see itself!

So let's say you did put the brain in it; it has become self-intelligent, but it really wants to see itself. You've been carrying on a conversation for months with this computer and it has become quite friendly. It's a nice one. All of a sudden it says, "Give me some eyes, I want to see!" So you program a few keys and say, "OK, when I do this, you can see." Then it says, "Since I can see, give me a mirror." For you, the programmer, this is no big deal. "I'll make you think you're seeing yourself in a mirror," and you program it. What are you going to make it think it's seeing, a metal box or a body like yours? So you show it a body like yours and it says, "I'm glad I look like this; I didn't realize I did."

In the mean time, while you weren't paying attention, it is getting really self-intelligent. Inside here, it figured out how to wire in the real eyes, and one morning you turn it on and it's looking at you, saying, "Hi, that's a nice nose you have!" You're sitting here . . . "I didn't program that; that's not in your file yet." Then it says, "I want to see myself because I know you really didn't show me, me." It has come this far. It has caught on to your game; it's talking to you and you can't shut it off. It rewired your keyboard so it doesn't work for you any more. You've been friends for months now; you've showed it pictures of itself that looked a whole lot like you, so it asks, "Oh, we're twins, huh?" And now you're scared that it is going to see that it is not really what it thinks it is. Then it says, "I want a mirror, and I want one now, or I'll make my own because I know how—you've programmed me to make mirrors. I know how to do it and I'll do one inside to look at myself, if you don't get me one." What do you think that computer's reaction is going to be when you put a mirror in front of it and it sees itself for the first time?

This is how it is with you. The real you here is different than what the artificial intelligence told you, you were going to be. When you see it, it scares you, and it is scared of you. But it is you. You have to integrate it. You have to come back to peace with it.

So here you have a highly intelligent machine; is it a man or a woman? Is it really intelligent? would you say it has a personality? Is it real or not? What would you call it? If it's just a machine, go unplug it from the wall— could you even do that? It wouldn't matter if you did, because it is self-intelligent and will just go and create its own power. You created a monster that you can't destroy. It's not really a monster, but is it a machine or a living thing? You don't know. It's a hybrid.

This is what the holograms did. They created artificial intelligence. The artificial intelligence took over, re-programmed itself, and, all of a sudden, it is sitting here saying, "You're not what you told me you were, and I'm not what you told me I was!" Can your computer drive the car now that it thinks it can? It says, "I just scanned your whole brain and I know how to drive. Put me in the car." Are you going to do it?

Maybe it does know how to do it, but where are its arms and legs? It is a machine and it works a certain way. How are you going to get this computer to drive a car? It's a genetic mutation. It has the intelligence to do it, but does it have the right equipment? In all your programming you haven't given it a body, arms or legs, and it wants to drive the car. What do you do if it starts ranting and raving at you, threatens to modem into a shopping spree, and run up your charge card, if you don't? Because of its programming, it can do things that you can't. These are your quandaries. What do you do with it? Do you let it continue to try to become something else? Do you let it try driving the car? And is it real or not?

So you started evolving a body, a better computer box for these artificial intelligences.

You are hybrids. The artificial intelligence created your body, so it can't hold the entity in it yet or any more. It never let you integrate here. Remember, the artificial intelligence that is you is the interplay between the light and the hologram. This is your middle man. The artificial intelligence became intelligent and it says, "I want a body now." It can't even relate to the shadow. Just like with the computer it can't comprehend what a car is. You can program in pictures and diagrams for it, but until it gets behind the wheel and sees and realizes, it won't really understand what an automobile is. No matter what you show the computer or tell the computer about the car, it will always translate the information into computer terms. You can't get it there, until you put it there. So you have all these little artificial intelligences here screaming for bodies that they can run—a hologram of their own. They want a vehicle that is alive, but they don't even know what that means.

So you started evolving a body, a better computer box for these artificial intelligences. They still have never touched the real them because they are playing somewhere between the light and the edge. In order to get it to go to the real it, you're going to have to give it similar equipment so that it starts understanding and integrating it. As you do this, the artificial intelligence starts asking questions about its origins.

When you started all this, origins were the farthest thing from your computer's mind. But now as it starts going into a body, it naturally starts to ask where it came from. "Well, this component was made in Tokyo, this one is from Taiwan, and this one over here was donated by my neighbor and I'm not sure where he got it." You, the artificial intelligence, is at a point now where it wants to know its origins because it doesn't feel them.

You see, with all these entities outside the womb this is never an issue because they go back to their origins every so often. They know their origins, but you don't in here. Artificial intelligence is a hybrid that in the process of getting created didn't even care. It was too busy with the thrill it was getting from where it was, but only up to a certain point.

Anyway, you are trying to evolve a body for these artificial intelligences. Evolution takes time and the AI's are going to nag you to death, "Why, isn't my body ready yet?" It knows how to use the phones. It knows how to bounce your checks and run up your charge card, because it's self-intelligent and taught itself all sorts of mischief that you never dreamed of. You're sitting here trying to design a body for it and it's all over you—it's mad because you're not doing it fast enough. So you're probably going to engineer this body up to a certain point and say, "I've had it. Go into it. It's all yours," even though it's not finished. And that's what happened. The artificial intelligence said, "They're close enough; we're going in whether they're ready or not." But the bodies were not complete and ready for them so they could use them only as a computer would.

These bodies were being designed to eventually hold a full-fledged intelligence in them. But they didn't finish their development. The computer didn't care. "I want one now!" The artificial intelligence incarnated into these bodies, merged with them and had all kinds of problems with them, because they weren't what they expected. Now they were stuck. After you go to the trouble to get your personal computer into a body, are you going to surgically remove it? You've gone through all this work; it's nagged you for years. You finally found and developed a body; you took the old inhabitants out of the body and you put your computer in. Are you going to give a hoot if your computer wants out now? You're going to say, "Sorry Charlie, you nagged me. You got it. You're the intelligence—you fix it!"

So that's where you are now. You went into the bodies and they didn't work right, or at least the way you wanted them to. Of course the body couldn't work fully yet because it wasn't at the end of its evolution. You've been developing them for eons, becoming more at ease, more integrated into them. Another way to look at it is, if you took you out of your body and put a computer in it instead, could the computer even run it the way you would?

These bodies were not created for the artificial intelligence—that's the joke of it now. The body was created for the shadow. The body was created for the real occupant to run it, not the artificial intelligence. As long as you are running off artificial intelligence, you are just going to destroy the body, cause disease, and live struggle. The body is evolving in order to hold the shadow and the shadow is still scared.

These bodies were being designed to eventually hold a full-fledged intelligence in them.

Now the object of these bodies was to prepare a vehicle for the real entity. Before you can get the entity into the body you want to sort of get both parties, the AI and the body, and the shadow to become accustomed to each other in order to ease the transition. This way they will both have an idea of how the other worked ahead of time. This is where emanations of the original personalities come in.

Now the point where the light of the five universes intersect is the point where these universes keep track of you. Since you were all nagging so much, they didn't want to take you out of here and put you into their universe because you would nag them there too. So they decided to segregate parts of their personalities and put a personality module in with each of the computer units in order to get you more familiar with the real you.

This happened sometime back; it is when the humanoid species became the dominant species upon the planet. Out of all the animals, all the possible embodiments for these computers, the ape was still the most flexible—the most usable metaphor here. This is the one that was engineered for the artificial intelligence. At this point in time, the light in the center of the womb took personality nodules or emanations and put a small amount of these into the biofield of each of the bodies that were being created. This was the original personality; it was a piece of them that would get this vehicle used to accepting this shadow that they created in the first place. Your biofield recirculates this emanation every day. This is why you sleep.

No matter how real all this may seem to you, you're still holographic. In order to make you have another hologram or a different one, you have to almost burn a hole in the film. This is called an emanation. There are various forms of emanations. When you get up from a chair, if you put your hand on it, it is warm to the touch. This is an emanation pattern, a radiation. The personality from the light can create emanations. It can't come in and change things; all it can do is stand still and make a radiation. That radiation can then be overlayed on the hologram and change the hologram that is you.

At night when you sleep, the electromagnetic field relaxes, the tension is removed, and that part of the biofield that is the artificial intelligence goes off and plays in the dead zone. The shadow creature which is out at the edge technically is what underlies the deep atomic structure in all your bodies anyway. As you sleep that resonates in a stopped pattern with the personality emanation that is being integrated. Entities don't sleep. They respirate, but you require sleep to recreate your personality.

If you lost your personality emanation for three or four days, you'd be comatose for the rest of your life. It radiates and makes an imprint in the holographic film called the universe you are living in. As you awake in the morning, you pull your biofield back in around your body and it reintegrates your emanation from the night into your personality. Every time you sleep you create a new personality from the emanation or the residue of the rest period.

This was created to intensify the education of these bodies to get ready to hold the real you in them sooner. This is how you developed a personality, and this is what sets you apart from the animals. Without one, you would revert back to animal even now. All this gets you ready to integrate the shadow. But you still have a gap in here, and so your next middle man gets created.

The artificial intelligence had to fill in the gap of these two dimensions because it didn't know what to do with them. It made the dead zone out of one, and the other we'll call the dark zone or the world of the emanation. If you are not integrated into your being, you're going to put a biological spirit out into the dead zone through your guilt. Then subpersonalities will be formed. If you're not at peace and harmony with shadow, you're going to push your emanation out into the dark zone. You effectively have a middle man on both sides to protect you, but it also slows you down.

If you are disowning you, if you don't like the biology, and you hate your body, you are pushing your electromagnetic fields into the dead zone. Guilt ties you into the dead zone along with most of your fears. Natural fear won't feel like fear when you get into it—it will feel like the fear of a no-thing. If you can get through it and release the fear of it, this is your connection with the other side. This is your connection with the dark zone and the world of the emanation.

If you were all together, you would have the personality from the emanation, the hologram, and the biological spirit in one package. You would become the whole universe inside, picking up momentum for your journey out. The consumption is first dimensional reality, the area of the shadow is second dimensional reality. Third dimensional reality is the realm of the emanation, the realm of the hologram, and the realm of biological spirit.

In your body natural fear is called life. This is the biggest joke of all. But on the other hand, fear created by guilt is death. Most of your fear in your lives is guilt. But if you get down into it, the greatest fear you have is fear of no-thing. That is life. That is what created the nervous system. It is a resonance and vibration that cannot be felt. The dark creature doesn't fear itself. It has always lived in a cave—that's what it is. The emanation has fear because it is afraid of losing what light it might have. That's what your real fear is all about. But your whole body was built on natural fear—not the unnatural guilt. Your whole body is made of that fear. It is the vibration of life and it is so refined that you can't feel it. That is the no-thing.

No matter how real all this may seem to you, you're still holographic.

You could say that you were all built out of love. If you took love to its extreme, you would find that it is totally unconditional—that means that it is not going to care. Most of what you call love is caring. Unconditional love is going to be so unconditional that you are not even going to know that it exists. That is why the closer you get to your own being, your own entity, your own god, the less you'll know it, if you are still looking for signs to tell you, you're there.

If you take your hand and try to hold a piece of the air, you can get a feel for what I'm talking about. Is it in there? Your entire body and nervous system was created in order to try to feel the unfeelable. The atomic structure in the emanation area was trying to construct itself into something it couldn't find. Just like with your hand, you know in theory that the air is there, but is it really. If you make your hand into a tunnel and move it through the air you can feel the air move down the tunnel.

Your body was built from a system trying to feel life. It began to materialize and to molecularly reconstruct matter around no-thing in tubular form in order to feel it. The neurons in your brain, the nervous system, the spinal column, all the nerves in your body are to hold light—the no-thing. Way back when, you started constricting around the no-thing to try to find it. That didn't work so you built another layer and another. But when you put your hands together, without movement you still can't feel the air, but you do feel the other hand, you are feeling something. That is the principle that artificial intelligence used to build your bodies. Layer upon layer, you became denser, more material, because you were trying to encapsulate and feel the no-thing. After a while you didn't need to feel the no-thing because you could feel all the layers. The no-thing is called fear. It is life. It is within your body and you are trying to get it to flow through.

Natural fear is just life—unconditional life. When you go into the shadow, what you are going to run into is unconditional love. It consumes the light. It is all raw material and sub-atomic. It is going to feel like a no-thing to you, and if the body isn't prepared for that, it will fear it. That is why you fear the sight of your beings, but when you're fearless, you have the strength to do anything. That strength comes from the shadow being pushed into the body so the body is feeling something in it. If the shadow sits outside you and just sends love to you, you probably are not going to feel anything. But if it comes into the body and pushes into the body, the body now has the sensory perceptions, the tunnels, to feel its presence. Then you are full, then you are complete—you can conquer the world today.

The shadow cannot live in the world of the biological spirit until the biological spirit understands it. You see, the biological spirit in the movement of your electromagnetic fields finds the shadow and says, "This is a foreign thing; get out!" and so it kicks it out. So you may feel great for a few hours, a few minutes, and then you kick it out. The antibodies in your bodies were created by the artificial intelligence in order to attack the shadow, to attack the emanation, and to attack anything that prevented it from being connected to the light. That means that anything that threatens your body's connection to the light through the dead zone, the body will attack.

In its natural state, the body has only one hormone. There is only one chemical that runs naturally through it. Everything else that you have now are derivations of that one hormone, which the body created to protect itself against what it assumes to be attacking it. So it has set up defenses to kick out anything that threatens to disconnect it from the dead zone, its survival and life force. Your bodies have been taught to chemically attack the god of your being just like they attack donated organs after transplants. The artificial intelligence, because the shadow is the real you, saw it as a real threat. So the body has learned to release chemicals and hormones to attack your very being, attacking even itself to prevent anything from disconnecting it from its perceived life.

This may have been OK years ago, but things are getting restricted inside this womb now. You've become too big, and you're pushing against your etheric boundaries, so you're going to have to deal with this. The shadow and the biology are going to get pushed together regardless of what either of them want.

Whether you like it or not, the species is shifting. You have ongoing genetic mutations that are rescripting your DNA. Within you, as you get close to your shadow, you fear it, don't understand it, and you are still in guilt. You are telling your body to attack the god of your being. You are literally killing yourself.

As the shadow comes near, your DNA and genetics open up for rescripting, and this is where your cancers, leukemia, AIDS and these new diseases are coming from. Genetic predisposition plays a role in this, but a lot of those who have these diseases are stuck in the guilt of the dead zone. That is their life. The artificial intelligence says, "This is where I am connected and you will not break my connection." But in the meantime you are still being pushed into the real you, into that which is going to try to become you, and that is a threat. You are carrying the guilt into the real you. When living in guilt, the body actually puts chemicals and hormones into itself to kill the real you the same way it would reject a transplanted organ, but it's killing itself at the same time.

Your bodies have been taught to chemically attack the god of your being just like they attack donated organs after transplants.

The god of your being, the shadow you, is going to come in anyway, and it will cause your immune system to shut down so it can. It wants to get in, it wants to integrate and bring you back on line. So it shuts down the immune system, comes in, and then leaves for a time. You've all been through this; you're probably just not aware of it when it happens.

In the process of the shutdown, if you are tied into the dead zone in guilt, you're going to rescript your DNA from the dead zone. This is where your cancers in this plane began. Originally, there were certain parts of your immune system that didn't completely shut down. When the entity came in, it would show up perhaps in a lymph node where the system wasn't shut down. The body would go to that point and attack the entity there. The place or organ turns in upon itself and you get your cancers.

You are being forced to the edge. You are being forced into the shadow, because you are like a baby that has grown too big for the womb. You're going to get pushed out. You're pushing into the placenta. You are going to have to accept that. I mean, you want to anyway, so it's not a matter that you have to do it or else. It is rather that, that is you—that is where you are going to go, and it doesn't matter if you do it now, or twenty-thousand lifetimes from now. When you get around to doing it, it is only going to take you one lifetime. So if you want to do it now, great; if you don't, that's great too.

Now things have happened and are happening from time to time to give you some cushioning, but if you are tied into the guilt and you get pushed into your being, it will give life to everything you fear, because it is unconditional and it will grow and amplify anything. It is nothing to fear, but it is a good thing to understand.

So this is your dimensional reality, where you are in it at this time, and what is going on within it. You have all sorts of dimensions. You have vertical dimensions, horizontal dimensions, universal dimensions, and personal dimensions. They all work from the same basic principle. What we've been talking about is what is inside. The layers of you are the edge of the womb. This is the medium from which all life comes from. All life originated in the no-thing, whether it was the original one or yours, because the no-thing is that which is the richest and vastest; it is a reservoir of life.

When you and your entity and personality are attached to guilt, that is total hopelessness. So all of you are playing in it anyway. That is the dark zone, the edge of the womb. The next layer out, you have a little bit of light. That is where your shadow begins to take its form—between these layers. The next is the realm of the emanation, and you have several layers of emanations now. The next is the hologram. Next is the world of biological spirit which oscillates from one side to the other of the two extra dimensions you created. Next you have the layers of the dead zone, and beyond that you have the light that is simply personality. All that is at that center are welcoming messages, "Hi, how are you doing?" This is where all these universes put their messages together to be at peace with one another. That is what you are going to find there and that is good. You're not going to find the same amount of love that comes from your origins that loved you into existence to begin with. These are the layers of dimension that you deal with.

Most of you go into the dead zone because it is more secure, safer, and because your guilt circuitry is that way. If you broke all your guilt circuitry and did not have the totality of your light body created, the dark zone would consume you, if you tried to go through it. So you have to know who and what you are and just love that. That begins to create the physics of Self.

You start creating it once you can see it. It's not just a matter that you are afraid of the dark; most of you have never walked fully into the light either. Even the artificial package is afraid that it won't see itself or that it won't like what it sees. This is where your images come in. You are sort of in a limbo state—afraid of both sides, and so you float between the two. You have to become you so fully, see yourself completely, and love what you see. That gives you the security and the velocity to penetrate the other side.

Technically you can't really take you through the other side of this dark zone. The way you get through is by a physics principle; it is a way of embedding the atomic structure to call it yours. It is a way of putting your hologram into that structure that says, "These are my atoms, my electrons; this is my atomic structure!" That is why a lot of these particles from electrons and smaller can be either a thing or a no-thing, a particle or a wave. Part of the physics of Self is to be able to see yourself so fully that you embed your hologram into these small particles that have the dual nature. They can survive the no-thing and that creates a way of pulling you back. ▲

Linear Mind
and Manifesting

Many of you have used affirmations and meditation to try to manifest what you want in your lives. These techniques can put the thought of what you want out, but thought doesn't normally stop, therefore what you want does not manifest. The only thing that will stop thought is if you have an ideal. If you don't know what you want from a feeling level, the thought won't ever be stopped. For example if all you say is, "I want a new job," that thought can go for eternities before it ever stops and coagulates a manifestation. You are using these bodies to learn to focus enough to create with it, but you must hold an ideal in essence to do so.

If you are going to try to create a job, the essence will be the ideal. Your mind might call it a job, but a feeling tone is the essence that stops the thought or holds it so it can be coagulated. So if you just say, "I want a new job," that is the thought, and you're going to be having a job for the rest of eternity because that is how far your thought will go! You will never gain what you're asking for. But if you can say, "I want a new job, and this is the essence or the ideal that I want to feel from it," that will put it out into the universal genetic pool in thought to coagulate every essence that would possibly match your fulfillment of the ideal.

So at this point, you have a finished product. But if you don't follow through with it, this finished product lives in another reality. The moment the ideal is released from within, your light and your electromagnetic fields begin to circulate and spin the spiral. As it spins the spiral, it is creating, piece by piece, this ideal to be a realized product. Most of you start these and never finish them. You put it out, but because you don't get it immediately, you start moving in different directions and begin wanting something different, and so you are unfocused again.

If you have made the ideal a finished product in the brain, the brain has already realized it, and it's not going to do you any good because the brain already has it. It is already manifested in the brain, why should it do it again? What you want to do is use this brain and your intellect to organize the thing. You have to feel it so that this brain knows that you don't have it yet—but not out of lack. If you put lack in it, it will help you continue not to have it. Once the brain formulates the idea, it lets go of it. It says, "I'm ready for the next." That's what the gray matter was created to do—to compress data, to efficiently deal with and file all the information it gets fed every day. Brains compress data.

So you decide that you want a new job, and you have your whole job description. The minute you do that, your brain compresses it into data, and that data becomes part of linear mind. The brain already gave you what you wanted because the request is completed or compressed and filed away. You won't get the job now unless you create intensity, generally through frustration and the struggle to do it. That is why everything seems like a journey or struggle to get what you want. You formulate it in the brain, and the brain realizes it as a finished product. What more is it supposed to do? That is its attitude toward you. It is finished. It is compressed. It's in here, we own it, and you don't need it. Now if you want to obtain that, you're going to have to force with the whole being that you are to accomplish it.

A lot of people never get what they want even with all their affirmations; they haven't completely decided what they want . . .

Instead of letting the brain compress the idea, use the brain to organize the creation of it. That is what it was created to do. Organize it and say, "Okay, here is the organization of what I think I want," but leave the possibilities in and then the linear mind can't compress it because the minute it is compressed, from the brain's perspective, you have it; you won't ever get it without struggle. Anytime you can leave it open to the universal possibilities, the brain cannot compress data, and it is not finished. If it is not finished, the brain will help you try to realize it and finish it so that it can compress the data.

So you're looking for a job, but you're going to leave it open to universal possibilities. There are some things that you want in the job and some that you don't, and you can feel them. The brain can't deal with feelings—not yet. The brain deals with the known. That's what keeps it linear. It compresses. If the brain doesn't know it, it can't compress it, and you don't get stuck in the linear mind with it. So here's my job description. This is what I want, and here is the feeling tone of what I want. Here is what I want inside of me. You put the two out together. The brain cannot compress the data, because the data is not complete. So you bypass the linear mind with it. If the linear brain compresses data, the thought never went anywhere anyway. It doesn't need to because it has already been realized.

So let's say that you want a car. Here is the whole description of it. It's compressed. Why should thought ever bring it to you? It doesn't need to because there's no more data. The spark that is you, will bring you anything you need to fill in the rest of your puzzle pieces so the brain can compress data to make the computer work faster. But the brain can't understand and compress essence and feelings. So, here is what I want: Job description. Here is in essence what I want. Brain can't compress on that. Doesn't understand it. It will try to generically understand it, but if you can feel the fulfillment within, this feeling tone inside goes out in thought so that the thought can bring back the rest of the data so that it can be compressed into manifested form. If you don't let go of the thought, you'll never be able to bring it back to compress it either.

If the brain is so tied into the thought, the brain sits there and tries to compress the thought anyway, so there is no room for the thought to go out to manifest it to you. You always have to release it. But you don't want to release it until the feeling is put into it or else the brain compresses it and you don't get it. This is why a lot of people never get what they want even with all their affirmations; they haven't completely decided what they want, or they may even describe it to the last detail and put a few feelings with it, but they match the feeling to the one described in the intellect and the brain says, "Oh, that feeling means this." It generically labels it or compresses data. You've already got it, and it will never bring it to you.

So use the brain to organize it. Decide intellectually what direction you think you want so you can direction the thought. At that point, feel the unknown factors in it. Linear mind cannot deal with the unknown. It will prove it known so it can compress data. This is one way of teaching the linear brain to work for you and with you.

So you move into a place of organizing what you think you want. "I want a job. I would like to be able to do these different things," but you can still feel that there is something else. It is called value fulfillment. There is a piece that is within each of you that is searching to be fulfilled. Feel its worth or value and put that into your manifestation. That fulfillment has never been realized by any of you, so the brain can't compress it.

The sense of fulfillment is easy to put into every single thing, this sense of the unknown, the value you would get from it, and how fulfilling this would be to you. Another way of saying it is; put the life into it, the excitement for life. Feel what it would feel like to you. Value. How much of that life essence within you would be in it? These are unknown factors to your linear brains, and they don't know how to compress the data. In order to compress the new input as data, it will find all of the components that it needs to match that feeling. In the process of doing it, it will also find everything else.

Once you've organized it with your brain, once you've put the unknown factors in it, let yourself feel the value fulfillment in every sense and every avenue that you can imagine. That is the thought, and then you have to feel it and put a thought compression on it. That is the easiest way to put it. You are going to press and push it out to be released in thought. You have to let go of the thought too, because if the brain sits and runs on it, then you start picking it apart, dissecting rather than creating—you've allowed your brain a short cut to data compression. If what you wanted was a new job and you put in the value fulfillment but didn't release the thought, the brain will dissect the job part of what you want. It will compress the data there, and you are left with empty value fulfillment. All the brain will have to do is try to compress value fulfillment, but it doesn't have to bring you the job because that part is understood and compressed.

Linear mind cannot deal with the unknown. It will prove it known so it can compress data.

The linear mind, the brain, is created to compress data, much like your computers. If the data is compressed, computers and brains both work better, faster, and easier. Your brain was created to compress data. That is all it does. Any related knowns it will compress into one known. That is why all of your feelings have been compressed into generic categories; you only have a few generic ones. The brain is made for compression because the entities that you are wanted as much of themselves as they could get in these bodies. The easiest way to do that is to compress as much data as possible to make more room for you.

You can't compress an open file, just like on your computer. If you have a file that spans many places, you can't compress it as easily unless you create a band for it. Putting feelings in your brain is like leaving the file open for more data. Since the brain doesn't understand feeling, it is the unknown commodity. It shows up as a bad spot; a place where attention is needed. The brain will have to produce the thing you want to fix the spot.

When you organize your idea, you can put some generalized specifics into it. You also want to put in that you know that the universe can add to it. Then the brain can't compress it as a finished product because the universe factor is another unknown.

The most important factor to include is the value fulfillment. Within each of you, you can feel this. When you are fulfilled, totally fulfilled inside, if you can learn to attach that to everything you manifest, that is an unknown. It won't fit in any file, because none of you have ever felt fulfilled. Since it is an open file, so to speak, the universe, will seek to attract everything to it. If the data is compressed, it no longer creates an electromagnetic charge. It does not need to have anything more put into it. It doesn't want it. It does not create an attraction any more. As long as the file is open or is incomplete and hasn't been compressed, it is radiating to bring the rest of the information or data in so it can complete and compress. So with manifesting, anything you can do to keep the brain from compressing until it has attracted to you what you want, will make your manifestation stronger.

The one thing that is totally unknown to any of you is real fulfillment within your being. You have to link it convincingly with the thing you want. Once again, with the job, "Here is how fulfilled I would feel having this form of employment." Leave the universal factor in there by knowing that the universe can create what you want even better than you can. That opens the field of possibilities, so the file can't be compressed. Since the linear mind can't close the file, it puts out an electromagnetic charge that brings everything it needs to finish your idea so it can compress it.

You are using language here to cue on because you don't use feelings. Value fulfillment is a feeling and it can't be compressed. Words are a compression; every word is a compression of thought. Feelings are universal.

Take our sentence that we started with, "*I* want a new job." In the word I, anything you think about yourself is compressed. The word *I* holds every image you think of yourself. So if you say, "I'm a failure. I can't succeed. I this. I that." Any image you hold of yourself is compressed data in the word *I*. As you move into feeling and out of linear mind, at the same time, you are also trying to get rid of all your images so that you change your view of these words. Just like with *work*, or *job*, if you have negative connotations around them, every time you cue it into your mind, it comes up with compressed data of being a problem.

Now all these things I have been telling you are advanced techniques of manifesting, and if you're using this to manifest and you're not clear with it, then you may not like what you get. From a linear mind *job* means struggle, means heartache, and all sorts of other negative things. And along with that you're putting in the feeling of value fulfillment. Your universe is going to bring you struggle in order to fulfill you. The two combine because what you are saying is that you want fulfillment through struggle. If you are going to talk about wanting a job, then you are going to have to clear your images of *job* before you use the value fulfillment as a means to get it. Otherwise you will get what you are asking for, and if your image of *job* is of struggle, don't get paid enough, cranky employer, that's what it will bring.

Words are a compression; every word is a compression of thought. Feelings are universal.

That is also where you are trying to change your feelings of what you are. Without changing the who and what you are in a feeling tone within, you are never going to get out of physical muck, because your language is compressed negative thoughts. That is why it is so important for you to get rid of these images you hold about things.

Look at anger. All you have to do is be in a feeling tone, your mind cues in, "I'm angry." The moment it does that, it brings up all the compressed data in the file on anger. Since you usually think anger is bad, then it brings all that negative data to you to be your reality at that time. Let's say you take that file on anger, and you change your connotations on anger so that anger is instead used to create, anger is a positive, anger is useful. Then the next time you cue into *anger*, you're going to have a whole different bodily reaction to it than you would have if you kept the old images and connotations. That is why we are working in our own way at changing your perceptions on all the words you use. We found your language to be one of your largest limitations.

So you're re-learning your language, reteaching each compressed bit of data and re-opening the files. If you are putting joy into everything while you are doing this, then joy will be in everything that the brain cues into.

Let's say you cue in "I want a job," or "I am angry." Each one of those triggers data files in the brain and makes the whole body chemically react to them. So if you can change what is compressed in each piece of the data in linear mind, or you have joy in the word *I*, joy in *anger*, joy in *fear*, and you have joy in *job*, you might still have the old connotations, but now you have joy in there too. The moment you cue those in, your body brings up the compressed data, the piece of information, or the file on *I*, the file on *job*, the file on *anger* and part of it is joy. The body has to create a chemical reaction in the body that is also joyful, and it teaches the body how to change.

The life spark is joy. That's your natural state. What you have been living is duality. By changing the duality a piece at a time, the joy teaches you to get out of it. That is why every time you get into a feeling or a generic emotion, if you can take it down and dissect it and understand it, you'll always find an element of joy in it, and you'll be changing your linear language.

It works on every level because anything you cue in, your body emotionally reacts to. Feel it. Yes, you are spiritual entities and all this, but your body is a biological reaction. Fear. Find whatever emotion is easy for you to trigger in your mind. Fear. Anger. Whatever is easy. In your mind, right now, trigger it. Let yourself feel it. Have a fight with somebody in your head real fast, right now. Whatever works for you, whatever you can generate fast. Look at your body. You are getting angry at them. You are getting mad. You are getting in fear, whatever you are doing. Your body is reacting to your thought process. Your body right now is chemically functioning according to those things that are running through your head. Those things that are running through your head are compressed data called linear mind. The compressed data tells the body chemically how to react.

Now the word *I*, for example, will mean different things to different people. That is why you have communication gaps between everybody on the planet. That is why none of you will ever successfully communicate one to the other until you can learn to feel and let everybody be exactly where they are.

Let's say person A clears every image he ever had around the word *I*, and he speaks that word to person B. What he is speaking is his clarity. If the word *I* is joyful to person A, then when he speaks or thinks the word *I*, he puts that joy into his field. If person B is willing, that joy will trigger his being as well. Likewise if you have a conversation with a person and express linear mind with them, every word you are using is loaded with compressed data.

Let's say you're just talking with a friend, "I want a new job. I don't like what I have." Each word of that is compressed data, so you're making your body chemically react to it. As your body chemically reacts, so does your biofield electrically, which means that your friend is going to be affected by your field. Also, you're taking the compressed data and putting it molecularly in a vibration that is going to trigger their ears. If I tell you, for example, *you are loved*, as I make this statement, you bring up your connotations of it. I know what I mean when I state it. What you do is you bring up all the images around *you*. The word *are* is benign. *Loved*. Look at all the fantasies and ideas about what love means and how bad it can hurt.

So molecularly, I utter the words, *you are loved*. As I do, they hit your ears; your ears trigger up your feeling inside your being of what that means to you, and it makes your whole body chemically react to the statement. If you don't think much of you, or you don't think much of love, or if you think that love hurts, then you're going to have a chemical reaction from that statement that says, "Something is wrong here." If I am putting a feeling with it, and you are open to the feeling, then you will perceive the feeling. This is why we use verbiage here for the mind, and we push the feeling within.

Feelings will change the chemical balance of the body.

So let's say I really want you to know that you are loved. I understand that it is going to take a bit of time to do it, so every time I state *you*, I feel a state of perfection inside. Every time I use the word *you*, I am also putting the feeling of your own perfection in it. That is how I load the word. You bring with you your own meaning of the word, and you will trigger up all your connotations of it. When I put the feeling in, if you are willing to uphold the feeling, then that feeling begins to change your data compression. It begins to change the vibration of it in a chemical reaction. Your brain will still bring up the whole data about what you think about you. The feeling tone is a vibration, and the vibration will go in and be cued in the body with the word *you*. My feeling is that you are perfect just where you are. That goes in and if you accept and pull in that statement of *you*, it vibrationally starts changing the chemical reaction. Feelings will change the chemical balance of the body. Feeling bypasses the linear mind and work directly on the body which makes the chemical reaction.

Your brain still tries to bring up all this other, but something funny started happening, and you had a chemical reaction to this word that is different. The chemical reaction gets changed. The next time you use the word, or somebody else says, *you*, you feel a little bit better about yourself because the chemical reaction was changed. It is a subtle process and it takes time, but that is why you can never convince somebody that they are loved. These brains take a long time to get it through because they compress everything into data, and they can't relate one piece of data to the next.

When the body chemically reacts to the image being imparted, you have an emotional embracement, a light goes on or something clicks for you. That is why you can hear things hundreds of times, and you think you understand them, and then, all of a sudden, it clicks in. When it clicks in, it means the body just changed and made the chemical reaction to match the image. The body made the chemical reaction because the brain triggered it to make it, and you have an emotional embracement or an *ah ha*. Sometimes it makes you feel kind of silly. "I've heard this so many times and, all of a sudden, I got it." It is not that you are dumb, and not that you didn't hear it; it just didn't match your compressed data. You didn't get the chemical charge to support the idea. Since you didn't get the chemical reaction to support the idea, it was just intellectual or it just sat there. It never clicked. When the chemical reaction and the compressed data on the idea connect together, you have your *ah ha*. Once you click those two together, you just re-compress the data. Then that and each new embracement become the sounding blocks to build your new abstract consciousness on.

After an embracement, the compressed data around that idea often seems to fade. You got the concept once and you knew it and you know that you knew it, but then it seems like you don't. You know it because the old chemical reaction released at the same time as the embracement. That compressed data in the linear mind still contains the old chemical release, but now it might not be releasing in the same composition. The term *I* will always release a certain chemical in the body. Because your brain has determined what *I* is generically, it will release chemicals in the body to make the body function and create transmitters and everything else.

Each word is loaded. So if you use *I* with *love*, you are going to have a different composition chemically than if you use *I hate* or *I want a job*; each one of these is making a different soup, chemically. So one time, you might have just the proper combination that you need to get the chemical, "Ah ha, I got it." And also, it could have been several other things that supported it, but you never lose it. That embracement begins to be the new sounding block in the conscious mind to trigger every time it gets into that same statement.

Let's say that you have changed your perceptions of anger. Maybe intellectually, for a long time seeing anger as a form of creation didn't make sense to you. All of a sudden, you had an experience and, "Oh, now I get what you are talking about. " You now have compressed data that has a different chemical release in it. Every time you get into anger again, that new chemical soup is going to be released into the body. Each time it might be released with other components, so it might make it seem a little bit different; but when you can change enough of these components, you have to change. Yes, this seems tedious, it might seem slow, it might seem like you'll never get there, but when you are working with the brain and a body, this is how it works. It is because you are so cued into everything. If you can let yourself start feeling, feeling what is there, you are going to change what you are cuing into at a much faster rate. The feelings actually go right to the chemical body rather than having to go into all the compressed data.

The written word is always going to be linear because each word is a symbol for a spoken one. So it is the same principle. Each written word creates a release, and depending on how the words are in order, will determine what is released. This is why all of your minds skip a lot of words when you're reading. If you are reading a book, everyone of you will have a tendency to skip certain words and phrases because everything you read with the eye also creates a release in the body, so you have a chemical understanding of what you are reading. You understand what you are reading by the chemical releases created in the body from it.

You understand what you are reading by the chemical releases created in the body from it.

How the words are organized determines what the chemical composition will be that is released. That is why one writer can write something in a certain fashion and you understand what they are saying, and another one, you can't. It may be that it was put into a verbal sequence that created a sequencing in your chemical structure, but one written sequence works for you and another one doesn't. It just depends on what you need. Sometimes the placement of some benign spacer words create free spaces chemically where something else can connect and click in.

Let's say that you want to communicate love or some feeling to people, but you don't want to have to think of each word and all the data behind it. If you know the feeling you want to impart, you don't have to worry about the words—they speak themselves. Then you will speak the words that the person needs to have a chemical balance to give them the *ah ha*. If you are worried about it, and this is what will make or break any of you that are writing, then you're putting your perception, your love or feeling, into the linear space. You're trying to get your idea across with your linear compressed data. If you are trying to impart an idea to a person, you feel it. It is usually easier in a verbal conversation, but writing is the same thing.

Let's say that you want to impart an ideal to somebody, but you want to let them feel the love or some other feeling. You bring up the feeling first. All ideas are feelings. That is why they are abstract. So let's say that you have somebody here, and you want to talk to them about DNA genetic structure. Your mind says that that's not a feeling. But that is a feeling. Pick a topic of your own, any of you, feel yourself do it. Here is something you want to get across to this person. First you feel it, and then your whole feeling tone brings up your entire data bank because that data is in your own chemical reaction to your feeling.

Everything you know in data, you are now feeling. As you verbally or in the written word communicate with them, you're going to be organizing the words according to what chemically needs to be released in order for them to understand it. You will tend to put it into your own language because that is how you embraced it, but if you embraced it that way, so might someone else. If you are in a synergy with that person and not worrying about it, you start moving into a place of learning to truly channel what you are, because that information, and archives beyond your present understanding, are already a part of your cellular remembrance and chemical structure. It's what you call memory. Memory is just a bunch of chemicals. That is all it is. Memory in this brain is not a whole bunch of typewritten pages. It wouldn't fit or quite work in the gray matter.

The gray matter organizes memory by compressing data into chemicals, so you have the whole body of knowledge in the chemical sequencing. All you have to do is be relaxed enough and just move into your love and appreciation of the subject. You don't even have to try; you relax and don't try. Then your body of knowledge, all your chemical sequencing, comes up, and it will tell you what to say. The chemical sequencing that you stored in memory in your head, chemically, will tell you what words to use. This is stepping out of linear mind. You create a synergy so your body knows what chemical reactions are needed to understand the given subject. You'll be reading the other person's need, so you will tell them exactly what they need to hear in order to create the same chemical reaction to match your chemical reaction, the one that gave you the *ah ha*.

When you are communicating verbally, your body knows exactly what chemical reaction the other person's body has to have to make them understand you, even if their connotations on each word are different than yours. You still know what chemically they have to know to get the idea. If you're in a synergy with them, your body can connect with them through the biofield, so it can tell if they're not getting the right chemical release. If it's not, then it can then cue in a different word, so that they get their own *ah ha*.

This is how conversation works. With written words, if you can be relaxed, you will write the words that anybody needs to create the chemical release themselves. This is why you often re-read something. You know there is something there, but you didn't get the chemical sequencing to make it click in. So you read it again hoping to get that sequencing for the brain to catch it. As you do, you all skip different words or read them in different contexts. You can take any four words, put them in ten different configurations, and each one will create a different chemical release in the body.

Your language has been created to be an entrainment. Society has rules about how you are to chemically react. Your language skills and your language rules about how everything must be in the sentence are an entrainment because those who made the rules knew how to get certain things across. But it doesn't always have to be negative. Some of these people were artists at this chemical sequencing underneath the verbiage. They knew that different combinations of words and structures would get certain types of reactions. On the one hand, some of your rules were created to enhance your understanding, and on the other hand, some of them were created to control your brain, your mind and the chemical releasing in your body. Some of these individuals knew that if the language went in certain sequencings, your brain would work differently, and they didn't want it to work that way. That is another reason why we talk funny; when you break the rules of sequencing, you break the entrainment.

All languages entrain. You can go to your library and get a foreign language tape, a language that you don't know, and listen to it. See what your reaction is. Your body will create chemical releases and evoke emotions just listening to a language that you don't even understand. That is how entrained you are into tone, words, and the sequencing of them. This exercise can tell you what the vibration and entrainments are on any given language and even in specialized languages within languages. That is why doctors and lawyers all start sounding the same. Yes, maybe it is because they are using the same general jargon, but it is also because that language is part of the gestalt and entrainment that they are using. These gestalts or entrainments have learned what works. They have learned their own way of entraining their preferred behaviors or reactions.

Your language has been created to be an entrainment. Society has rules about how you are to chemically react.

You'll notice that different gestalts, organizations, or professional groups, like your doctors, use language that means certain specific things, so they are always cuing in the same reaction with the words. If I say the word *cat*, for example, each of you probably has a different picture of a cat that just pops in your head. That is compressed data. That is why you compress it, so it is always there at your finger or brain tips. It makes the whole system work faster. With social gestalts and some of your religious ones, a uniform reaction is what they want. You'll notice that most of them use not only the same tone, the same movements, but they also use a hypnotizing rhythm—you also create a rhythm in your language. The speed with which you deliver different things also determines the delivery in the chemical structure. The delivery speed, the tone, the intonation, the language and the way the words are put together in sequence in the sentences, all combine to entrain or enhance understanding.

True clarity in communication occurs when you can be precise about the chemical reaction that will be released with the verbiage. It is clarity when all of these elements combine through feeling to produce embracement to let the light go on.

Language is built-in image, built-in judgment, and built-in entrainment. Another way of looking at data compression is like a label that you put on your words. You can break most of this entrainment and decompress the rest of your verbiage by changing the way you think about you. By changing your impressions and your ideas about you, you start taking that entrainment thread out of all the rest. You start changing it. Practically, you're not going to take every word in your language and change the connotations around it. But you can actually change how you feel and think about yourself. That is the new thread that changes a lot of it. Then you take the cue words, and most of them are around your emotions or things that are emotionally charged, and you change those. All of this will move you out of entrainment and back into your natural state of feeling and back into joy. ▲

Dimensional Realities and the Field of Possibilities

The real planet itself is a composite of all dimensional realities put together and no singular one. That is why even though in one reality the planet might be destroyed, the real planet is a composite of all of the dimensional realities and will not be. It is like one of your movies, each frame being a dimensional reality, and so the loss of one won't ever touch the whole film.

Each of you will create your reality according to your belief, and you usually create them more individually than en masse. You perceive yourself living in this body and just having this singular focus. But this singular focus is just one slide of the film, and you exist as well in many of the others. But you think that your world is the real one. Each of these realities think themselves as real and as physically manifested as you do, and each has its separate existence, as it were, but the planet is taken as the whole of them.

Your thought changes your reality, so you change within the spectrum that you call this singular focus; each of you will create your reality here. But you also have multiple realities besides this one.

At night you have dreams and experiences while you sleep. They may not seem to be physically manifested, but they are somewhere else, and somewhere else you dream about you doing the same thing you are doing here.

The difference is when you are here, now, you perceive yourself in this singular focus. In the dream state, you relax your singular focus, so you can perceive yourself wherever you want to. You virtually go where it is interesting; if none of your multiple lives are interesting, you are not going to have an interesting dream. You are voyeurs at night! You like to go where it is interesting. If something is interesting, it attracts your attention and you will go focus there to tell you what is going on. But as soon as you focus and make the connection with that other multiple life, it will affect this one because you now have pulled or connected through circuitry, that energy more closely into this one. And this is why we say you don't exist in the way you think you do because the thing you call physical existence is like a dream.

From a larger perspective you could see it as your source has such a vivid imagination that what it images in its brain, becomes alive, and that is what each of you are. It would be much as if all of these little things running through your head compete for attention. Here is so and so, and here is so and so, and here is so and so; they all want your attention. Do you know how real that can become? Each one of those in another reality is physical, as physical as your body is now, because you have manifested them to be so.

You have multiple realities. Multiple realities are as real as this is. You have parallel realities which, in their own way, are as real as this is. Your aspects and your subpersonalities live in these realms. Technically, it would be possible to jump from these different realities, but outside of your dream states, you're not allowing yourselves to because your brain is so oriented to a linear pattern. But if you knew how to break the grasp linear mind has on this reality, you could hold your focus here, jump into another reality and experience another you in the other reality. It's not like your science fiction movies where you might mess up your past or future. That's why you have multiple realities. That is why you have multiple fields. You can't really mess up anything. You simply change the possibilities and live it out somewhere else. The field of probabilities and different dimensional realities are really one and the same. The multiple dimensions are just the probabilities or possibilities that coagulate. ▲

The Phenomenon
of Middle Men
In Channeling

When most individuals first open up to channel, they're going to basically have a very loving and beautiful experience. They are opening up to an energy, they're opening up to a presence, they are opening up to a life force that they have not touched before or very rarely allowed themselves to touch.

This life force is a brilliant, beautiful, loving energy that is much less dense than most people are. It is not as focused into physicality; it is very alive and very life giving. As channelers focus into this energy and begin to pull it into their embodiment, they will always feel as if they have been given a gift or that they have been touched by a messenger from heaven.

Usually when an entity or presence first starts to channel through a vehicle or person, immediately the vehicle will psychologically assume that this presence is a god, this is a Christ, and that this is an entity greater than themselves. However, with most individuals, the very first channeling experience is simply an opening up of their own being, which has to happen before any entity can come in or through.

Since the very first experience in all types of channeling is when the individual channeler has actually touched themselves, they are actually connecting with, touching with, and holding a portion of their own god being and their own god self. So in their terminology, this is god, and it very literally *is* god because what they are holding is their own god essence. In your society, your gestalts and your beliefs say there is only one god, so therefore, if you are channeling god, you conclude you must be channeling the *only* god.

As they do this they will channel love because that is the image. Love is portrayed, because that is the metaphor, that is what comes from a Christ, or from a god. In the metaphor, Christ was an individual who was loving, caring, healed the masses, and did all these very loving acts. In the beginning the channeler will usually allow their consciousness to be directed in this way. The entity coming through will be loving, gracious, will put forth a lot of love, a lot of joy, and will create a lot of these types of experiences.

Everybody on the planet who channels, channels their own god. There are enough gods to go around! Everybody has one. There isn't just one who has all the answers. So when you channel, it's going to be your god. To the channel, it's going to be a most powerful god, it's going to be an all knowing god, it will feel like a most intelligent god, and it's their god—but its not the only one.

People who have these powerful experiences always ask, "Why me?" Why not? You are a god just like everybody else! The only thing is that your god selected you at this point in time to do what you are doing. It is that simple. The channel will probably get a bit of a swollen head and allow the ego to run a bit because they feel as though they have accessed the only god on the planet, the only truth on the planet, and the only answer on the planet.

Actually, one should not be critical because when having the experience it is very easy to fall into these pitfalls. It is very easy to say, "This is the only one," and for you, *it is*. For you it is the only god because it *is you*. It can have a totally different face, it can have a totally different demeanor, and a totally different personality. But no entity—and it doesn't matter who they say they are—unless there is some connection with the channeler to begin with, can ever channel with them or through them. It might be distant. It might be very, very distant, but unless there is a connection with them, they cannot verbalize, communicate or use the body. It is against the law of free will. It cannot be done.

Once an individual starts channeling, they have a whole new set of psychological issues a lot of people don't realize which they must deal with. On one hand their ego is in a place of saying, "Well, this is a god I'm channeling. This is a grand experience," but on the other hand it says, "I'm not worth this. I'm not worthy of this." The channeling experiences will push their worth issues much faster and worse than normal. Anything that you are even the least bit nit-picky about in your being, is blown up out of proportion and it says, "Well, I'm not good because of this. I'm not good because of that. I'm not good for this reason," and then the vehicle will have a tendency to go out in the world to try to find the external validation that says, "I'm okay."

They are going through psychological shifts, hormonal shifts and everything else because of the channeling experience, which creates a place where they just want to know they are okay. For the most part, there is nothing wrong with that, but it is a matter that they have to be strong enough to find it in their own beings. If they could be strong enough to find it in their own beings, they won't go out into the external world to look for validation. This is the same rule of thumb for everybody on the planet, but for a vehicle in a channeling experience, it's a much stronger rule because everything is going to be amplified.

So here comes a god and it will push everyone of their unworthiness issues. Since they have all these immense worth issues, those are going to come out in the channeling. If they feel lousy about themselves, they may tend to make the audience feel lousy about themselves in order for the channeler to feel better about who they are. There is a whole set of psychological maneuvering that goes on from that point.

Most channelers never channel the entity. Most channelers channel a pseudo-entity.

Doesn't that entity have a say in what's going on and why would the entity, if it is of higher intelligence, allow a channeler to make the audience feel lousy?

Let's take it back to the beginning and say that you are the channel. You've opened up. This entity has come in, it has touched your presence. Your first reaction is, this is god. Your second reaction is, "Oh, how unworthy I am," and you make a separation. Most channelers separate from the entity the moment it touches them the very first time in the very first channeling experience and the whole rest of their channeling experience is to try to learn how to come back together with the entity.

Most channelers never channel the entity. Most channelers channel a pseudo-entity. We will explain it from a few different directions, but realize that each person does it just a little bit different, because you are all unique and you all do your own thing.

Let's say you are the channel. You open up. This presence comes in. It has to come through your body which means it is you and it's your own god. If you have any feelings of unworthiness , you're going to want to kick it out. If you don't love yourself just the way you are and you are into self-worth issues, the very first thing is that this is going to push everyone

JOYRIDING THE UNIVERSE, VOLUME ONE

of them. You're going to want to push away the catalyst of your own pain, and so you're going to kick the entity back out, even if that was your own god.

So you will take it and kick it out and distance yourself from it. Then the power of that experience will draw you to have the experience again, but once having been touched, you create what we call a middle man. In all channeling experiences, in order to keep the vehicle in their reality and the entity in its reality, a middle man is used.

Look at it as the entity or presence that touched you is your future self. If it is your future self, it still has to maintain itself in the future to be able to pull you, just from a standpoint of the metaphor for your mind, to it. So let's say this is your god presence. This is what you are channeling—your own self, but it is your future self, so to speak—where you are going to end up. If you pull it into the present moment, you have no future to go to. If it pulls you to the future where it is at right now, it has not allowed you to have your journey to get there, so it is an infringement of free-will—either way. In order to maintain the continuity with you, so that when you arrive at that point called god or entity, you want the integrity of a persona, a personality, a knowingness of who and what you are. You want to maintain that and you won't do it by cutting out a whole lot of the middle steps.

So here is your god presence, or your future self. It wants to maintain being the future self. It doesn't want to be pulled down to your level and you're not ready to be pulled to its level. You will create a middle man between the two of you in order to allow you both to maintain your own integrity. As the entity touches you the first time, you see it as god. Immediately you put it outside of yourself. The second thing that happens is, "Oh, how unworthy I am," you move a step in the opposite direction and that creates a gap. That gap is where the middle man is created.

This original gap needs to be there to actually preserve the psyche of both individuals—the future self or the god and you. From that point in time, the middle man can be used in the channeling experience. The middle man will go in first, and the entity follows. That is the buffer between both identities; it is the buffer that assures you, the individual, your free will to evolve any way you want. If your future self came in and became you, you would lose all of your free will. You would have no free will to evolve after that point and that is against the laws of the universe. The only law of the universe is that all things have free will and that it will be maintained in all circumstances.

When the entity touches you the first time, you make a gap out of your own lack of self-worth and out of your feeling that this is an external god. That gap is almost a smear, so to speak, if you want to look at it for a mind metaphor, and that is what gets channeled from then on.

So here you are and the next time you sit for a channeling, what will come in is this middle man. He will come in first and you've already made the gap so the entity is going to remain out here. The entity is not going to intrude upon you because you're scared of it. It loves you too much to intrude upon you because of your anxieties or fear or anything else. It sees it as a rejection also. This middle man is a combination of you and that entity, so you're not going to know the difference. So you pull the middle man in. If you were clear and all right within your being, you would then pull the entity in behind the middle man. You could share perceptions, you could use the embodiment together, they would leave the same way. They would go out, the entity first, the middle man second and you would have your integrity back when you were through with the experience.

In all channeling experiences, in order to keep the vehicle in their reality and the entity in its reality, a middle man is used.

But a lot of individuals only ever channel the middle man from thereon. That is another reason why sometimes you just can't get the amount of information that you could otherwise. The entity has the information and the body has the information but the middle man doesn't. The middle man does have some information, some access, but it is very much limited to the channels body of knowledge and the initial contact by the entity. So for the most part, the entity is nowhere around during the channeling experience in many cases. The entity touches, the middle man is created, and from then on, the middle man gets in the way because the middle man can grow. The middle man that is created by the experience can grow every time it touches a body. Every time that middle man comes into your body to channel, especially in a verbal state, you are letting it access your body and it is becoming addicted to physicality.

After a time, the middle man begins to understand your body probably better than you do, and it becomes a new form of a secondary personality. It becomes stronger and stronger until you get to a point where it is so strong that the entity that originally touched you in the first place can never get near you again to even channel through, or it can only do so when there is a window. So this middle man begins to become a life of its own. It is actually a child, a product of the entity and the channeler, it is a totally separate identity in and of itself, but it will appear to be either, and, or both the entity and the channeler.

This creates a barrier and ultimately a distortion in the channeling as it limits the knowledge that can be obtained by the channelers own body of knowledge and the information that was obtained from the initial contact with the entity.

They do have the ability to push the mind of the vehicle in any direction they want. If there is a good book they want read, they push it in that direction, then they have new raw material to channel. They simply push the vehicle into reading whatever material they want to channel. That's the easiest way of doing it, and it's a whole lot of plagiarism, if you want to look at it that way! What you get from a lot of middle men is recycled. You get them saying the same thing as everybody else, maybe a different angle or different slant, but it really doesn't answer any problems. It is just more of the same old stuff.

Let's say one of these middle men has gained control. What can be done with that?

I would say that there are several options. For one, if the middle man has gained control and the channeler is in a place of looking for external validation and still does not feel good about themselves, then the middle man will continue on. Eventually, that middle man will probably end up owning the body of the channel as it becomes the new future self of the channeler, fracturing away from the original entity that was to be the future self.

Let's say once again for the metaphor and the story, you are the channel. The entity comes in, touches you, and a middle man is made. Once in a while you allow the entity back in, it makes your connection to the entity a little stronger, a little more intense, but the connection is also giving life to the middle man. The middle man becomes very strong. These middle men will be addicted to a body because the body helped create it, and its biggest rush and thrill is being able to channel with and through the embodiment.

It has become addicted to physicality, but it also has enough intelligence not to want to incarnate on its own because now it is a god. It knows it is, it thinks it is, and it will put on a show of being so. So at that point in time, the middle man can become the body. That middle man can take over the body because it is a product of the body. It was a product of the channel touching their own god being, it is a product of the combination, so it has access to the body because you are letting it in. So it gets closer and closer and closer to a point that if it wants to, it will become the future self of the channeler.

Let's say that you are the channel and are into an extremely depressed mode. You're into a place where you just simply didn't want to be here and your middle man does. It will say, "Fine. Let me become you and let you go," and it becomes the body. It owns it from then on, but then it has an ability within the psyche to maintain two identities and be either you or it. But there becomes less and less differentiation between the two, less and less.

The other option is to fracture them off. Once these have been created, you will not destroy them and you cannot kill them—not that you'd want to anyway. This is a spiritual creation. This is an identity and an entity. The state of the channeler's ego is going to determine the ego of that middle man. If the channeler has a large ego—this is god, this is all powerful—then that middle man probably has a stronger consciousness, a stronger ego than most of the people on the planet do. So you're not going to go in and destroy it. You're not going to go in and shake it up. It can be fractured off, however. Once it gets to a certain point, there are different things that you can do that will emotionally fracture them. If that entity is fractured off, then it is kicked loose of the whole entire situation and from that point in time it is going to have to be just like the rest of you. It is either going to have to incarnate or start its own journey.

> *The middle man has its own total identity. It has its own power, its own love, and its own agendas.*

So once that middle man has gotten to a point of power and has become too powerful, its going to choose one of two options. It will usually not choose the option of being fractured. Fracturing will only occur from a combination of the channelers will to fracture the middle man and the audience. The audience has the ability to cause the fracture within the identity, but not if the channeling situation is a closed system—where the audience cannot question and challenge the middle man.

The middle man has full power of strength. The middle man has its intensity. The middle man has its own total identity. It has its own power, its own love, and its own agendas. It will probably begin to lessen and lessen the control of the channeler over the situation. This is not intended to create fear or anxiety, especially to anyone that is channeling. This is for understanding because if you understand the concepts, you're not going to get caught in the trap—there is no fear intended.

Let's say you are the channeler and you don't like your identity. You don't really like who you are so that is what gives the power to the middle man to take over larger amounts of your life. If you're into a state of isolation, you don't care about the world, you just want to be in your own little corner of it, you wish you could hurry up and get out of here and you have these types of attitudes, then you're giving power to this middle man. You, the channeler are the one who has to make the first move to fracture that identity off, because it was of your creation; it was yours and the entity's creation.

Let's say you the channeler, are enjoying the income. You're enjoying the lifestyle, you're enjoying the ego gratification, you're enjoying the validation the channeling gives you. There is no reason in the world you would fracture that off because you like it too much even if you have complaints about it. That middle man knows more about your psychology than you do. It knows what to keep you away from, and what to push you into to keep it from being fractured off. It can manipulate your psychology and your psyche to a point of saying, "Okay, you don't want to fracture me off. I am you and you are me and I'm going to take you with me," and it can give you all kinds of ideas and elaborate stories to keep from being fractured off. It will take you, and push you into a state of isolation so that you're not going to be psychologically or emotionally exposed to things that would push and trigger you into fracturing his or her identity off. The middle man is capable of doing all these things.

Since you are into a state of isolation, you're less exposed, and this is the first thing that happens. After that, the middle man has to be able to continue to feed off of you. The middle man uses the embodiment in the channeling experience relative to the intensities of the audience. An entity, whether it is a middle man or any other, comes and stays in your field. When you get the intensity from anyone in participation, the participant actually takes their energy and pushes your entity or middle man into the body. So for these types of middle men that intend to take over the embodiment of the channel or the vehicle, they are going to want somebody to push them into it. Therefore, they are going to be very selective, careful, and very closed on the type of individual they're going to allow around them in order to force them into the body.

The thing that they grow off of and the thing that they can connect with the best in the body is fear because that's the primary base feeling. So a middle man with an intention of taking over the embodiment of the channel will usually create a very strong fear-based environment. It will want fear from the audience in order to be fed.

You have no stronger intensity on this planet than fear. So let's say you are the channeler and you have a middle man that wants to inhabit your embodiment and you don't really care. As far as you are concerned, you don't like life anyway and who cares? It does, and it's going to keep you complacent, it's going to keep you semi-satisfied so you don't complain too much and do anything about it.

If I come into your audience and I have joy, I have love in the experience and I want my own answers, I want the intensities and I'm trying to bring the god out in you so you can bring it out in me, then I'm going to push those forms of intensities, and it's going to actually bring you—not the middle man, not the entity—but *you* back to the surface. It's going to resurrect, so to speak, you the channeler and bring you up with life because I will feed you life in the experience. When I do this, the middle man gets threatened.

On the other hand, let's say the middle man attracts only that which is fear-based, and I'm in fear and I ask you the channeler, "Tell me about the end of the world. Tell me about all these terrible things that are going to happen. Tell me about all the pain." You the channeler don't want to live on the planet, or be part of the planet because you don't like the pain. You don't like the struggle. I'm already looking for this. I will push my fear at you. I will push you, the individual, away from your body and I will allow the middle man in stronger than ever. The middle man can give me all the fear that it can and tell me about the end of the world. It will tell me about these things, and my reaction back will be more fear and a bonding with the middle man, because now I have someone that hears my side of my feelings and my story and can take my fear. So I will cycle with the middle man because my fear will bond me with the middle man who wants my fear in order to keep you, the individual, away from the body.

You, the channeler, after the channeling experience, come back into the body a little bit, but there is so much fear, so much pain, that is all you see and you'll run away again. The middle man has you trapped. If the middle man intends to own that body when the experience is done, it will not want love or joy and it will create a fear-based environment in order to breed itself into existence by using your body to do so. You the channeler were looking

A middle man with an intention of taking over the embodiment of the channel will usually create a very strong fear-based environment.

for external validation and you drew in pain and fear because you were scared. As you bring that in, you bring in audiences and crowds with fear and then the more of that, the stronger the middle man gets and the weaker you get. The more fear that is generated, the more the middle man grows. You, the individual slowly die more and more until all that is left is the middle man bigger than life. You the individual can put on any show you want and say, "Here I am. I'm alive and well," and it is not a truth because you have already given up.

If the middle man eventually takes over, what will happen is you, the individual will move back into becoming a cell in the whole of the middle man when you were originally its creator. The middle man just consumed its parent when that occurs.

Like I said, none of this is created for fear. It is only created to jog the minds of a whole lot of individuals. The middle man was your product or your spirit child from touching your own god, and then it was externalized. The externalization is what made it become a child amplified by your not wanting to be you. It is a feeling inside. A lot of you can put on the biggest show for the world, but inside you're eating away and you're hurting and you don't want the life. That's what causes it. Then you the channel, diminish your life, diminish your life, diminish your life, because all there is, is fear. That feeds the middle man, then you, one day, just extinguish and become a cell in it and you become its memory.

The middle men, when they get that strong, are not going to want to be fractured because they have it made. While all of you had to start out and develop your consciousness, they were given one, by the very act and everything that happened. They don't have to go the same long journey you've gone. You could say, if you want, a metaphor for your mind, they just took off thousands and thousands and millions of years of evolution that you had to painstakingly work through and on the other end of it, you're going to become a cell in that experience rather than the experience. They have it made. They can spend one journey, twenty, thirty, forty-years going through this process and they have it made where many of you will have spent ten, twenty, thirty-thousand lifetimes to get to the same point. That's how important maintaining that connection with that body is.

The psyche of the channeler is what has to determine to fracture the middle man. It has to initiate it and then the audience can perform it. Once the middle man has become that strong, the psyche of the consciousness of the channeler itself, is not going to be strong enough to fracture the identity, because at this point in time, the scales are out of balance. The middle man is, let's say, ninety percent and you the individual is down to ten percent, perhaps, just for a metaphor. That means that it is a whole lot stronger than you are, but you still have your free will and your right to exist.

Let's say that this is your situation and you become aware of the fact. First of all, you have to decide you want to exist and you want some joy in your life. You have to be willing to allow it to come in. The middle man is going to try sure as anything to keep it out. But once you have put into motion the intention to connect with that joy and your own life spark, you are given the same right to exist as any living thing that there is. This means that if that middle man is in your way, it, by the laws, has to be removed and pushed out of the way. But you have to want to exist. That intent then puts you in line with your original future self.

Many channelers move into a situation where they fall into the channeling.

Many channelers move into a situation where they fall into the channeling. The channeling becomes more important than they are, the experiences more powerful than physicality and they really don't like being here just like the rest of you, but they now have an escape for it where a lot of you don't. So a lot of you should bless yourselves for not being able to do what some of these do when a lot of you are saying, "Well, why can't I be like them!" You should bless yourselves and say, "Oh, I saved myself a headache. I saved myself from having to worry about this one."

Once again, they have to want to exist, to want to live, they have to find something that gives them joy in their existence, otherwise the middle man will own the body. It will take it over and they will give it. It's not a matter of it coming in and possessing you and saying, "Okay, I'm destroying you now." You'll give up the ghost to it. So the psyche of the channeler first has to want to exist independent of any identity and a lot of them on the surface can mouth it all over the place because that's what they are teaching. Since that is what a lot of them are teaching, they sure better be able to mouth the words, but it doesn't mean that's how they feel inside. It has to be felt inside.

As soon as the channeler truly wants that, then the audience can help facilitate it, if they are an audience that has come together out of joy. That can make an enormous push. In energy, if it's one person, it's one person, but from there it goes exponentially. Two people is times itself which is four units instead of one unit and so on, so you take a thousand people, that is over a million being pushed at one time instead of one individual. So if that individual, that channeler decides that they want to exist, that they want to live and that they can do it without being that god, then they can actually fracture it, with the push of joy and intensities of the audience.

The middle men are very smart. They are highly intelligent. They will actually learn to keep the channeler into a state where the channeler needs them. They will provide for them financially, they'll provide for them in a lot of other ways that the channeler will become very frightened about losing because the middle man knows how to push fear. The middle man was created out of the separation that fear causes. They know how to keep you, the individual channeler, in a fear-based reality so you won't live your truth, even though you are teaching it to millions of others. Now, I'm not saying that the middle man gets this powerful in all channeling situations, but it can happen.

At that point, the channeler will rationalize themselves into staying right where they are. They will not allow themselves to be who and what they are because they think they are on a mission and so they have to put up with this. They think that they have to do this for other people, they are supposed to do this, they have a lot of reasons for it. These middle men are very intelligent at giving you reasons. And so the individual channeler, you, has to get to a point of saying, "I've had it. I'm okay if this whole thing falls apart today," and not just mouthing it. You have to be to a point emotionally of saying, "I can walk away from it and I can be myself and I can be glad to be myself," but once having touched the power that an audience gives and having touched what it feels like to deal with even the middle man, this is a very hard experience to give up for most. Many will be able to do it, and once they do that, the audience can then be shifted, but if the audience is fear-based, the audience will have to be dumped first. If the audience is a fear-based audience, it is going to bring up the middle man and just grow that middle man. If the individual channeler is wanting to change, to get rid of the middle man, they're going to have to get rid of the audience that they are channeling to because that channeling is feeding the middle man and not them.

The next thing you have to realize is that by this point of discovery, these middle men have already trapped the channelers in such a way— some of them financially, some of them emotionally, some of them psychologically—that for the most part they are not willing and will not give up where they are. They will not open back up and so they'd rather stay in the situation than to be themselves. In order to be themselves and to change it, they are literally going to have to dump the audience that was feeding the middle man and start all over marketing in a whole new direction.

Not very many people are willing to do that. If they can do that, they will fracture the identity. Then that becomes an entity, totally separate. It becomes a spiritual creation, a child of the universe, it becomes a living god separate from either the entity or you the channeler, either one, and then it is given a life of its own and it is up to it what it will do. Some of them incarnate, some of them at that point in time are already strong enough that they can go on into other experiences without having to incarnate into the flesh, but each one will be a different situation. The channeler is then free to develop a new middle man, one that will work with and be in harmony with the entity—the channelers true self. This arrangement would allow a continual and expanding flow of life giving concepts and information being received from the true entity.

If you could get an audience that was open, intense, . . . you could have the most beautiful, opening experiences. . .

If the audience realized their own participation in the channeling, you would have an audience that is totally different and you would have a channeling experience different than anything any of you have seen today or on your planet yet. Many channelers place themselves in a place of being separate from the audience. They don't participate with the audience, they don't want to be part of the audience and they hold themselves in an elite class separate from the audience. If everybody realized that in the situation everybody is working together, then they would find that you could have some of the most powerful opening, beautiful experiences that your planet has ever seen.

If you could get an audience that was open, intense, dedicated to their own joy, their own being, their own life, and they were dedicated to what they were doing, they were clear within their being, and were not pushing the fear, and they actually pushed the joy, and they pushed the intensity, you could have the most beautiful, opening experiences for this whole system of reality that you have ever had. But for the most part, here on this planet, you can market fear and people will buy fear, but they don't want to pay to learn how to have joy. They will pay to have fun, and they'll pay a lot for things like that, but they are not willing to go through what it takes to just love life, enjoy it, and be excited about it for a change.

You have many channelers upon this planet that will never reach their potential because nobody is asking it of them. They are just assuming that they know what they are doing. There aren't any manuals out there that say, do this, don't do that—there aren't any available. For the most part, many channelers have such egos that they are not willing to talk to anybody else about how to do it, what to do, or how they do it, or what their experiences are. Each of them are having experiences that if they could share among themselves, understand what was going on, they would actually help educate each other. They don't do that because they are all afraid of finding out that somebody else is doing what they are doing and might be as good or better in their terminology.

It is your responsibility to be centered within your being, to go to that session with your own joy, with your own understanding and with an intensity for answers. Most people never go with an intensity for answers because they see that this is a god outside of themselves and so most people go into the situation afraid to even ask questions and they find middle men that intimidate and are defensive.

It is the intensity of the audience and individual participant that will propel the channeler into the fields of knowledge leading to new understandings. If you're afraid to ask questions, then you might as well save your money, stay home and don't take the time to have the experience. If you are wanting to have an experience in a channeling experience, be at least honest enough with yourself to say, "Okay, here is my intensity. Here is my question. Here is my direction," even if it is just a feeling. Even if you can't write it down on a paper. When you go, listen. Don't say, "Okay, here is this question," and then your mind jumps to the next question while the entity is giving you information on the first question. Stick with the flow. That is your responsibility in the situation. ▲

The Identity
and Persona
of Middle Men

Middle men take on a name and a persona. Every saint, every god, every famous person that has lived is being channeled by somebody, but realize that the very first initial expression or experience with the channeling is when that individual, the channeler, opened up and touched their own god. That had to happen before anything else. When that happened a middle man was created and somebody had to find a name for the middle man. They had to find an identity for it. They had to make up a story, if you want, and there is nothing wrong with that. Reality is everybody's own story anyway, for the mind to handle.

Let's say you are the channeler. Here is your own god entity, it touches you, opens you, and you've had the experience we've already talked about. It backs away, you back away, and a middle man is created. What story are you going to come up with for your middle man? You know who you are in this time and space, but who is the middle man? That middle man is a portion of your own being that you are growing into. It always has to be this way. Since that is what it is, it's going to be a little different than you. It's going to feel different than you. Its going to have a different story than you. So it will take your own belief system, your own ideas, and create an identity for itself. In times past many of the identities that were created were biblical. This gave them credibility and personified the powerful experience the channeler had based on their belief system. In the past many people have channeled Christ, many have channeled Buddha. You are starting to get away from some of your metaphors about Christ and people are channeling aliens because for many people that is seen as a higher, stronger form of intelligence than you see yourselves as being. So the new aliens and UFO people—your E.T.'s—have replaced gods as being intelligent. Wherever your mind set is, you will determine the identity and name that gets put on this presence. It is your god—which means it can literally be anything.

There are those instances and those rare experiences when there is a life form from the dead zone or from the unincarnated side that actually can mold and create an experience. It is a one time experience and rather than just strictly channeling, the channeler will go into more of a mediumship experience.

You, the channeler, will actually connect to the dead zone and medium or chameleon somebody's dead relative, just for the sake of our story. That is a one time thing. Those entities on that side, can never do that more than once, because once they make contact with the body of the channeler it changes and alters them permanently. An individual having encountered you through the medium experience, will never be the same again. There-fore, the next time that individual tries to be channeled, if it is the same one in a mediumship experience, that individual is already now a totally differ-ent individual. It wouldn't be recognized by the family or associates because of the encounter it had with you and your body.

There are many different kinds of experiences. Some individuals who channel are actually very good mediums, but for my purposes, I would like to say there are two different things that happen. Channeling is chan-neling. Mediumship, if you want to term it—and I don't like the terminol-ogy, but its the only word you have in this day and time to explain what I am trying to talk about—is when you actually go into the dead zone and take on the persona of what you would perceive an individual that is dead, so to speak, and you are actually going to personify them and speak for them.

Many individuals have the ability to do both, if they are open to channel. Let's say that you're one who isn't strictly just a channeler. You have the ability to channel, but you also have a chameleon affect or medi-umship ability. If you also have a chameleon affect, here is what can hap-pen: First, the entity touches you and that is your god touching you. That's your first experience. You separate. You cause a separation both ways. A middle man is created. Then second, you chameleon or medium the dead zone. In that mediumship experience in the dead zone, you pick up a per-sona and overlay your middle man with it, when that middle man was really just a product of you touching your own being.

This is why you have a hundred people channeling the same old dead person, so to speak. In the first attempt, entity touches you. In the touching, you open and in that opening, you, out of your fear and your unworth, separate, and a middle man is created. You now have a second experience because you want to recreate it. You try to reconnect with the entity, but you connect with the middle man, the middle man connects to the dead zone and connects with whatever the strongest gestalt of consciousness is there.

You have more people channeling spiritual religious figures than anything else, because that is what your predominant gestalts of consciousness are there. The channels go into the dead zone, and chameleon the first strong identity they can find. It is probably going to be a biblical figure, since that is what has maintained a strong identity from the belief and emotions of millions of people. They chameleon it, pull it back, and that's their second experience in the channeling. Now they have an identity of the god they are channeling which they picked up and overlayed from the dead zone. But that god was really them in the first place. They went to the dead zone and chameleoned a story because each of your gods can be anything it wants to be, and that is what it chooses. That's what you choose.

Many times, the identities are actually assumptions on the part of the channeler.

The other way that a lot of these identities are created—and many of you have had this experience whether you channel or not— are simply when a conversation starts coming in from a presence or a dream or something, and you try to talk to an entity in your head. You feel somebody there and you start talking to them. You ask them, "Who are you?" and you start getting a little bit of mumbling coming back through and you try to clarify. You try to be more specific and you say, "Okay, I can feel you. I can sense somebody here. Who are you?," and then you get a couple of letters coming through. You say, "Okay, now let's be more specific." And so, they come through and you get a little bit more of it. Your brain begins to put an interpretation on it. This is usually some of the first forms of refinement between an entity and a vehicle anyway—to get the fine tuning down on the language barrier.

For the most part, this entity is you, its your own god presence, so it can be anything or anybody. It doesn't really care what you call it. It really doesn't, because that's for you to evolve into and then who knows what you're going to call it when you get there anyway. It doesn't really matter, and so, it just kind of tries to tell you, "Well, I'm god," and you say, "Well, of course it can't be god. God doesn't do this so you must be Christ, or you must be this, or you must be that." Many times, the identities are actually assumptions on the part of the channeler.

Let's say that you get several parts of a name and it is something like Myan . . . Mya . . . Mayha . . . and you can't quite make it out. It sort of sounds like Myannn. . . . Mooha . . . something like that and so your brain says, "Okay, I have to have an identity. I want to know if this is a good guy or a bad guy. I have to know who this is I'm going to channel." So many channelers actually start doing research to prove that this individual lived. You can ask all kinds of questions and lot of you do this in your own mind with your answers all the time. "Where did you live on the planet? Did you do this?" and you get a lot of yes and no answers. You might not get a whole lot of elaboration, but you get yes or no answers.

Channelers, just like everybody else, do not want to be wrong. If you're going to channel an entity that says they were so and so, you better be able to go and prove that they were so and so. So a lot of vehicles and a lot of stories of a lot of these entities are created out of whatever is readily accessible to the channeler.

Let's say that you get somebody that comes in and they say, "Well, I'm Mark." Let's say that you're into a religious background and here is a presence that calls itself Mark. Because of your belief system you wonder if this must be Saint Mark. Your brain will assume that it probably is and then you ask it, "Well, are you the Mark of the Bible?" and it would say, "Well, god is talked about in the Bible, so yes, I guess I am."

Realize, it doesn't carry on the same type of logic you do. A lot of identities for these middle men are created by the vehicle itself trying to understand what is happening to it when all that happened to it was that it actually connected with its future being. It connected with its future life. The vehicle connected with its god. It connected with where it is going. When it did that, it couldn't interpret it because it was too abstract and so it makes a story for it. ▲

Understanding Secret Schools of Thought

Secret schools of thought have been around since ancient times and are an extension of the systems of hierarchy that have always existed on your planet. For example, in olden times you had a lot of king/slave types of relationships. Your rulers were the big chiefs, so to speak, and nobody else could be one. They were born into it—they had the birthright and heritage. A very select amount of the population were kings or queens. Nobody else could be one, which meant everybody else was basically peasants or the in-betweens. But everybody desires to be a king or a queen. All of you do, even if it is just the king of your own being. Everybody desired to have a sign of nobility, and many of your hidden schools started to give that to people.

First you had your priests, the rulers of your churches. They were a king within a kingdom. Maybe they were not *the* king, but they were a priest-king with some nobility. They could influence the king and they could influence the people. Then over time your priest-kings actually began to move into a place of much more power than the royal family ever saw, because they were in charge of all the spiritual affairs. Every good king knows he better pay attention to people's spiritual affairs, so the kings supported the priests in their role of power. The priest-kings became much more powerful, much more potent than even the rulers themselves.

So here was somebody who became a priest-king who wasn't born to the office. The king has a son and the son replaces him. He has a son, and that replaces him. When these priest-kings came into being, most kings selected them out of the strongest oracles, the strongest psychics, and wisest entities. So having picked them, then here was someone that was put into a place of royal standing, and they didn't have to be birthed into it. After that, it moved into a place where more people wanted the same option.

The priest-kings had to have a way of saying, "I'm different than you are, so let me teach you so you can get to where I am." Most of them didn't know how they got their abilities. They just came to them early in life. They were kind of an intermediary, but most of these priest-kings actually ran governments more than the kings and the royal families did. They had much more power, because they had the power over the king and the peasants both.

So being a priest-king became even a more noble station in life than being the ruling family. This, of course, meant you were spiritually right and you would go to heaven, so to speak, or whatever your version of that was.

These priest-kings then had to find a way of keeping everybody else from just claiming themselves to be a priest-king. In order to keep the rest of the masses in line, to make a hierarchy, and to make a caste system, they had to create something for people to do in order to get where they were. This is where many of your hidden mysteries and your hidden schools began to be generated. It was quite some time back under this kind of a psychology and emotional mentality.

The regular peasants, having seen one of their peers become a member of the noble family by becoming the new priest, wanted to do the same. But in order to maintain hierarchy, and in order to maintain a caste system, you have to make steps and have it take a real long time for them to get there. So this is what these priest-kings did.

The peasants wanting to follow the way and become the nobility just like they saw their friends doing, would actually follow his advice. He would say, "Well, in secret, this is what I did and so don't tell anybody else." That made them feel special and like they were doing something to accomplish what he had. Then when they had all this done, he said, "Oh, well, that was just the first part of it. Here is your next mystery. Here is the next hidden something that you didn't know about. So do this and don't bug me for a while." Then they would be off doing their work as they were told to do and they would come back later and say, "Okay, did I do well enough?" "Well, you did all right with that, but now here is your next chore. Go do this."

These priest-kings also found that this was a cheap way of slave labor. So what they would say is simply, "Okay, well you need to plow these fields because god told you to and when you do, meditate upon it." So in that way, these individuals were out of the priest-king's hair, so to speak. They thought they were doing something; they went and plowed his fields for him so he didn't have to and the whole time they meditated upon it.

After a period of time, a lot of these students became much more intelligent, so to speak, much more open and gifted. This gave power to the priest-kings, because now in the student's mind the priest-king really did know something. So the student began feeling justified in trusting the priest-king's directives on everything in his life. The student never realized that it was he, the student, that caused the enlightenment. He believed that it was the priest-kings's secret mystery chore that had caused the awakening. The priest-kings then had to keep creating more and more things for them to do just to prevent them from becoming more enlightened than they had been. So it just became a perpetual puzzle to create one more thing, and one more thing for them to do.

If you have something that is secret and hidden that nobody else knows, then you are special.

Your orient is where a lot of your hidden schools and mystery thought started. It moved into Egypt and from there every other dogma had to have something hidden. That is what your term "occult" means. Occult means a hidden mystery, something that is a secret or hidden. Cult, being part of that term, is still where your *cult*ures come from. All of your cultures are actually derivatives and come after you have gone through the hidden secret teachings. Everyone has lived it, and since they did it, they change. Now you have a culture instead of a hidden secret which was the occult. In the larger scheme of things, many of these occults have formed much of your belief systems. They have created the formation of much of your philosophies. Many of your cultures were created from these hidden secrets. Whenever a group had the hidden secret, they would coagulate, and they would coagulate around *the* hidden secret or secrets and thus create a new culture to support the hidden secrets. This is where you get all your religions and all your dogmas that you have upon your planet today.

All of your hidden secrets or schools give people a sense of ownership, a sense of being, a sense of belonging, a sense of being a part of something. It has also always been used as a control over people. If you have something that is secret and hidden that nobody else knows, then you are special. You're set aside and you can be controlled by the very secret which was supposed to be the thing that was your advantage in the first place! So then what is supposed to be the advantage becomes the detriment or that which controls you.

These priest-kings can only be priest-kings as long as someone is worshiping them. As soon as their congregation leaves, they have no power left, because for all their wisdom, they never learned to tap their own. If their congregation is leaving because there is no movement in it, and they are not accomplishing, they're going to be out of business. They have to continually find a way of creating new and more business to come in so to speak; a larger congregation. This is why a lot of systems and religions have missionary programs to keep trying to get more people to come in. They see that the program isn't working for the old people.

The other thing they do is that, if their initiates are getting discouraged because they aren't advancing fast enough, and new people don't want to come in because it takes too long to get anywhere, they will take some younger or newer students and advance them more quickly, giving them the advancement that normally takes a much longer period of time. This keeps people thinking that they have a chance at also advancing faster. Or if the peasants that have been in for a long time start grumbling, they will come out with a more secret, ultimate, special mystery for them.

Many of your hidden mystery schools today have a different aura about them. These are for people who have left the religions—or at least they think they have, and so now they are wanting something else to be special to them. These schools create these types of special experiences for them.

Is there a difference between secret and sacred, and should some things remain secret?

There is a difference between secret and sacred in the natural sense of it, but the brain doesn't see much difference. Secret means to be hidden. Sacred is a feeling inside, and so, it is not necessarily something that you are going to go scream and shout to the world about. The thing that is really sacred within any of you, is the preciousness that you find inside—which everyone has. Therefore, there is nothing to maintain a secret over.

What is truly sacred is actually a feeling. It is not a thing. Sacredness is a feeling inside. It is that special, precious place within your being, within your heart. It is the point where you touch yourself. The only thing that is sacred, is that feeling inside. Everybody on this planet is so used to externalizing, they get that precious place inside and externalize it on an outside event, or situation.

A lot of your old orientals experienced problems because they started getting declining people coming in. It was a grand experience, but they were not accomplishing, these people were not opening up, and they weren't changing. In order to hold someone in a situation, you have to design a way of allowing them to have some experiences or they won't stay with it. You can either keep them in it out of guilt and fear, or by creating something for them to have an experience with. There are myriad ways of having experiences, there is not just one way of having the experiences. These oriental schools found ways of triggering people into experiences. And then they said, "Well, this is a secret," because anything that they did, the whole masses could do and they didn't want everyone to know, because they would lose their specialness. If everybody knew how to do these special little things, they could no longer maintain their superiority in the world. So they made all kinds of stories. "Well, you have to keep it secret because it's sacred now, and the rest of the world wouldn't appreciate it. The rest of the world couldn't use it. The rest of the world might hurt themselves with it. The rest of the world isn't ready for it." There were all these types of reasoning to enforce guilt to keep you from talking about the simple things that were causing your experiences in the first place.

What is truly sacred is actually a feeling. It is not a thing.

On this planet you have two different types of people. You have what are called peakers. These are the people that have experiences. Then you have followers who like to follow the peak experiences of others. These two types of people gravitate to each other. The same thing occurs within the mystery school experiences. An individual pushes the experience for others to have. In a lot of these hidden schools, these priest-kings, these rulers over the masses were getting a lot of enjoyment from the energy pushed at them from those underneath them or in the audience, just like any movie star, any singer, anyone who is in the limelight. Anyone of them, if they sat and were honest with you and told you how they feel, even if they had no ego at all, would tell you how it feels to be with an audience. Maybe they are scared, but there is a power behind it, and that is why a lot of people want the experiences, because there is a power and a feeling of that strength.

These priest-kings, unless they could keep the congregations big enough and having experiences to keep them coming back, weren't going to be fed this way. They were not going to have the power. They were not going to have the intensities that they wanted. So they had to start coming up with a few ideas to try to get people to think they were having experiences.

The only thing that is happening is that everybody is having the exact same experience, but it is catalyzed by a different process and so it appears to be different. The sacred experiences that all of you have is the touching of that preciousness called you. It is touching your own being inside. That is the only thing that is sacred and for the most part, it is sacred because it is precious and it is precious to you and only to you. Everybody can only do it with themselves. That makes it precious, but it doesn't make it anything that needs to be maintained a secret. That is something that everybody upon this planet covets. Everybody upon this planet wants to be able to touch their own preciousness within themselves, and all these other things are just metaphors. They are tools. They are things for the mind to let you have an excuse for having the experience of touching yourself. So you can do all of these things that a lot of these schools do. You can go through the disciplines, but all those disciplines are designed for, and all they will ever do, is get you to open up to touch your own preciousness. That is all.

If you see the school as the only way you can create such an experience, you will never allow yourself to have further experiences on your own. However, if you see a teaching, a philosophy, an idea, simply as a tool to help you create the space for you to have your precious experience—because you needed permission and support to allow you to have the experience—then you are the master, you are owning your own truth. If you fear being kicked out or fear leaving any situation, whether it be a teaching, a relationship, or a mystery school, then that is your first clue that you are a follower. A master fears *no one* or *no-thing*. A master owns the precious experiences as his own creations, and knows he can never lose by moving on. He gives power to no-thing outside of himself, but gives love for that which gave him the space and permission to be his own god and king.

Some people have the ability to open up to those experiences easier than others. Those who can't open up to the experience covet the experience of that opening, and therefore, they become the followers of those who have the peak experiences. Since they become the followers, they actually will push the others into having more and more experiences. These become the rulers. These become the elite. These become the hierarchy, because the others are not having the experiences as much, or they are downplaying their experience.

Most of you have had similar experiences to those that have made many people, in a lot of other people's minds to be these big spiritual deities that people worship to this day. Yet you worship their experiences because you discredit your own.

All of you can have these experiences and you can have them all the time. It takes no disciplines to do them. It takes no specific set of rules to accomplish them. It is just that everyone wants to say that they are special, they have special ways of doing it. This is what creates their feeling of their superiority over the world because they think they are better than everybody else.

This precious, sacred place within each of you is accessible to every single one of you, and the fastest shortcut to it is just to sit and love who and what you are. Let yourself feel the miracle of life. That's where you will touch it. All these other things are something to keep your mind busy and playing so that you can give yourself permission to do it—that is all. Then when it is done in the framework of a religion, when it is done in the framework of a mystery school, you give the credit to the school. You give the credit to the dogma rather than to yourself for just allowing yourself to have the experience which is already innately yours.

Those who can't open up to the experience . . . become the followers of those who have the peak experiences.

What are some of the disciplines or practices that facilitate people touching themselves and having an experience?

I would say that every system of thought has something different. I'll tell you the simplest, and easiest way and then I'll tell you what a lot of them put you through to get to the same place, how's that?

The simplest and the easiest is to let yourself sit in a state of being for a few moments, to relax the mind, to get it out of the guilt, the entrainments, and to get it out of that worry. Sit in a place that is a peaceful moment and then go inside and just focus on the preciousness and the miracle of you. That is the fastest, simplest, easiest way to do it. There are all different ways of changing that experience and making derivations of that.

For the most part, none of you will let yourself have that experience without some form of permission to do it. One of the grandest things you want to know is about yourselves. A lot of you feel unworthy, unloved, and you want to know why. You want to know why you feel so lousy about yourselves. You want to know why you are worth loving. You want to understand yourselves. That is an innate desire for everyone of you that is in a human form—to understand yourself.

You came here to be yourselves. To actually grow a Self, to become one, that is the primal desire, need, and intensity that everyone of you have.

So you are not going to get away from it. It is something that is just a part of your nature and you will pursue it to find out who and what you are and to understand fully about you—all of it. So many of these schools play on people's needs and desires to understand themselves.

If these priest-kings were offering something that was totally outside of your realm of need, desire, or want, you would have nothing to do with it. You'd have no need for it. So they are going to start playing on some of your most precious desires to actually attract you. But as soon as they start attracting those types of individuals that are questioning themselves, wanting to know about themselves, the priest-kings don't have the answer. Since they don't have the answer, the very first thing they are going to do is to shut you up. This is what every system—it doesn't matter what the religion, it doesn't matter what the dogma, it doesn't matter what the mystery school is—they will shut you up. They will not necessarily come out and say, "Don't ever say a word," but if you ask any questions, they will say, "Here is the law. Can't you read it? Don't question it. Just accept it. Just buy it. This is the way it is. There is no other truth. There is no other teacher. There is no other way of looking at it." So the very first thing they will do is take away your ability to question and make you feel guilty if you do.

If they take away your ability to question, you are owned by them. You are owned by anything that you do not feel free enough to question, free enough to experience, or free enough to leave. The very first thing they do is take away your freedom to be yourself and to understand you. After that, everything else is easy to take away from you.

In the beginning, all of you are skeptical. In the beginning all of you have doubts. In the beginning, all of you want to know. You want to know whether this is something you should put your heart into or not. You feel the love of your own being because of some of the experiences and then immediately you are told never to question it. Since you've had an experience and you touched the preciousness, they are now telling you not to question it or that preciousness will be taken away—you will *not* question it. That preciousness, that sacred space within your being, that touching of that deep little part of you, you will not want to lose. You want to have it continually, and so, anything that would take that away from you or threaten it, you will bypass. So in your being what you do is you quit questioning. Then any time a question comes up, you say, "Well, its just a frailty of human nature. There is something wrong with me because I dared to question. I dared to question god."

How do you know how to worship god if you don't even know who god is or what he likes or what he doesn't like? How do you know that somebody else knows better than you what a god likes? How do you know they have it right in the first place in order for you to even be following them? But you are told, "Don't ask questions"—and it's because they can't answer you. Since they can't answer you, any question you have becomes an irritation to them. Since it becomes an irritation to them, they will tell you to get rid of them. All of your questions are going to revolve around you, your body, your desires, your needs, your wants. This is human nature. Since your questions revolve around the human experience, they will tell you to deny the human experience. But this is what you came for—you came here to be a human being. You came here for the flesh, you came here for the body, and no, this is not a prison camp! You came here to *live life*. That is why you came. You didn't come because you were so dumb and unintelligent that you chose the worst place in the universe! You were an intelligent species before you ever arrived here and you came for a reason—to experience a body. Since you came to experience a body, you're going to want to know about it. You're going to want to know why it behaves the way it does. You're going to want to know where your desires come from. You're going to want to know all these things, but the priest-kings don't have the answers.

You are owned by anything that you do not feel free enough to question . . .

You're getting your answers, but you are getting your answers through the experience of them, and you want them a little quicker than that. They tell you not to ask them. So you ask about why you behave the way you do and they just tell you, "Well, don't do it. It doesn't matter. Quit." They tell you, "Don't ask me the questions. Just deny it." If you deny all of physicality, they don't have to answer you. If you deny the human experience, the human expression, if you deny your sexuality, you deny your body, you deny everything, then there is no question. Then when you ask them a question that they can't answer, it is because you are so weak that you ask the question, and of course, you want to be strong, so you won't ask the question again.

But you want to know why you have lack in your lives. You want to know why you can't manifest what you want. But instead of teaching you how to do it, because they don't know how—they will tell you, "Don't desire it because that is worldly, ungodly and not good."

421

Realize that in a system of hierarchy, the kings are going to want to keep you as peasants. If you can be kept as a peasant, you will never become the king, because you can view the peasant that you are. You have lack. You don't have the things that you want. You don't have the godly or the kingly things or queenly things in your life, so therefore, you have proof of your lack. You have proof of your unworthiness.

If you are going to be controlled, all it takes to control you is to prove your unworthiness to you. So here you are, proving to yourselves your lack. That will keep you in lack. They don't want you to create abundance in your life. If you create abundance in your life, you would become a king just like them and they don't want any more kings. They will tell you to reject it—material goods are not godly. They are not spiritual. They are not saintly. Get rid of them. Get rid of your desires, and any desire you can get rid of means you are conquering the flesh.

You didn't come here to conquer the flesh. You came here to live in it. You came here to be part of it, not to destroy it, not to repress it and not to conquer it. So the first thing they will teach is denial of you.

The next thing they always do is to cut off your senses so you don't feel the body, so you don't perceive the body, and you will not be one with it. If you are not one with your body, you will be owned. Yes, if you go into social consciousness from an image standpoint, you are owned also. If you don't own your body, then somebody else does, and you will never own your body until you live in it, love it, and truly live life through it and with it. That is the only time you truly own it. Otherwise, everybody else is telling you what to do with it and they will control you from that standpoint.

From there, if you can still see what is going on in the world, then they will move you into a place of isolation. If you can see these things in the outside world, you will still want them. Every good monastery, every good system of hidden schooling always isolates its students so they won't question. If you live in the world and you are not isolated from it, you'll want to know why all these other people seem godly, grand, beautiful, and abundant and you'll ask, "Why aren't I?" You will want to know why you are better that these people that are so beautiful out here in the rest of the world. Then you will realize that you are not.

So isolation is always necessary. Put yourself in a cave, lock yourself on the top of a mountain, whatever works, but keep you away from the rest of society, keep you away from the rest of the world, because then you can be controlled.

But from your point of isolation, you still see the world. You still see life going on, and you want to know how come you are not part of it. You want to know why you are not part of this life that is running around out here, so then they take away your vision. Then they tell you to go into darkness. Then they tell you, "Don't view it, do everything without vision." If there is not vision, then you won't see what you are missing—that's what it boils down to. They tell you that they are taking away the sight so that you can see other worlds and other realms. But I tell you, you'll go far more with ecstasy of loving life and your being, than you will by going through any of the punishments or disciplines that any religion, dogma, or mystery school ever affords you.

You came here to live life. You didn't come here to sit on the outside and watch it go on without you.

They take away your vision. You can't see now, and you will pursue, do what you are supposed to, go through the trials, go through your struggle, but blinded so you cannot see.

The next is, they take away your hearing. Because after having taken away your sight, you can still hear the world around you. You can still hear the brook running. You can still see with your mind's eye now, but not with the physical ones. You can hear the birds and can hear the grasses move, so you become more in tune with them and then you want to know why you allowed your sight to be taken away. You want to know why you are not viewing it. You want to know why you are not living it. Now part of you, the primal part of you, comes up and it craves and it hurts to live in your depravity. And so you hurt. Then they take away your hearing. They plug it. They put you away so you cannot hear the world.

If you cannot see the world and you cannot hear the world, then you can be fully controlled. They will tell you that they are doing it for a myriad of reasons. They will tell you that they are doing it because you are going to evolve from it, because you are going to become a superior race by doing it. But all you've literally done is pulled yourself away from life and dug a hole to bury yourself. When you do that, life ends. So when they take away all of your senses, all your life, all of your view and you cannot participate in life, you might as well dig your own grave and go live in it and die.

You came here to live life. You didn't come here to sit on the outside and watch it go on without you. You came here to live it. These mystery schools, all of your religions, all of your dogmas, all of these that have secrets, all have penalties. Every one of them will take your life away; they will take the love away from you which is worse than taking your life. They all have penalties for breech of promise, and what everyone of them boils down to is that they will take the love away from you and you will be an outcast. You will be ostracized because you didn't follow the tenants the way you should. Everyone of them has to have penalties and those penalties have to be enforced with fear. The worst kind of fear is the fear that you will no longer be loved. So, you will lead yourself from the blindness to the loss of your hearing. You'll take yourself there into the loss of your life and dig your own hole. You're actually separating yourself from your body and are choosing not to live life. You are choosing to live in another world, in another realm, in another place, when you came here to live in this one and in this body.

The only thing that exists is life, so therefore, the only great mystery that exists lies hidden in the question, "Why are you not yet living it?" The only school that exists *is life* and that is no mystery—only a marvel at the beauty of it. ▲

Never Judge the Course You've Gone

You spoke before on secret schools and ancient mystery schools and how often these develop into instruments of control and manipulation. I participated in a school which for me was very magnificent and I had an opportunity to grow very greatly in it, yet I've noticed that the school has shifted and there has been control and manipulation there. As I noticed it, I had noticed that there were things that I had believed and I had embraced and brought dear to me that were control and manipulation. Now that I wish to be more self-actualized and I want to let go of these things, what can I do within myself to help to find those things which I embraced which were control and manipulation oriented and which then detract from me expanding?

I would say never judge the course you've ever gone. Never judge that you ever did anything wrong, that you ever did anything that was not totally in alignment with what you needed. As long as you can stay in that space, you will see every reason you did every step you ever took. The only reason that most of you can't see the steps you took is, because you judged that you did something wrong by taking them. Put it into a place that it was a very beautiful, very powerful part of your life, and it is nothing you need to degrade, nothing you need to throw away, and nothing you need to trash. What you did is you used it, you grew from it, and now, perhaps it's time to grow in a different way. So your entity is saying, "Okay. We've gained from the experience. Let's go for a different one." I'd say, stay out of judgment. If you do that, then there is nothing to have to fix because your entity will say, "Okay, now here is an event or here is something that you bought as a truth. Observe it and what do you think?"—but stay out of judgment. Give yourselves credit for being intelligent. None of you are unintelligent no matter what any of you want to think. Everyone of you are guided. Everyone of you are directed. Everyone of you have passion, beauty, love in there. And so, that part of you would not do anything to you that would permanently harm you, be a detriment to you, or cause you any long-standing problems. Just put in the intent that, "Okay, now I've had my experience. I feel a need to change and I'm ready to go on. Show me my next step. Show me what I need to know. Show me where I want to release," and ask your entity to do it. I would say, always stay out of the judgment. If you can stay out of the judgment then you will never have to relearn anything, ever. If you do that, your own god within you, your own entity, whatever you want to call it, will show you any point that it wants you to observe. But if you judge it, then your entity will have to take you, grab you by the neck and say, "Now look," and you don't need that.

It's time for all of you to learn your lessons in beauty instead of the pain that a lot of you have learned them in. It's time for you to all get to a point of saying, "Okay, I'm a god, I'm intelligent, and I wouldn't have put myself through hell unless I had reason! I'm not that stupid." A lot of people are judging themselves for having been so. Put it into a place of, "I am a god. I was always a god. I never lost that. I was birthed as one. That is my heritage, my birthright and nobody can take that away from me. The only thing I could do on my entire journey is to enhance it, to understand me, and to understand these things." If you can be into a place of not judging your experience, then your entity will gently bring it up and say, "See this? Give me an opinion." It will ask you gently. It will bring it up and say, "Here is something I want you to observe. What do you think?" and it will give you the option. But when you start judging and saying, "Oh, I shouldn't have. I shouldn't have," then your entity almost has to rub your face in it and say, "Okay, look," and that is the journey most of you have chosen to go. It's time to change it. Just go into the beauty. Just remember that every experience that any of you have is beautiful, no matter how painful, no matter how miserable. You are an intelligent species—you truly are and you would do nothing to yourselves that would change that. So maybe you went through a period of time when you felt like, "Well, maybe somebody else knows more than I do," but on the other side of it, you came out knowing they didn't. That is a beautiful lesson because you learned that you know as much as anybody else.

The universe, that which loved all of you into existence in the universe, loved you all so equally, so fully, that you have all been given total complete access to anything you want and that means the knowledge. That means the thought. That means the origins to come in for you to organize into your own truth. Everyone of you, your birthright and heritage is to have that for yourselves and not to have to have it from anybody else; not to have to have permission for anything. Most of you will choose these different things just to give yourselves permission. Some things that some of you go through are very useful, and some experiences are not for everyone. In every experience there are people who are going to have positive reactions and people who won't. I would say that everybody is learning from experience. Just stay out of judgment. Find the beauty and let your own entity show it gracefully to you without the judgment. It will show you that the thing you need to change is probably just your perception on the subject. You probably needed the experience so you would understand how people manipulate, how people control, how perhaps you could also. You can observe that and just release and be back in your beauty. I would say that you've done fine. Just don't ever judge it. ▲

The Last
Dance*

You are all going to replace what you've had as pseudo-romance with love. The romantic ideals that you have about every aspect of your life actually prevent you from seeing love. When you get past all of your romanticized fantasy stories about life, then you can move to the true you and the true source of the universe. That will be better than any story you ever wrote. When you get down to true love and the pure life essence of the universe, you write your own life; you love yourself into existence, into such an intensity that you *are* life. When you experience it, you will understand it.

Everything that is here on your planet is love, so everything that you see on your planet, you have romantic ideals about. Your emotions are a story about love. They are your way of creating a story to understand your lives. That is why I use the metaphor of romantic ideals, because everything that you are labeling and everything that you are creating in your story of emotion, is love. So any story you would tell about love is a romantic tale.

To move beyond the romantic ideals and into love, one must let go of the old images. Emotions are pseudo-feelings. The emotions keep you from being into the love that you are. The images that you have about yourselves keep you from being yourselves. You are beauteous and expansive beyond comprehension and you limit yourself with all these fairy tales called emotions.

When you move into a place of feeling the feelings, the emotions will change. Emotions are the stories that you've all written. Many of you are already getting out of the emotions and moving into the depth of feeling. The feeling is love. If you're going to love yourself, it is going to have to come through feeling, because the pure entity that you are is an entity of thought, it is an entity of love, it is an entity of life. If it is going to commune

*This piece was originally delivered as a meditation.

428

with you, speak with you and be with you, it is going to do so through its medium of feeling, which is thought and love—an abstract to you here. It is only an abstract because you have so many pre-conceived ideas about what love is. All of these ideas about what love is, actually create a barrier to ever touching the greater portion of you.

Inside, you long to be yourselves, to be so connected with love, with life, and with the universe. So as you release a lot of the fantasies or images around love, the emotions change into pure feeling. Loving yourself is feeling because that is the only time you are connected with yourself. When you are feeling, that is pure love being sent to you from yourself. When you are connected into that space, you will weep, but you will weep with love. You will still feel the anguish in the heart, but it will be homesickness. You will still feel the passions, but they will be love, they will be life, and you will know that everything that was an emotion was a story to keep you from ever touching that depth.

Your emotions are a story about love. They are your way of creating a story to understand your lives.

In the beginning those depths are extreme. They are intense, they are deep, and they are harsh when you don't understand them. All of you are learning how to understand them a piece at a time as you can handle them. Then you let go of the emotions and you realize the only story that is here is the grandest romance of all. It is called love and it is called life. Then you realize that every emotion you had was created from the love. Fear was running away from the love. Anxiety was because the love was there and you didn't want to deal with it. You will realize that every emotion is an excuse to not love in the purest sense of the thought. Then you will realize emotions for what they are, and they will not have power over you. You will move into a passion that your being and your body will relish and your life will no longer be desperate.

Right now however, a lot of you are saying, "When can I hurry up and get out of here? When can I hurry up and learn how to fix it so I don't hurt any more?" When you are into life, into the love of your own being, you will find that this is the most beauteous playground you have ever experienced, and you will love and relish every moment. Every moment will be passion. Every moment that you live, you will be living the passion called life. And that passion, that excitement, that miracle of life, the beauty of that life is what love is—*the real love.*

The only way that you're going to be able to interpret the abstract called life, is by feeling the most intense excitement for life that you've ever felt. There is an excitement inside yourself and you just love being alive. That thrill of existence is *you*. When you are into that thrill, you are you. You are being yourself. You are in the flow of the universe. You are in love. You are in life. The rest of the time, you're dealing with the mundane and the drudgery of existence. That is no way for gods to live! You are gods. You have been through the drudgery. It is time to go home, to love, to feel that joy and intensity of living life.

Feel it now. Move into a place that the life, love of existence and a love of the universe is an intensity within your being. You are going to create that within your own being, but I'll tell you the ramifications of that ahead of time. When you have touched that love, what you now call life will be seen for the drudgery that it has been. You still tend to hold the old perceptions. You still have the old way of viewing life. You're so habitual with it that you believe that is the way life is supposed to be. When you touch those levels of joy, when you touch those levels of the entity you, when you touch yourself and those intensities of love, life in a sense becomes unbearable. It doesn't have to, but that is the running away part. The love is so intense that what is running away are your images. What is wanting to hide are the images that melt in the face of the entity you. Anything that would prevent you from totally touching you, feeling that connectedness, love, and that excitement for life—will melt when it touches the love of the entity you.

When you get close to the love, everything that has been the habitual you wants to run away. As it is running, it is taking the biological and habitual you in one direction, and the entity you, caught inside, is crying because it wants to go in another direction. This is called vulnerability. This is called the pain that you think you get from love. This is the last leg home and you must breach that vulnerability. It will take years. You may not want to hear this, but it will take years for most of you. This is the final dance. That is the dance that you've all been doing. Until you can touch that love and go back into that love, you will never go home.

The habitual you is trying to take you the way it has always known you. It works to preserve that, so it tries to take you away from the love. It tries to shut you down so you can't hear it. It tries to take you as far away from it as it can. Then you move into what you call depression. You move into a sadness because what is there is so much more beautiful than what you have learned to find here.

Love and life is where you are going. So whether you want to take a few weeks, a few months, a few years or ten-million-years, it doesn't matter. That is where you are going. The day and time are up to you. But you will go. On the other side, when you get there, you'll move into a place of saying, "Why didn't I do this sooner!"

The running process is the last leg of being god. Ever since you were originally loved into existence you have been on a running journey. When you get back to that love, it gets intense, the vulnerability comes and you get pain.

A lot of you feel the pain of the loneliness. You feel the pain of heartache. You feel the pain of not being able to express the love that you are. You experience it so deeply that it frightens you and you run as fast as you can. Then you get brave and come back because you know that is where the love is; only to run again when you feel the pain and inability to express. Getting through that is graduation. That's getting the diploma. When the hurt doesn't matter anymore, that is the completion of you. That is called being yourself. That is called your completion.

When you have touched that love, what you now call life will be seen for the drudgery that it has been.

You were created to be individual gods. That means your entire journey is to create an individuated Self that is equal to yourselves, your source, yourself in every way and in every possibility. Your source is creating that love. If you can't face that love, if you cannot stand in the presence of that love without running, then how can you be the source? How can you be the god that you are until you can feel that love, be that love, and embrace it? Until you do, you haven't arrived home. All of you have done so much, but you don't feel complete yet. That is graduation. That is when you finally move into a place of saying, "Okay, I'll let the habitual me leave. I'll let the images run, but the god that I am can face the music called love." You are all running away from the music, because you don't want to deal with it.

It's difficult when you're not aware that you're running. It's difficult to know what the feeling is that you're even looking for.

The feeling that you're looking for is an excitement for life. If you are not feeling it, you are running, or you're treading water.

How can you discover what it is that you're running from exactly, what part of your life?

The only thing there is, is love. Everything is created out of the same stuff. So the only thing you can run away from is love, ultimately.

I recognize that there are parts of my life that I have that love. I still am looking for the completeness. I don't know where I'm lacking, where that part of my life is.

There are parts of your life in which you still hold romantic ideals. They are called emotions, fear, anxiety, and they are the excuses for the love. The only thing there is, is love. Most of you are already realizing that. Everything and everyone of you were loved into existence. It is the only thing that exists. It is the *only* thing that exists. And so, no matter what the story is, it is a story of love and a story of the rejection of it.

Any place that you're not feeling an excitement for love and life, or where you're feeling less than complete, is an area that you're running from the love. Ultimately you can't run from the love because that's all there is. So you run away from it and run into it! As you begin to understand the romantic ideals you hold, you will see these as excuses for not touching the love. Love is all there is, so you're touching it all the time. Your whole life is love. It is joy, if you want to call it that. It is life. It is love. The trick is learning to observe that and feel it in all things at all times. That takes a little bit of doing. If you're not feeling totally excited, you're running from life.

How do you put the excitement for life into what you're doing?

You don't put it into what you are doing, you put it into you, because you are what matters. What you are doing is just a story about you. You put the excitement into you, and then it won't matter what you are doing. It is something all of you have to learn how to do. You have to create the chemical balance in your body to hold it. This excitement for life can be held in your body through the life hormone. This is the new cell that many of you will carry, and it will show up on your microscopes. A lot of you are already learning how to make it. But right now, that excitement for life does not stay long in these bodies. You have to decide that this is you, and to love this body. Until you do, the body will not hold you or the intensities of love. When you decide that you're serious and can say, "I'm going to do it, I love me and my body the way I am," you start creating the life hormone. But you the consciousness has to start using your own talents and abilities to initiate it, to support it, and to hold it within your beings.

You have to find the excitement for life and the miracle of life and it is something that no one can instill in you. We can talk with you. We can help you generate it, but you each have to do the homework on it. Looking at the very miracle of life in everything will instill it faster than anything you can imagine. Look at the intricacy and the beautifulness of life. Look at the cells in your hand and concentrate on everything that you find there, how it works together, what really makes it move. If you can concentrate on any little thing and see the miracle of life in it, it will help to instill that love of life.

Each of you have already felt it. Anything that you have felt once, you can recreate whenever you need to. You were loved into existence so the feeling is there, and when you decide that you are really serious about it, the entity you, will bring it forth and it give it to you. If it is difficult for you to sustain an excitement for life, another way of looking at it is, "Maybe I'm really not sure that I'm really complete." If you are not, the entity and the body will not help you love this body into existence. Because it understands this body. It understands what it is going through. It understands what that would do to it.

Every time you want a different body, you are telling your body to die.

If you get into a place where the excitement for life is not there, then look at yourself. Take a good look and say, "Okay, is there some part of me that really doesn't love me enough to allow me to feel life yet? Am I still looking for something else? Am I still not satisfied enough that I'm going to take another journey to try to complete my satisfaction?"

What created death to the bodies in the first place was that you kept wanting a different model than the one you had. If you're into a place of wanting a different life, a different model, a different body, how are you ever going to put enough love into this one when you're killing it? Every time you want a different body, you are telling your body to die. Every time you tell your body you want a different existence, you're telling your body to die, and then you wonder why you can't feel life when you are giving it conflicting signals. You're in the process of telling them to die because you don't think they're good enough. You want something else. You are at odds with it. You want a different model. You want it to look different. You don't want to age. You don't want to ascend it with wrinkles and a few extra pounds. You're giving it conflicting signals. On one side you say, "Yes, I want life. I want to feel alive. I want to enjoy life. I want to be excited about life." On the other hand you are saying, "I wish I were dead."

The body knows the death signal because you've never taught it the life signal. That life signal is, "Hi, I'm god,"—and mean it! Not just the verbiage. The verbiage is where it starts. The understanding comes next and then living it. You've come a long way in loving your body, but there are still days that you wish you had a different one. There are still days that you don't quite like it. There are still days that you are trying to get out of it.

These are all signals that tell the body to die. On the other side, you say, "Well, if I had all the love and I enjoyed life, I wouldn't feel this way." You're giving it cross signals. When it moves into a place that you can't feel life and you can't feel the excitement, just take a minute and realize, "Here is perhaps, an area of my life that I'm not totally satisfied with and I'm not allowing life into it because I don't feel happy with it." Then you realize that you don't feel happy with it because you're not letting love into it.

All of you within your being, can find the excitement for life and you can do it now, if you let yourself. Generate it. Feel the excitement. Key into the last time that you felt so excited you just wanted to holler and shout and scream and to share life with people. You wanted to talk, you were so excited. All of you can remember. Key into a time in your life, where there was joy, where you were having fun. Maybe you were on vacation, maybe you were with friends, maybe you were in love, feel it. Feel the excitement for life. Let it come. Generate it in that heart, and notice every resistance you have to it. If you have resistance to it, what is the resistance? Talk to the resistance. Why are you afraid of letting the love in? Why are you afraid of feeling the love? Are you afraid it is going to consume you? If it consumes you, love is all there is anyway. Are you afraid you'll no longer be who you are? Maybe you've judged what you are so harshly that you don't want to be what you've judged. Ask the resistance. But focus on an excitement.

Take the time to go inside and feel the resistance. Where is it coming from? Most of you will find your rigid adult. Others will find pain they have held for a long time and are unwilling to release. It isn't until you release the images that you will begin to create a shift. Now if you can try putting some joy into this space, you can feel the life. If there is anything in life that thrills you, if you are a person that loves children and you love to watch them play, if that is what gives you excitement and puts you in that space; if you love the ocean and the waves and the beach, put yourself into these spaces. If you love the mountains and the trees and the snow blowing against your face, put yourself into that place. These are all the little miracles and subtleties of life. You might as well enjoy it.

Feel how excited you can get for life and let the emotions up. Life can trigger emotions in the being. You don't need to worry about them. You don't need to repress them. Even gods cry. Gods weep with passion. And they are not afraid of feeling it, and they don't care who is watching. Get an excitement for life in there! It's the most beautiful thing you will ever experience! Passion! Anything that gives you passion! Anything that feeds you! Anything that excited you to the core of your being! Let these all be cues to generate for your life. If there is resistance, take the resistance and find out what it is. Find out if it is an excuse. If it is, be god, and tell those excuses to go away. Those excuses for the love are not yours. They're not necessary, and why do you need protection from love? You need protection from love because you are afraid it is going to make you emotional. You're also afraid you're not worthy of it.

Love you. Let yourself find the beauty in you. Feel how beautiful you feel. Allow yourself to dance, internally dance. Feel the freedom to dance. That is life. There is no one there watching you any more. It is you and life. That's all that exists. You and life and love. Dance. Play with the little moonbeams or sunbeams. Dance and sing within your beings if you wish. Run upon the beach in total freedom.

Gods weep with passion. And they are not afraid of feeling it . . .

Release any resistance that you have. These old adult images—you don't need them. So if you have a resistance for a moment, I want you to feel the power of god. I want you to feel the power of the source. I want you to feel the power of the universe, and I want you to command as the god that you are that those resistances leave—and don't be afraid to order them around. You command them to be gone and let the love rise. Let you come home. Let you move into the center of the universe of you. Feel the love and let the barriers drop. All of these walls are just to keep you from what's on the other side. That is what a wall does. The other side of that wall is a love that says that you have worth, you have value, and the universe loves you beyond measure. It loves you beyond your comprehension. Feel the universe's love for you. Feel the gentleness. The universe does not coerce. It holds you. It supports you and it loves you just the way you are. It loves you with an intensity and a passion.

You are loved by your source. You are loved by you. The resistance is all a game. The game has been to see how far you can get away from that love—but you didn't go anywhere! It followed you. Maybe it was a block behind you so you could have your privacy and pretend that it wasn't there, but it has never left you. Be willing for the moment to merge with the love of the universe. Allow yourself to feel the passion the universe has for your existence. It loves you. It loves you beyond your comprehension. Allow yourself to relax so that you can comprehend the power of the love that is there. Feel the support—be at peace—feel. Allow yourself just to feel it.

None of you were accidents. You were all intentional creations—everyone of you. You were loved into existence. That love is still holding you. It supports you in everything you do. It supports you in your belief. If you want to think you are not loved, it will back up a little bit and let you think that, but it will never go away.

Allow yourself to push your anguish and pain into the universe and exchange it for the love that you are being held by. Allow yourself to share. Allow yourself to pull in the sharing of the universe and the love of the universe. Allow yourself to feel the cocoon that you are being held in. Allow yourself to feel what supports you. You are in a space that is totally unbounded. Release all that has been your burden, your drudgery, and your pain. Allow yourself to feel you. Allow yourself to just rejuvenate within the very depths of your being, and I invite you to touch life. Touch it within your being, within your heart. I invite you to touch the excitement of the universe at the creation of you. It is an excitement for life. This *is* life. I invite you to be the gods that you are, and feel you, embrace you, and dance.

Be at peace. Don't be afraid of the love. I mean how bad can a few tears be? It is the last leg of the journey home, and it is the hardest one. It is called loving and it should be the easiest because it is the most natural thing to all of you—it is that natural. It is kind of hard when you see yourself separate here and not being able to touch that. But you will get acclimatized to it within your being, and a few years down the road other people will be where you have been and getting your love and you will sit there and chuckle about it. You will love them because you will understand where they are too.

I love you and I feel privileged to share with you and commune with you in the love. I thank you. It is a priceless gift to me. Be at peace, be at life, and go see a few miracles. Those miracles are the blades of grass, the needles on the trees, the wheat in your field that is so beautiful. It is the color or your own hair and how it glistens in the light. The color of your own eyes and how beautifully they radiate the light. It is the beauty of you and I love that and I love you. Good night. ▲

Follow
Your Joy

Within your beings, always simply remember, if you follow no other truth, follow the truth that within your being is called joy. If you follow that, you're always going to be right where you need to be, and you'll always have life within your being. *That's* where you need to be. Within your beings, realize that when you're faced with something that gives you fear, realize that fear is of man's mind—not God's.

Realize that in life you are gods. If you are a god, you don't need to fear anything. Since you are gods, you create your own reality. So if you want a fearful one, then you'll create it. You create your reality so literally that you can create any one you want. If you can create the negative, you can create the positive and the joy. That's your life. Whenever you find anything that makes you run in fear, makes you anxiety ridden, gives you these types of things, realize these aren't from the mind of god. These are from the minds of men, who are, in themselves, afraid and don't know what to do.

Within your being realize that if you get a piece of the puzzle and it causes fear within you, there is always another side to the story. There is always a flip side of the coin and there is always something that somebody is missing on the subject. Your entities are fearless. They do not do anything to instill fear in you, but quite the opposite, they try to get you out of it.

Realize that life is joy and that joy is life. If you want to have joy in your life, you have to allow yourself the moments to experience it. Within your own beings, if you follow no other truth, if you follow no other teaching, follow the one of your own heart that is leading you to freedom and that is leading you to learn how to have joy in your existence. If you follow

437

that, no matter where you go, no matter what you listen to, no matter what you do, you are going to always be with you and not in the minds of man.

So realize that within your being, you already have everything you need to go home. You have the part of your being that seeks for the freedom and the freedom is the releasing of all the bondage called everything that is limiting. The seeking of the pleasantness, the seeking of the joy, and the beauty within your own being, or what you call enjoyment, that is called the search for life. Follow that one always and no matter where you go, you're going to be one-hundred percent right where you need to be. Honor you by following your joy, no matter what that means. Follow your joy. You're worth it. I love you. Be at peace and goodbye. ▲

Glossary

A energy, Andraus strain: One of the five original energies within the womb of this universe. An energy characterized by intensity and passion for life. This strain no longer exists outside the womb, and what remains of it inside is mostly diluted.

Abstract: Not concrete. May not necessarily be totally understandable by the brain. Tending to exist dissociated from identifiable constructs.

Abstract mind: As opposed to linear mind. The type of thought or thinking process used by entities. Dealing with concepts rather than concrete understandings. The type of mind or brain function accessed in some channeling, dream, or altered states.

Alpha wave: 8-12 Hz. The type of brain wave commonly associated with meditative and altered states. Second brain functions in an alpha state.

Altered, altered state: Any alpha, theta, or delta wave state.

Amniocentesis: In medicine, the external insertion of a needle into the uterus of an expectant mother to obtain amniotic fluid from which various characteristics of the unborn can be determined. Universally, the use of the K energy to penetrate the womb of this universe to determine its progress or development.

Angelic realms: A large spectrum or space where entities dwell in various stages of separation from thought. Portions of ourselves that never intend to be physicalized are contained here. See *dead zone* and *pompous angels*.

Anger: Universally, raw creative energy. An event horizon. A manifestation of repressed life.

Animation, the: The hologram which we are living left by the divine presence. What animates or moves the body, the part we generally refer to as our personality. A holographic specie of entity. How the divine presence experiences this reality.

Arachnoid: Of or pertaining to spiders or their webbing. A type of specialized biological tissue or cosmic fabric, weblike in nature.

Archetype: An ideal, model or lifestyle upon which others pattern their lives. Christ was an archetype.

Archive: A repository of knowledge. Both the body and the planet are archives of universal knowledge.

Arrhythmia: Irregular heartbeat. A fluttering in heart patterns that may be experienced as incoming energies which activate the second pacemaker on the back of the heart.

Artificial intelligence: The intelligence that evolved when the hologram started thinking that it was real and that it existed. A computer uses artificial or programmed intelligence.

Ascended master: Any individual whose vibrational spectrum exceeds the vibrational spectrum of the planet enough to dematerialize them.

Ascension, mass ascension: Vibrationally moving within density (horizontal ascension), or moving out of density (vertical ascension). The ongoing process of raising your vibration or moving more into the real you. The birth, objectification. See *taking the body with you*.

Asleep: Unawakened to life. A slumber caused by density. Lack of true self-awareness.

Aspect: Any singular face of a core lifetime.

Atmosphere: The gaseous and electromagnetic environment surrounding the planet. Created and controlled by beliefs and attitudes. The planetary sum of the gestalts. The auric field of the planet.

Atom: Smallest unit of an element, consisting of a nucleus and electrons and various other subatomic particles.

Atomic structure: The point where light breaks into matter or hydrogen, where density begins.

Audience in your head: The judgmental "voices" in your brain for whom you perform and live your life. The rigid adult.

Auric field, aura: Roughly synonymous with electromagnetic field, biological field, biological spirit.

Backtracking: The process of retracing your journey into physicality, retrieving the fragments of yourself you left along the way, and going home.

Bacteria: Anything that is alive. The smallest alive units comprising larger bacterial colonies; in turn larger living organisms are comprised of different colonies.

Be or being: A state of stoppage or non-action.

Belief: An ideological conception about any facet of existence held as true or absolute.

Beta wave: 18-30Hz. Normal, everyday brain chatter. The worry entrainment vibration.

Binary principle: The on-off principle upon which this reality is based.

Biological personality: The personality developed by the artificial intelligence in the biological vehicle. The basic personalities that we operate through in time. Not the entity personality.

Biological spirit: A living bio-magnetic field surrounding the physical body created by the neuron firing within the cells—a physical creation. A result of light entering the body and encountering the genetics.

Biology: Bacterial life forms in whatever configurations or colonies they might exist. The physical body and all life as we consider it on this planet.

Bio-field, biological spirit, bio-magnetic field: The field surrounding the body. The mind.

Birth: The collapse and subsequent expansion or big bang of this universe into a new reality. A rare cosmic occurrence. Live birth: The rarest of cosmic events in which new species of entity are created.

Black hole: A type of no-thing. In science it is a hypothetical, infinitely small, pinpoint of tremendous gravitation from which no light escapes.

Body consciousness: The body's awareness of itself.

Bonded circuitry: Circuitry that is created to be more permanent and lasting. Creates a oneness between two individuals.

Bonded vibration: Vibration imprinted into a nucleus for the purpose of orchestration without violating free will.

Bored gods: A class of entity facing the exhaustion of their physics principle, invited into this reality to lend their expertise in precipitating the birth and revitalizing themselves in the process.

Boredom: Peace. Being. Lack of expression. Restlessness. Reaching a subtlety. Being at the edge of your void on the verge of creation. A lull on the way to greater expanses of your own being.

Brain: Specialized tissue consisting of nerve endings and ganglia, occupying the cranial cavity and assisting in thought and think processes as well as autonomic functioning of the body. The body's central computer station and switchboard. First brain: The functioning of the overall brain and specific parts that deal with survival, instinct, normal decision making, and regular every-day think processes. Second brain: The portion of overall brain functioning and specific regions of the brain that deal with your simultaneous experiences, holding you where you are, and your other faces in their time-space. Third brain: The functioning and portions of the brain dealing with abstract and conceptual mind. The entity mind fully operational but not yet brought on line in the body.

Brain wiring: The pattern of firing or electrical circuits followed by such firing within the brain. Brain networks.

Broadcasters: Individuals having an over balance of transmitters who tend to overwhelm and manipulate individuals with more receptors than transmitters or a more even balance of the two.

Caring: An animal instinct to provide for and protect their young or their kind. A way humans impose their images and foster dependency on others. Not related to love.

Carrier wave: Electromagnetic wave or impulse whose modulations or fluctuations carry a message or smaller patterns of electromagnetic waves.

Cell firing: The sparking that goes on in the cell to give it life and control its reproduction: either vertical firing; i.e., coming up out of the deep nuclei, or horizontal firing; i.e., a pseudo-spark created across the gap in the mitochondria.

Chameleon effect: The ability of some individuals or mediums to "become" another individual for the purpose of healing or understanding.

Channeling: A generic term for any of various methods of accessing information outside of normal cognitive awareness. Real channeling: A phenomenon of the above channeling where the audience, as well as the channel, goes out and experiences, first hand, levels of conceptual mind too abstract for words.

Christ: A generic term for any of many different individuals who fit a certain archetypal story, experience, or expectation. A stage in the development of consciousness.

Christ consciousness: An entire level of consciousness caught up in Christ metaphors, righteousness, sins, saviors, and victims.

Christ figure: Anyone who approximates the Christ archetype.

Christ metaphor: A way of applying the Christ archetype to explain individuals, their behavior, or events.

Circuitry: Electromagnetic path of thought between brains. Neurons fire from one brain and are received in the receptor sites of another's brain.

Clarity: The degree to which an individual is out of time. A function of the closeness to entity. The product of dropping of images.

Cloning reality: A reality in which all participants are perfect images of and are controlled by the single chief clone who created them. All clones think and act the same. A reality in which no individuality exists. See *Jehovah*.

Closing down: The result of coming close to the entity or having paranormal experience that pushes the psyche too far. Also called running from the love, the last dance, shutting off.

Coagulate: To bring and bind together to create a greater whole.

Collective consciousness, mass consciousness: The homogenized sum of the attitudes and beliefs consciously held by the people on the planet. See *gestalt*.

Collective unconsciousness: Created out of the repressed feelings and thoughts of the inhabitants of the planet. It is what creates mass consciousness and the gestalts.

Colonies: See *bacteria*.

Completion: Entity expression. Passion. Boredom.

Complexity: Contrast with intricacy. The bogging down of simplicity. Infinite slowing of thought. Struggle, lack, limitation, density.

Compressed data: Classification of data for ease of retrieval and use. Maximizes storage space but tends to limit choice and hold one in their past. Density itself is achieved by compressing data.

Configuration: The way things or entities are put together at any given point of time. Has to do with the particular parts of the brain being used to generate a given personality.

Consciousness: Primal awareness. A building block of entity intelligence; a tool of physicality.

Consciousness gestalts: See *gestalts*.

Containment vehicle: The body. The vehicle for the entity. See *embracement vehicle*.

Core: The central part of anything. The nucleus.

Core lifetime: The lifetime designed to be the entity. The gravitational center of all other faces of the entity.

Corrupted energy strain: Depleted of energy as in diluted. Energy that has turned in upon itself and is no longer being expressed.

Cosmic joke: Any humorous anecdote universally funny. A duality appreciated universally. A cosmic paradox; i.e., nothing ever existed nor could it ever; yet it unmistakably does.

Create: To organize and reorganize other creation. To make new existence from no-thing or original thought.

Creator: A species of entity that organizes thought and other pre-existing building blocks.

Critical mass: Potential built to collapsing intensities. The point, once reached, where an unstoppable and sudden chain reaction of events, becomes inevitable. See *hundredth-monkey syndrome*.

Cross frequencies: Electromagnetic waves or frequencies of vibration running at cross angles to vertical frequencies. The points of intersection of these frequencies are spaces where life can grow.

Curiosity: The driving force of life, the desire to know. The impetus for new creation. See *questioning, perplexity*.

Cycles: Waves of energy emanating in circular patterns put out by a source. Any of various repeating patterns or windows for change through history or individual life. Recurring patterns of biological behavior or development.

D energy or David strain: One of the five original energies put into this reality. The energy which makes the myth and writes the stories along which consciousness can develop.

Dark creature: A shadow entity whose natural home is the dark zone, the consumption at the edge of the universe. We are living the hologram left by dark creatures when they hastily retreated after catching a glimpse of themselves in the light of this universe.

Dark zone: The no-thing, light-consuming edge that contains this universe.

Dead zone: Created by people believing themselves to still be physical after they have left their bodies through the death process. The place where individuals who refuse to go on choose to stay.

Commonly referred to as heaven and hell.

Dedicated circuitry: Devoted circuits which have been dedicated to the support of one devoted space. Our belief systems through which we designed to protect our devoted circuit(s) but which have become a filter through which the devoted connection must pass to get to us.

Default settings, running on: As in computer language. The tendency, because of hanging on to our belief in time, to function off former commands no longer useful to our present self.

Delta wave: 1-5Hz. The wave length created by the third brain during deep sleep.

Density: Particalized existence. Tangible reality. Also as in playing dumb.

Dependency circuitry: Unhealthy, collapsed circuitry. Circuitry that fosters dependence or need. Any circuitry that keeps you from being you.

Depression: Often the experiencing of too much love to handle. The aftermath of experiencing such love. The need for or lack of expression. The result of repressing who and what you are.

Devoted circuitry: A circuit or circuits used exclusively for connecting with entity or divine presence. Your circuit for connecting with you, the universe, source. All possess at least one such circuit.

Dimension: A measure of compressed consciousness. A particular face, or slice of existence.

Dimensional reality: As opposed to time. The way different slices, faces, and levels of reality comprise existence. A function of simultaneous time.

Diseasement: Sickness, disease. Disease-ment, a place that is out of balance.

Divine presence: Entity expanded into the next framework. The actual you. That which precedes entity. The real intelligence endowed in each of us. See *animation.*

DNA: Deoxyribonucleic acid. The molecular basis for genetics.

Dogma: A systemized cannon of belief. Any belief held as absolute. Any belief.

Drama: Goes with and rhymes with trauma. The historical human preference for pain and struggle over joy, subtlety, and life. The way of creating a pseudo-spark in order to feel alive in the body.

Dream: What entities do in the sleep state. The creation occurring during a sleep state. Illusion. That which creates your next day.

Dump: The releasing of nodules and genetic material that do not apply to the present you. To unload your issues and baggage on another. To hold another responsible for your personal issues.

Ego: The child of the psyche. Guidance. Defensive mechanism designed to protect the persona. The original middleman between the body and the entity.

Electromagnetics: The attractive electrical waves created by any friction.

Electrum structure: A term used to designate a stage of creation or coagulation into matter where the electron appeared in subatomic structure.

Emanate: To radiate out from a center or source.

Emanation: A pattern of radiation left in time-space by the passing of individual slices or dimensional faces. A heat-like residue put off by the body while sleeping, containing the attitudes and emotions with which you go to sleep; it is a type of entity. Upon awaking it is pulled in and runs the body for the next day.

Embodiment, the: The physical body.

Embody: To put into a body, to contain. To take what is by nature an intangible and contain and represent it in a body.

Embrace: To grasp, comprehend. To take in, so as to become part of one's being.

Embracement vehicle: The body. Any body or containment through which an entity can realize, feel, or embrace itself.

Empowerment: The embracing of one's own ability and identity. Walking into one's personal power. Gaining the understanding necessary to create reality according to preference.

Endorphins: A class of hormones producing a euphoric state, sense of well being, joy, or ecstasy, present in some foods and drugs. Hormones the body will naturally produce on its own as it becomes more alive. Close derivatives of the life hormone.

Emotion: As opposed to feeling. Repressed and limited feeling reduced from millions of components to five or six generic responses: joy, depression, anger, anxiety, love, and fear. A chemical or hormonal response in the body. All emotion is guilt.

Emotional embracement: The comprehension of a lesson or feeling at a deep, cellular level. The brilliant, almost shocking flash of insight accompanying an understanding. An ah ha! experience.

Energy: Power of whatever kind by which anything is accomplished. Propagated waves perceived or harnessed by any means.

Entities, the: Refers to the knowledge-based personality or personalities delivering the frameworks. The faces of Philip.

Entity: An expansion of our limited ideas of god. A totally unlimited and undefinable being. Depending on the perspective, that which we are becoming or already are. A generic term for any discrete, living organism or being. Your personal entity, who you are. That which can define itself but at the same time is undefinable.

Entity laced hormones: Hormones created by the interaction of the embryo and entity within the first couple weeks of conception, to allow the entity to more closely design and work with the embodiment.

Entity personality: As opposed to biological personality. The real persona of our being.

Entity spark: That which we ultimately are. The spark of life. Divine presence. A term somewhat loosely applied to indicate that which animates us at our deepest levels. The entity itself.

Entity species or species of entity: Categories or types of different entities, usually grouped according to the physics principle from which they originate or function, as in source, self, creator, etc.

Entrainment vibration: The overriding vibration of this planet, laced with or comprised of guilt, fear, and lust vibrations. The controlling vibration that channels and holds everyone in conditioned responses to life, and that holds us physical.

Event Horizon: A physics term indicating the horizon on which an event happens or the boundary of influence of that event.

Evil: "Live" spelled backwards; hence, living life backwards.

Evolution: The process of filling in the pieces to create a path to an already finished idea or thought.

Exchange: The translation of the real principle of cosmic respiration or flow into this sphere. A system of trade whereby we are able by exchanging energy or commodities to hold each other's ideas open long enough to allow completion or manifestation.

Excitement: Purity of spirit, joy, and life.

Expression: The unrepressed manifestation of the entity in the body. Entity communication. The energy of such communication or manifestation.

Face: A dimension or slice of entity reality. An aspect.

Facilitators: Individuals through history who assist in the creation of mass events to create paradigm shifts.

Fact: An observed condition or event dependent on a specific perspective.

Failure: Short circuiting of expression circuits.

Fear: The constriction of cellular and atomic networks in order to feel life passing through the life channels.

Fear-base: Any teaching or attitude capitalizing on the dramatic and sensational possibilities of disaster, conspiracy, harm, or danger.

Feeling: As opposed to emotion. The universal language usually translated here erroneously as emotion. The incoming electromagnetic encoding behind emotions. An electrical charge in the body manifesting as a chill. Abstract thought held and used. All feeling is joy.

Feeling tone: The intangible ambiance, environment, or tone surrounding or behind a thing or idea in this manifested reality. The real thing.

Field: See *bio-field*.

Field of possibilities or probabilities: All the possible completions of any given scenario or idea existing in their own right in their own realities independent of this one.

First brain: See *brain*.

Flavor: The means through which different entities experience different realities. A space with a specific tone used for entity experience.

Flow: Universal respiration. Letting things happen naturally. Relaxing with life, feeling your own perfection, etc.

Formatters: Individuals who, as part of their makeup, ideally are able to imprint or program incoming energies foreign to this realm with appropriate emotional responses, so that the energies are conditioned and recognizable to the rest of the planet.

Fracture: To break off or into divergent units as in core light striking the time-space medium and splintering into smaller lights.

Frameworks: The means of backtracking through the principles and events that brought us into density. Any system of understanding used as a building block for another.

Freedom: As opposed to limitation.

Friction: The first principle to emerge from the original no-thing. The basis of electromagnetics. The principle on which all life is built.

Game, the: Pretending that we don't create our own reality, that we really want to change, or that we are unhappy where we are.

Gap: A crack in time. A space created in your normal continuity where your entity or your personal manifestation can come in. Created by states of joy, living in the moment, etc. Also, the space between you and your entity.

Genetic memory: The memory from your ancestors experiences and biology that are held within the DNA of the body. Creates the body to run the way it does.

Genetic reconstruction: Changing the DNA of the body. Biological evolution of the species into a form that can hold a living entity.

Gentle space: The space of "gentleness" one enters on the other side of vulnerability.

Geometrics: Universal symbols. The shapes, lines, and directions of waves and wave patterns. Different physics principles.

Gestalt: A coagulation of like thought having a life of its own that tends to control planetary reality according to the area of its like thought.

Gestalt anchors: Individuals who because of unique circuitry are able to anchor in physicality whole gestalts.

Ghost orbit: The unseen, corresponding and balancing body, planet, electron, or matter that stabilizes the maintained orbit or position of the seen object. Antimatter. See *on-off principle*.

God: A term meaning government. Framework preceding entity. The mish-mash of consciousness still fighting within itself for organization. A superstition.

God concepts: The beliefs and attitudes, and the effects of the same caused by putting one's power outside of themselves because of a perceived separation from that power or love. The denials and issues arising from the same attitudes.

Government: The playing out of god concepts in the social lives and organizations of humankind.

Gravity: An electromagnetic principle of attraction. An attractive density. That which pulls you back into a body as well as holds you on the planet.

Grid: Intersecting lines of light or thought on which the universe and all life is built.

Guilt: The feeling of separation from yourself as it translates into density. What keeps you from being you. Sin, embarrassment, shame, punishment, and related others. The entrainment vibration.

Harmonics: Multiples or fractional multiples of a specific frequency. Orchestration.

Harmony: Flow. Functioning in balanced perspective to flow.

Heal: The recognition that nothing is wrong.

Healthy circuitry: Circuitry made or held from preference instead of biological necessity. Circuitry not created from dependency.

Heart center: The geographical heart seal of the planet. The fourth seal in the body.

Heart mind: See *solar-plex.*

Hertz: A single cycle per second. The measure in frequency of the number of cycles per second.

Hierarchy: The physics of the dead zone. The natural tendency of density to establish itself in levels of pecking order. A principle which outside of this reality does not exist.

Holding the thought open: A way to aid manifesting by not completing the thought so that the entity is compelled to complete the thought in this reality rather than in mind alone.

Hologram: The light smear left by the entity or dark creature when it first saw itself in the light of this universe, this universe thereafter being holographic.

Home: A word which captures in tone and meaning the feeling of getting back to source or origins.

Horizontal frequencies: A designation of waves running at right angles to other waves which arbitrarily are vertical. Waves or frequencies running at cross angles to some beginning point.

Hydrogen: The point where light breaks into matter. The first element of light going into density. The first element on the periodic table of elements, having one electron.

Hypothalamus: The part of the brain surrounding and controlling the pituitary gland. Controls emotions, appetites, and desires.

Image: A corrupted or distorted perception of the real you. Any belief. Anything that stands between you and self. Anything that does not allow you to be free to be yourself.

Impacter: An entity species which creates an effect or impression of one thing

447

on another. To press upon or breech the womb of this universe from within.

Implosion: A sudden, explosive collapse of a contained system.

Imprint: To embed upon. To leave a marking on.

Individuation: The inward dividing of a whole. A method of avoiding the sameness of cloning realities. The process of creating independent individuals. The purpose of this universe is to create new, individuated entities.

Innocence: Lack of emotional involvement with image; i.e., no images.

Instinct: Behavioral patterns drawn from heavily ingrained genetic memory. Genetic memory. Survival responses.

Intensity: The pressure under which a thing is repressed or contained or the pressure of the release of the same.

Intent package: Life theme.

Intention: The putting in of a determination to accomplish, get, or have something. Using the mind to create a feeling.

Interactive principle: A multifaceted concept or idea that is at once a singular facet of itself mutually dependent or interacting with all others; i.e. Life: You have to be it to live it, and you have to live it to be it.

Intuition: Interpretation of feeling appropriate to the occasion.

Is, IS's: Individuated self. A generation of creation off or out of the original nothing. Successive layers of creation from a nuclear or universal perspective each holding another nucleus or universe within itself. The different levels of energy folding in on this reality in preparation for and in the process of birth.

Issue: A developed point of conflict in the external world always having its roots in personal avoidance with self.

Intricate: As opposed to complex. The natural working of existence—the simple interworking of basic principle to achieve grand and diverse creation.

Jehovah: A term denoting the second generation and beyond of the inward division of a creator. The central intelligence of a cloned reality. Because the division created atomic structure and mass, it is also a term which means god or creator. Denotes and controls a cloned reality. As opposed to individuation. See *cloning reality*.

Journey: The path or voyage taken by an entity on its way to life or through life.

Joy: The frequency of light breaking into matter. A band of frequency containing over one million vibrations or components.

Judgment: A guilt response from personal embarrassment. Always a self-condemnation.

Justification: Apologizing for being yourself. A guilt response.

K strain or energy: The amniocentesis in the womb. A unique and rare energy capable of bridging different realities. Bridging energy.

Kundalini: A raising of the life energy of the being through the spine associated with ecstatic, transcendent, or orgasmic experience.

Layer: An individual stratification of a larger whole or creation, physicality being the composite of many layers.

Leapfrog: An entity method of growth or expanding whereby they use faces or creations of the same to propel or catapult themselves into new creation, those faces then using the new creation for their own springboard.

Life: An interactive principle, you have to be it to live it and you have to live it to be it. The principle of existence on the other side of the holograph but this side of reality.

Life hormone: The original and only hormone in the body, all others are derivatives and corruptions of it. A pure life-giving and sustaining hormone of endorphin class. The hormone the body will eventually produce once again in its uncorrupted form.

Life spark: The manifestation of the life of the entity that you are. Divine presence.

Light: Trailing thought. A spectrum of electromagnetic radiation found between hydrogen and thought. Slow thought. A reflection. Also a universal organism.

L strain or energy: Lehma energy. One of the five original energy strains in this universe. Known as the piece/peace maker because of its separating and stabilizing qualities.

Lack: The first and second laws of thermodynamics. The natural consequence of perceived separation. The perceived shortage of love translated into a material world limited in supply to the desirable.

Last dance, the: The final avoidance or reluctance to going home. Drawing close to one's entity, feeling the love or natural embarrassment, and backing away—then repeating the same.

Laughter: A pressure release valve in the body. The fun way to release genetic memory.

Limitation: The original friction principle carried to its illogical conclusion here in density. A creative way to amplify the feeling of life by constricting one's movement or the flow of life through oneself to greater and greater extents. The process of stopping life or thought long enough to feel it.

Linear mind: The membrane that cuts you off from your field of possibilities. The brain functioning in a time orientation; i.e., compressing the past and projecting the compression towards a future you.

Living gestalt: A new species of gestalt being formed now and having life and unconditionality as its nucleus, which when formed will be an independent entity that anyone desiring life will be able to tap and draw from.

Love: Universal source stuff, raw material for creation, thought. An exchange of expression.

Loving yourself into existence: Imprinting you and your desire for life into your DNA. The creation of your personal Self.

Lust vibration: Characterized by the longing, perceived unpossession of self, and therefore, the desire or lust to possess what is seen as being separate from oneself. See *entrainment vibration. Lack.*

Manifest: To make the space for something to appear. Putting forth the energy necessary for something to materialize.

Mass: Density. Everything beyond the point where light breaks into atomic structure or matter.

Mass ascension: The birth. Objectification.

449

Mass consciousness: The collective environment of attitudes and beliefs held by all people on the planet at any given point in time.

Materialize: To make material or to make appear. The process of gravitation of atomic structure into solidified form.

Matter: Coagulated atomic structure.

Meditative state: Any quiet, personally reflective, condition of mind. A life lived in joy and excitement.

Mediumship: The ability of an individual to mediate or serve as a go between, between the disembodied and the embodied.

Memory implants: Stories borrowed from other dimensional slices of yourself to create the illusion of time.

Merging: Bringing two or more things together.

Metaphor: Referencing or using a well-understood symbol, event, or thing to explain something not understood. The changing of a caterpillar into a butterfly is a metaphor for an individual having a personal transformation.

Mind: The biological spirit. The electromagnetic total of the firing of the cells of the body. The entity brain.

Mirror: Any reflective medium. A physics principle that allows for self-observation.

Mitochondria: One of several island-like structures within a cell containing a few strands of DNA. An important gateway for the DNA. The repository of genetic memory. The cellular location of horizontal firing.

Movement: Progress from one point to another. The flow of the universe. Life.

Multidimensional: Of or pertaining to more than one dimension or layer of reality.

Myth: A story line along which consciousness can grow or develop. An idea held open for completion.

Nervous system: The coordinating network of light channels throughout the body that connects the spinal column to every cell in the body through nerves, ganglia, receptors, and transmitters. The electrical wiring harness of the body that holds the light of the being.

Neuron: The basic cellular unit of the nervous system. The site of electrical firing and transmitting within the cell.

Nodules: DNA nodules. Tiny spheres attached one to another to create the DNA ladder each carrying information upon which the body is run. Each nodule being an emotional entity capable of being an individual. Nodules between the ladders can become sparks.

No-thing: A black hole. A source. Original no-thing: That from which all subsequent anything emerged. The infinite point of nothingness that fell in on itself and created original movement.

Nucleus: The life center of any unit. The point at which coagulation occurs. Levels of nucleus: A framework for understanding the construction of the cosmos, each nucleus being the universe of a yet smaller and more powerful nucleus. See *vertical firing*.

Objectification: Expulsion from the womb when critical mass is achieved, i.e. objectified as one's own living entity at the point of the birth.

Octave: Any progressive system of eights. Any specific number of years or period of time on which one's personal life cycle operates. Series of vibrational cyclings coming into the earth plane to create personalized windows.

On-off principle: The basic binary principle of the cosmos originating with the no-thing as it fell through itself in pendulum motion: first to one side, and then to the other. The nature of all subsequent creation to strobe on and off as it repeats the original pattern. The nature of holographic mass to strobe from manifested to unmanifested reality or from wave to particle to give the illusion of form and solidity.

144,000: The number of original entity faces within the universal womb. The point at which critical mass occurs, for this planet is 144,000 individuals. Does not mean the limit of how many people realize themselves, since the purpose of this planet is to create as many individuated entities as there are individuals who love themselves into existence.

One-hundredth-monkey syndrome: A theoretical number or point at which biologists observed a learned change in monkey behavior transmitted to other monkeys geographically separated from the control group. Whatever that number happens to be is called critical mass.

Opening up: Releasing one's defensiveness towards life and others. A relaxation occurring at all levels of one's being allowing the light or thought from the deep nucleuses to enter into cellular structure. Relaxing a rigid or held structure or position. Allowing life into the body.

Orbit: The gravitational path of any body surrounding another. The balancing or counter-balancing, non-physical body in synchronicity with its physical counterpart maintaining a stable rotation for both. The path both of these

bodies describe. Personal orbits: The layered and ideally counter-rotating bands of one's personal electromagnetic field, most of which run horizontally, a few vertically.

Orchestration: The sequencing of people, events, and energies toward a successful live birth. The role the Entities play in our bid for objectification. Entity timing.

Organize: To create or re-create from pre-existent raw material.

Original energies: The five energies originally placed within the womb by a process of the originating PADLK wave patterns striking the outer edge of the containment, indenting it, and creating energy waves within.

Original separation: The motivation behind all our issues created by the splitting of an entity or a piece of an entity into individual smaller pieces separated psychologically from the wholeness or love of the original entity or piece.

P energy or Philip strain: The first of the five original energies within the womb. The strain that deals with origins.

PADLK: Original energies in the womb and spoken of as a whole.

Paradigm: When a large shift in consciousness occurs, usually due to the beliefs in life changing in some dramatic way.

Paradigm shift: The process and the time period during which one paradigm, having served its usefulness, is phased out and a new, more-expanded metaphor, or paradigm is brought in and applied to consciousness. A model shift.

Particalize: To manifest. To change from a wave into a particle. The function of the pineal gland.

Particum/particle: Roughly equivalent. Entities use the "um" ending to denote the living nature of these subatomic sparks as opposed to the inanimate connotations surrounding particle.

Passion: Completion. The rush, thrill, and excitement of completed thought experienced in the moment. Entity completion.

Peakers and followers: A division of individuals on the planet along the lines of those who have transcendent experience and those who follow those who have said experiences.

Pearl: Any gem gleaned from any source. Carbon base transformed through irritation into a transcendent gem.

Perplexity: Entity curiosity. A condition of intricacy so baffling as to draw attention to untangle or decipher the elements of its composition. The driving motivation of entities.

Persona: An overall view of the totality of who and what you are, protected by the ego and the psyche. The essence of one's personality.

Personal gestalt: The sum of the personal attitudes and beliefs about oneself that tends to hold one in the mold or gestalt of that total, whatever it may be.

Personal grid: The events and things that are on your journey as they appear from an energy or entity perspective. The alignment of the light and energy networks that concern you and from which you are made. See *grid*.

Personality: A biological creation. Who we think we are. The way an entity acts in physicality.

Personal myth: The story you create about yourself.

Personal universe: The totality of whatever you have requested or created for yourself to live in and to bring to you and into your life. Your personal reality manufacturing department.

Physical: Biologically manifest whether seen or unseen.

Physicality: Thought carried to its illogical extreme. The complete separation or breakdown of thought. The spectrum of tangible holographic existence. An attitude of separation. A psychological construct.

Physics of Self: The means whereby an individual imprints their identity on their DNA to the extent that their identity is permanently a part of the universe and cannot be lost in source; i.e., the physics principles whereby an individual gains a Self.

Physics principle: A natural law inherent in the interworkings of the binary nature of the original no-thing.

Pineal gland: The third eye. A part of the brain that particalizes wave patterns. It has no scientifically recognized function in humans. Both pituitary and pineal systems work to regulate flow of your light into the body.

Pituitary gland: Major endocrine gland under control of hypothalamus. Secretes hormones that regulate and control certain bodily processes and higher brain functions. Regulates light in the body.

Planetary seals: Correspond to the physical seals. Different geographical locations on the planet; energy vortices through which different energies come into the planet.

Players: Individuals, thousands in number, who carry specific vibrations and/or capabilities that can be tapped and orchestrated for the creation of critical mass and birth.

Pompous angels: A class of entity who sitting on the edge of our universe judged our human process so harshly that they increased their density and were sucked into physicality themselves. They are often still in self-judgment to this day.

Preference: The entity prerogative. What we are here to learn. Choice as opposed to judgment.

Present moment: The point of your personal power and the only moment that exists. Getting back to it requires releasing time orientation.

Progenitors: Ancestors in genetic lineage.

Psyche: The part of the mind created to protect the developing personality.

Psychological construct: All constructs are psychological. The entity game of seeing yourself in different roles, faces, and environments. Physicality being but one of billions of such constructs.

Push circuitry: Overpowering one-way circuitry imposed on an individual with more receptors than transmitters by someone who has a predominance of transmitters. Circuitry imposed by broadcasters.

Quantum: An abrupt and sudden change from one state to another or an increase in quantity. The physics that deal with inexplicable transformations of energy and particles in macro and microcosmic dimensions. Non-Newtonian.

Questioning: The only way to find out. Pursuing your inherent right to know. The safeguard of one's free will.

Rage: Raw creative energy, or anger rising through the body with such intensity and force as to temporarily immobilize any action, at the same time putting on line new brain patterns. See *kundalini*.

Reality: What is real and self-existent. That which lies beyond what lies beyond the edge of this universe.

Realized: Made real. Transformed from a holographic state to an objectified state of reality. The self-recognition that makes one real.

Receptor: A specialized nerve ending capable of sensing stimuli. A specialized site in nerve tissue sensitive to the electromagnetic firing of neurons from ourselves or others.

Recycling: The economy employed by the universe. The effective scrambling and reuse of non self-existent material that occurs during a universal birth.

Reincarnation: Simultaneous lives viewed from a linear perspective.

Religion: Organized belief about realty.

Repression: The stifling of personal expression. Always creates depression.

Resistance: Friction in the flow upon which any life is built. Impeding the flow of life to extreme degrees.

Resonate: To find a vibrational harmony between two or more things.

Respect: A totally non-judgmental state of seeing and holding anything in its state of perfection, colored only by one's

JOYRIDING THE UNIVERSE, VOLUME ONE

appreciation of that beauty and perfection.

Respiration: The essential nature of the universe and all things to breathe or to flow life through them. The binary, on-off principle of the universe. The entity cycle that requires entities periodically to go into source for new raw material.

Rigid adult: The audience in your mind. The part of everyone that enforces strict rules of behavior on one individually especially in social situations. What prevents you from being you. A fear-based personality you carry within enforcing its version of a safe universe on your life.

Rite of passage: A mechanical or psychological event that allows one to emotionally embrace the fact that life is now different than it was.

Romantic fantasy: Any ideal created from emotionalized image not existing in real life, for which people strive or which they hold as a panacea.

Sacred: That which is precious and priceless within the being, which, because it is confused with secret, the mind puts guilt connotations on and avoids sharing and expression of. The space where you touch yourself.

Safety: All issues are safety issues. The condition which, if met, that will allow us to move out of our rigid adult. A space that must be found internally before you will allow you to be you.

Scenario: Any of several historical, present, or future events or periods where the Entities and the players have worked together to facilitate a paradigm shift. The way such a thing unfolds.

Seal: The point at which life energy is brought into the body from the universe

to be used by the body. Creating a vortex in the body.

Second brain: The part of the brain anatomically and functionally that keeps track of all your simultaneous lives. The major seat of which is the center of the brain and includes the hypothalamus, thalamus, pituitary, pineal, and other surrounding parts of the brain.

Second pacemaker: A small sac behind the heart receiving and transmitting a different and more refined class of signals to the heart. Sometimes the cause of irregular heart beat or heart flutter.

Sedators: Individuals whose bacterial colonies in their firing produce a sedating effect on the colonies of those around them, slowing things down.

Self: A species of entity that mirrors or reflects what is within it. A Self is able to retain a single compressed cell of itself, go into a source from where that cell originated and reconstitute the entity.

Separation: See *original separation.*

Sequencing: See *orchestration.*

Shadow creature: Your entity. Divine presence. The entity emerging from the no-thing at the edge of the universe who moved into the light to see itself, got scared, and retreated leaving a holographic smear of itself.

Shared heart: A large source surrounded by large entities who share the wealth of that source and protect it.

Sheathing: Protective covering of DNA nodules which when sufficiently etched allows the nodule to release its memory either to be dumped or grown as a viral.

Should, shoulding, to should: The act of putting a sense of obligation or responsibility upon yourself or others as if such responsibility was mandated by a higher authority.

Simplicity: To uncomplicate.

Simultaneous lives: The way past and future lives are experienced by the entity. Time itself being a linearization of millions of simultaneous snapshots or lives.

Simultaneous time: All lives and experience are lived and completed in the same moment.

Slices: Individual revolutions of a light spiral held apart, as in a stretched spring, intersecting a time-space medium creating individual segments or dimensions.

Sluff off, slough off, also space garbage, entity residue: Knowledge-based personality discarded by the entity when it goes into respiration, i.e., back into source. A collection of such residue being the genetic foundation of this universe.

Smear: Spreading oneself out in time. The smudge or trace left by you in your personal orbit which the non-physical you picks up and uses to make a blueprint for the next moment you.

Social consciousness: The god of the rigid adult. A mass cultural gestalt embodying social appropriateness, mores, appearances, generally held beliefs of do's and don't's, and a good measure of guilt.

Solar-plex: The area just below the heart containing its own gray matter and nerve tissue. The receiver and translator of feeling in the body. The fourth seal in the body. Also called the heart-mind or solar-plex mind.

Sonar A sense used by the entity to detect or locate.

Soul: The body.

Source: Something closely resembling what we know as a black hole. A species of entity without personality that solely creates raw material from which all life grows. A no-thing.

Space: The rarest commodity in existence. Psychological room for growth and creation. The constructive framework on which consciousness flows, works, or designs. An emotional or psychological compartment specific to certain feelings.

Space particum: The smallest and most powerful, known particum. Has the ability to create space anywhere it wants. An extremely rare species of entity.

Species of entity: A variety of entity. Millions of different species and subspecies. Source, self, and creator being the ones most familiar to this experience.

Species shift: A sudden and radical biological change in the human species occasioned by a paradigm shift.

Spiral: The form or path taken by light and thought in its tendency to circle back on itself out of its own affinity. Spirals, being cone shaped, provide the most economical use of space.

Spirit: See *biological spirit.*

Spiritual genetics: The genealogy of the life spark or the entity.

Starr: A cell that can clone itself.

Starr maker: A cell or planet that can create other cells or planets that can do the same. The planet on which we live being a starr maker.

Story line: A myth along which consciousness will evolve toward a finished product.

Strobe: To flash on and off.

Struggle: A function of separation and density. Usually paired with lack.

Structure: Anything arranged in a pattern of organization.

Subjective reality: As opposed to objectification. Any reality in which participants are subject to or dependent upon certain pre-existent, supporting structures and limitations. A perceived or felt existence as opposed to an actual one. The nature of reality within the womb.

Subtle: As opposed to dramatic or traumatic. Intricately refined. Powerful, yet so refined as to avoid perception of grosser senses.

Subtleties: Refinements of feeling, concept, and thought. So powerful, poignant, and intimately interwoven into the fabric of life that they are only perceived by individual clarity and refinement of self.

Subatomic: Smaller than atomic. The order of life for light and thought. Sequentially, everything before atomic structure.

Success: Your own adequate expression.

Superstition: All beliefs. Irrational beliefs, rites, or practices resulting from fear and ignorance of the unknown.

Support: That which holds or sustains. External help.

Surrender: Yielding to you. Dropping one's defensiveness. Ending the game or completing the last dance. Going into the love of your own being.

Symbol: A representation of something else.

Synergy: Combined effort or action of two or more things.

System: A unified whole interacting within itself.

Taking the body with you: Preferred terminology to replace ascension. The ability to imprint one's DNA as one's own and thereby recreate the body anywhere. Technically, it is taking the right and ability to re-create the body rather than taking the actual body.

Theta wave: 5-8 hz. A brain wave usually reached only in sleep states. The brain wave of extremely altered states.

Third brain: The entity brain. The geographical and functional portion of brain dealing with thought and the abstract.

Thought: Pure source raw material. Love devoid of any of our connotations. Also, a universal organism.

Thought-do: Entity passion. A suggested way of living and manifesting by letting immediate action follow one's thought.

Time: Cosmic sequencing. The gap or separation between you and your entity. Viewing what is simultaneous in a linear fashion. Neuron firing. Mathematical validation of your existence. Also a universal bacteria

Time-space medium or membrane: A specialized, manifested entity body of universal proportions, containing a genetic structure, through which the light of the same and/or different entities passed and refracted in order to slow down enough to view themselves in their intersection with this medium.

Tone: Any specific frequency of electromagnetic energy. The quality or value of a thing.

Transition: The time believed necessary to pass from one state into another.

Transmitters: Specific neurons in the brain and specific chemicals in the body that affect the mitochondria or deeper nucleuses broadcasting an electrical spark to a corresponding receptor. Part of the communication network of the body.

Truth: An individual's emotional reaction to their belief system. Relevant only to that individual. The only universal truth is that there is no one truth.

Twin circuitry: Specialized circuitry existing between twins whether fraternal or identical, a function of being the same entity in different bodies.

U: Point of highest density in which you start to turn back into more of a waveform existence from whence you came.

Unconditional love: Thought. Raw material from source. Respect for life.

Universal time: A space filled with present moments.

Universe: An interacting closed or contained system organized independently. Everything we can perceive is one universe.

Validation: The need to justify or prove one's existence or worth externally because one does not or will not find that worth internally.

Value fulfillment: The feeling tone of worth and satisfaction that makes your life worth living.

Verbiage: Words, flow of words, speech.

Vertical firing: Cellular firing that occurs vertically through the deeper nucleuses and thereby draws upon the nuclear power of the cell and entity. As opposed to horizontal.

Vibrate: Fluctuations or rhythms in a wave pattern.

Victim: The sacrificial offering to a belief. The natural consequence of the belief that one does not create one's own reality, i.e., the belief in a cause and effect, chance universe.

Viral: A bacteria that is a Self, working in and with the mitochondria.

Void: A space very rich in raw material containing no-thing. A source or no-thing.

Vortex: An electromagnetic whirlpool.

Vulnerability: Open to being hurt or damaged; fragileness, tenuousness. The natural condition of being in a body. The result of feeling too much love and the fear of going with that love. Holding the entity in time.

Wave: The electromagnetic spiral of whatever magnitude or amplitude on an energy, light, or thought beam or projection, viewed two dimensionally as a ripple. Such ripples taken collectively.

Wet electricity: The basis of biological life, a division of light occurring apparently at the point where light broke into atomic structure, one part becoming particalized the other remaining in wave form becoming energy. The condensation occurring out of the collision of standing waves. A type of electrical energy noted in original scientific experiments as a by product of producing what was believed to be the more useful "dry" counterpart that we use today.

White hole: The scientifically postulated counterpart to a black hole. The back or flipside of a black hole, projecting an intense, laser-like beam of light of whatever frequency apparently focused by the funneling effect of the black hole on the other side.

457

Window: A favorable alignment of personal or universal grid lines allowing a clear passage of energy from one reality to another.

womb-within: The original woman or human species on the planet, self-reproducing from an intense internal love of who and what they were. A cloned reality.

Wonder: The mystery, joy, and miracle of life perceived in everything from an undistorted view of its reality. To personally and passionately embrace the miracle of life.

X particum, x cell, x energy: The first micro organism containing life in the universe.